Popular Musics
of the Non-Western World

POPULAR MUSICS
OF THE
NON-WESTERN WORLD

An Introductory Survey

PETER MANUEL

New York   Oxford
OXFORD UNIVERSITY PRESS
1988

Oxford University Press

Oxford   New York   Toronto
Delhi   Bombay   Calcutta   Madras   Karachi
Petaling Jaya   Singapore   Hong Kong   Tokyo
Nairobi   Dar es Salaam   Cape Town
Melbourne   Auckland
and associated companies in
Berlin   Ibadan

Published by Oxford University Press, Inc.,
200 Madison Avenue, New York, New York 10016

Oxford is a registered trademark of Oxford University Press

Library of Congress Cataloging-in-Publication Data
Manuel, Peter Lamarche.
Popular musics of the non-western world.
Bibliography: p.   Includes index.
1. Popular music—History and criticism.
I. Title.
ML3470.M33   1988   780'.42   87-34861
ISBN 0-19-505342-7

9 8 7 6 5 4 3 2 1
Printed in the United States of America
on acid-free paper

Preface

It is only relatively recently that popular culture has come to be recognized as a not only legitimate but important field of scholarly inquiry. At the same time, its study continues to be discouraged by a traditional academic disdain for the subject matter, a tendency to take its presence and impact for granted, and a fear, on the part of researchers, of being associated with the commercial journalists who contribute most of the literature on the subject. Hence popular music is often all but ignored even in works that pretend to be exhaustive studies of musical culture.

Yet scholarly interest has increased dramatically in the last decade, as it becomes clear that the rise of pop has been the most significant event in twentieth-century music. Socio-economic and technological developments accompanying modernity have engendered a proliferation of new styles, instruments, performance contexts, and musical meanings—in short, an entire new realm of music with a larger collective audience than any art form in previous history. Popular music has special importance as a socio-cultural phenomenon, for it embodies and expresses the new social identities which emerge as products of urbanization and modernization throughout the world.

In 1968 Alan Lomax voiced what was then a growing concern among music-lovers, namely, the fear that the inability of traditional cultures to maintain their musical integrity and distinctiveness against the onslaught of Western pop would lead to a "cultural grey-out." In *Folk Song Style and Culture*, Lomax raised the specter of centuries-old communications structures "being swept off the board," of vulnerable oral traditions being forgotten, such that whole cultures are "left with a sense of belonging nowhere and we, ourselves, losing our local roots, become daily more alienated." Indeed, the slick packaging and calculated mass appeal of Western pop, as well as the economic and political hegemony of the culture that created it, have promoted the spread of rock, disco, and the sentimental ballad to the extent that there are few, if any, countries on earth where they do not have audiences. "Cultural glitter-out" might seem a more appropriate description of the documented disappearance of innumerable traditional ethnic styles when faced with the raucous competition of pop and modernity in general.

Today, however, we can happily observe that the unfortunate mortal blows dealt to many traditional musics and cultures have been balanced by the extraordinary proliferation of new non-Western pop genres; most of these, while borrowing Western elements, in their own way affirm modernity and express the contradictions and complexities of modern culture. In doing so they perform a social function that traditional musics can no longer fulfill.

Fortunately, the last two decades have seen a marked increase of studies of non-Western popular musics, as scholars of various disciplines recognize the importance and, very often, the inherent appeal of these new musical forms. It is the aim of this book to contribute to an understanding and appreciation of these forms by describing the major traditions in a single volume, in a manner which seeks to be at once readable, and informative to the specialist.

This volume concerns itself only with popular musics that are stylistically distinct from mainstream Western styles (rock, disco, slow ballad, etc.). Thus, the primary distinguishing criterion used here is style rather than country of origin. Here, we are not concerned, for example, with the music of Greek pop singer Nana Mouskouri, since her music conforms to a standard Western sentimental popular style; however, this text does treat Greek *rebetika* and *bouzouki* music, which, although incorporating elements of Western music, are stylistically quite distinct. Similarly, although Japan has a highly developed music industry, mainstream Japanese popular music is outside the scope of this book because, with the exception of *enka* vocal inflection, it is stylistically indistinguishable from Western popular musics. Traditional genres are, however, discussed in this volume insofar as they are relevant to the development of modern popular styles.

The emphasis here on non-Western styles means that this volume cannot pretend to present an exhaustive, holistic treatment of popular music in any given society. In most of the cultures discussed here, Western-style music plays an important role in an ongoing dialectic relationship—often both symbiotic and competitive—with indigenous or syncretic popular musics. A thorough exploration of this relationship, although essential in fully understanding even the non-Western hybrids themselves in context, is beyond the scope of this study. Rather, it is the author's hope that the documentation provided here may be useful to those wishing to explore further, within individual cultures, the complexities of contemporary musical life in general.

Even within the realm of non-Western popular musics, this book cannot claim to be a comprehensive, definitive survey. No one person can acquire profound expertise in every major popular music worldwide, and as a result, it is inevitable that some area experts may find fault with the treatment of their regional specialties here. The author well realizes the audacity of undertaking a study of this scope; at the same time, the need for such a broad survey is overwhelming. In view of these conditions, wherever possible, data presented here have been acquired from the author's original research; however, secondary sources (primarily in English, Spanish, French, and Portuguese) have been crucial, especially in areas the author has not visited. Such sources vary in availability and quality. A voluminous body of literature, for example, exists regarding African popular music, and the interested reader is naturally urged to consult such sources for further studies. Also worthy of special mention are the publications and recordings by John Storm Roberts and the excellent film series and book of Jeremy Marre, "Beats of the Heart." This text, however, makes no pretense of attempting to do justice to all the extant research, but endeavors rather to synthesize and compile the most important data in a single, accessible volume. It is regrettable that some areas (e.g., Central Asia, Burma) have been neglected because the author has been able to acquire neither first-hand data nor useful secondary sources.

Acknowledgments

While retaining full responsibility for the contents of this work, I would like to express my profound gratitude to the numerous scholars, musicians, and others without whose assistance this text could not have been written. In particular, I would like to thank Jane Sugarman, R. Anderson Sutton, Walter Feldman, Isabel Wong, Pham Duy, Scott Marcus, Andrew Kaye, Lynn Dion, Niloofar Mina, and Charles and Angeliki Keil for their constructive comments on individual chapters. Gratitude is also due to Yohannes Haileyesus, Yan-Zhi Chen, Alicia Svigals, Dinis Paiva, Harry Leroy, Mehmet Yorukoglu, Olavo Alen, Juan Villar, Don Niles, Kavalam Pannikar, Phil Barbosa, Tim Newman, and my editor Stephanie Sakson-Ford, as well as the numerous contributors of photographs who are acknowledged in the text. Needless to say, I am also indebted to Virginia Danielson for contributing the chapter on Arab music. In a more general sense, Nazir Jairazbhoy, my mentor for many years at UCLA, has continued to serve as a model of scholarly integrity and depth for me. Finally, I would like to acknowledge the loving support and indomitable good humor of my wife Beth, who has had to share me with this book for over two years.

New York City   P.M.
September 1987

Contents

Popular Musics
of the Non-Western World

. . . It is a question of the Third World starting a new history of Man, a history which will have regard to the sometimes prodigious theses which Europe has put forward, but which will also not forget Europe's crimes. . . .

Frantz Fanon

CHAPTER 1

Perspectives on the Study of Non-Western Popular Musics

Definitions

Much has been written about the distinctions between folk, classical, and more recently, popular musics. It is often easy to regard such discussions, whether justifiably or not, as gratuitous exercises in abstract taxonomy, and it is clear that they are generally of more import to musicologists than to performers or audiences. Nevertheless, world musics often do lend themselves to broad, if occasionally ambiguous taxonomies, the clarification of which helps us to understand the nature of these genres in terms of the attributes they share or do not share with others. Moreover, many cultures themselves do distinguish between folk, art, and popular music styles. Hence such categories often can and should be employed as "-emic" constructs in understanding ethnic music from the perspective of its own culture. What should be avoided is not the use of clearly defined classifications, but rather the tendency to attach ethnocentric, class-centric, or idiosyncratic values to such concepts. At the same time, in order to understand the relationship between these different kinds of music, one must define the underlying, generally unarticulated criteria which distinguish them.

Many of the handy distinctions between folk and classical musics do not help us when the notion of popular music is introduced. In traditional societies, it may be useful, for example, to distinguish folk music from art music by regarding the latter as the music of the dominant classes in a society, but the appeal of modern popular musics may fall across a wide spectrum of classes. Similarly, popular music has been distinguished from art music with the criterion that art music needs some sort of subsidy, whether from state or private sources, whereas popular music is able to survive commercially. Again, however, this criterion does not distinguish popular music from folk music, neither of which needs subsidies. Hence, contemporary criteria for distinguishing popular music tend to be based on other factors.

While the term "popular music" has been used in a general sense in English-language writings to distinguish music "of the people" from art music associated with elites, there is clearly need for a term, or the narrowing of this term, to describe the new forms of music that have arisen in this century in close relationship to the mass media. Referring to the broad concept of popular music as "people's" music, the editors of *Popular Music* write:

> . . . there is at the very least a significant qualitative change, both in the meaning which is felt to attach to the term and in the processes to which the music owes its life, when a society undergoes industrialisation. From this point of view popular music is typical of societies with a relatively highly developed division of labour and a clear distinction between producers and consumers, in which cultural products are created largely by professionals, sold in a mass market and reproduced through mass media.[1]

This statement articulates some of the most crucial distinguishing features of popular music, especially its association with and dissemination by the mass media, and the reproduction of popular musical products (especially recordings) on a mass basis for marketing as commodities. The alleged correlation between industrialization and popular music should, however, be qualified if the statement is to be applicable on a global basis. India, for instance, may have highly developed heavy industry, but film music may be quite popular in some rural areas that are not remotely industrialized. Similarly, industrialization is extremely limited in Afghanistan, but a sort of urban popular music (*kiliwāli*), disseminated primarily via radio and cassettes, has indeed arisen there.[2] More specific distinguishing criteria of popular music are offered by Nettl:

> . . . a working definition of popular music in Western society appears to have several ingredients: 1) it is primarily urban in provenience and audience orientation; 2) it is performed by professional but not very highly trained musicians who usually do not take an intellectual view of their work; 3) it bears a stylistic relationship to the art music of its culture, but a lower degree of sophistication; 4) in the twentieth century, at least, its diffusion has been primarily the mass media of broadcasting and recording. It is normally assumed that popular music existed before these mass media came into existence, but it is difficult, in the period before the twentieth century in Europe and America, to distinguish between the three styles (i.e., classical, folk, and popular music).[3]

These ingredients may constitute the basis for a working definition of popular music in non-Western as well as Western societies, with certain qualifications and clarifications. We should, for example, exclude the notion of auto-didactic learning from the "training" which Nettl describes as limited, since the education and learning of self-taught musicians may be extensive. Further, a popular music may well be more sophisticated in certain parameters than the art music of its culture; aside from sophistication in such matters as producing and mixing of recordings (which should not necessarily be regarded as extra-musical parameters), there are, for example, certain kinds of rhythmic complexity in a James Brown song (not to mention jazz) which are not found in Mozart's symphonies (although the reverse may also be true). Moreover, the realm of musics which are diffused primarily through the mass media is distinctive and substantial enough that we may well wish to exclude from our definition of popular music those related genres referred to by Nettl which predated these media, regarding them as urban folk musics or, if need be, in a category of their own.

We may also wish to add other distinguishing criteria of popular musics. First is the distinction—more meaningful in traditional societies than in Western culture—that popular musics tend to be secular entertainment musics whose production and consumption are not intrinsically associated with special traditional life-cycle functions or rituals. Further, popular music in capitalist societies usually involves a "star system," wherein the media promote personality cults around the musician's life-style, fashions, or private life; ultimately, this promotion aims to distance the musician from the public in order to weave an aura of fantasy and glamor about him. Finally, high turnover of repertoire is a characteristic feature of popular music, where the media strive to promote continual interest in the most recent releases of an artist.

Distinctions are bound to remain ambiguous in certain cases. Indonesian *kroncong* and Portuguese *fado*, for example, existed as urban folk musics well before the advent of the mass media. They have since, however, been absorbed into recording and broadcast repertoires and are marketed and consumed much like any other pop genre. Modern *fado* may be "enhanced" with orchestral or synthesized accompaniment in typical pop fashion, but many recordings of *fado*, and most of *kroncong*, do not differ substantially in style or orchestration from their traditional predecessors. Are we, then, to consider them popular even if their present form is similar or identical to one we would call "folk"?

Similarly, classical and folk musics may well be commodified as commercial recordings and disseminated extensively via the mass media, and there are certainly many avid aficionados of art music who seldom attend live performances. Distinguishing these genres from popular music may rest upon such factors as the relatively low profit of record sales for performers and composers, the peripheral relationship of folk music to the commodity market, and, above all, the fact that traditional musics evolved independently of the mass media. Such inevitable ambiguities should remind us that generic categories are not airtight and are to some extent arbitrary.

Popular Music and the Mass Media

It should be clear that the most important distinguishing feature of popular music is its close relationship with the mass media. Popular music, as we are employing the term, arose hand-in-hand with the media, is disseminated primarily through them, and is embedded in a music industry based on marketing of recordings on a mass commodity basis.

Incipient popular song first appeared in nineteenth-century Europe and the USA in connection with the spread of sheet music and, to some extent, the first music reproducing media, *viz.*, the music box and the player piano. The proper evolution of most popular music, however, occurred in close connection with the advent of the phonograph. By 1900 the phonograph was being widely marketed for home use throughout Europe and the USA; by 1910 it had become entrenched in the third world as well. As the medium spread, its impact on music itself increased. Both traditional and modern genres recorded on discs—especially before the advent of the LP—were subject to new time constraints. The studio itself constituted a new performance context, isolated from the actual audience. The musical performance, recorded and reproduced as a "sound object," was alienated from its performer, who frequently had no control over its dissemination. As musical performances became commodities that could be bought and sold on a mass scale, a new realm of financial considerations entered the practice of making music. The nature of the dialectic between economics and aesthetics changed dramatically. One socio-economic class—the corporate bourgeoisie—established an unprecedented degree of financial control over world music, to the extent that roughly half the records sold today are produced by a mere five multinational companies (CBS, EMI, Polygram, WEA, and RCA).[4]

In many cultures, recording technology had a dramatic effect on musical life within a short period after its introduction. As early as 1910, for example, a recording engineer traveling in the Caucasus mountains could relate the infatuation of the rural Cossacks with their phonographs and worn records.[5] Even in societies where few could afford turntables, records could be played on juke boxes, or, as in Egypt, by itinerant entrepreneurs who, carrying spring-driven phonographs from village to village, would play requests for a small fee. As technology improved, international commerce increased, and interest in the phonograph grew, record companies were established throughout most of the developing world. Today there are few countries where records have not been widely marketed.

While radio may not be the first mass medium established in a given country, it is usually the most widespread, generally disseminating more music to more people than other media. In India, for example, while radio did not appear until 1927—twenty-six years after the introduction of commercial phonograph records—it now reaches 90 percent of the country's population (while newspaper circulation totals only 16 percent), and over a third of radio time is devoted to music.[6] Music heard on radio is only indirectly related to the commodification of music, since the broadcast is not purchased by listeners; the indirect ties, however, are profound, since music on commercial radio serves to attract an audience for advertisements, and the selection of repertoire is primarily determined by this need. Moreover, radio song selection may be strongly shaped by corporate intervention through payola or rigging of polls, both in state-owned stations (for example, in India[7]) as well as in commercial stations. The audience of radio broadcasting may be limited in poor countries by the cost of ownership, but one radio may, of course, serve many listeners; it is a common sight in an Indian town, for example, to see a dozen or more listeners standing around a cigarette or betel-nut stall, listening attentively to the shopkeeper's transistor.

In countries like India, the price of an inexpensive radio (around $20 in the 1970s) remains prohibitive for a large sector of the population. The considerably lower capital investment required for a movie—often as low as 12 cents in South Asia—has undoubtedly contributed to the importance of cinema as a medium for dissemination of popular music. Because of such economic factors, the appeal of the cinema, and its ability to add a new sort of visual dimension to music, several popular musics have developed in close association with cinema; aside from Indian film music, examples include modern Arab urban music, the tango, Indonesian *dangdut*, and Chinese mass music. Typically, these musics are incorporated in the form of musical interludes woven into the plot, whose cinematic context obviously has considerable effect on the music's impact and meaning. Antoine Hennion has argued, in reference to French sentimental popular music, that while a listener may consciously notice only the melody of a song and assume that it is what appeals to him, in fact, it may often be the orchestrated, slickly produced accompaniment that appeals to him on a deeper, albeit unperceived level;[8] in the case of popular songs in cinema, the cinematic context—including the immediate visual setting, the relationship to the plot, the singer's demeanor, and the frequent use of dance—provides other layers of meaning which naturally color and influence musical perception.

Television may supplement or, in some cases, replace the dissemination of popular music via cinema. In the affluent USA, television has been described as "the central cultural arm of American society"; in underdeveloped countries, access to television may be limited to middle and upper classes, but even in developing countries like Egypt, television may constitute, along with radio, the predominant dissemination medium. In Egypt, the rise of television and music programming therein—whether contemporary performances or song segments from old films—has gone hand-in-hand with the decline of cinematic musicals;

unable to compete with television in the realm of music presentation, modern Arab cinema has on the whole forsaken the artificial introduction of song segments for a more Western, straightforward narrative approach. As is the case with cinema, the visual context of a television production of a song sequence may profoundly influence apprehension of the music itself.

Video is becoming an increasingly widespread medium for dissemination of popular music, especially in a region such as South Asia, where such music is often embedded in cinematic musicals. Video technology, whether in the form of feature films or independent musical segments, may offer viewers greater access to mediated musical performances than do cinema and television. The effects of the spread of VCRs, however, are mixed. In further privatizing entertainment, they contribute to the atomization of the audience, wherein the culture of the living room replaces that of the coffee house, theater, and concert hall. A Pakistani correspondent has described the VCR boom in his country:

> Reducing the consumption of the arts to the confines of the home means there is no artistic community left, either for the artists or for the audience. There is no sense of participation, of mass catharsis. . . . Instead, one is left with fragmented and alienated domestic ghettos.[9]

Cassette technology, the most recent mass medium, may prove to be as revolutionary as radio has been. Simple cassette players are far cheaper than phonograph systems, and cassettes are less expensive than records and can offer more recorded music time. Most important, perhaps, is the potentially low expense of cassette production, especially in comparison with that of records, films, or videos. Throughout the third world, the last fifteen years have seen the flourishing of innumerable backyard cassette industries, duplicating cassettes, printing labels, and marketing "product" through local outlets with very low initial investment and operating costs. The backyard cassette industries are able to respond to diverse regional, ethnic, and class tastes in a manner which is not characteristic of record or film industries; the latter are mostly corporate- or state-controlled and hence tend to seek or create as broad a market as possible. Cassette technology, in other terms, offers the potential for diversified, democratic control of the means of musical production, and has engendered many new forms of music which have arisen as pop stylizations of regional folk musics. West Javanese *jaipongan* is one particularly striking example of a vital pop form which has emerged as a grassroots regional expression, independent of centralized, corporate music industry manipulation and promotion. Moreover, the advent of cassette technology is having a much greater impact in the third world than in the developed countries. In the West, cassettes merely constitute a somewhat more convenient alternative to records, which themselves have been widely distributed for generations.

But in the developing world, cassettes are now reaching many rural or lower-class audiences who previously had no access to, not to mention control of, recorded music.

Certain broad trends are noticeable in the development of the media in the non-Western world. In the early period of recording technology, production of 78 RPM discs lay mostly in the hands of multinationals like EMI. Throughout the 1950s and 1960s, the greater technological sophistication required for LP production tended to perpetuate the concentration of the recording industry in the West and a few cities elsewhere.[10] Nevertheless, by this time the evolution of hybrid urban pop forms was well under way in many countries, under the influence of urbanization, modernization, exposure to foreign musics, and the spread of the mass media. In the late sixties, the advent of silicon chips/integrated circuits and the compact cassette dramatically expanded the music industry worldwide. The cassette boom of the seventies, as we have seen, extended recording production and consumption potential throughout the world. This period saw the simultaneous concentration and diversification of the music industry, for while the "Big Five" record companies came to control over half of all record sales, at the same time, smaller record and cassette outfits proliferated, producing local music under local control for local audiences.[11] Correspondingly, as the expansion of the media in the seventies further increased exposure to, and often dominance of Western pop, at the same time, the flowering of regional independent recording companies contributed to the boom of non-Western pop styles. The emerging pop musics, moreover, began to gain new state and popular acceptance as vital expressions of national culture; several have of course found markets in the West itself.

The increased access to recording technology has greatly promoted illegitimate and parasitic sectors of the music industry, especially piracy (unauthorized duplication of recordings for commercial purposes) and bootlegging (marketing of unauthorized recordings of live performances). On the local and short-term levels, such activities may lower consumption costs and offset corporate, state or multinational control of music dissemination; thus, for example, underground distribution of progressive *nueva canción* ("new song") in Chile has enabled this dynamic genre to escape total censorship under the repressive Pinochet regime.[12] On the other hand, rampant piracy may stifle the growth of any regional recording industry, as has been the case in Tunisia.[13] Moreover, it deprives recording artists of royalties.

Mass Music or People's Music?

The most profound and persistent theoretical question in the study of popular musics (and of popular culture in general) concerns the relation between popular music and the aesthetic and ideological needs and aspirations of the individual, ethnic group, or class. Discussions have centered around the degree to which popular music can be regarded as a genuine grassroots expression that responds to and fulfills emotional needs, or, alternately, whether it should be recognized as a creation of corporate (or state) culture industries that exploit, manipulate, or even create taste rather than respond to it. Does popular music rise from the people who constitute its audience, or is it superimposed upon them from above? Does it reflect and express their attitudes, tastes, aspirations, and worldview, or does it serve to indoctrinate them, however imperceptibly, to the ideology of the class and gender which control the media? Does popular music enrich or alienate? Can popular music challenge a social order? Do listeners exercise a genuine choice among musics, or can they only passively select preferences from the styles proferred by the media?

While these questions have been discussed and argued extensively, most of the debate has been restricted in scope to Western popular culture, such that its applicability to non-Western music is often unclear, limited, or in need of qualification or revision. The following discussion attempts to summarize salient aspects of the mass culture-popular culture argument in the context of world musics, with the aim of suggesting some of the complexities involved.

Defenders of popular culture insist upon the richness and diversity it offers to consumers and its ability to strengthen democratic institutions through a harmonious pluralism; they cite the relation of popular culture to education, mass media, and technological and economic progress as components of modern society which promote humanism, individual autonomy and fulfillment, and popular participation in sociocultural decision-making.[14] These favorable evaluations are more often conveyed implicitly than explicitly, particularly in the capitalist world. Bourgeois ideology, ever reaffirming the value of popular culture and its ability to satisfy the consumer, pervades the media, whether via *People* magazine, television commercials, or middle-brow laymen's literature on popular culture itself. Indeed, the very fact that popular culture is so widely and unquestioningly accepted may contribute to the paucity of scholarly articulations of its merits—these often taking the form of academic rebuttals against radical critiques.[15]

In spite of the general public acceptance of popular culture, and perhaps because of a common intellectual antipathy toward it, in the realm of scholarly or philosophical literature, attacks on popular culture seem to outnumber apologies for it. The criticisms tend to fall into two broad schools of thought: conservative elitism, and neo-Marxist critical theory, which reach their shared negative appraisal of popular culture (or, more disparagingly, "mass culture") from the perspectives of diametrically opposed ideologies. The former approach, drawing from the earlier writings of Nietzsche, finds twentieth-century expression in F. R.

Leavis, Ortega y Gasset, and, most notably, T. S. Eliot. While Leavis blames industrialization for destroying the humanistic integrity of traditional culture, Eliot sees secular democracy as the villain, in that it threatens class hierarchy and, by extension, high art. For Eliot, modern mass culture is an expression of the brutish domination by the coarse majority, which threatens *from below* the high culture which is the most precious asset of civilization and which can be maintained only by a privileged elite minority. The culture of the lower classes, which in traditional "folk" society could merit a place in national culture, in modern times becomes significant only as a menace to the survival of the dignity, integrity, and sophistication of the intellectual aristocracy. Explicit or implicit in this aesthetic is a romantic nostalgia for the precapitalist past, a poor understanding of modern class relations, and a contempt for the common man—features that have greatly limited support for such conservative critiques among scholars.[16]

More influential in scholarly circles have been the radical critiques of mass culture that view the culture industry as an instrument of anaesthetizing manipulation superimposed upon the masses, alienating them from themselves and obscuring iniquitous class relationships. This critique received its fullest articulation in the work of the Frankfurt School—Adorno, Marcuse, and Horkheimer. Of these, Adorno's writings are most immediately relevant, since they concentrate on music and contain specific discussions of popular music.[17] Adorno is most concerned with popular music as a threat and contrast to "serious" music, that is, classical music. Popular music, he argues, is a banal, standardized, artificial entertainment form which, instead of challenging its audience to listen actively and intelligently, offers "pre-masticated" formulae that rely on a system of conditioned emotional reflexes in the listener. Popular music thus accepts or even invites the commodification which is the fate of most art in the modern world; indeed, popular music, to Adorno, is produced from its very inception as a fungible item for sale in the market place. Adorno's elitism thus has affinities with that of the conservatives discussed above, but he differs in seeing mass culture as a form of domination *from above,* serving to alienate, manipulate, and obscure class consciousness among a potentially progressive working class.

Adorno's provocative views on popular music, despite their insights and influences, have been much criticized, especially for his shallow familiarity with such music, his elitist distaste for practically any modern music outside that of the Second Vienna School, and his failure to see how popular music can in some cases challenge rather than passively accept a social order.[18] Yet the most substantial limitation of Adorno's approach to popular music is its exclusive (and admitted) concentration on Western bourgeois society (especially Nazi Germany and New Deal America), whose culture industry has allegedly all but erased vital folk musics. Part of the problem with Western culture, he argues, is that "there is no longer any 'folk' left whose songs and games could be taken up and sublimated by art."[19] Implicitly, then, the nature of popular culture might differ substantially in less developed, non-Western countries enjoying, from this perspective, the advantage of historical backwardness. While Adorno does not appear to have had any sympathy for or interest in non-Western cultures, his arguments do at times suggest that the rich surviving folk cultures of such countries, having escaped commodification and "outwitted the historical dynamic," could constitute the bases for a vital popular culture.[20] In this sense, even Adorno's harsh critique leaves room for a favorable view of non-Western popular music.

Herbert Marcuse's similarly pessimistic appraisal of modern society and culture, most explicitly articulated in *One-Dimensional Man*, presents mass culture as a totalitarian system promoting false (and often consumerist) needs and values and thereby serving to maintain an unequal social order through *consent* of the dominated classes rather than through brute force. "Can one really distinguish," he asks, "between the mass media as instruments of information and entertainment, and as agents of manipulation and indoctrination?" (*One-Dimensional Man*, 8). Marcuse's approach thus bears close affinities to Gramsci's theory of hegemony, which stresses the role of culture as an indoctrination to bourgeois ideology. Interestingly, Marcuse suggests the possibility that non-Western, technologically backward countries might modernize in such a way that would avoid the alleged totalitarian effects of industrialization (*One-Dimensional Man*, 47–48). Thus, like Adorno, he hints at the distinctively vital role that non-Western popular cultures could perform by virtue of the very uneven development of technology, the mass media, and commercialism of these countries. This view is shared by other writers such as Marothy, who attributes the vitality of popular music to its "infusions from below," that is, from the lower classes.[21]

One feature of Western popular music singled out for special contempt by Adorno is its heavy reliance on standardized formulae governing style, text, melody, formal structure, harmonic progressions, and the like (*Introduction to the Sociology of Music*, 24–26). Standardization is indeed an undeniable feature of popular music; in part, it derives from the reluctance of producers to risk stylistic experiments or innovations when very few records (currently about one out of twenty in the USA) actually make a profit. In many cases, the development of popular culture has led to a net decrease in the number of musical styles produced within a given region. Top 40 formats in radio programming can streamline and limit the variety of music available to the public. Variations within particular styles may also decline.[22] Improvisation is often deemed too risky and unpredictable to be included in recordings, and in subsequent live performances musicians may attempt slavishly to reproduce the recorded version of a song rather than incorporate spontaneous improvisation. The decline of text improvisation in calypso is one example. Instances of stylistic standardization also abound in non-Western pop music. Indian film music producers, to cite an extreme example, prefer to employ a handful of well-known playback singers rather than hazard an unfamiliar voice or style; this extreme homogeneity of vocalist selection is all the more notable given the extraordinary linguistic, class, and ethnic diversity of the North Indian audience. Similarly, one could point to the use of formulae in most folk-derived pop forms, such as the exclusive I-IV-I_4^6-V progression of the South African *kwela,* or the predictable harmonies and rhythms of Latin forms like the *cumbia* or *merengue.*

Naturally, one should not expect the variety of popular music to equal that of art music. Further, art musics (not to mention folk styles) themselves rely on formulae. The difference, according to Adorno, is the creative, vital, dialectic relationship between active form and inherited convention in "serious" music. Yet interesting as this concept may be, it must nevertheless remain ambiguous and subjective. Dismissing most popular music as beneath contempt, Adorno and other Frankfurt theorists do not provide any theoretical or methodological framework for a detailed analysis of popular music which could illuminate the mechanisms of such an alleged dialectic. Moreover, Adorno's overemphasis on standardization cannot explain the variety that does exist in popular music, or the need, which he himself recognizes, to sound somehow different in order for it to sell.

Another criticism of popular music and, generally, of most music in modern society, is that it tends to be produced by specialists and consumed passively by audiences who exert no real influence on its production, aside from buying or rejecting what the media offer. Such a situation alienates the listener from his own potential as a musician, and deprives him of any direct feedback or control over the body of music from which he chooses his favorites. By contrast, traditional classless societies may regard everyone as musically talented to some degree,[23] and even in traditional stratified cultures with musical specialists, non-specialists may frequently make music, often out of social obligation, and they can influence performers (such as the bard in the teahouse) by requesting repertoire, offering direct comments on the music, proferring or refusing tips in an intimate face-to-face situation, and the like.

Just as dance halls in the USA and Europe have increasingly forsaken live music for recorded disco, in the third world there are innumerable instances of recorded music replacing live performance, both for functional uses (e.g., in a Hindu temple) and for entertainment. The glitter of new, imported, synthetic music is one factor frequently contributing to the preference for piped music. More important in many cases is the high cost of hiring groups to perform the new pop styles. In Jamaica, for example, amateur informal folk genres like mento have been all but forgotten since reggae and Western pop came into vogue; but because sound systems for bands are so prohibitively expensive, live performances of reggae—or any other popular music—have become rare, except at select events like the Sunsplash festival.

In general, the increase of passive consumption leads to a decrease of topical contemporaneity, as song texts expressing immediate concerns relating to social function or socio-political issues give way to sentimental doggerel. Trinidad calypso texts were formerly composed daily as commentaries on the events of the previous twenty-four hours. Now, as the music industry encourages calypso artists to seek broader audiences and compose hits with texts that will not become obsolete overnight, contemporaneity is less crucial a goal. Meanwhile, the vogue of ten- or fifteen-piece bands and correspondingly complex charts limits repertoires of many calypso singers to only two or three songs per season.[24]

The degree of genuine choice exercised by the popular music consumer has also been a subject of debate. It is clear that the mass media may democratize culture by offering listeners an incomparably greater diversity of music than they would otherwise experience. The Indian villager of the nineteenth century might be familiar only with the amateur folksongs of his particular village, but today the radio alone could expose him to popular and folk musics from countless other areas, as well as Indian and Western art musics; the East Javanese owner of a cassette player need not restrict his listening to local music when the local cassette stall offers everything from Sundanese *jaipongan* to the Rolling Stones.

While the consumer may be theoretically free to choose from a wide variety of musics, his taste may be manipulated to a large degree by music industry promotion. Only such manipulation, for example, could explain the ubiquity of Lata Mangeshkar's voice in Hindi film music, whose audience is so extraordinarily diverse. While promotion and marketing techniques often fail, it is difficult to question Adorno's statement (echoed by Marcuse, Hauser, Gramsci and others) that "the mechanisms of distribution carry at least as much weight as that which they distribute" (*Introduction to the Sociology of Music*, 34). These mechanisms have been used to create homogeneous mass audiences—even though, properly speaking, there are no masses, only ways of viewing people as masses.

Similarly, Marcuse argues that the celebrated freedom of choice is in fact deceptive and superficial, and that the nature and presentation of the goods offered reinforce an alienating, commodifying market system (*One-Dimensional Man*, 7–8). A defender of the democratization of culture in modern society notes that the products of "high culture" (not to mention pop culture) now reach a greater audience than ever before, and insists, "a Beethoven symphony remains a Beethoven symphony regardless of whether it is sold in a supermarket or a 'quality' record shop."[25] Yet Marcuse illustrates that when once revolutionary works are revived by the media as classics, "they come to life as other than themselves; they are deprived of their antagonistic force" (*One-Dimensional Man*, 64). Similarly, just as an Egyptian wedding song may have a special meaning in the context of its traditional rendering by a group of village women, when a stylized version of that song is presented as a pop song on the radio, its aesthetic and ideological meaning may be grossly altered. One cannot simply insist that a wedding song remains a wedding song regardless of whether it is sold in a supermarket or sung by a group of rustic women at a wedding. In this sense, the diversity of popular music offered by the media is tempered by its presentation as an easily commodified "sound object" among so many others.

Frankfurt School theorists argue that this reified mode of presentation tends to negate any role popular music might play as social criticism. Even revolutionary art, they assert, loses its oppositional content and function when it is harmlessly digested into the "harmonious pluralism" of modern mass culture. Thus, for example, while bebop was consciously conceived of by its creators as a negation of or even rebellion against white, corporate, commercial domination of American society, this same music—in a disarmed, non-percussive style—is now incorporated into Muzak, used in shopping centers to promote commodity consumption. "Time and time again," writes Adorno, "jazz became a captive of the culture industry and thus of musical and social conformism" (*Introduction to the Sociology of Music*, 34). Rock, the great counterculture music of the 1960s, is now intimately linked with corporate capital. The use of rock and other once-oppositional popular musics in advertisements is especially notable. In the mid-1980s, Johnny Nash's reggae hit, "I Can See Clearly Now" was used in a commercial for window cleaner, and "Mack the Knife," whose text was written by Marxist playwright Bertolt Brecht, appears as the theme for a McDonald's ad: "It's Mac Tonight." Meanwhile, the Shirelles' 1961 hit, "Dedicated to the One I Love" John Weiner points out, "is now used to suggest that if you are dedicated, you should serve bran flakes to the one you love."[26]

Everywhere popular music texts seem to dwell predominantly on sentimental love; while this aspect of popular music contrasts with the wide range of social commentary, political satire, and alternative world views often expressed in traditional folk musics, it is generally taken for granted. But an ideology—such as the depoliticized passivity promoted by so much popular music—is most powerful when it is taken for granted and appears as the only natural way. In this capacity, mass music can serve to obscure, distract, and anaesthetize, especially in a socially exploitative situation where a genuine *vox populi* art might instead urge reformist activism.[27]

As suggested in the discussion of cassette technology, the ideological relationship between society and popular music may depend to a large extent on who controls the (musical) means of production. Are music making, packaging, and dissemination in the hands of a corporate music industry, or are they carried out on a grassroots level by backyard cassette studios producing for local markets? In many cases, production control may be mixed; moreover, many non-Western pop musics may be corporate (or state) music industry stylizations of lower class, grassroots traditional musics. Decoding ideologies of such popular genres may be difficult and subjective, as the class structures of their parent societies are invariably complex and contradictory themselves. In general, working class artistic expressions are contradictory when ownership of the means of (musical) production rests with a more dominant class. The development of modern Texas-Mexican popular music is illustrative: as this music became more commercially successful, the social criticisms and political contemporaneity of the folk *corrido* gave way to the apolitical sentimentality of the pop *ranchera*. Thus José Limón observes that modern Tex-Mex pop, rather than expressing a clear message of Chicano solidarity in the face of Anglo domination and discrimination, instead becomes at best ideologically ambiguous.

> For the Mexicanos it may in part be an exercise in cultural affirmation, but this comes at a literal and metaphorical cost, as certain other nonaffirming, socially debilitating ideological effects are also conveyed through the musical complex. As with so much of mass media culture, the result is a contradiction.[28]

Similarly, as Marothy notes, "social classes are not sealed off by walls," and a grassroots genre like jazz, once absorbed into the commercial market, can no longer be regarded as the undiluted expression of any one class, but rather as "the product of an *incessant, intricate mutual effect* resulting from the tastes and efforts of both the capitalist and working classes."[29] It is in this sense that scholars like Richard Middleton and Stuart Hall stress the importance of analyzing popular culture neither as pure resistance nor as superimposition, but as the arena of negotiation, and "the ground on which the transformations are worked."[30] Most importantly, popular music—like art in general—must be seen not as an abstract, autonomous phenomenon, nor as a passive, superstructural reflection of a technoeconomic base, but as an active participant in mediation and expression of broader conflicts and tendencies.

Because of the potentially contradictory nature of popular music expression, it should not be dismissed as either an undiluted *vox populi*, or as superimposed, monolithic, dominant ideology. That is not to say, however, that one may complacently satisfy oneself with the facile assurance that "the answer lies somewhere in between." Difficult and controversial as the task may be, decoding musical ideologies, with careful attention to musical and extra-musical parameters, remains the ultimate goal of understanding musical meaning. Frankfurt School critical theory may provide an essential critical perspective, but a comprehensive theory of popular music must be updated to consider the impact of new technologies (such as cassettes) and new socio-economic developments; it must not be permitted to substitute simplistic denunciation and dismissal or, alternately, idealization and romanticization, for rigorous analysis and discriminating critique; and most importantly, it must be broadened to encompass a global scope.[31]

Popular Music and Socialism

The tendency of popular culture studies to restrict their scope to the capitalist world has long since constituted an anachronism, as for several decades roughly a quarter of the world's population has been living in some sort of socialist or communist society. Of course, some essential aspects of popular music are inherent to media dissemination, and are thus not unique to capitalism. In socialist as well as free market economies, popular music ultimately entails commodification, the reinforcement of passive consumption rather than communal performance, and the alienation of the performer from the musical product and the personal audience. Moreover, in socialism as in capitalism, the musician may well compromise his style in order to reach a wider audience and command a larger salary; thus socialism may certainly accommodate a kind of commercialism, although it may be labeled differently—for example, in Cuba—as "facilism" or "populism."

At the same time, there are important structural differences between socialist popular culture and its capitalist counterpart. Superstar hype tends to be negligible; commercial promotion of artists is inconsiderable, and there is no need for the state-run entertainment industry to create alienating auras of fashion and fantasy around musicians. Music is not tied to advertisements or to the promotion of bourgeois consumerism. Insofar as all citizens under communism are wage-earning proletariat employed by the state, one cannot speak of *class* hegemony in the capitalist sense—although this is not to suggest that distinct *levels* of power and affluence are absent in such societies. Further, even in middle-income countries like Cuba, the professional musician may enjoy an economic security beyond the reach of most aspiring professionals in, for example, the USA. The effects of such cradle-to-grave security on artistic creativity may be arguable, but they should not be ignored.

In socialist countries the constraints and pressures on musical style and content tend to derive less from market concerns than from bureaucratic or ideological factors. In the case of music, these constraints may range from relatively mild (as in Cuba) to brutally totalitarian factors (as in China under the Cultural Revolution). Invariably they are more conspicuous and overt—although not always more onerous—than the pressures exerted by the market in the capitalist world; as such, the excesses of the Zhdanovs and Jiang Qings, together with the relative intolerance of dissent in the socialist world, have led to the bourgeois assumption that artistic freedom and communism are simply incompatible.

Aside from the hazards of becoming embroiled in vitriolic polemics, a discussion of the functioning of popular culture in socialist countries continues to be hindered by the paucity of extant case studies; while smug, ignorant dismissals and over-idealistic paeans are not lacking, Western scholarship has produced few inquiries employing an informed, dispassionate perspective which is at once open-minded and critical. At this point we may merely suggest that the limits that have been and are still imposed upon artists in the socialist world may not be structurally inherent to socialism; in that sense, such a socio-economic system— regardless of its other assets or defects—may continue to offer one kind of alternative to the dialectic contradictions which popular music may never transcend under capitalism.

Urbanization

One of the most important aspects of the study of popular music is its relation to urbanization, especially in the context of the developing world. The musical styles discussed in this book are the products of societies which have undergone socio-economic transformations unprecedented in their rapidity and profundity. The demographic growth of cities has in itself reshaped societies. Statistics tell familiar stories throughout the world. The case of Mexico is typical: the population of Mexico City grew from 470,000 in 1920 to over fifteen million in 1986, and a once predominantly agrarian nation is now two-thirds urban in residence. Many cities have emerged from virtual emptiness; Karachi, a small fishing village until the late nineteenth century, now contains over 10 million inhabitants. The rise of urban popular musics is thus a reflection and a product of the emergence of vast new urban societies that scarcely existed a century ago.

Urbanization and modernization effect qualitative as well as quantitative social changes. Pre-capitalist forms of barter and payment in kind give way to wage labor and a money economy; provincial outlooks are replaced by nationalism; land ownership becomes the exception rather than the rule; the individual or the nuclear family rather than the village or extended family becomes the socio-economic unit; traditional forms of social stratification are replaced by new ones, whether capitalist or socialist; and new bureaucracies, mass media, and work patterns emerge. For many, the changes wrought by urbanization and modernization are accompanied by considerable alienation, exploitation, and impoverishment. As such, the creation of a new social identity assumes a crucial rather than incidental role in survival and adaptation to the new environment. To those immersed in the struggle, popular music may serve as a powerful and meaningful symbol of identity, functioning as an avenue of expression and mediation of conflict. Popular music, however much it may sound to the naive ear as a crude imitation of other forms, may serve as a metaphor for the creation of a distinctive world of common meanings and shared cultural ideologies on the part of the new urban classes. For the city dwellers of the developing world, neither traditional "folk" forms nor imported Western styles may fully express social identity. Rather, new musics are generated which syncretize and reinterpret old and new elements in a distinctive metaphorical expression. As Coplan has written:

> Musical composition in this sense involves the reinterpretation of new elements within existing cultural models, and the reshaping of those models to facilitate adaptation to changing situations. Popular music thus provides a multiplicity of meanings accommodating a range of manipulation, interpretation and choice, and supplies a measure of solidarity in an environment characterised by social insecurity, dislocation, and differentiation.[32]

The evolution of popular musics, then, must be seen as paralleling the evolution of new societies. The course of musical evolution thus emerges as the product of the musical resources available to a society, and, equally as important, of the extra-musical conditions and attitudes that guide musicians in selecting, recombining, and creating new styles. With music as with history in general: man makes musical history, but he does not choose the way he makes it.

Rapid urbanization often brings together members of distinct ethnic, racial, linguistic, and/or tribal origins. Such groups may find themselves interacting with and living alongside one another, and confronting shared socio-economic challenges. The traditional ethnic identities of formerly discrete groups may tend to weaken in cities. In most of urban Africa, ethnic identities remain strong, but in certain conditions— such as when ethnic groups mix in neutral contexts like mining towns— migrants may come to think of themselves in occupational, class, or national terms as well as in tribal terms. Popular music again plays an important role in mediating, forming, and expressing this reorientation of social identity. Coplan has described how South African *marabi* music, performed in proletarian beer gardens, became an important vehicle in the development of a pan-ethnic urban consciousness; similarly, he relates how the polyglot use of several distinct languages within individual highlife songs has helped promote that music as a lingua franca genre among its tribally diverse audience.[33] In North India, popular music lyrics in the lingua franca Hindi-Urdu tend to predominate. Popular music may thus develop as a common denominator style both from the homogenizing effect of urbanization as well as from the natural attempt of the commercial music industry to seek as broad a market as possible; lingua franca popular music thus becomes both an agent and a function of the formation of pan-ethnic social identity.

Nevertheless, it should not be assumed that musical syncretism and acculturation are inevitable responses to urbanization and the cohabitation of diverse ethnic groups. Indeed, in many situations, popular music may serve as one of the few and most important realms in which a community can express and reinforce its own distinct identity. In this fashion, for example, the variety of ethnic popular musics among immigrant groups in New York City may be said to function as preservers of ethnic pluralism rather than as agents of homogenization; thus Arab urban music, disseminated in clubs and recordings, may be meaningful to Arabs in New York City precisely because it is distinctly Arab, not because it offers potential for hybridization with American pop.

Popular Music and the Lumpen Proletariat

One of the most remarkable features of the evolution of popular musics is its association, in numerous cultures worldwide, with an unassimilated, disenfranchised, impoverished, socially marginalized class. This lumpen proletariat comprises a heterogeneous mixture of hoodlums, pimps, prostitutes, vagrants, sidewalk vendors, drug addicts, musicians, miscellaneous "street people," and assorted unemployed migrants. They share a common status on or beyond the periphery of stable, "respectable" society—the economically and socially assimilated working and middle classes. It is paradoxical that these marginal misfits in their milieu of bars and brothels should be so crucial in the development of new musical forms, especially since the genres they create are often destined later to become celebrated as national expressions. Nevertheless, it was exactly such groups, rather than the middle or working classes, that gave birth to such diverse and vital forms as *rebetika*, modern *kroncong*, reggae, steel band, the tango, and, last but not least, jazz.

In such societies, why should so much creative energy be associated with despised and isolated social groups? The answer depends to a large extent on the particular cases involved, yet certain general patterns of patronage and preference do emerge cross-culturally. In many newly urbanizing societies, the elites tend to emulate and identify with either traditional high culture or with Western culture. The comprador nature of many of these emergent aristocracies ties them financially, as well as ideologically and culturally, to the West. Such elites, aside from attempting to distance themselves from rural culture, have often regarded with scorn the indigenous hybrid cultural forms that were emerging in the slums and red-light districts of their cities. Thus, the Buenos Aires turn-of-the-century upper class emulated Parisian fashions rather than the crude and rustic tango, and the Javanese aristocracy of the same period patronized traditional courtly entertainments.

More difficult to explain is the limited creative role, in these societies, of the assimilated middle and working classes. In some cases they may have remained too attached to their traditional rural cultural forms, or, alternately, too intent on obsequiously imitating the elites they aspired to join. In other cases, their puritanical and single-minded work ethic may have led them to regard music in general as frivolous and distracting.

The lumpen proletariat, in contrast, possesses an "unbound" creative energy. On the one hand, they are generally denied access to the high culture of the aristocracy; the turn-of-the-century Argentine pencil vendor could scarcely cultivate an interest in Debussy even if he had wanted to. On the other hand, the traditional music of the countryside was alien to them. The lumpen proletariat are city dwellers, bred in the urban slums where they manage to devise a bohemian *modus vivendi*. Hence, they are inherently predisposed to new forms of cultural expression. Moreover, being social outcasts, their creativity is not circumscribed by the orthodox conventions of middle-class society. The raucous trumpet playing and sensuous dancing of Storyville bordellos may have shocked the prudish New Orleans middle classes, but the black tavern clientele, denied entry to bourgeois society, cultivated no such snobbish attitudes or inhibitions.

Victor Turner characterizes such marginal social groups in terms of their *liminality*. Liminal classes would include, for example, the unassimilated migrants from the Greek countryside who poured into Athens in the first half of the twentieth century, and came to constitute important sources of *rebetiko* culture. Turner stresses how such groups can be seen as transitional—in this case, between rural folk society and urban working- or middle-class society. Alienated from rural culture, denied access to bourgeois culture, and "stripped of all secular status," the liminal groups, he argues, tend to have an acute sense of social identity. "Usually they are highly conscious and self-conscious people and may produce from their ranks a disproportionately high number of writers, artists, and philosophers."[34] The traditional low status of musicians in many societies has also often been both cause and effect of their association with the liminal classes.

The musical forms created by the lumpen classes may eventually be accepted, in pure form or not, by middle-class societies. In some cases the impetus could be external—for example, it was only when the tango became wildly popular in Paris that the Argentine urban elite belatedly embraced it as a national form. In other instances, it has been the gradual assimilation of the lumpen proletariat into society that effected a simultaneous incorporation and "nationalization" of its musical styles; such appears to have been the case with the evolution of *rebetika*, albeit in a diluted and emasculated form, into a genre patronized by the Greek middle class.

Acculturation

In the preceding section we discussed some of the class inter-relationships involved in popular music within a given society. Much scholarly attention, particularly in the realm of popular music, has been directed toward the process of acculturation. Musical syncretism is frequently a consequence of cultural contact. Its occurrence is clearly related to a host of broader factors pertaining to the relationship between the two or more cultures involved. On the purely musical level, scholars have observed that the degree of stylistic compatibility between the musical systems in contact also appears to be an important factor.[35] "Central traits," it has been suggested, are the least likely to be altered in such syntheses. In many cases it may be difficult to identify such central features, although the study of syncretic musics across cultures strongly suggests that vocal style is among the most fundamental traits and is generally the most resistant to change. Thus, for instance, one can find many examples of popular musics from India, Iran, and China which are thoroughly Westernized in every parameter except vocal production.

The most conspicuous forms of acculturation, including those lamented by Lomax in the Preface, involve Western influence—specifically, the adoption of Western musical elements (such as instrumentation, harmony, and vocal style) by non-Western musical cultures. This transculturation has become so widespread and deeply rooted that Western disco, rock, and slow ballad have become international styles, promoted by a network of multinational corporations. Yet Western society is by no means the only large culture to have global impact, as is illustrated by the influence of Indian film music in countries as diverse and distant as Yugoslavia and Indonesia.

Acculturation can, of course, operate in different contexts. An ethnic or racial minority can exert a prodigious effect on the music of the dominant culture enveloping it, as with the influence of Afro-American music on mainstream American popular music, or, for that matter, the incorporation of Uighur rhythms and melodies into Chinese mass music. Acculturation can occur between two smaller societies of similar size and can become highly complex when musical styles and characteristics are exchanged back and forth between two culture groups over an extended period. The musical "round trip" between Africa and the Caribbean is particularly notable. Descendants of African slaves in the Americas developed dynamic hybrid musics synthesizing African-derived rhythms and Western melodic and harmonic patterns. Some of these styles—especially the Cuban *rumba*—became widely popular in the Congo and other parts of Africa from the 1950s on, and they generated new hybrids of native African and Afro-Caribbean music. These, in turn, excited the interest of Caribbean musicians in the seventies, stimulating the development of new pop forms like Haitian "mini-jazz."

Cultural borrowing is seldom completely indiscriminate, and is often limited to elements that are in some way compatible with the host culture's musical system. Moreover, a recipient culture may adapt foreign elements in distinctly idiosyncratic ways that substantially alter their function, context, and meaning. The uses of harmony, for example, in Greek, Balkan, and Turkish popular musics could not be called functional in the Western sense, since the chordal vocabularies derive not from European common practice but from the tonal resources of the modes used. Thus, for instance, a song set to the familiar *Hijaz* mode, with its characteristic flatted second and sixth degrees, would employ major triads built on the tonic and the lowered second and sixth degrees, along with minor triads on the fourth and lowered seventh degrees.

Meanwhile, Indian pop music uses Western harmony in its own distinctive way. Most Indian pop songs are set to diatonic modes (often resembling Western major, minor, and dorian). While conception of a melody may remain basically modal, a subdominant or dominant chord may be added to a sustained sixth degree or seventh degree, respectively, present in the melody. The resulting harmonic practice thus resembles Western pop harmony and common practice more than do the Greek and Turkish conventions. Nevertheless, the similarity with Western functional harmony may be shallow, and may not extend to the realm of the listener's perception; in order to understand the function of harmony in such songs, we must know how South Asians themselves perceive it, and to what extent it creates the same dynamic tensions and resolutions that it does for Western listeners.

Naturally, different South Asian audiences may perceive harmony in different ways, according to the degree of their acculturation, and harmony itself may be used in varying manners in different songs; thus, generalizations may be difficult, and one must remember that acculturation is not simply a question of the borrowing or syncretism of musical elements, but involves an understanding of the phonemic significance of these elements to native listeners. For the Westerner, hearing such acculturated elements with *native*—in this case, Indian—ears may be even more difficult than learning to appreciate unacculturated Indian music on its own terms, since Western listening habits are more likely to intrude when Western elements like harmony are present. In this sense, a holistic study of musical acculturation must transcend the level of sound structure to encompass change, or stasis, in musical *meaning*.

Borrowed and inherited musical elements are often simplified in the process of acculturation. Thus, for example, a hybrid form like highlife has neither the polyrhythmic complexity of traditional West African music, nor the sophisticated harmonies of its Western influences, like jazz. Coplan observes that, in this sense, the acculturation process can be likened to the formation of pidgin languages, wherein aspects of the parent languages are simplified in the hybridization process.[36] Detractors of the new popular musics are apt to criticize what often appears to be the naive, indiscriminate borrowing of hackneyed Western clichés, and the simultaneous abandonment of rich traditional musical practices.

Musical acculturation often involves sensitive issues regarding national identity in relation to the West. An acculturated popular music can constitute a remarkable metaphor for a culture's self-image in the world; insofar as popular music can help shape that image, it is natural that heated polemics should arise over the ramifications of musical form and content. Indeed, in most of the developing world, popular musics cannot be fully understood independent of the legacy of the colonial past and the imperialist present. On the one hand, Western musical styles are often identified, explicitly or not, with progress, technology, modernity, and power. National musics, by contrast, are often seen as quaint and backward; ironically, they may even be associated with colonialism, especially in cultures where such musics were previously patronized by comprador elites. Aside from such considerations, the spread of Western musical features around the world may also be seen as a reflection of the fact that Western music (like many other musics) does of course have a great deal to offer.

On the other hand, a nationalist may well regard the imitation or borrowing of Western musical features as an illustration of Western hegemony, in the form of an obsequious (and often inept) aping of one's former colonial masters. The dominance of the "Big Five" multinational record companies can be seen as perpetuating this exploitation. To a Frantz Fanon, the poolside combo playing crude versions of Frank Sinatra hits in an upper-class club in Morocco would be but another instance of "black skin, white masks," and one more chapter in the ongoing degradation of the once-vital cultures of the third world. As Fanon's work itself reflects, the problem of reconciling national and Western cultures can be particularly acute and difficult for the educated middle classes—especially those who have been trained in the West and yet remain loyal to their homelands.

Regardless of one's appraisal of the merits or faults of musical syncretism, the process of such acculturation is inexorable. It is true that in most of the developing world, folk music may continue to occupy a place, whether as a peripheral commercial genre, an artifically preserved museum piece, a tradition upheld by isolated groups, or a persistent yet marginal alternative to mediated musics. But increasingly, the entire world in which folk traditions were embedded is changing or disappearing. Television, cinema, and radio have irrevocably shattered the insularity of traditional rural life. The antenna emerging from the huddle of sun-baked huts alters the image of the Algerian village far more than its simple appearance might suggest, for to the peasant exposed to American TV, or to Indian film music, the village will never look the same, and traditional rural music will never sound the same. In a word, there is no turning back.

One should, however, remember that Western-like features in ethnic pop musics are not necessarily borrowed from the West, but may in some cases have originated out of indigenous precedents or processes; that is, diffusion should not be confused with polygenesis, and modernization should not be considered synonymous with Westernization. The adoption of "song-like" formal structure in some non-Western popular genres may be a case in point. Since the Renaissance on, there has been a strong tendency for Western musical pieces to be sectionally structured, goal-oriented, discrete units with a clear sense of dramatic climax and closure; genres as diverse as sonatas, pop ballads, Tin Pan Alley tunes, and Beatles songs all exhibit this "song" format. Such an organized format contrasts with open-ended, expandable or compressible approaches used in narrative epics, *juju* music, *ch'in* variations, and, indeed, most musical genres outside of Western bourgeois traditions, which often operate more through repetition and variation of short motifs.[37] Use of closed "song" format in Western music has been related to ideological and socio-economic factors. Shepherd argues that manipulation and juxtaposition of large musical sections are related to the advent of literacy (enabling information to be stored indefinitely), technology (engendering an objective view of time and a greater ability to control nature), and positivism (with its progressive, rather than cyclical view of history).[38] Marothy observes how the appearance of sectional "song" forms, using symmetry, recapitulation, and climax, was contemporaneous with the advent of European capitalism, and he treats use of such formal structures as expressions of the bourgeois worldview, in which the individual, rather than the family or communal group, is the socio-economic unit.[39] Hauser similarly notes the appearance in Renaissance painting and literature, of a rationalized aesthetic which demands logical conformity of all parts of the work of art to the whole, in contradiction to the aesthetic of the bardic epic or the Byzantine panel.[40]

Thus, when musical forms in developing countries abandon or alter traditional elastic, additive, loose structures and replace them with "song"-like forms possessing a clear sense of dramatic climax and closure, it may be difficult to ascertain whether such a change is due to simple Western influence, or rather to changing local tastes deriving from socio-economic developments within the culture itself. Modern popular renditions of formerly strophic genres like the Urdu *ghazal* or the Mexican *son huasteco* often superimpose a kind of closed song format, through introduction of new sections, climaxes near the end of the song, and the like; such a development should not necessarily be attributed to indiscriminate Westernization, but may instead reflect internal class evolution and the subsequent rise of a bourgeois aesthetic.

CHAPTER 2

Latin America and the Caribbean

Latin American and Caribbean popular musics have exerted remarkable influence worldwide, exceeded in this respect only by modern Afro-American pop styles. Their development has been a complex and on-going process of synthesis of styles and features from disparate regions and classes, and as such it constitutes a particularly challenging and rewarding field of cultural ethnological study.

Bred primarily from fusions of European and African-derived musical elements, Latin American popular musics have, on various occasions in the nineteenth and twentieth centuries, returned to both Europe and Africa to form integral and at times even dominant components of popular music taste. The alleged Spanish importation of the sarabande and *guaracha* from Mexico in the seventeenth century would constitute among the earliest instances of a European metropole absorbing a style from its own frontier colonies. In the nineteenth century, such "infusions from below" would increase, as the Cuban *habanera* caught the attention of composers like Bizet, and, on less aristocratic levels, the Luso-Brazilian *modinha* contributed to the evolution of the Portuguese *fado*. In some cases, the new European hybrids were stylized, modified, and re-exported to the New World; as a result, much of Latin American music cannot be regarded simply as the offspring of European and African parents, but rather as the issue of complex processes of musical miscegenation and cross-fertilization.

The emergence of the mass media greatly expedited such cross-fertilizations and exportations, most notably, perhaps, in the case of Cuban styles which enjoyed vogues in the United States, Africa, and elsewhere. Interchange between Afro-Caribbean and African popular musics has increased dramatically since 1945, with styles and sub-styles from Kenya to tiny Martinique emerging and developing their own international cult followers. The interest in ethnic, racial, and cultural roots that has emerged in the last few decades has further deepened and accelerated the syncretic process, as has the coexistence of large immigrant communities in centers like New York City.

While the popular musics of Latin America and the Caribbean have developed almost entirely from European and African sources, much of the traditional syncretic music of the Western Hemisphere is strongly influenced by Indian elements. This influence is perhaps most clear in hybrid forms like the contemporary *huayno* of the Andes, but it is by no means confined to that region. Nevertheless, Indian contribution to modern popular music styles has been negligible, for a number of reasons, including: the absence or social marginality of Indians in the most influential sources of popular music (such as Cuba, Brazil, and Argentina); colonial repression of indigenous musical practices, as a strategy in the subjugation of the numerically superior Indians; the tendency of syncretic popular musics to emerge in urban areas, where Indian society has been less prominent; and, perhaps, the inherent vitality, versatility, and contemporaneity of the Afro-European hybrids.

As a result, most of the genres considered in this chapter represent diverse developments of European and African musical elements. Colonial demography was naturally a primary factor in shaping such hybrids. On the European side, individual national musical styles (such as those of Spain and Portugal) tended to be most influential in the colonies of each metropole, although historical conditions, such as the Franco-Haitian exodus to Cuba around 1800, led to considerable overlapping of colonial boundaries. Similarly, the contributions of distinct African regions and ethnic groups were shaped by colonial spheres of influence in Africa; hence, many of the slaves brought to Portuguese colonies were from Angola and the Congo, while the British drew heavily from the West African Fanti and Ashanti. As the majority of Cuban slaves were imported in the nineteenth century, the Spanish colonists found the internally divided Yoruba to be particularly vulnerable to depredations.

Many specific features of neo-African traditional musics in the New World (such as particular rhythms and lyrics) can be traced to their African sources. Some of these features have persisted in contemporary popular musics. On the whole, however, it is easier to speak of more general African characteristics that have been retained. These would include: an emphasis on rhythm and percussion; overlapping call-and-response vocal format; linear, open-ended forms as opposed to closed, sectional "song" format; repetition of short melodic and/or harmonic units; frequent association of music with dance; and the use of certain African-derived instruments like conga drums.

The European influence is most manifest in the use of such features as harmony, Western instruments, text forms, and, in many cases, bel canto vocal style. Hispanic heritage in particular survives in a predilection for triple meter, guitar and related instruments, and the use of

"Andalusian" harmonic progressions (especially A-minor G-major F-major E-major).

Cuba

The international popularity and influence of Cuban music styles in the nineteenth and twentieth centuries are phenomena without parallel, especially considering Cuba's relatively small size. The genteel *habanera* was merely the first, and hardly the most consequential Cuban style to be exported. Subsequent genres, incorporating more neo-African influence, came to enjoy a far broader appeal, both in Cuba and abroad. For many decades, Cuban-style boleros and *danzones* were dominant genres throughout the Hispanic nations of the Caribbean basin; since the 1940s, modern Cuban dance music, especially the *son*, provided the basis for the *mambo* and *rumba* crazes in the USA and Africa, and continues to constitute the backbone of the music now called "salsa."

The international vogue enjoyed by these musics, so incommensurate with Cuba's size, must derive from a combination of factors. Prior to the advent of the mass media, Cuba's central and accessible location certainly facilitated contacts with Europe and elsewhere, to an extent uncharacteristic of more isolated colonial cities like Lima and Mexico City. A primary factor, however, must have involved the inherent appeal and accessibility of Cuban popular music. While the causes of these may be ultimately impossible to ascertain, one factor must have been the substantial degree to which neo-African musical practices were tolerated by the colonial authorities and even accepted by society at large. Related to this acceptance was the subsequent evolution of musical styles that incorporated relatively even blends of European and neo-African features; the appeal of these musics to a large degree transcended class and racial distinctions in Cuba itself, rendering such styles particularly suitable for export.

Nevertheless, Cuban national musical culture developed considerably later than that of Mexico and Peru. After Cuban gold reserves were exhausted, Cuba, along with Puerto Rico and the Dominican Republic, long remained a neglected and sparsely populated backwater of the Spanish Empire. It was not until around 1760 that interest in Cuba's agricultural potential began to promote substantial immigration. Subsequently, the colonists began to import large numbers of slaves to work on the sugar plantations and replace the indigenous Indian population, almost all of which had perished or been exterminated in the sixteenth century. By the late 1700s, blacks outnumbered whites on the island 340,000 to 291,000.[1]

The British occupation of Havana (1762–1763), although brief, provided an early impetus to trade and economic activity in general, contributing to the opening of the colony's first theater in 1776. This and other subsequent theaters often featured *tonadillas*—light dramas with musical interludes—that were important vehicles for the development of national musical styles in Cuba, Mexico, and elsewhere.[2] On the whole, however, contemporary Cuba was a provincial outpost in comparison with neighboring Saint Domingue or, for that matter, Mexico City. Around the turn of the century, the Haitian revolution precipitated the immigration of several thousand Franco-Haitian refugees—white and black—who came to exert a considerable cultural impact in eastern Cuba. Most important from the perspective of musical development was the introduction of the *contredanse* (Sp. *contradanza*), a stylization of the English "country-dance" which had spread to Haiti via Brittany. In the colonies, the *contradanza* soon evolved from its rustic, collective European form into a genteel, light-classical genre patronized by the growing colonial bourgeoisie. As the genre became more distinctly Cuban, its name changed from *contradanza habanera,* that is, the Havana-style *contradanza,* to simply *habanera.* In the course of this evolution the form also acquired the distinctive short, recurring rhythmic ostinato which pervaded several other syncretic genres in colonial Latin America:

In the 1880s, the *danzón,* standardized and promoted in the compositions and editions of Miguel Failde (1853–1921), came to replace the *habanera* in popularity. For some forty years hence the *danzón* remained the single most popular Cuban dance genre, and it continued an attenuated existence through the 1950s. Unlike the *contredanse,* the *danzón* was a couple dance, and as a musical form was cultivated by musically literate composers. Also in keeping with its bourgeois European character, it was in a sectional rondo form; most typically it consisted of an eight-bar thematic section ("A"), repeated once, leading to a contrasting section ("B"), a repeat of the "A," followed by a "C" section of a more lyrical character, and concluding with a repeat of the "A" theme—thus its form could be schematized as ABACA. In the early twentieth century a coda was added, which generally consisted of instrumental solos over a medium tempo, harmonically static vamp.

The *danzón* was primarily instrumental; initially it was played by an "outdoor" military-style ensemble including timpani and brass instruments, but in the early twentieth century this *típico* ensemble came to be replaced by the *charanga francesa,* consisting of enlarged rhythm section (piano, bass, timbales, and other percussion), two violins, and a flute.[3] From its inception, the *danzón* reflected neo-African influence in its incorporation of an "obsessive" isorhythm—in this case, the *cinquillo,* which had been imported from Haiti, where it remains an important rhythm in *voudoun* music.[4] The *cinquillo,* indeed, is the most distinguishing feature of the *danzón:*

Neo-African influence had been an important element in Cuban music since well before the development of the *danzón*. In the late 1700s, chroniclers were describing Afro-Cuban percussive musics and dances like the *chuchumbé;* one such contemporary description related how "the talent, for the dancer, lies in the perfection in which the hips and lower back are moved, while the rest of the body is more or less immobile."[5] The same, indeed, could be said for modern Cuban dance styles. African influence increased dramatically in the nineteenth century, both in the crystallization of neo-African genres and in the incorporation of neo-African features into syncretic styles like the *danzón*.

A number of factors contributed to the strength of the African strain in Cuban music and culture. The majority of Cuban slaves were imported in the nineteenth century—indeed, as late as 1873—such that fresh infusions of African talent continued until a later date than anywhere else in the New World. Many of the slaves lived on large, isolated plantations in the countryside, where their musical practices continued in relatively traditional forms. At the same time, black cooperative societies called *cabildos* flourished in the cities and provided dynamic contexts for the creation of new Afro-Cuban music and dance, especially for the large number of free blacks. Colonial authorities tended to tolerate neo-African musical practices; in this respect they differed from their Northern European neighbors in the USA, who lacked the Mediterranean peoples' cosmopolitan tolerance and required an ideology of virulent racism to legitimize oppression of blacks in an otherwise democratic state.[6] Finally, many blacks became professional musicians, since whites regarded such a vocation as disreputable and, indeed, generally preferred the vitality of black performers. As a result, as early as 1831 a chronicler related that music performance in Cuba "was in the hands of people of color."[7]

By the latter half of the nineteenth century, the public preference for black or mulatto dance musicians had become widespread, and Cuban music had finally surpassed imported styles in popularity. On the European-derived side of the musical spectrum lay art music, the emerging *danzón*, and neo-Hispanic *campesino* music (*zapateo,* and the more text-oriented forms of *décima* or *punto cubano*); also gaining popularity was the *canción,* a languid, sentimental ballad typically sung by male *trovadores* in Italian bel canto style with guitar accompaniment.

African-derived genres included the musics associated with *santería* and other Yoruba and Bantu cults, *congas* used in Carnival masquerade processions called *comparsas,* and more importantly for the development of popular music, the various styles of *rumba.*

Rumba, a secular Afro-Cuban music and dance genre, appears to have crystallized in the late nineteenth century, being performed both by rural and urban blacks as informal entertainment. The *rumba* ensemble generally consisted of a lead vocalist, a chorus, and at least three percussionists. Several types of traditional *rumba* have been identified, with the *yambú, colombia,* and *guaguancó* being the most important. Of these, the *guaguancó* was the most popular and most influential in the later evolution of Cuban dance music. The *guaguancó's* percussive accompaniment combines improvised parts with standardized ostinati. The most characteristic of the latter, and the trademark of the *guaguancó* is the *tumbador* isorhythm played on two lower-pitched congas, shown below. This is combined, most typically, with a "two-three" *clave* pattern (or variant thereof)—played on a pair of hard wooden sticks bearing the same name—and one of a set of standardized ostinati beaten on the side of a drum with the *palitos,* a pair of thin wooden sticks.[8]

Over this basic composite rhythm, syncopated improvisations are performed on a higher-pitched conga drum, the *quinto.* The similarities between the *rumba's* percussive structure and that of West African drum ensembles is obvious: The *quinto's* function is analogous to that of the improvising master drummer, while the *clave* and *palitos* patterns may be seen as counterparts to the time-line.

The *guaguancó* is best regarded as consisting of two sections—the *canto* and *montuno*—with a short introduction called the *diana.* In the *diana,* the lead vocalist sings a few introductory phrases to non-lexical syllables; in the *canto,* he sings an extended narrative text, which is often loosely improvised, and may be punctuated by short choral refrains. Eventually, the lead vocalist signals the commencement of the *montuno,* which is in the form of call-and-response with the chorus. Both *canto* and *montuno* are of indeterminate length. Melodies used in the *canto,* and the loose two- or three-part harmonies of the *montuno* refrains reflect clear Spanish influence and often suggest simple repeated chord progressions. The *rumba* could be performed in any social gathering, whether in a *cabildo* or on a street corner. It would invariably accompany dance, which in the *guaguancó,* consists of couple dancing (without touching) where the male symbolizes his domination of the woman with swats, kicks, and, at climactic moments, stylized pelvic thrusts (*vacunao*) aimed at the woman's pudenda. *Rumba* texts are generally topical, concerning love, the *rumba* itself, or neighborhood or national events, and are often a vehicle for socio-political satire.

Roughly contemporaneous with the emergence of the *rumba* was the early evolution of a genre that was eventually to dominate Cuban popular music: the *son*. The *son* appears to have originated in eastern Cuba, influenced both by Afro-Cuban musics as well as rural Hispanic-derived genres. The latter influence was evident in the use of simple chordal harmony, quadratic verse forms, the mandolin-like *laud*, the guitar, and the related *tres* (bearing three double or triple courses generally tuned D-G-B). From the Afro-Cuban side came the use of bongos, *clave, botija* (a blown jug), and the *marimbula*—an enlarged descendant of African *mbira*-type thumb-pianos—which is used in Cuba and elsewhere in the Caribbean as a bass instrument. Also essential to the *son* instrumentarium is the *güiro*, a gourd scraper presumed to derive from indigenous Indian musical practice.

In the early twentieth century, the *son* arrived in Havana, where it emerged into historical daylight. By 1930 it was the most popular urban dance genre, and the sextets and septets that specialized in *son* put an end to the hegemony of the *charanga* ensembles.[9] Particularly influential among the new groups in this first stage of the urban *son* were the Sexteto Habanero, the Septeto Nacional (of Ignacio Piñeiro), and Miguel Matamoros' Trio Matamoros. While most *son* musicians were black or mulatto, the genre's popularity soon extended beyond racial, class, and ethnic lines. The *son's* vitality and importance, indeed, stemmed from its dynamic synthesis of European and Afro-Cuban elements, to the extent that it eventually became recognized as the preeminent national genre of Cuba.

The dramatic vogue of the *son* coincided roughly with the advent of the mass media. Player pianos and music boxes had already found their way into many middle-class homes, but victrolas and radios soon became far more common. Cuban radio, from its inception in 1922, played an important role in disseminating popular music. As Díaz observes, while radio stations did promote foreign music, until the forties they tended to rely less on recordings than on live studio performances— partly because the latter were so cheap. This practice not only favored Cuban music over imported forms, but also tended to promote lesser-known groups and songs.[10] Aside from thus democratizing musicians' access to the media, the radio had a number of other effects; Díaz notes that the *charanga francesa's* greater suitability for broadcast fidelity struck the death-blow to the old, horn-dominated *orquesta típica*; moreover, radio amplification eliminated the need for strong singing voices, promoting demand instead for suave and intimate voices with more distinct personalities; finally, the radio further weakened racial barriers in music, for while black artists might be prevented from performing in the most exclusive clubs or homes, no such discrimination existed on the radio—for "the voice has no color."[11]

In the standard *son* ensemble, as first popularized by the Sexteto Habanero, upright bass replaced the *marimbula* and *botija*, and a trumpet was added. Individual rhythmic parts were simplified, although the *bongocero* was free to improvise throughout. In spite of the Spanish preference for triple meter (retained in the Cuban *zapateo* and *punto*), the *son* was performed in 4/4, usually at a moderate tempo (M.M. ca. 120). Its Afro-Cuban affinities were less evident in style than in the use of *clave*, bongo, and a bipartite formal structure paralleling that of the *rumba*, that is, a narrative first section, followed by a *montuno* in which responsorial vocal parts would be sung over a simple, repeated harmonic ostinato. The initial section, while corresponding loosely to the *rumba's canto*, acquired the character of a Europeanized "song," with an extended, closed harmonic sequence—occasionally 32-bar AABA form—providing the background for solo or duet vocal lines.[12]

The next stage of evolution of the *son* is best represented by the ensemble of Arsenio Rodríguez (1911–1970), a blind *tres*-player and bandleader whose group was a predominant trendsetter in the forties and fifties. Arsenio's ensemble included piano, second trumpet, and, in some cases saxophone, as well as an expanded rhythm section using *timbales*, conga, and cowbell (*cencerro*) along with the more traditional instruments. The individual instrumental parts were standardized to produce complex, intricate composite rhythms.[13] Moreover, the trumpets, instead of improvising in a traditional desultory manner, were incorporated into tight pre-composed sectional arrangements in a fashion obviously influenced by contemporary swing bands. Arsenio's mature style, in a word, established what were to become the norms of subsequent Cuban dance music and salsa. Arsenio's prolonged residence in New York City further laid the foundations for the subsequent vogue of Cuban dance music among Latino communities there; thus, as Díaz notes, by the forties "salsa was already complete in the legacy of Arsenio."[14]

Cuban dance music, while having the *son* as its backbone, comprises several other important genres, especially the *guaracha, bolero, chachachá, mambo,* and more ephemeral styles such as the *pachanga.* In the context of modern dance music the distinctions between some of these genres may become blurred, although their evolutions are generally quite discrete.

The *guaracha* dates (in some form) from seventeenth-century Mexico, whence it was exported to Spain. By the nineteenth century it was flourishing in Cuba as a lively, up-tempo dance song popularized in brothels.[15] The *guaracha* bears considerable affinity to the urban *son,* although it differs in its satirical and often bawdy texts, its alternation of verses and refrains (as opposed to *canto-montuno* form) and, to some extent, its rhythm.[16]

In the 1950s, the *chachachá* replaced the *danzón* as the staple genre of the still vital *charanga* ensembles. Popularized by the Orquesta Aragon and, more specifically, by composer and bandleader Enrique Jorrín, the *chachachá* enjoyed considerable vogue in the USA, albeit in diluted form. The *chachachá* resembles the *son montuno* in its medium tempo (M.M.ca. 110), composite rhythmic structure, and variable form structure. It differs primarily in its association with *charanga* ensembles rather than horn-based *conjuntos; chachachás*, like much of *charanga* music, are often sung in unison by two or three singers, occasionally in a rather effeminate vocal style.

The *bolero* is a slow, romantic ballad, most easily distinguished by its bass pattern (half-note, 2 quarter-notes, where bass is present).[17] *Boleros* may be performed by *charanga* groups, dance *conjuntos,* or in the standard Cuban trio format of vocals, *maracas,* and two guitars.

Mambo is a particularly imprecise term. It appears to have been first popularized in the mid-1940s by the *charanga* ensemble of Antonio Arcaño, Arcaño y sus Maravillas. We may recall that in the early twentieth century the *danzón* had acquired a coda consisting of a syncopated, percussive vamp over which instrumental solos could be improvised. In subsequent decades, this coda became increasingly long, while the preceding sections were shortened or partially omitted. Arcaño extended this Afro-Cubanization process by further truncating, or in some cases, entirely omitting the opening sections, stressing instead the instrumental vamp.[18] The true popularization of the term *mambo,* however, was the work of bandleader Pérez Prado, who applied it to the up-tempo, primarily instrumental big band arrangements that made him famous in Cuba, the USA, and Mexico. Prado's antiphonal sectional writing and his big band format were clearly influenced by contemporary swing, but his rhythms were entirely Cuban and represented an important step in the re-Africanization of Cuban popular music.

Modern Cuban Dance Music

Cuban dance music reached something of a peak in the 1950s, with the flourishing of Benny Moré, Félix Chapottin, Miguelito Cuní, Niño Rivera, the Sonora Matancera, and others. Much of the vitality of this period derived from the incorporation of Afro-Cuban elements into mainstream styles, which paralleled an increased recognition of the neo-African contribution to Cuban culture in general.[19] The clearest manifestation of this recognition was the merging of the *son* and *rumba* in a manner that achieved a balanced synthesis of European and neo-African features. From the perspective of the *son,* the chief developments were: an increase in tempo (often to as much as M.M.220), a heightened rhythmic intensity, standardization of the "song"-*montuno* form, and a proliferation of song-texts extolling the *rumba* and Afro-Cuban heritage in general. Alternately, the trend could be regarded as a modernization and Europeanization of the traditional *rumba guaguancó,* consisting primarily of the addition of Western instruments, fixed arrangements, and more sophisticated harmonies. Indeed, in this fashion several traditional *rumba* compositions have been transformed into popular dance songs by modern *conjuntos* and salsa bands.[20]

This particularly vital period of Cuban music coincided with the further extension of the mass media on the island. By 1950 several Cuban record companies and radio stations were flourishing, and nearly 90 percent of homes had radios; television had also become an important medium, and soon only eight countries in the world had more televisions than Cuba (over 200,000 at this point). Live music abounded everywhere from exclusive cabarets like the Tropicana to public buses, where strolling artists earned local renown performing on busy routes for handouts.[21]

By the 1950s Cuban dance music had become a dominant musical style not only in Puerto Rico, but in much of Africa and among Latino communities in the USA and elsewhere. In Puerto Rico and the USA (especially New York City), this music eventually came to be known as salsa. The term "salsa," although common in usage, should not be taken to denote a distinct musical genre; in fact, salsa style does not differ in any significant respect from that of Cuban dance music of the fifties.

We have mentioned the intricate composite rhythm achieved by the interaction of several standardized rhythmic parts in the Cuban dance music ensemble. The "two-three" *clave* pattern is cited by some musicians as an underlying structural component even though it is frequently absent.[22] The counterpart of the *palitos* in the modern dance *conjunto* is the cowbell, which may play the traditional *palitos* pattern given above, but more often plays the ostinato shown in Example 1 below, or a variation thereof. The conga rhythm is less regular, but generally features two eighth-notes played on the fourth beat of each measure. Piano patterns, which will be discussed in greater detail, play important rhythmic roles; in the *montuno*, they, along with the cowbell and vocal refrains, generally form two-bar "closed-open" groupings by stressing the downbeat of the first bar while eliding that of the second. The most remarkable rhythmic feature, however, is the anticipated bass pattern, in which the first beat of the measure is skipped (or tied), while the note played on the fourth beat anticipates the harmony of the following bar. All of these parts are shown in the excerpt below:[23]

The *montuno* section of the *son/rumba* may contain instrumental solos, featuring *timbales*, piano, trumpet, *tres*, or other instruments. These improvisations may occur in the format of "calls" to the choral "response," but frequently they are extended solos performed over the repeated harmonic and rhythmic ostinato of the *montuno*. The individual instrumental styles are themselves worthy of greater analysis than is possible in this volume; Crook has made some general remarks about percussion style, and one may note that the trumpet style, although distinctively Cuban, is heavily influenced by jazz.[24] The piano style, both in accompaniment and solo, is particularly distinctive and crucial to the ensemble's sound and hence merits some further consideration here.

Cuban piano style bears some notable affinities to jazz—especially in the frequent omission of the root from chord voicings—and most

Cuban dance pianists appear to be familiar with jazz. The Cuban style differs, however, in its greater stress on volume and percussive intensity, both in accompanying and in soloing. Comping, for example, consists not of the irregular, loose accentuations of jazz piano, but of steady rhythmic/chordal figures that play an essential role in the intricate aggregate rhythm of the ensemble. These figures typically alternate triple-octave pitches with two-octave diads in standardized rhythmic patterns which, as mentioned, stress the first beat of every alternate bar. These characteristics are illustrated in the following examples, which show some typical ostinati played over a common *montuno* chord progression; of these, most typical is the first, with its characteristic alternation between the fifth and sixth scalar degrees:

Improvised piano solos similarly reflect the stress on volume and rhythm in the juxtaposition of double- and quadruple-octave melodies, syncopated arpeggios, and other effects, as shown in the excerpt below.[25]

Another important set of popular genres in the first half of the twentieth century are those collectively referred to as *trova*, including the *criolla, clave,* and, most important, the *canción. Canción* literally means "song," but in Cuba and other Latin American countries it generally denotes a slow, sentimental ballad not meant for dance. The roots of *trova* and *canción* lie in the nineteenth century, their primary models being Spanish *canciones* (*boleros, tiranas,* and *polos*), German *lieder,* French *romanzas,* and especially Italian operatic arias. Products primarily of the urban petty bourgeoisie, the *trova* songs dealt with love, the Cuban countryside, and nationalism.[26] The most celebrated composers of traditional *trova* were Sindo Garay (1866–1968) and Pepe Sanchez (1856–1918). From the thirties on, the *canción,* resisting any Afro-Cuban influence, came increasingly under the sway of North American popular music. This last trend contributed to the rise in the forties of *filin* (from "feeling"), a more unabashedly sentimental *canción,* still typically performed, in *trova* tradition, by one or two vocalists with guitar accompaniment. In subsequent years, the *canción* effectively merged with the mainstream international slow ballad, acquiring all the commercial, artificial mannerisms of the latter while losing whatever distinctly Cuban character it ever possessed.

Cuban Popular Music since 1959

The Cuban Revolution has had prodigious effect upon the socio-economic contexts of musical life in Cuba, although its actual impact on musical styles is less tangible, aside from the advent of *nueva trova.* In the early 1960s, nationalized state institutions replaced nearly all of the private sector, including most aspects of the formerly commercial music industry such as nightclubs, recording companies, radio stations, and concerts. The revolutionary government has regarded the promotion of national culture as a high priority; moreover, it has enthusiastically promoted Cuban popular music as a vital part of national heritage.[27] Hence, in spite of shortages of funds and a host of problems accompanying the bureaucratization process, the first decade of the revolution saw a "remarkable improvement of material facilities for cultural expansion."[28] While record production appears to have stagnated somewhat,[29] radio transmission tripled,[30] prices were lowered at the now nationalized clubs, conservatory education was provided for talented students, and elaborate amateur and professional competitions and forums were established (such as the Adolfo Guzmán competition and television shows like *Para bailar* and *Todo el mundo canta*). At the same time, many musicians emigrated, taking advantage of the United States' policy of accepting refugees from certain communist countries.

As in most of the Western world, rock music and the mainstream sentimental ballad enjoy great popularity in Cuba, and the Cuban government makes no attempt to discourage their dissemination. State ambivalence toward jazz persisted until the early 1980s, by which time a number of Cuban jazz musicians achieved international renown and the government belatedly turned to promoting them, and jazz in general.

Cuban dance music has continued to flourish, paralleling, in many cases, the development of salsa abroad. The most noteworthy groups of the 1970s and 1980s have been Los Van Van—an expanded *charanga* ensemble—and Irakere. The latter is a sort of Cuban supergroup, led by composer-pianist Jesus "Chucho" Valdéz, performing eclectic syntheses of Afro-Cuban cult music, modern jazz, and rock over a foundation of sophisticated Cuban dance music. Van Van is best known for their popularization of the *songo* rhythm; in other respects their music is fairly conventional, if tuneful.

On the whole, however, the revolution does not appear to have generated any dramatic new developments in the realm of dance music style; rather, its impact has been in such matters as the attempted democratization of access to musical education and performance, some increase in politicization of song texts, the demystification of performers and avoidance of "superstar" promotion, the disassociation of music from commercials and from the capitalist market in general, and the creation of an ideological climate which promotes a different aesthetic apprehension of music on the part of the listener.[31]

Nueva Trova

Nueva trova, the Cuban efflorescence of the pan-Latin American "new song" movement, is the most original musical development in Cuba since 1959, and reflects, more than any other Cuban music, an intimate association with the ideology and socio-cultural climate of the revolution.[32] The movement first appeared in the mid-1960s, and eventually received official sponsorship from the government and the Casa de las Americas, an important cultural organization in Havana. The affinities with music of Joan Baez, Bob Dylan, and other North American singers were reflected in the use of the term "protest music" at this early stage. Exponents of the genre eventually came to disparage this label as excessively negative, and in 1972 the term *nueva trova* came into vogue. While many *nueva trova* songs do in fact protest against imperialism, sexism, and exploitation, underlying such themes is a more positive vision of mature, egalitarian emotional relationships and a just, humane society. Capitalism, with its attendant social inequalities and its network of imperialist international relations, is not regarded as the means to achieving such a society. Rather, *nueva trova* song texts reflect affinities with the progressive lyrics of poets like Neruda, Vallejo, and Guillén. Poetic style ranges from the surreal and esoteric to the simple and unpretentious; on the whole, however, the literary standards of the lyrics are high. As often as not, subject matter may be personal relationships rather than explicit social commentary, but these matters are seen as integrally related in the concept of a progressive, humane society. Hence, for example, the deliberate avoidance of machismo, objectification of women ("your pearly teeth"), of hackneyed romantic rhetoric, and of the ritual cursing of "faithless" women so common in many traditional Latin American songs.[33]

From the musical perspective, *nueva trova* is highly diverse. The movement's name reflects its affinities with traditional *trova*, particularly the *canción*, and the legacy of nationalistic hymns and *décimas* which date from the nineteenth-century anti-colonial struggle. Many *nueva trova* songs incorporate traditional rhythms, instruments, and text forms (such as the *décima*) in a conscious attempt to reinterpret and adapt Cuban musical heritage to the new society created by the revolution.[34] The influence of the *son* and *guajira* is particularly strong, for example, in the music of Pablo Milanés. Other musicians are somewhat more eclectic in style. Many of Silvio Rodríguez's songs are closer in style and spirit to North American soft rock. While Rodríguez and Milanés most typically sing while accompanying themselves on acoustic guitar, Sara González tends to favor an upbeat ensemble backing, occasionally with a Brazilian flavor.[35]

In accordance with their sense of solidarity with *nueva canción* colleagues in Latin America, *nueva trova* musicians often incorporate elements of music from Venezuela, Puerto Rico, and, especially, the Andean *altiplano*. Sometimes, the presence of such elements may be more symbolically than musically functional, as when the group Manguaré uses Andean flutes and drums in a song whose style and texture remain that of tame North American folk-rock. The emphasis on texts and the goal of appealing to a pan-Latin audience may also contribute to the frequent use of a bland, mainstream *canción* style, which may not be new, not to mention revolutionary. Thus, *nueva trova*, as a set of musical styles, should be comprehended as a reinterpretation of traditional Cuban *trova*, as a regional variety of the pan-Latin *nueva canción*, and as one efflorescence of the cluster of socially conscious musics that emerged in the Americas as a whole (including the USA) in the sixties.

While right-wing governments in countries such as Chile and El Salvador attempt to exterminate *nueva canción*, Cuban officialdom extends full patronage and encouragement to *nueva trova*. The movement, as Carrasco states, has in fact become "a sort of mass youth organization with representatives all over the country";[36] the members, who number over two thousand, meet regularly to discuss thematic and artistic problems, and they also participate in national forums like the Guzmán competition.

Puerto Rico

Puerto Rico, since its European discovery, developed as a sister colony to Cuba in the Spanish Empire. In many respects, the evolution of Puerto Rican culture paralleled that of Cuba. As in Cuba, Puerto Rico's indigenous population was largely annihilated in the sixteenth century, and the island remained a relatively neglected backwater of the empire, which concentrated attention and resources on the more lucrative Mexican and Andean regions. Development of Puerto Rico increased in the late eighteenth and nineteenth century, especially as dismemberment of the empire heightened the island's strategic importance. African slaves were imported to work the cane plantations, although they do not appear to have exceeded one third of the island's population at any time.

Puerto Rican musical culture developed along roughly similar lines to that of Cuba, and in fact was directly influenced by its musical trends. Thus did the Puerto Rican *danza* evolve as a counterpart to the Cuban *danzón*, and the *guaracha*, evidently imported in the nineteenth century, established strong roots in Puerto Rico. Of the Hispanic-derived rural folk musics, the most important are the various forms of *seis*. The *seis* is typically performed by a solo vocalist, accompanied by *güiro*, *maracas*, guitar, and the *cuatro*, a smaller guitar-type instrument with five doubled courses. As a dance genre the *seis* could be viewed as a counterpart to Cuban forms like the *zapateo*, while the more text-oriented *seis con décima* is analogous in function and form to the Cuban *décima* or *punto guajiro*. The *aguinaldo*, using similar instrumentation and style, developed as a characteristic genre performed in Christmas season.

On the whole, this heritage of Hispanic-derived folk genres, rich as it may be, did not play a crucial role in the development of Puerto Rican popular music. *Seis* and *aguinaldo* persist as folkloric musics, but they have not been modernized or stylized as commercial popular musics dependent on the mass media. Indeed, it may be said that Puerto Rican traditional music has in general played only a limited role in the evolution of popular music on the island. Puerto Rico and its emigrant community in New York have developed remarkably vital and influential popular musics, but these have been overwhelmingly dominated by Cuban, North American, and more recently, Dominican styles.

The two Puerto Rican traditional genres that have developed into modernized popular styles are *bomba* and *plena;* neo-African influence is clear in both, and as such they represent the black and mulatto contributions to the island's musical culture.

The *bomba* is strongly African in character; it developed among the black communities in coastal towns where the sugarcane mills were located. The antiquity of the *bomba* is obscure; Vega claims that it emerged in the seventeenth and eighteenth centuries, while López Cruz regards the arrival of black Haitian refugees around 1800 as a crucial catalyst in its evolution.[37] The genre became obscure by the mid-twentieth century and never achieved wide popularity outside the black and mulatto communities, as did the *rumba,* for example.

In other respects the *bomba* may be regarded as a Puerto Rican counterpart to the Cuban *rumba.* It developed as an informal secular entertainment genre, accompanied by social dancing. The ensemble consists of vocals and percussion. The text, generally of topical nature, is rendered in alternating stanzas and responsorial sections. The accompanying percussion ensemble may include a variety of instruments (such as *güiro, maracas,* and cowbell), the most important of which are the *bomba* barrel drums from which the genre derives its name. Of these, the larger, lower-pitched *seguidora* provides supporting ostinati (along with sticks beat on the side of a drum or another hard surface), while the player of the smaller *requinto* improvises throughout. A variety of rhythms are employed in the numerous types of *bomba. Bomba* is danced by couples, who do not touch; at times, lively, competitive interaction occurs between the *requinto* player and a male dancer.

The *plena* is of greater importance in the development of popular music, because it flourished later and achieved much wider popularity among the Puerto Rican population as a whole. Like *bomba, plena* emerged among lower-class black and mulatto communities in coastal towns, especially Poncé and Loiza Aldea. While the origins of the genre lie in the later part of the colonial period,[38] its heyday was the second and third decades of the twentieth century. *Plena* accompanies a social couple dance of somewhat lighter character than that of the *bomba,* and lacking the competitive interaction with the drummer.

Much of the *plena's* charm lies in its narrative, colloquial texts, which typically relate or comment upon contemporary events of local or national interest. The text stanzas, sung by a solo male vocalist, alternate with short choral refrains or responsorial sections.

A variety of instruments may be used in traditional *plena.* The most important of these is the *pandereta,* a Spanish-derived tambourine without jingles. While the lead *pandereta* player improvises freely throughout the performance of a piece, other *pandereta* players provide supporting rhythms—generally a simple quadratic pulse emphasizing the downbeats. Rhythmic support may also be provided by *güiro,* cowbell, conga, or bongos. The *plena* ensemble usually incorporates at least one European-derived melodic instrument, such as a harmonica, *cuatro,* or guitar. Further, *plena* harmonies, although simple, may incorporate modulation, unlike those implicit in the *bomba.*[39]

While the *plena's* blend of European and Afro-Caribbean features won it many middle-class listeners and practicioners, it remained most popular among the lower classes. In the late 1930s, under the onslaught of imported popular musics, *plena* declined rapidly, and in its traditional form the genre survives only in a folkloric capacity. Nevertheless, more modernized and stylized versions of *plena* did emerge as commercial genres, and have persisted as peripheral features of the Puerto Rican popular music scene.

In the 1930s Puerto Rican culture came to be heavily influenced by external forces. Urbanization and the advent of the mass media increased contact with imported musics, and Cuban musical styles began to dominate the cities, relegating indigenous genres to the sidelines.[40] At the same time, Puerto Rico's dependency on its new colonial master, the United States, became dramatically more acute. Under North American rule Puerto Rico became a source of cheap labor and a captive market for goods produced by the metropole. Agricultural depression in the thirties occasioned the first wave of emigration to the USA, particularly New York, whose upper East Side came to accommodate a sizeable expatriate community of improverished refugees from Puerto Rican slums like La Perla. Such emigration enabled Puerto Rican culture to establish new roots in an urban environment, while at the same time contributing to the continued North Americanization of the island itself.

While Cuban popular music was beginning to dominate the Puerto Rican popular music world, some attempts were made to revitalize *plena* as a contemporary commercial genre. In the thirties Manuel "Canario" Jiménez greatly popularized a somewhat modernized version of the *plena* in Puerto Rico and in the New York barrios. Canario's repertoire included newly composed *plenas* as well as traditional favorites such as "Santa María" and "Cortarón a Elena." He retained the traditional *plena's* melodies, harmonies, mixed male and female choruses, alternating verse and chorus structure, and the topical, often nationalistic subject matter; at the same time, he supplemented the genre's traditionally sparse melodic instrumentation with piano, two or three horns, and a bass, which occasionally played in the anticipated Cuban style.[41] In the next decade, Cesar Concepción further commercialized and diluted *plena* by incorporating it into big band format. Concepción's *plenas* were traditional in their formal structure and text content, but in their orchestration, style, rhythms, and replacement of *panderetas* with congas they differed little from Cuban dance music. Moreover, they lost what has been described as the "proletarian character" of Canario's music, instead becoming "salon *plenas*" which some Puerto Ricans came to regard as febrile and archaic.[42]

In the mid-1950s, congero/bandleader Rafael Cortijo and his vocalist Ismael Rivera burst upon the Puerto Rican music scene with a dynamic and rejuvenated *plena*. Most of Cortijo's music consisted of Cuban-style *rumbas* and *guarachas*, but he became widely celebrated for his use of modernized *plenas* and, occasionally, *bombas*. Although Cortijo's instrumentation and style resembled that of Concepción, through Rivera's earthy singing and a generally "hotter" style, he recaptured the proletarian rawness of the traditional *plena*. Many of Cortijo's texts, in their use of *barrio* slang and a certain malevolent suggestiveness, became quintessential expressions of the "Newyorican" culture of the housing projects and slums.[43] The vogue of television in the fifties further contributed to Cortijo's popularity.

Since Cortijo's death in 1982, interest in *plena* has dwindled, and the genre is seldom performed outside of folkloric contexts. Puerto Rican salsa groups continue to play predominantly Cuban-style music, while the young—both in the island and in the USA—are increasingly drawn to rock. In the eighties the Dominican *merengue* has invaded Puerto Rico and New York in force and further weakened indigenous styles like *plena*. As Newyoricans now outnumber those living in Puerto Rico, and the island itself is increasingly choked with cars, billboards, and Burger King restaurants, the renewal of Puerto Rican national culture—including *plena* and *bomba*—seems less likely than ever.[44]

The Dominican Republic

Throughout most of its history, the Dominican Republic has been afflicted with an unusually high level of violence, chaos, and socio-economic disruption. This persistent adversity has tended to hinder the development of the rich spectrum of musical genres extant in, for example, neighboring Cuba. Nevertheless, the Dominican Republic has fostered one national dance—the *merengue*—which has become one of the most important pan-Latin popular musics of recent decades.

Early Dominican history to some extent parallels that of Cuba and Puerto Rico. Within a century of the European discovery, the indigenous population of Hispañola—estimated at one million—had perished, and large numbers of African slaves were imported to toil in the mines and plantations. After the inconsiderable gold reserves were exhausted, the colony became a haven for pirates and stagnated to an even greater extent than did Cuba and Puerto Rico. Unfortunately, while these two islands experienced economic and socio-cultural renaissances commencing in the late eighteenth century, Spanish Hispañola suffered further catastrophe and decline. From 1822–1844, the harsh Haitian conquest and domination of the Dominicans ruined the local economy, engendered a heritage of racism and contempt for African-derived culture, and precipitated the flight of the educated Hispanic upper classes, who took with them their own European cultural traditions.[45] Political and economic chaos persisted until the North American occupation (1916–1924), by which time a white, Hispanic-oriented aristocracy had begun to re-emerge. By the nineteenth century Dominican society had become relatively homogeneous from the racial perspective, in the sense that the vast majority were mulattos; however, until the twentieth century the formation of an integrated social fabric remained inhibited by a weakened Hispanic cultural legacy and a rejection by the middle and upper classes of the island's African-derived heritage. In the twentieth century, however, relative political stability and opposition to the North American occupation eventually contributed to the growth of a nationalism which further promoted the rise of the *merengue* as a national music and dance form. The *merengue* was also incorporated into the salsa repertoire, and in the eighties has enjoyed an unprecedented vogue in Puerto Rico and New York.

The early origins of the *merengue* are unclear, and its evolutionary relationship with the Haitian *méringue* and with Puerto Rican, Columbian, and Venezuelan namesakes is ambiguous.[46] The genre appears to have become popular in the Dominican Republic in the early nineteenth century, and by the mid-nineteenth century it had assumed its classic form as a dance song in fast quadratic meter with an accompanying ensemble of *tambora* (a double-headed drum), *güiro* (or *güira*), and a guitar or *cuatro*. In the 1850s, composer Juan Bautista Alfonseca (1810–1879), motivated by the current nationalism and romantic interest in folk culture, popularized a stylized version of the folk *merengue* among the Dominican upper classes. This salon *merengue,* employing an expanded ensemble including violins and flutes, was often disparaged as immoral and crude by more Eurocentric elements of the aristocracy, and virtually disappeared by 1900. Austerlitz has illustrated how the persistent ambivalence toward *merengue*—both as a national genre and as an African-influenced lower-class creation—has reflected the ambiguity and contradictions in Dominican national identity.[47]

In the northern, densely-populated Cibao valley, the folk *merengue*—the *merengue típico cibaeño*—continued to flourish, with its topical texts serving as important means of oral communication and social commentary. In the 1870s the accordion was introduced to the island and soon came to replace the guitar in the *merengue* ensemble; some groups also incorporated a Cuban-style *marimbula* (Dominican *marimba*) as a bass instrument. Over the next forty years, alongside this *típico* format—which later came to be called *perico ripiao*—developed a dance-band *merengue* ensemble using horns—especially saxophones.[48]

In the twentieth century, greater socio-political stability and resentment against the eight-year US occupation heightened the rise of Dominican nationalism. While elite disparagement of the *merengue* persisted, the genre gradually came to constitute an important symbol of national culture for an increasing number of Dominicans. The despotic dictatorship of Rafael Trujillo (1930–1961) helped to definitively enshrine the *merengue* as the country's foremost musical genre. Trujillo was of humble class origins and regarded the landed gentry with disdain; once in power, he promoted the Cibao *merengue*, both for propaganda purposes and as a populist and nationalist symbol.[49] The national radio station established by Trujillo in 1946 further disseminated both *perico ripiao* and the dance band *merengue* throughout the country.[50]

The Trujillo era was a golden age for the *merengue* in the sense that it received such enthusiastic official patronage and faced little competition from imported musics; at the same time, strict censorship sharply circumscribed the genre's traditional role as a vehicle for grassroots socio-political commentary. In the decades following the assassination of "El Benefactor," North American rock and Cuban-style salsa made substantial inroads into the Dominican music scene, especially since the *merengue* was associated by many with the negative aspects of the Trujillo regime.[51] At the same time, however, the genre regained some of its status as a medium of social commentary and expanded its impact in Puerto Rico and among the growing immigrant community in New York. The *merengue*, under the leadership of stars such as Johnny Ventura, adapted to its new international audiences by the use of faster tempi (up to M.M. 172), more elaborate arrangements, lavish stage presentations, and, in some cases, a free usage of instrumentation and stylistic features borrowed from rock.

Most *merengues* consist of two parts: the *merengue* proper, containing vocal stanzas sung over variable chord patterns, and the *jaleo*, which generally features call-and-response vocal and instrumental patterns sung over oscillating tonic and dominant harmonies. (In this sense the *jaleo* corresponds to the *montuno* of the *rumba*.) "Classic" *merengues* from the 1920s to the 1960s often contained an eight-bar march-like introduction called *paseo*. Modern pop *merengues* may have a somewhat more complex structure: The following format is typical:[52]

instrumental introduction
verse
mambo (instrumental *jaleo*, during which the singers dance)
verse
mambo
coro (call-and-response vocals over simple harmonic ostinato)

The *jaleo* derives much of its dynamism from fast, precomposed passages (also called *jaleos*) played by the saxophones, often in parallel thirds; improvised sax solos may also occur in the *jaleo*. The most distinctive feature of the *merengue,* however, is the fast composite rhythm produced by the continuous sixteenth-note *güira* pattern and the *tambora* ostinato, as shown below. The saxophone *jaleo* patterns often interlock with this rhythm. The bass generally emphasizes the downbeats with regular half-notes, although Cuban-style anticipated bass is sometimes used in *jaleos.* If present, the piano generally reiterates Cuban-style *montuno*-type ostinati. Most of these features are evident in the following excerpt from a typical *jaleo:*[53]

It would be an understatement to point out that the *merengue* lacks the complexity of the Cuban *son,* or of salsa in general. Its rhythm, although lively, is simple, and the choreography is elementary. Harmonies consist primarily of tonic-dominant alternation, not only in the *jaleos* but often in the opening *merengue* portion as well (a factor which renders the two sections less distinct than the *canto* and *montuno* of the *son*). Sophistication is generally most evident in the saxophone *jaleos,* which often consist of intricate, high-speed arpeggio patterns employing staccato attack, repeated pitches and other technically difficult effects; tight (*apretado*) execution of the arrangements is essential.

Since the late 1970s, the *merengue* has reached an unprecedented level of popularity, not only among Dominicans and Puerto Ricans but also among other Latino communities (such as Central Americans). New York barrios that once resounded with salsa now throb to the pulse of *merengues* by Wilfrido Vargas and Johnny Ventura. While many contemporary *merengue* texts deal with sentimental love, a number deal, in one way or another, with contemporary urban life and thus serve as mediators between the values and worldview of rural peasant life and New York City.[54] Correspondingly, many groups tend to divide their time between New York and Santo Domingo in order to establish audiences and reputations in both cities. It is not unusual for an aspiring singer or bandleader to record an LP with studio musicians in Santo Domingo in order to acquire club dates in New York City—reversing the traditional procedure wherein local renown is a prerequisite to record contracts. As of 1987, most prominent groups and stars continue to originate in the Dominican Republic; La Gran Manzana ("The Big Apple") is one of the few major bands emerging from New York—a city which *merenguero*

Wilfrido Vargas is fond of describing as "a province of the Dominican Republic."[55]

The *merengue* boom has thus made heavy inroads into the popularity of salsa. The contemporary *merengue,* with its simple choreography and slick stage presentations, seems assured of a continued vitality, if at the expense of the rustic unpretentiousness and topical contemporaneity of the traditional *perico ripiao.*

Salsa

Salsa has come to be recognized as one of the most dynamic and significant pan-American musical phenomena of the 1970s and 1980s. In its various regional forms it is the single most popular dance music style among Puerto Rican and Cuban communities in their homelands and in the USA, and it enjoys great appeal in Central and South America as well.

The very term "salsa" is itself ambiguous, and its use reflects some of the contradictions and complexities of the genre. On one level, as Singer and Friedman note, salsa is to Latinos as "soul" is to blacks;[56] salsa—literally, "hot sauce"—is spicy, zesty, energetic, and unmistakably Latino. On another level, the term is often used as a convenient rubric for the *conjunto*-based Cuban dance styles as well as the modernized *plena, merengue,* and *cumbia.* The occasional accommodation of these genres under the label "salsa" illustrates the similarities in instrumentation and arrangement styles, as well as the extent to which the respective audiences of these genres tend to merge.[57] Moreover, to some, the conception of *merengue, son,* and the like as regional efflorescences of a unified pan-Latin sound represents a potential Latino solidarity. To others, however, the recycling of Cuban music under an artificial, obscurantist label is but one more example of North American exploitation and commodification of third world primary products.[58]

While the term "salsa" may comprise the several Latin music genres mentioned above, stylistically its backbone consists of Cuban dance music—particularly the modern *son* that evolved in the 1950s. Salsa tempi may tend to be somewhat faster and its horn sections larger, and some salsa texts do reflect the particular social contexts of their origins, but the primary distinction between salsa and Cuban dance music is non-musical: salsa is produced outside of Cuba, primarily by Puerto Ricans and Cubans living in New York City and Puerto Rico, and also by stylistically similar groups based in Venezuela, Mexico City, and other Spanish-speaking countries of the Caribbean basin (where it may be called *música tropical*). While the term salsa is now extremely common in usage, it is seen as artificial by many Latin musicians.[59]

Although salsa may not be stylistically original, it is highly significant as a socio-cultural phenomenon. For millions of Latinos salsa is not only the most popular dance music, but is also a link between tradition and modernity, between the impoverished homeland and the dominant United States, between street life and the chic night club, and between grassroots culture and the corporate media. Salsa is a musical lingua franca shared by separate Latino nations and communities, and a forum where the conflicts and contradictions involved in such encounters are mediated.

While many cities in the Caribbean basin and elsewhere function as regional centers for salsa, New York City has been by far the most crucial in its mature development. The major record companies—particularly Fania—have been based in New York and it is in that city that the Puerto Rican community, along with other immigrant groups, has established salsa as an expression of Latino ethnicity in a social context otherwise characterized by Anglo economic, political, and cultural domination.

Cuban dance music had achieved a presence in New York City as early as the 1930s, when it was imported by Puerto Rican immigrants and a few enterprising Cuban groups. One of the latter, led by Don Azpiazu, established the Cuban *son* (under the misnomer *rumba*) as a peripheral American pop genre with his hit "The Peanut Vendor" ("El Manicero"). As the barrios continued to swell with new immigrants, and North Americans grew increasingly fond of Cuban music, more Cuban and Puerto Rican groups sought their fortune in New York City. In downtown clubs, Anglo as well as Latin bands (such as that of the Spaniard Xavier Cugat) played diluted, sweetened versions of the *son* for local audiences while the uptown, East Harlem clubs offered more authentic music to immigrants.

It was in the next decade, however, that Cuban music acquired a special vitality of its own in New York. In general, this was due to the continued growth of the immigrant community, the maturation of the big band dance vogue, and the boost given to small record companies by the juke-box industry and the musicians' strike of the early forties. More specifically, the establishment of New York as a center for Latin music resulted from the local success of a generation of brilliant bandleaders. Most important among these were Arsenio Rodríguez, Machito (Frank Grillo), and Tito Puente, who led dynamic Cuban-style big bands and together with Pérez Prado further popularized the *mambo*. Also worthy of mention is the charismatic bandleader Tito Rodríguez, who was renowned, among other things, for his acrobatic break-dancing thirty-five years before that term was invented. This period also saw excursions into Cuban music by American jazz artists such as Dizzy Gillespie.

These successful bands continued to flourish in the 1950s and, in some cases, through the 1980s. As the *mambo* was in full swing in the USA, Cuban *charanga* ensembles popularized the *chachachá*, which was then adapted to big band format by Puente and others. As Roberts notes, the over-commercialization and dilution of the *chachachá* and the rise of rock and roll subsequently circumscribed Latin music popularity among the Anglo market,[60] but continued growth of the barrio insured the perpetuation of Latin dance music in the city; more specifically, the influx of Cuban refugees after 1959 reinforced Cuban dominance of Latin music in New York, not to mention Miami. The overwhelming predominance of Cuban music persisted, despite the fact that most of the prominent bandleaders emerging in the sixties—such as Ray Barretto, Johnny Pacheco, and Eddie Palmieri—were not Cuban.

It was not until the late 1960s that the term "salsa" came into vogue and was applied to the music that Tito Puente and others had been playing for twenty-five years. The rubric was popularized by a Venezuelan radio station and, more importantly, by Jerry Masucci, the Italian-American founder of Fania Records, which emerged as the largest producer of Latin dance music recordings until being sold in the early eighties.

The 1970s were the true heyday of salsa. Radio dissemination, record production, and the number of top-quality bands increased dramatically. At the same time, as Roberts notes, there was a stylistic "return to Cuban orthodoxy" as bandleaders spoke of "grassroots purity" and generally forsook the big band format for the standard (and more economical) Cuban *conjunto* of a rhythm section with a front line of two to five horns.[61] Established stars like Celia Cruz and Eddie Palmieri were joined by a host of fresh talent. Generally singled out for special critical acclaim is the music of bandleader Willie Colon and singer-composer Ruben Blades. These two artists, who have collaborated on several LPs, are celebrated for their stylistic eclecticism and distinctive arrangements. The Panamanian-born Blades, one of the most prominent salsa artists, owes his popularity primarily to his fine voice, compositional talent, cinematic successes (especially the 1985 "Crossover Dreams"), and a dynamic and exciting stage presence, which lacks the manneristic sensationalism of singers like Oscar d'León. Blades also has an acute socio-political consciousness and avoids the trivial lyrics that, partly due to industry pressures, prevail in most salsa songs. Hence, Blades, believing that salsa can and should be a kind of "urban folklore," composes songs about barrio life, social ills, American imperialism, and Latino solidarity.[62]

Don Randel has illustrated Blades' innovations by comparing a typical song of El Gran Combo, "Lírica borinqueña," with Blades' "Decisiones." Both are set in a conventional, brassy salsa style; but while the text of the former evokes a nostalgia for a pastoral, rural Puerto Rico, Blades' lyrics narrate, with biting humor, urban scenes of teenage pregnancy, extra-marital philandering, and catastrophic drunken driving. Moreover, Blades' skillful, almost imperceptible use of irregular line and stanza lengths lends his delivery a uniquely conversational spontaneity. As Randel observes, Blades has indeed "crossed over"—not from a

Latino to an Anglo audience, but *with* a tradition-oriented emigrant audience to a modern, urban, international Hispanic audience.[63]

Blades' complaints about the music industry reflect salsa's embodiment of the ideological contradictions inherent in most popular music. As Blades and other critics argue, salsa's effectiveness in expressing the concerns of its constituency is limited by the corporate music industry and socio-political environment, which encourage escapism, reaction, and passivity rather than reformist commitment and mobilization. Newyorican community leader Felipe Luciano asserts:

> What has happened is that, due to the influence of record companies who want to dominate the market with a bland salsa sound, our music, almost insidiously, takes on a status quo role, a pacifist and defusing role. It takes people away from having to look at the reality of their own lives and at the shit-encrusted walls they have to work in.[64]

On a specific, mundane level, the superficiality of most salsa lyrics reflects the political passivity of the New York Latino community. The potential political power of this bloc of over three million is formidable, and could constitute a significant threat to the powers that have traditionally controlled the city; yet only about 11 percent of New York Latinos actually vote.[65] It is in this context that critics such as Blades and Luciano deplore the often explicit pressure exerted by the music industry to avoid confronting social realities in a manner which could divide or disturb a politically heterogeneous consumer group.

In the 1980s salsa is perceived as being on the defensive. Many younger Latinos in New York and elsewhere prefer rock to salsa, which they perceive as archaic. Even within the sphere of Latin dance music, standard Cuban-derived salsa has been reeling in recent years under a *merengue* onslaught. The *merengue*, in spite of its repetitiveness, has been enjoying an unprecedented vogue because of the simplicity of its choreography, the willingness of Dominican bands to play for meager wages, the bands' slick stage acts, and increased Dominican migration to New York City. Puerto Rico—formerly the bastion of Cuban-derived salsa— is now heavily inundated with Dominican *merengue* bands; the island has been particularly vulnerable because it has little control over its immigration policy and, unlike other Latin American countries, "Puerto Rico has no protectionist laws that require promoters to hire local bands alongside foreign ones, and radio stations to mix local with imported music."[66]

It is generally agreed that salsa is at best in a period of transition. One may hypothesize that the relatively low socio-political consciousness of the pan-Latino and Newyorican communities has left their cultural expressions particularly susceptible to North American influence, as well as media manipulation. It remains to be seen if a genuine musical "urban folklore" will emerge out of the remains of a style which itself, although dynamic, is inherited from the fifties.

Colombia

Of all Latin American countries, Colombia has perhaps the most diverse musical heritage, to which people of Indian, African, and European descent have each made significant contributions. Despite a considerable amount of miscegenation, Colombian society has always been relatively fragmented along class, racial, and regional lines. This poor integration has been manifested in a history of violence, as well as in the persistence of musical diversity. Since the advent of the mass media, modern Colombian popular musics have reflected, on the one hand, a degree of enhanced national cohesion subsequent to the cessation of civil wars, and, on the other, the vicissitudes of the drug trade which has come to dominate social and economic life in much of the northern and central regions.

The most important Colombian popular genre, and that which has won the largest international audience, is the *cumbia*. The traditional *cumbia* has been until recently the most popular dance of the Atlantic coastal region. In its folk form it is played (generally without vocals) by one of two ensembles consisting of drums and either duct flutes (*gaita*) or a simple cane clarinet (*pito*). In the accompanying dance, which is performed at night, women circle around the musicians, holding candles in their hands, while the men dance in a more assertive fashion around the women. *Cumbia* is assumed to be primarily of black or mulatto origin, as is reflected in the African origins of the word *cumbia* and of the drums. However, the *zamba* communities (of mixed Indian and black descent) are also believed to have contributed to *cumbia's* evolution and, more specifically, to the use of the *gaita*.[67]

Cumbia appears to have evolved in the nineteenth century, for descriptions of similar dances date from this period.[68] By the mid-twentieth century a more popular, commercial variety of the *cumbia* had come into vogue, incorporating vocal couplets and refrains, and played by a dance band using horns, bass, and Cuban-style rhythm section. The modern pop *cumbia* preserves the simple quadratic meter of its predecessor and retains the rhythmic ostinato that most clearly identifies the genre:

In the traditional ensemble this pattern might be played on the *guachos* rattle; in the modern *cumbia* it would be rendered on *güiro* and/or *clave*, and it could be beat with a stick on the side of the *timbales*. The bass generally moves in the pattern of a half-note followed by two quarter-notes (although as in the Dominican *merengue,* Cuban-style anticipated bass is frequently employed); the piano completes the classic *cumbia* format with a chord on the second beat of each bar, as in the following excerpt:

The harmony of the *cumbia* is simple, although more varied than, for example, that of the Dominican *merengue.* Its tempo is moderate, and the modern choreography—performed ballroom-style—is relatively accessible, which may explain its popularity among Central Americans and Mexicans less skilled in the virtuoso Cuban dance styles.

Cumbia has become essential to the repertoires of Tex-Mex *conjuntos,* and it is frequently performed by salsa bands in areas such as Los Angeles where Central Americans and Mexicans (as well as Colombians) congregate. Puerto Rican and Cuban audiences, however, take little interest in *cumbia.*

During the 1970s and 1980s, *cumbia's* popularity in Colombia has been rivaled, if not surpassed by that of *vallenato. Vallenato* is another rural folk genre which has developed into a commercial popular form, although its style, audience, history, and ethos are very distinct from those of *cumbia.*

The earliest references to *vallenato* date from the beginning of the twentieth century, when it appears to have emerged in the northeastern rural regions of Magdalena, Cesar, and Guajira, which continue to be its strongholds.[69] From its inception the *vallenato* audience appears to have been tri-racial, although Indian musical elements are not clearly manifest.[70] *Vallenato* originated as a recreational song of the cattle-ranching cowboy culture, disparaged as crude and rustic by the bourgeoisie but cherished by its own audience as a favorite entertainment at cockfights, taverns, and parties. Although the *vallenato* traditionally accompanies a couple dance, its texts have always been regarded as important vehicles for social commentary.[71]

The traditional *vallenato* ensemble consists of an accordion, a stick rasp called *guacharaca*, and a small, two-headed drum, the *caja* (lit., "box"). This ensemble thus closely resembles the accordion-*güiro-tambora* format of the Dominican *merengue*, which according to Otero, was an important formative influence on *vallenato*.[72]

The word *vallenato* properly denotes the aforementioned ensemble, a musician therein, and, in a generic sense, the music performed by such a group. The *vallenato* repertoire, however, comprises a number of distinct genres. These include *cumbia, son,* the obscure *puya* and *tambora,* and most importantly, *paseo* and *merengue.* Despite the alleged influence of Dominican music on the *vallenato,* the Colombian *merengue* bears little or no relation to its Caribbean namesake. While the latter is in duple time, the *vallenato merengue* is in triple meter; in the modern ensemble the bass plays in 3/4, while the accordion and *caja* articulate figures in 6/8. The Colombian *paseo,* in quadratic meter, is believed to derive from the *paseo* introduction to the classic Dominican *merengue.* The *paseo's* rhythm may resemble that of the *cumbia,* although more syncopated bass patterns may also be employed. The formal structure is irregular but generally alternates verses with simple refrains sung in parallel thirds. Harmonies are simple, often alternating between tonic and dominant.

In the 1940s, Julio Torres, Guillermo Buitrago, and others popularized a more commercial *vallenato* that came to be widely disseminated through radio and records. The new *vallenato* generally incorporated electric bass and percussion instruments like the cowbell and the *tumbadora* drum. In other stylistic aspects it came under the influence of Mexican *norteño* and Tex-Mex music.[73]

The development of commercial *vallenato* in recent decades mirrors the profound changes in Colombian society and economy during this period. On one level, the spread of the mass media and capitalist relations into rural life is reflected in the extent to which *vallenato* has become a major concern for the record companies. The annual *vallenato* competition at Valledupar, for example, is financed and allegedly rigged by record companies to promote their chosen stars.[74] Another equally tangible illustration of *vallenato's* contemporaneity is the subject matter of its texts. While a large percentage concern sentimental love, many texts are political in nature, railing against corruption, poverty, and other social ills; leftist content is not uncommon.[75] Conversely, a number of texts are paeans to local magnates of the marijuana and cocaine trade, who are known to bestow lavish gifts on singers who praise them.

Modern *vallenato,* indeed, reflects the degree to which the illegal drug trade has corrupted and disintegrated Colombian society in the northern coast regions. Since the 1960s, the marijuana and cocaine boom has subjected the populace to the lawless violent influence of the drug mafiosi, whose domination over social, political, and economic life the civil authorities are unable or unwilling to challenge. While injecting large amounts of cash into the region, the drug trade has inflated prices, promoted violent crime, exacerbated machismo and prostitution, and increased dependency on the vicissitudes of North American drug demand. *Vallenato* has, in its own way, flourished under the patronage of the drug runners, largely at the expense of *cumbia* and other traditional musics. A local musician reported:

> *Cumbia*, for example, was once heard everywhere. But when the mafia arrived, they brought their brash corrupted vallenato music to replace it. Today that's all you hear on the street.[76]

Just as many traditional *vallenato* singers were kept as employees of ranch owners, so are several contemporary composers and vocalists maintained as virtual praise-singers by potentates of the drug industry.[77] Other performers sing of the drug runners as folk heroes, or they lament the lives ruined by the volatile and often ferocious drug trade.[78] The cocaine boom of the seventies, in general, is intimately connected with what has been described as a contemporary *vallenato*-mania, helping to transform a rustic and ingenuous folk music into a thriving and boisterous adjunct to fiercely competitive and often corrupt drug and record industries.

Mexico and the American Southwest

Mexico, the largest Spanish-speaking country and second-largest Latin American nation, has developed an appropriately substantial and active popular music industry. The extent of the contemporary music scene is illustrated, among elsewhere, in the proliferation of commercial radio stations, totaling 486 in 1971, most of which offered primarily popular music.[79] Much of Mexican popular music is widely distributed outside the country's borders, in other Latin American countries, as well as among immigrant communities in the United States.

At the same time, however, the vast majority of the popular music produced in Mexico has been and continues to be based on imported styles—especially the mainstream, international style of sentimental slow ballad. Earlier in this century, Cuban genres like the bolero and *danzón* dominated urban tastes. Mexico has excelled both in the quality and quantity of production of these genres, but there is no need to discuss them at length here since they are not, on the whole, distinctively Mexican. Significantly, it is the peripheral northern regions and the Chicano communities in the USA that have produced the most distinctive popular musics, namely, the closely-related *norteño* and Tex-Mex styles.

Mexico's modern music is overwhelmingly European in character and derivation. In spite of the country's predominantly mestizo demography, Indian traits in its popular musics are negligible, if not wholly absent. Similarly, while African slaves constituted a significant component of Mexican urban culture in the seventeenth and eighteenth centuries, it would be impossible to pinpoint any African-derived features in contemporary music (except those which have been borrowed from rock music).

In general, it may be stated that Hispanic traits—such as triple meter, Andalusian harmony, Spanish dance names, and accompanying *zapateado* dance—are most evident in mestizo folk musics, particularly the regional varieties of *son*. As in other Latin American countries, Spanish-language popular theater—especially the *tonadilla*—played an important role in disseminating both Hispanic-derived forms as well as emerging national folk styles.[80]

In the early 1800s, partly due to a growing nationalistic antipathy toward Hispanic political and cultural domination, Italian musical influence began to permeate musical life in the Mexican heartland. Among the urban aristocracy, Italian operas of Bellini, Donizetti, Rossini, and others became the favorite musical entertainment, along with salon music in similar Romantic European style. More significantly, the fondness for bel canto singing appears to have spread to the lower classes, not only in Mexico City but throughout much of the country. Italian influence, and bel canto style in particular, were the primary factors in the emergence of the urban Mexican *canción*, a term which, as in Cuba and elsewhere, generally denotes a sentimental, amatory song in slow tempo, not associated with dance.[81]

Before discussing further the evolution of the Mexican *canción*, whose importance and popularity continue to the present, it would be appropriate to consider a form of urban popular music that enjoyed a vogue from the 1920s to the 1950s, namely, the songs performed by trios such as Los Calaveras, Los Hermanos Martínez Gil, Trio Los Panchos, and many other outstanding groups. These songs were rendered in suave, polished three-part harmony, generally accompanied by acoustic guitar, *requinto,* and light Cuban-style percussion. Most of the songs were boleros which, whether of Cuban or Mexican composition, were performed in wholly Cuban style. The trios' repertoire, however, also included a distinctively Mexican genre, the *huapango*.

Traditionally, the term *huapango* denotes the variety of Mexican *son* derived from the Huasteca region. The *son huasteco* is archetypically performed by a trio consisting of violin and the guitar-like *jarana* and *guitarra quinta;* the *huapango* differs from other regional *sones* most notably in its use of falsetto breaks and its distinctive 6/8–3/4 rhythm, in which the downbeats are consistently muted and unstressed in the instrumental accompaniment. The *huapangos* performed by the urban trios may be regarded as stylizations of the folk *huapango*. Unlike their rustic predecessors, the commercial *huapangos* are written by known composers and sung in slow tempo, often in bel canto style wherein the falsetto breaks are exaggerated into extended solo or group passages.[82] Moreover, in accordance with bourgeois rather than pre-capitalist aesthetics, the additive, strophic form of the traditional *huapango* is modified or forsaken to incorporate sectional "song" form with a clear dramatic climax and definitive sense of closure.[83] Finally, of course, the *haupangos* of the urban trios were widely disseminated by and inextricably associated with the mass media.[84] The sublime boleros and *huapangos* of the trios continued to enjoy considerable market popularity until the 1960s, when they were overwhelmed by the sentimental *balada romántica*.

The *balada* itself may be regarded as a modern commercialization of the Mexican *canción*. In its most traditional form, the *canción* could be sung by one or two vocalists with guitar accompaniment. With the advent of the mass media, a *canción romántica* with more elaborate orchestral background came into vogue. In effect, the Mexican *canción*, like its counterparts in Cuba and elsewhere, merged with the international mainstream sentimental ballad, producing what is referred to in Mexico as the *balada romántica*. This genre enjoys tremendous popularity in Mexico, and Mexican *balada* singers have acquired substantial audiences elsewhere in the Hispanic world. However, the genre is wholly international in style (as well as production, distribution, and consumption), such that there are only idiosyncratic rather than regional differences between, for example, the musics of Mexican singer José-José, the Spaniard Julio Iglesias, and Engelbert Humperdinck. Given its overwhelming popularity in Mexico, the *balada romántica* is worthy of study,[85] but as mentioned above, its international style renders it outside the scope of this book. Various authors have attempted to identify certain features which lend a distinctive character to the Mexican *canción*—in particular, the histrionic bel canto vocal style, and certain characteristic melodic and accompanimental figures,[86] but on the whole, while the *canción* has established deep roots in Mexican culture, it remains an imported style. The same, naturally, applies to the tangos, *boleros*, and *danzones* of composers like Augustin Lara (1900–1970).

A uniquely Mexican flavor is, however, unmistakable in the *canción ranchera* sub-genre, which first emerged in the late nineteenth century. The early *canciones rancheras* were peasant songs originating in the rural *haciendas;* during the rule of Porfirio Díaz (r. 1877–1911) these were incorporated in stylized form into urban theater music, especially in Mexico City.[87] Mexico's dramatic urbanization and, in particular, the migration of landless peasants to the cities further popularized the urban *ranchera* music, which came to occupy an image analogous to that of country and western music in the United States. The real vogue of the *canción ranchera*, however, coincided with its incorporation into the mass media: radio, records, and especially the cinema of the thirties and forties. Mexican films of this period featured singing and acting stars like Jorge Negrete and Pedro Infante. The films, in accordance with the predominantly lower-class audience of the *canción ranchera*, were swash-buckling adventure dramas incorporating plenty of action, romance, and music. Nevertheless, although produced *for* the working classes, they were products of an urban, capitalist entertainment industry, with all the attendant promotion of superstars, fantasy, and glamor. It should not be wholly surprising, then, that such films, far from addressing socio-economic problems in a frank and progressive manner, tended to extol machismo and an individualistic, self-indulgent life style;[88] many song texts expressed similar world views, denouncing fickle women and celebrating male independence and drunken self-pity.[89]

The *canción ranchera* has continued to be one of the most vital aspects of the Mexican popular music scene. Its distinctive Mexican character lies in its virile, melodramatic vocal style, in the custom of singing the choruses in parallel thirds, and most visibly in the accompanying ensembles; these generally consist either of a *mariachi* group— typically, two violins, two trumpets, guitar, *vihuela*, and bass *guitarrón*— or a *conjunto* featuring accordion and the guitar-derived *bajo sexto*.

The *conjunto* ensemble and, to a large extent, the *canción ranchera* itself, are strongly associated with the *norteño* and Tex-Mex musics of the northern border regions. The latter constitute perhaps the most distinctive Mexican and Mexican-American popular musics, and their development and social ethos have been well documented, most notably in Manuel Peña's studies on Tex-Mex *conjunto*.[90]

The northern (*norteño*) regions of Mexico—which until 1848 included what is now the southwestern USA—traditionally constituted a frontier region with relatively limited cultural, economic, and political ties to the central Mexican hinterland. Until 1800 the region was sparsely settled, populated only by Indians, missionaries, and small traders. Immigration increased in the nineteenth century, and the area attracted substantial numbers of northern Europeans—especially Germans and Czechs—who brought with them their own musical traditions. Given the legacy of anti-Spanish nationalism and the remoteness of the Hispanic elite, the region's inhabitants came to adopt as their own the accordion and musical genres like the waltz, redowa, schottische, mazurka, and, above all, the polka.

While central Mexicans tended to regard *norteño* culture as provincial, northerners themselves gradually came to develop a sense of regional identity. This perspective became more focused after the Mexican Revolution, in which the northern regions played a crucial role under the leadership of Pancho Villa.[91] In the twentieth century this regional awareness fused with popular romanticization of *lo ranchero*, with its dashing, macho cowboys in their sequined *charro* outfits, its world of adventure, bravado, and romance, and, notably, its colorful music.[92]

Many features of *norteño* culture and music were common to both northern Mexicans and their Mexican-American brethren living in the lands that in 1848 had been stolen by the United States. But the Mexican-Americans—now oppressed, marginalized second-class citizens in what was once their own country—have lived since then in a socio-political milieu which is in many ways distinct from that of northern Mexicans, who, although mostly poor, have not been subject to the same sorts of racist discrimination. Chicanos, moreover, have been subject to pressures to assimilate and, at the same time, to identify defensively with their own Mexican heritage; accordingly, some cultural distinctions between the two groups began to emerge, and *norteño* (northern Mexican) and Tex-Mex or Tejano musics—although similar enough to be regarded by many as identical—developed along paths which are best seen as closely parallel rather than fused.

Before the 1930s, *norteño* and Tejano entertainment music generally consisted of vocal forms like the narrative, topical *corrido*, and instrumental dance pieces—predominantly polkas, redowas, and the like—played on *ad hoc* ensembles using various string and percussion instruments. By the 1930s the accordion had become the central and indispensible instrument in the dance ensemble, popularized in the recordings of Bruno Villareal and others. After 1935, under the influence of Narciso Martínez, Santiago "El Flaco" Jiménez and Pedro Ayala, Tejano *conjunto* music entered a new phase of development, featuring the use of the twelve-stringed *bajo sexto* bass-chordal guitar, the *tololoche* or contrabass, and a "snappier" accordion style using staccato treble lines and de-emphasizing the left-hand bass patterns of the old style.[93]

In the decade after World War II, Tex-Mex *conjunto* music, as performed by Tony de la Rosa, Valerio Longoria and others, assumed the modern style and form that persist today. Drum set and alto sax were added, archaic forms like the schottische were dropped, and the vocal *ranchera corrida*—or *ranchera* sung in polka rhythm—became the dominant genre in the repertoire. The polka tempo declined from its sprightly pre-war speed to a more moderate level at 110 to 120 beats per minute. The large record companies that had previously dominated Tex-Mex recording withdrew from the field, leaving small, local producers to fill the gap. Finally, the public ballroom dance became a regular feature of the Tejano musical world. (*Norteño* music, meanwhile, continued along more traditional lines, adopting vocal genres but eschewing the drums and sax.)[94]

The 1960s and 1970s were vital periods for both Tex-Mex and *norteño* musics. The dramatic population rise and urbanization of northern Mexico, combined with greater activity and sophistication within the regional recording industry, gave great impetus to *norteño* music; *música norteña*, indeed, has become the rage not only in the north but throughout much of Mexico, so that *norteño* singers like Chayito Valdéz and Ramón Ayala are national superstars.[95] The vitality of Tejano music also continued through these decades, marked in particular by the innovations of the Conjunto Bernal, which introduced three-part harmonies along the lines of the acoustic trios discussed above.[96]

By virtue of its history, style, and the language of its text, Tex-Mex music is an important symbol of ethnic identity for Texan Chicanos. Manuel Peña's studies have further illuminated the overwhelming working-class character and associations of Tejano *conjunto* music, contrasting it with the big band *orquestas* that perform swing charts, *cumbias*, and Cuban-style *música tropical* for middle-class Chicanos. The latter tend to scorn *conjunto* as crude and provincial, and they avoid the humble taverns and noisy dance halls where it is performed.

Since *conjunto* is so clearly associated with an oppressed and marginalized ethnic proletariat, its relationship to the cultural hegemony of the dominant Anglo majority is a matter of some interest, both for the study of popular music in society as well as of Chicano culture. Fortunately, the subject has by no means been ignored, although it is clear that *conjunto's* social role is complex, contradictory, and in many ways ambiguous.

Peña, while clearly aware of the contradictions implicit in the *conjunto* complex, tends to stress its role as a symbol of resistance against Anglo and middle-class Chicano hegemony. Moreover, it is the music's *style*, he argues, which by its very nature expresses and affirms proletarian Tejano identity. In a milieu that effectively discourages explicit confrontational socio-political messages, such sentiments can be conveyed only symbolically, as in the case of the "defensive, counter-ideological" expression embodied in *conjunto* music.[96] In this regard it is also significant to recall that much of the Tex-Mex record industry is in the hands of small, local, Chicano producers, who record, press, promote, and distribute their records with little interference from the corporate music industry.[98] Some song texts by artists like Little Joe Hernandez explicitly confront socio-political issues.[99] Peña further argues that Tejano dances constitute not escapist sprees but secular rituals wherein the reality of their cultural independence and solidarity is confronted and reinforced.[100]

In other respects, however, *conjunto's* alleged counter-hegemonic stance is questionable. Peña himself notes that the vast majority of *conjunto* texts, unlike those of many folk *corridos*, are completely depoliticized, dealing instead with unrequited love as experienced or imagined by the male. Moreover, he acknowledges that Tex-Mex music failed to become identified with the Chicano socio-political mobilization that emerged in the sixties;[101] instead of becoming a *nueva canción*-type vehicle for protest and agitprop, *conjunto* has become commercialized, effectively neutralized, and absorbed, like so many other potentially oppositional phenomena, into the fabric of American bourgeois capitalism.

José Limón further questions the degree to which *conjunto* style and performance context can be regarded as counter-hegemonic. Noting the depoliticized texts and the commodification of *conjunto* through records and public dance halls, Limón regards as problematic an approach that celebrates Tex-Mex *style* as a symbol of class consciousness, arguing instead that Tejano music and dance are cultural contradictions that "contain both elements of nationalistic/class resistance and acquiescence to the dominant social order."[102] From this perspective, the public dance, with its drinking, occasional fights, and sentimental songs, could well be regarded as an escapist flight from social reality rather than an affirmation of solidarity.[103] In sum, Tex-Mex *conjunto* music seems to be a particularly clear embodiment of the ideological contradictions that pervade most popular music. As Limón concludes, working class as well as middle class cultural expressions are fraught with contradiction, because these classes do not fully own the means of production.[104]

Argentina

Argentina's renowned gift to the world of popular music, the tango, in its own country is much more than a music and dance genre. Argentinians regard the tango as the quintessential expression of their own national character, and they trace in its evolution the history of their urban society and identity. Hence the tango has been the subject of a vast body of literature, written especially, although not exclusively by Argentinians.

The origins of the tango have been the subject of much debate, which, due to the national and racial issues involved, have not always been dispassionate. One school of thought traces the tango to the Cuban *habanera*, which enjoyed prodigious popularity in mid-nineteenth-century Buenos Aires, where it was often referred to as the *tango americano*. Another related genre that may have played an evolutionary role was the contemporary Andalusian tango, which was disseminated in Argentina in the 1870s by Spanish *zarzuela* theater troupes.[105]

Skeptics of these supposed relationships point out that the Cuban *habanera* was genteel and bourgeois in character and patronage, while the Argentine tango was, in its early stages, despised by the native aristocracy for its associations with the lumpen slums and brothels. Moreover, the Andalusian tango, in its most representative flamenco manner of rendering, bears little resemblance in style or choreography to its Argentine namesake.[106] Hence, some writers have asserted that the genre emerged from an Afro-Argentine tradition by the same name, played at informal dances and in street processions by black *candombé* clubs.[107]

What is certain is that the early creole tango emerged among the outlying slums (*arrabales, orillas*) of Buenos Aires in the 1880s, incorporating elements of topical *payada* songs and the syncopated, African-influenced *milonga* dance genre. In the subsequent "guardia vieja" ("old guard") period of the tango (roughly 1885–1913), the genre was strongly associated with the lumpen proletariat world of brothels, thugs, and unemployed street people. Many of these were former soldiers who were left without occupations after the demilitarization following the decline of *caudillos* (regional strongmen) and the cessation of war with Paraguay. Others were former or frustrated peasants who were driven to the *arrabales* with the concentration of land holdings in large estates. Yet most were immigrants—from Spain, Italy, and elsewhere—who had come to Argentina to seek their fortunes but instead found themselves living in squalid slums, unable to participate in the economic progress enjoyed by the native elite. Throughout the "old guard" period these immigrants constituted nearly half of the population of Buenos Aires.[108]

The failure of the Argentine economy to absorb these immigrants, their subsequent hopelessness and disillusionment, and the contempt with which the native aristocracy regarded them, all contributed to a profound sense of alienation among the urban poor. The rapid growth of Buenos Aires—from 187,000 in 1869, to 663,000 in 1895, to its present three million—further exacerbated the sense of dislocation and rootlessness. The shortage of women intensified traditional machismo, leading to the male domination of public life, a weakened family structure, and the emergence of brothels which by 1900 employed some 20,000 to 30,000 prostitutes.[109]

The "old guard" tango emerged as the archetypal expression of the male condition in the *arrabal*. The genre was most typically performed in brothels and bohemian cafes; its choreography epitomized male aggressive domination; and, most concretely, its texts, full of *lunfardo*-derived argot, portrayed the frustration and defensive machismo of the archetypal tango man. The latter was epitomized in the figure of the *compadrito*, a lazy, dishonest, knife-wielding, womanizing dandy, who, although maintaining a violent and tough appearance, was invariably suffering the wounds of romantic betrayal. Hence, tango lyrics, like those of Portuguese *fado*, Greek *rebetika*, and Mexican *canciones*, often portray their subject drowning his sorrows in a bottle of wine, self-indulgently lamenting the cruel fate he has suffered at the hands of an unfaithful woman. The texts further encompass fatalism, reproach against a cruel society, nostalgia for the childhood barrio now engulfed in the city, and worship of the mother-figure; many texts from the "old guard" period describe brothel life, using thinly-veiled obscene metaphors.[110]

The exaggerated machismo portrayed in the tango has provided fertile field for Freudian interpretation, which has related the *compadrito's* stance to such factors as the matriarchy prevailing in the home as well as in the brothels owned and managed by madames. Such interpretations have been extended to the socio-economic realm;

Matamoro, for example, suggests that the absence of a father lamented in some tangos may reflect not only domestic life but the sense of social dislocation resulting from the emergence of a class—the unassimilated, immigrant proletariat—which had no history and no sense of incorporation in the national social fabric.[111] The tango thus came to express the resentment felt by the immigrants toward the disdainful gentry and, at the same time, the resentment of the dispossessed creole natives against the unwanted waves of immigrants.[112]

Chapter 1 discussed how popular music may be an important vehicle for the expression and consolidation of identity in the urbanization process. This phenomenon is particularly clear in the case of the tango, which served as a profound symbol of lower-class identity in the hostile, alienating, and insecure world of the *arrabal*. Also mentioned was the important role that the lumpen proletariat can play in the development of popular music. As suggested, the "unbound" creative energy of the lumpen class, its freedom from the cultural inhibitions of the aristocracy, and the crucial need for the creation of a new class identity may all contribute to the emergence of dynamic new forms of popular music. This phenomenon is nowhere more manifest than in the emergence of the tango in the *porteño* (Buenos Aires) underworld.

The earliest tango, closely allied to the *milonga*, was in some respects more distinguished by its choreography than its musical form, which varied considerably.[113] Typically played by a trio of violin, flute, and harp, the primitive tango was an instrumental dance form in 2/4 reiterating the familiar *habanera* ostinato. By 1900, the standard ensemble came to consist of piano, violin, and the concertina-like *bandoneón*. Texts, when present, were informally improvised or based on stock patterns. The Argentine elite—Eurocentric and yet obsessed with the image of a mythically "pure" national culture—regarded the early tango with scorn because of its ethnic "impurity" and its brothel and underworld contexts.

In the second decade of the twentieth century the tango became the most popular dance of the British and Parisian bourgeoisie. At the same time, a progressive "pact" between the Argentine urban proletariat and the latifundist oligarchy brought to power the radical party led by H. Yrigoyen. The tango's international vogue, the rise of liberal politics in Argentina, and an increasing professionalization of tango musicians led the Argentine elite to belatedly endorse the tango; or, as Matamoro puts it, the aristocracy came to "re-invent" the tango as their own private genre. The tango in this phase of its development—roughly, 1913–1930—donned a smoking jacket, in the familiar metaphor, and entered the domain of the bourgeois cabaret, the dance hall, and even the formal concert hall. Meanwhile, alongside this aristocratic "new guard" tango persisted a more populist and earthy tango associated with "old guard" musicians like Francisco Canaro and Roberto Firpo.[114]

Musically, the tango underwent a number of significant changes in this period. Around 1917, the popularization of Samuel Castriota's "Mi noche triste" ("My Sad Night") inaugurated the era of the *tango-canción*, recasting the tango as a vocal song with instrumental accompaniment. While the trio format persisted, larger ensembles also appeared, especially sextets with piano, contrabass, two violins and two *bandoneones;* ensemble arrangement assumed a new importance in the music. Instrumental styles were refined and codified by a generation of "new guard" musicians, including pianist Juan Carlos Cobián, ensemble leader Julio de Caro, and *bandoneón* virtuosi Osvaldo Fresedo and Pedro Maffia. This period also coincided with the zenith of vocalist Carlos Gardel (1887–1935), whose music epitomized the refined, sophisticated *tango-canción* style. Gardel, however, is even more important as an embodiment of Argentine aspirations and identity due to his rise from poverty and illegitimacy to fame and fortune, his reputed kindness and generosity, his good looks and suave urbanity, and, finally, his untimely "martyrdom" resulting from an airplane accident.[115]

The tango also assumed a definitive shape in this period. The duple meter of its primitive ancestor gave way to a steady, medium-tempo 4/4. A loose strophic form became standard, with five sixteen-bar verses. The *habanera* ostinato is often masked by an impetuous composite rhythm which could be schematized as:

The histrionic bel canto vocal style of the mature tango strongly reflects Italian influence. Instrumental styles exhibit considerable virtuosity, particularly in the Romantic piano figurations. Melodies, on the whole, are carried by the violin and *bandoneón*. Much of the ineffable tension and dramatic intensity of the tango derives from the juxtaposition of march-like stacatto phrases with suave, song-like legato passages, and the histrionic sudden changes in ensemble dynamics.

The creation of Gardel's superstar status, and of the mature tango in general, were intimately connected with the rise of the mass media in Buenos Aires. Tango dominated both radio and the record industry, and promoted the sale of cheap victrolas and radios from the late twenties on.[116] Cinema—especially the films featuring Gardel—became an even more important means of dissemination, further popularizing the dance among the predominantly working-class audience.[117]

At the same time, however, the increasing connection of the mass media with the international, USA-dominated entertainment industry gradually exposed the tango to an unprecedented degree of competition from other musical genres. Thus, on the one hand, the North American film and record producers readily promoted Gardel, especially in the era before the advent of dubbing, when Spanish-language films were needed to penetrate the Latin American market. On the other hand, the

Argentine public was inundated with a variety of foreign musics, from Frank Sinatra to jazz. Thus, Dariel Canton notes that while in 1925 tangos constituted 90 percent of record sales, in 1950 they totaled only 40.5 percent.[118]

In the 1930s the tango underwent a significant decline, which has been related not only to competition from foreign popular musics but also to the disillusionment, political oppression, and economic decline following the right-wing military coup of 1930. With the repression of the popular political activism of the Yrigoyen years, tango lyrics became even more fatalistic and bitter.[119]

By 1940 a new tango boom was underway, reflecting the proletarian ferment and mobilization that precipitated Perón's rise to power in 1945. Again, the vitality of tango—as both a proletarian and aristocratic genre—paralleled the reforging of a class alliance between these potentially antagonistic groups, in this case under Peronist populism. The bourgeois aspirations and expectations of this period, it has been suggested, may also explain the absence of revolutionary social criticism in the tango.[120] In this new heyday:

> Tango brought to the new proletariat an evocative, cultivated and sentimental literature, a product of the new economic and cultural situation. Behind its apparent evasion, tango fulfilled important functions such as the restitution of feeling in the submersion and marginalisation of the industrial town, the affirmation of a national dance and the exploration of an identification with the past.[121]

The mass media further popularized tango both as the preferred dance genre and as an ubiquitous "dramatic synthesis" expressing the dreams, frustrations, and nostalgia of the *porteño*.

In the mid-1950s the worker-oligarchy alliance again unraveled, resulting in Perón's downfall and a new disenfranchisement of the lower classes. As the Argentine economy fell further under foreign domination, the tango was superseded in popularity by imported musics. The sixties and seventies generated a somewhat self-conscious revival of the genre, whether as a "museum piece" or in the form of modernized stylizations by composers like Astor Piazzolla. However, with the advent of rock, and Argentina's immersion in international cultural and economic life, the young have, on the whole, lost interest in the genre. While the tango remains an important symbol of Argentine identity, its significance is more as a historical artifact than as a contemporary phenomenon. Indeed, the verses of "Mi Noche Triste," which once inaugurated the tango's heyday, now seem more appropriate than ever:

> La guitarra en el ropero todavía está colgada,
> nadie en ella canta nada, ni hace sus cuerdas vibrar . . .

> The guitar still hangs in the closet;
> No one sings through it, nor makes its strings vibrate . . .

Brazil

Brazil, in accordance with its status as Latin America's largest country, has been an important center of popular music. While linguistic differences have to some extent limited Brazilian impact on other Latin American popular musics, the *samba, bossa nova,* and in some cases, their nineteenth-century precursors have exerted considerable influence not only in the United States but in Portugal and its African former colonies as well.

The evolution of Brazilian popular music invites certain comparisons with that of Cuba. The importation of large numbers of African slaves led to a rich heritage of neo-African musics, including those associated with the Yoruba-derived *candomblé* cult. At the same time, the colonial and post-colonial urban elites fostered genteel light-classical musics which, themselves European in character, were subsequently exported to the Portuguese metropole. Finally, in the twentieth century, urbanization and the mass media contributed to the rise of syncretic popular genres—especially the *samba*—which blended European and African elements in such a manner as to acquire, to some extent, the status of national musics.

The most important ancestors of the modern *samba* were the *lundu, modinha,* and *maxixe.*[122] The *lundu,* in its original form, was an African dance and music genre of Congo-Angolan derivation. Introduced to Portugal and Brazil, it was wrathfully condemned by aristocratic observers for the perceived eroticism of its choreography.[123] Nevertheless, in the latter half of the eighteenth century, the Brazilian urban elite came to endorse a stylized form of the *lundu,* transforming it into a genteel, albeit syncopated salon dance. The aristocratic adoption of the *lundu,* indeed, was the first musical expression of the nationalistic and nativistic sentiments which had animated Brazilian literature a century before. The term *lundu* hence came to be applied to a variety of songs, dances, and instrumental compositions which incorporated elements (especially syncopation) of their neo-African precedents.[124] The acculturated *lundu* was most often accompanied by Portuguese *viola, violão* (guitar), or occasionally, piano. Behague characterizes the urbanized *lundu* by its simple harmonies, large melodic leaps, and stereotyped syncopations including the figure

The *habanera* ostinato is not uncommon in such pieces.[125]

While the traditional *lundu* appears to have expired in the early nineteenth century, the salon *lundu-canção* ("*lundu*-song") enjoyed considerable vogue until the latter part of that century.[126] Roughly contemporary in popularity was another bourgeois song form, the *modinha.* Although regarded as vaguely Luso-Brazilian in character, the *modinha* was informed more by Italian arias than by any folk relative. The genre retained some vitality until the close of the nineteenth century, by which time it had come to be set frequently in waltz rather than binary meter.[127]

In the latter half of the nineteenth century the term *maxixe* gradually came to be applied to Brazilianized versions of the polka, tango, and *habanera* which enjoyed popularity among the urban upper classes. In the final decades of its vitality the *maxixe* acquired a more distinctively national character—especially in the piano compositions of Ernesto Nazaré (1863–1934)—and thus came to be regarded as the first urban dance of Brazilian origin.[128] The *maxixe* continued to employ syncopated ostinatos, including variations of the familiar *lundu* and *habanera* isorhythms. While the genre declined in the early twentieth century, it is considered by some to be an important precursor of the urban pop *samba*.

The most conspicuous predecessor of the commercial *samba*, however, is the street music and dance genre of the same name. While several types of *samba* are found throughout Brazil, the most influential is that which emerged in association with the pre-Lenten Carnival festivities of Rio de Janeiro. In the nineteenth century Carnival was celebrated by revelers throwing water-filled balls of wax at passersby and, more importantly, by groups of costumed dancers marching to brass band music. By the early twentieth century the event had become a popular annual diversion, whose musical accompaniment included an assortment of marches, *maxixes, choroes,* and other pieces. In the second decade of the century these genres came to be largely replaced by the urban *samba*. The *samba* may be performed throughout the year at various formal and informal occasions but reaches its climax at Carnival in Rio de Janeiro. In 1928 the processional Carnival *samba* groups were formally organized into "schools," which would compete for prizes awarded by a selected jury. The Carnival *samba* became a focal activity for residents of the *favelas* (hillside slums). *Samba* processions, like their Cuban *comparsa* counterparts, became increasingly extravagant, combining elaborate floats, sumptuous costumes, narrative or topical themes (in the case of *sambas de enredo*), intricate group choreography, and, of course, *samba* music.

The *samba* itself comprises a choral melody with instrumental accompaniment. The vocal part generally consists of verses sung by a solo male, alternating with refrains rendered, generally in unison, by a female or mixed chorus. The arched, quadratic, diatonic melodies are wholly European in character; an analysis of characteristic motives and phrases would reveal many typically Lusitanian features. The texts occasionally deal with contemporary topical or socio-political events; more often, they concern unrequited love, Carnival, or the *samba* itself.

The musical accompaniment to the street *samba* is dominated by the *batería* of percussion instruments.[129] These perform intricate syncopated ostinati over the steady binary pulse of the *surdo* bass drums. Chordophones—especially the ukulele-like *cavaquinho*—are often present, although they are generally inaudible. Brass instruments are also in common use, to the displeasure of purists. Ensembles range widely in size, from informal groups of around a dozen musicians to massive and accordingly cacophonous entourages of over two hundred.[130]

The 1917 recording of Ernesto "Donga" dos Santos' "Pelo telefone" inaugurated the incorporation of the *samba* into the mass media. The early commercial *sambas*, despite their name and their frequent use in Carnival processions, bore strong affinities with the *maxixe* and, to some extent, the *modinha*.[131] By 1928 the more sentimental, slow-tempo *samba-canção* ("*samba*-song") had emerged as a distinct genre and with radio and record promotion gradually came to be the most popular national urban dance. The commercial *samba* incorporated several features of the street *samba*, including the vocal format, melodic style, and the binary *surdo* pulse. The latter was generally reinforced by the bass, with a sixteenth-note anacrusis eventually added before each downbeat. The accompanying syncopated *batería* parts were frequently present, albeit often in simplified form. Also common, however, was a horn section modeled on contemporary North American swing jazz. The choreography often resembled a polished form of the *maxixe*,[132] although in recent decades a variety of informal steps have come into vogue. In general, one may speak of a continuum of styles, from pieces virtually identical to street *sambas*, to more sentimental and "sweet" songs with heavy orchestration, muted percussion, and a softer, more intimate vocal style.[133] The most important exponents of pop *samba* until the fifties were Noel Rosa (1910–1937), Jose Luis "Caninha" de Morais (1883–1961), Pixinguinha (1898–1973), and Ary Barroso (1907–1964). In the late 1950s, a reaction against the increasingly "sweet" ballroom *samba* developed, resulting in a greater diversity of performance styles. While a "mainstream" sort of *samba* remains the standard fare for innumerable groups, another course of development led to *samba* styles heavily influenced by American rock; yet another trend led to the emergence of *bossa nova*.

Insofar as the *samba* is intimately associated with the proletarian *favelas*, one might expect its themes to reflect the social realities of a nation whose extremes of opulent wealth and abject poverty are perhaps the most conspicuous in Latin America. A few *samba* composers (such as Zelia Barbosa) do in fact attempt to confront social issues in their lyrics. Nevertheless, the very importance of *samba* to its constituency has led it to become exploited by the government and the dominant classes as a vehicle of propaganda or, more often, simple avoidance of controversy. The lavish state subsidies of *samba* schools are cited as the single most effective means of ensuring that song texts will be free from subversive sentiments. On occasion, *sambas* with explicit pro-government content have been promoted by paternalistic leaders.[134] Carnival itself, many believe, functions more as a "safety valve" for releasing tension than as a celebration of urban folk culture per se.[135]

Meanwhile, the content of commercial *sambas* has been strongly influenced by the censorship which prevailed for decades in the state-run radio. In the atmosphere of harsh right-wing military rule, political dissidents have regarded with ambivalence the songs promoted by vocalists like Carmen Miranda and Francisco Alves which blithely praise hard work and morality.[136] Since the resumption of partial civilian rule in the early 1980s, a more open and free ambience has led both to greater socio-politicization of song texts, as well as new levels of banality and even pornography in lyrics and performance acts.[137]

Around 1960 the *bossa nova* emerged as a vital and somewhat controversial new style. The early *bossa nova* may be regarded to some extent as an extension of the "sweet" style of *samba-canção*. However, its early exponents—especially João Gilberto, Antonio Carlos Jobim, and Baden Powell—incorporated jazz elements in a manner which rendered *bossa nova* significantly distinct from *samba*. Most notable in *bossa nova's* innovations are the complex, jazz-inspired harmonies employing altered chords and unusual progressions in a melodious rather than dissonant fashion.[138] The influence of "cool" jazz and a prevailing aesthetic of understatement are also evident in the non-percussive, albeit syncopated instrumental accompaniment, and, indirectly, in the soft, intimate, almost whispery vocal production.

Despite its overtly innocuous, muted quality, early *bossa nova* inspired a degree of controversy. Detractors of the style denounced it as the illegitimate progeny of jazz and *samba*, and, perhaps more significantly, they attacked its perceived elitism. The genre was indeed the product of the urban middle and upper-middle classes, and, in its early stages, it was regarded as one reflection of the optimism and complacency of its constituency.[139] The refined harmonies, highbrow apolitical texts, and references to posh districts like Ipanema all suggested orientation toward elite, educated listeners, rather than populism or, for that matter, crass commercialism. (The soft, non-percussive quality of *bossa nova* also rendered it unfortunately suitable for dilution as "cocktail" music.)

In the mid-1960s a new social awareness developed among *bossa nova* musicians; this development coincided with the rise of mass political mobilization under the Goulart government and the right-wing military coup which ensued in 1964. The most important figure in this "modern" phase of Brazilian popular music was Chico Buarque (b. 1944), several of whose songs eloquently portray poverty and urban alienation. In keeping with the *bossa nova* aesthetic, many of Buarque's lyrics were of extremely high literary calibre.[140] Buarque's texts have been criticized as being conservatively fatalistic rather than activist,[141] although given the harsh state repression of dissent under military rule, performance of overt protest music would have been perilous.

It remains to mention the *tropicalia* movement which developed in the late 1960s under the inspiration of Caetano Veloso, Gilberto Gil, Gal Costa, and later, Milton Nascimento. *Tropicalia* paralleled the rock vogue in the USA, reacting against extant musical clichés and complacency, and against the perceived vapidity and corruption of the upper classes.[142] *Tropicalia* comprises a wide variety of musical styles from rock to Dadaist collage techniques. As a distinct movement *tropicalia* appears to have eclipsed in the early seventies.[143] Since then, Brazilian popular music has remained unquestionably vital, as evidenced by the continuing successes of performers like Veloso and Nascimento. Nevertheless, while much of contemporary Brazilian pop retains a national flavor, the influence of rock is so overwhelming that such music tends to fall outside the purview of this volume.

Nueva Canción

The last Spanish-language genre to be considered here is not associated with any one nation but is rather a pan-Latin movement which has emerged out of the background of underdevelopment, North American imperialism, and rising socio-political consciousness in several Latin American countries since the 1960s. While no music can be holistically understood in a vacuum, *nueva canción's* relationship with its socio-political contexts is particularly visible, not only for the explicit social content of many of its song texts but also for the political significance it has for its audience.[144]

The development of Cuban *nueva trova* has been discussed in terms of its relationship to North American "protest" music, to Cuban nationalism, and to pan-Latin goals of social justice and fraternal solidarity. The context of the Cuban revolution renders *nueva trova* a special, albeit vitally important efflorescence of *nueva canción*. *Nueva canción* outside of Cuba, while sharing many features with *nueva trova*, emerged to a large extent from its own distinct socio-political backgrounds, which must be apprehended separately.

The development of *nueva canción* reflects a complex of socio-political trends affecting Latin American youth from the 1960s on. These included rising discontent with domestic political repression and social inequalities, increasing awareness of North American imperialism fueled by the Dominican intervention of 1964 and the Bay of Pigs invasion of 1962, and resentment of mass media domination by commercial North American music. The last factor was, of course, a product of the spread of the mass media and of their potential as vehicles both of national as well as imported musics. A few governments—notably Argentina and Chile—had previously enacted stipulations requiring substantial percentages of music played on the radio to be of national origin.[145] These policies promoted a vogue not only of traditional music but of singer-composers like Violetta Parra and Atahualpa Yupanqui, who offered their own idiosyncratic renditions of folk music to increasingly politicized and nationalistic audiences. Such music laid the foundation for a socially conscious reinterpretation of traditional musics.

Atahualpa Yupanqui's music combined uniquely expressive guitar accompaniment and an intimate, semi-melodic vocal style with poignant lyrics often portraying the sad plight of the Andean Indians. While Yupanqui was persecuted and exiled for his communist beliefs, his music acquired a considerable following not only in his native Argentina but in other countries as well.

Particularly receptive to such trends was neighboring Chile, which emerged as the true cradle of *nueva canción*. In the 1950s and 1960s, urbanization, unemployment, and increasingly conspicuous income inequalities contributed to a growing political consciousness that manifested itself in a wave of political mobilization and ferment. The populist rhetoric of liberal President Eduardo Frei (r. 1964–1970) served only to heighten expectations and discontent with the limited land and labor reforms enacted. Such conditions led to the election in 1970 of the socialist Salvador Allende, under whose presidency mass socio-political mobilization reached a peak.

These developments coincided with a dynamic surge of musical creativity. The spiritual founder of the musical movement was Violetta Parra (1918–1967) who integrated a love for national music with a keen social awareness. Parra collected hundreds of Chilean folk songs and composed ballads and socio-political songs on folk models; moreover, she promoted such music through publications, her own performances, and through a folk music center she founded ("La Carpa de la Reina"), which became a nucleus for the urban musicians determined to forge an alternative to commercial and trivial imported musics. Parra's work was carried on by her children, Isabel and Angel, who also composed committed songs and operated a focal *peña*, or coffeehouse featuring folk music.

The new music that had been evolving in the *peñas* became known as *nueva canción* after a large festival in 1969 in Santiago incorporated that name. By this time the genre had become allied with Allende's *Unidad Popular* party, and many of the most popular songs dealt with specific political events. A mood of optimisim, activism, and social commitment via radical reform pervaded song lyrics. Singer-composers Victor Jara, the Parras, and other musicians attained considerable popularity.

An important component of the Chilean *nueva canción* was the incorporation of elements of *altiplano* Indian music. In some cases, the use of Andean music was folkloric; groups like Inti-Illimani and Quilapayún often performed relatively straightforward, if "cleaned-up" versions of *huaynos, sanjuanitos,* and other Indian genres, using traditional instruments (such as *quena, sikus,* and *charango*). In other contexts, the *altiplano* instruments and musical features were incorporated into new compositions. The use of Andean music symbolized nationalistic pride (although Indians constitute only 5 percent of Chile's population), a conscious rejection of prevailing North American commercial music, and an expression of solidarity with the exploited and impoverished Indians. (What is less clear is the extent to which the marginalized Indians themselves identified with the *nueva canción* musicians, most of whom were from urban middle-class backgrounds.) By wearing ponchos and using instruments and stylistic features of Hispanic, African, and Indian derivation, the students sought to symbolize "the formation of a Latin-American (as opposed to national) cultural and political consciousness and identity expressed by the new politically active generation."[146]

While emerging from a common socio-economic condition and embracing a unified ideology, *nueva canción* comprises a number of heterogeneous musical styles. The "folkloric" reinterpretations of traditional *altiplano* musics and the use of Andean elements in new compositions have been mentioned. Other songs have been based on traditional Hispanic-derived folk models, especially the *cueca*, which is the most popular folk dance song of Chile, using a *huapango*-like 6/8 meter. *Cueca* texts have traditionally addressed a wide range of contemporary topics, and the use of the genre by *nueva canción* composers like Victor Jara perpetuated the tradition of nineteenth-century *cuecas* depicting the struggles of the Chilean working classes. Many songs are ballads written in a generic Western style, such as Violetta Parra's "Gracias a la vida," which became a sort of anthem for the new movement. Rock elements have also been introduced in some songs. A final category of songs are the simple, rousing, singable tunes like "La batea" which are designed for collective performance at rallies.

The Chilean *nueva canción* movement was at its peak in 1973 when a military junta, supported by the CIA, overthrew the elected Allende government. The junta, led by Augusto Pinochet, sought to eradicate Marxism and demobilize the population by outlawing labor unions, political parties, mass rallies, and all forms of overt dissent. A "cultural blackout" was instituted under which all artistic expression was rigidly censored. *Nueva canción* was effectually banned; its leading exponents were exiled, imprisoned, or, in the case of Victor Jara, tortured and killed. The government informed a meeting of folklorists that use of Andean instruments like the *quena* and *charango* was prohibited.[147] Imported North American commercial music again dominated the media.

The coup did not, however, signal the end of *nueva canción*. Chilean groups like Inti-Illimani and Quilapayún continue to play in exile. *Nueva canción* has flourished, albeit on a lesser scale, in other Latin American countries. In particular, the Nicaraguan revolution of the late seventies inaugurated a prodigious flowering of local new song in that country, whose most distinguished exponent has been Carlos Mejía Godoy. Argentina has fostered a rock-oriented variety of new song. International festivals of *nueva canción* have been held in Cuba (1978), Mexico (1982), Nicaragua (1983), Ecuador (1984), and Argentina (1985).[148]

In Chile itself, the growing availability of cheap cassette recorders has facilitated the wide dissemination of *nueva canción*, especially, for example, the music of Silvio Rodríguez. Meanwhile, a subdued, oblique form of new song, under the rubric *canto nuevo*, has managed to establish itself despite the totalitarian censorship of the Pinochet government.[149] *Canto nuevo* has been popularized by live concerts, irregular radio broadcasts by the Catholic Church station, and Alerce Records, which, together with the Nuestro Canto concert agency, has been testing the limits of state repression in an ongoing indirect confrontation. *Canto nuevo* texts are necessarily more subtle in their dissidence, and a new poetic imagery of protest has arisen.

Stylistically, *canto nuevo* departs in some respects from *nueva canción*. The *cueca*—a staple of pre-coup and exile groups—now tends to be avoided by some *canto nuevo* musicians, because in modern Chile it has become associated with the political right. In particular, the Pinochet regime has promoted groups like the Huasos Quincheros, which perform depoliticized *cuecas* and other central Chilean genres; texts to such songs present an idealized, artificial image of a bucolic, peaceful Chile, ignoring social realities and constructing a new "folklore of the landlord."[150]

At present, *nueva canción* continues to be a significant musical phenomenon in Latin America. Its popularity, however, remains strongest among progressive, middle-class youths—especially university students; the poor and exploited, in whose name *nueva canción* is sung, tend on the whole to prefer apolitical, regional folk and pop styles, as well as international genres like rock and the sentimental *canción*. In terms of mass appeal, *nueva canción* constitutes but a peripheral, albeit persistent alternative to these styles.

The ideology which animates *nueva canción* is explicitly opposed to cultural imperialism and the manipulation of taste by the corporate music industry. Moreover, it opposes economic exploitation in general and envisions art as a vehicle for socio-political enlightenment and mobilization rather than as a commodity to be passively consumed. Accordingly, the music's character is anti-commercial in its subject matter, its avoidance of sentimentality and pop clichés, its folk affinities, and the absence of superstar hype and promotion. The movement has always placed considerable emphasis on live performance, whether in intimate clubs or collectively at large rallies.

Nevertheless, the *nueva canción* vogue has from its inception been intimately connected with the mass media, and, as mentioned above, it was originally aided by state-imposed restrictions on foreign music imports and subsidies of local records. The partial dependency on the mass media, including the commercial recording industry, has clearly exerted some pressure on the movement and has caused a degree of inherent tension, for example, between groups who have recording contracts and those who do not.[151] The occasional use of commercial styles (such as that of the sentimental *canción*) has also generated some criticism.[152] Further, one may regard as paradoxical the frequent use of lingua franca North American "protest" or ballad styles to express nationalistic opposition to US cultural imperialism. Finally, despite its anti-elitism, *nueva canción* remains associated primarily with urban educated youth, and one could argue that some of its preferred styles—from ballads to the harmonized and standardized renditions of Andean *huaynos*—are inherently bourgeois in character. Thus, such internal conflicts as exist in *nueva canción* can be seen as inevitable products of its ambivalent relationship to the commercial mass media and of the class orientation of its constituency.

Despite these considerations, *nueva canción* constitutes perhaps the most widespread, organized, and deliberate challenge to corporate music industry manipulation by any artistic movement. *Nueva canción* exponents have sought to use the mass media themselves in ways which counter the media's negative effects. The artists have attempted to incorporate and reinterpret a wide variety of stylistic elements—including some from commercial musics—in order to create a new syncretic art form based on an aesthetic opposed to corporate manipulation. Finally, the middle-class background of many *nueva canción* enthusiasts itself illustrates the important role that disaffected and socially conscious elements of the bourgeoisie can play in progressive or even radical reform movements.

The French Caribbean

The French Caribbean islands—Haiti, Martinique, Guadeloupe, and Dominica—constitute a relatively distinct cultural and musical area. Their heritages of traditional music are not identical, due in particular to Haiti's early attainment of independence in 1804, which weakened its ties with France as well as with its former sister colonies. Nevertheless, in the twentieth century the mass media and increased transport, trade, and communication have enhanced the natural linguistic and cultural affinities between these islands. These affinities are especially evident in the realm of popular music and have themselves contributed to the international popularity of syncretic French Caribbean musics.

Secular music in Haiti has traditionally received less scholarly attention than music of the neo-African *voudoun* cult.[153] Nevertheless, it is evident that by the time of independence, creole dances had emerged which synthesized European harmony and song forms with African-derived elements. The most important of these early syncretic dances was the *carabinier*, which, in both salon and rustic folk forms, acquired the status of a national dance in the early 1800s, even though it was frequently condemned by the Eurocentric elite. The *carabinier* itself evidently derived from genres like the polka, fandango, berceuse, minuet, and *contredanse*, while incorporating rhythmic features from more Africanized dances like the *chica* and *gragement*.[154] By mid-century the *méringue*—apparently a close relative, if not a descendant of the *carabinier*—had emerged as Haiti's predominant secular dance. The *méringue* complex, like that of the *carabinier*, comprised bourgeois as well as folk forms; the salon *méringue*, whether played on piano or by a chamber ensemble, typically concluded genteel dances in the latter part of the nineteenth century.

The Haitian *méringue*, not surprisingly, is closely related to the Dominican *merengue*, and scholars in both countries claim its origin for their own fatherlands. In their folk forms, both are quadratic-metered dance songs using simple harmonic ostinatos and a characteristic sixteenth-note drum roll preceding the alternate downbeats; both frequently employ a bipartite formal structure consisting of a verse section followed by a call-and-response section (the *jaleo* of the *merengue*). The Haitian *méringue*, however, is markedly slower than its Dominican counterpart and tends to use guitar more than the accordion-based *merengue*.

The introduction of radios and records to Haiti in the 1920s led to an inundation of Cuban and North American music, which came to supplant local music in cabarets and brothels as well as on the media.[155] In the forties, the *méringue* regained its popularity—albeit in a strongly Cubanized form—in the music of bandleaders Weber Sicot and, more importantly, Nemours Jean-Baptiste. Jean-Baptiste adapted the *méringue* to *mambo*-style big band instrumentation and rhythmic patterns, coining the term *compas direct* for his innovation. For his part, Sicot is credited with popularizing the rubric *cadence* for his similarly modernized *méringue*.[156]

In the sixties, younger musicians influenced by North American rock introduced trap set and electric guitar to the *compas* ensemble. Such music came to be referred to as "mini-jazz"—"mini," because the ensembles were often smaller and the performers younger, and "jazz" to denote a degree of fashionable North American influence. The model for the guitar style, however, was not the USA but the Congolese music that was coming to dominate African pop as well. One evident vehicle for the transmission of Zairian music to Haiti was the substantial number of Haitians who taught French and other subjects in Zaire in the years following that country's independence. Consequently, Haitian *compas* came to incorporate the intricate interlocking guitar patterns of Congolese pop, although they are often overshadowed by horn and vocal parts.[157] By this time, New York City, with its growing Haitian community, had emerged as a center for *compas* performance and recordings. Miami, Montreal, Paris, and the other French Caribbean islands are also important *compas* centers.

While *compas* may seem on first hearing to have a rather generic

Afro-Caribbean sound, there are several features which distinguish it from stylistically similar genres such as soca. *Compas* style, which has changed little since the sixties, retains the *méringue's* traditional bipartite structure, moderate tempo (M.M.ca. 114), and the identifying drum roll before the downbeats. Other elements in the genre's composite rhythm are a steady bass pulse and an ostinato played on cowbell and bass drum:

The traps player generally limits himself to playing a quarter-note pulse on the bass drum and, more importantly, a *cinquillo*-type pattern on the closed high-hat or a simple three-three-two ostinato on the cymbal.[158]

As is the case with the Dominican *merengue,* an aspiring musician or group often feels obliged to produce an LP (often using synthesizer instead of live acoustic instruments) as a prerequisite to obtaining club dates. Once successfully promoted, the band can then struggle to become one of the handful of groups with regular engagements and international tours.

Compas enjoys great popularity in Martinique and Guadeloupe. More closely associated with these islands, however, is *zouk,* a similar genre which reflects a closer orientation towards disco. The samba-like *biguine* of Martinique is also adapted as a modern pop genre by local musicians; in the latter idiom it may become practically indistinguishable from *compas. Zouk* bands—particularly the Guadeloupian Kassav'— are also greatly enjoyed in Haiti, reflecting the growing unity of the French Caribbean as a contemporary musical area.

Jamaica

Jamaica, lost by Spain in 1655, is heir to British rather than Hispanic and Italian musical influences. Thus, missionary-inspired choral singing, simple common-practice harmony, and relatively straightforward rhythms persist today rather than the Andalusian harmony, bel canto singing, and fondness for hemiola found in the Hispanic nations of the Caribbean basin. British colonial repression of neo-African percussion-based musics also served to dilute the rich African rhythmic heritage found, for example, in nearby Cuba. Yet Jamaican popular music found its own vital transculturated voice in reggae, which has exerted an international impact remarkable for such a small nation.[159]

The immediate folk precedent for the emergence of modern Jamaican popular musics was mento, a strophic topical song related to calypso. Mento's ad hoc accompanying ensemble generally included guitar, which provided a steady ostinato also characteristic of later popular genres:

By 1950 most Jamaican youths had come to regard mento as quaint and archaic. Enjoying far more appeal were contemporary American pop styles, especially rhythm-and-blues, which was popularized to some extent by radio, but more extensively by disc jockeys with portable sound systems.

In the mid-fifties, ska emerged in the growing urban slums as a distinctively Jamaican reinterpretation of R&B. Ska employed the instrumentation and general style of R&B, and many early ska songs were simply cover versions of American hits. While a triplet-syncopated shuffle beat was occasionally present (as in the top-40 ska hit "My Boy Lollipop"), more often a "straight four" tempo was used, synthesizing R&B and mento rhythm. Typically, the traps would stress beats two and four (at a tempo of M.M.115-140) over a "walking" quarter-note bass, while the guitar would strike the "and" offbeats in a syncopated mento style.

Ska was from its inception associated with the urban poor; accordingly, it was spurned by the small Jamaican middle class until acceptance in Great Britain and the USA earned it some local as well as international attention.[160] While most ska lyrics made no pretense of profundity, O'Gorman notes:

> Above the heavy beat of the Ska and the often tentative and inhibited attempts at improvisation in what was then more often an instrumental form, there began to be heard the voice of the "little man" whose grudge against a seemingly oppressive and unjust society began to take positive shape and find expression with greater and greater confidence.[161]

The occasional interjection of socio-political contemporaneity into song texts became more frequent in the 1960s, as Jamaican and African nationalism, American civil rights agitation, Rastafarianism, and the awareness of socio-economic injustice in Jamaica all intensified. Around 1965, as Jamaican popular music began to transcend ties to American trends, ska evolved into a more sophisticated style dubbed "rock steady."

Rock steady was seldom purely instrumental; like ska, it was primarily dance music, but its rhythm was more relaxed. Most authors assert that the ska rhythm "slowed down" in transit to rock steady. In fact, the tempos of the two genres are generally the same; only the rhythmic density has changed. The guitar, instead of strumming nervously on each eighth-note upbeat, now stresses only beats two and four;[162] the bass, rather than playing "even fours," emphasizes beats one and three. Most notably, the drums play a much less functional and conspicuous role; often they are virtually inaudible, or they merely add occasional desultory accents. Their time-keeping, intensifying role had been taken over by the bass, which was now louder, more active, and less pedestrian than the "walking" ska bass.

The crystallization of reggae around 1969 marked the emergence of a truly Jamaican popular music. Stylistically, reggae constitutes more a maturation of rock steady than a departure from it. Reggae's emergence coincided with several broader phenomena. First, Jamaican music enjoyed a prodigious boom in Great Britain, the USA, Africa and elsewhere, boosted by the cult status of Jimmy Cliff's 1968 film, *The Harder They Come*. The Jamaican recording industry developed in size, overseas distribution networks, and technological sophistication. Jamaica's most brilliant popular musician, Bob Marley, rose to stardom. Rastafarianism became a significant social, religious, and even political force and grew even more closely associated with popular music. Last, but not least, reggae's heyday was intimately linked to the socio-political ferment and activism that led Michael Manley and the People's National Party (PNP) to power in 1972.

The role of the mass media in the evolution of Jamaican popular music has been distinctive in several ways. Popular musics invariably involve an interaction between live performance and consumption of recorded or "mediated" music. Marked dominance of mediated rather than live music contexts, as in the case of Indian film music, may indicate corporate hegemony rather than grassroots expression, but such would not appear to be the case in Jamaica. Aside from individual radio and record listening, the norm for Jamaican dance music has generally not been a live band but rather the sound system, operated by a disc jockey. The sound system, indeed, has occupied a unique place in Jamaican music. Since the fifties and sixties, mobile disc jockeys have offered a wider range of dance musics—local and imported—than live groups could provide, and, moreover, they are cheaper. As Sebastian Clarke notes, even the Jamaican record industry was originally oriented toward use by the deejays rather than market consumption: "The sound system operator was cutting records for his 'sound' . . . and was not concerned about releasing records."[163] The advent of dub has further enhanced the role of the sound system; dub "deejays" even regard themselves as being closer to grassroots sentiment than the live bands since they can deal with a wider range of contemporary topics in a given context.[164]

Similarly, reggae and its predecessors evolved more as studio recording arts than as live performance genres. Name bands often consisted simply of regular session musicians backing up a lead vocalist; in live shows groups would often perfect means of imitating studio effects like reverb and echo.[165] Yet studio domination in Jamaica does not appear to have enforced conformity to corporate guidelines, either in style or in content. Most Jamaican records have been produced not by multinationals but by small, locally-financed ventures, often using primitive recording equipment.[166] Such conditions have left Jamaican musicians vulnerable to unscrupulous and ruthless exploitation both by local and foreign distributors, but they have also prevented artists from becoming too distanced from the socio-political realities that inform daily life as well as music.[167]

Ska, rock steady, and reggae were the product of lumpen proletarian "rude boy" and Rastafarian subcultures, both of which challenged, in their lifestyles and dress as well as music, the Eurocentric, conformist status quo upheld by the small Jamaican bourgeoisie. While most of the song texts were trivial, several celebrated pan-Africanism, black power, social reform (if not revolution), and the welfare of the common man. Reggae, then, provides another illustration of how the disenfranchised and despised lumpen proletariat may be the source for a dynamic popular music, which, as in the case of tango, achieves broad national acceptance only after earning foreign renown.

Rastafarianism has been an important theme of Jamaican popular music since the 1960s. Indeed, the publicity that reggae has lent Rastafarianism has led some foreign listeners to assume that many or most Jamaicans are Rastas, when in fact they constitute only a small minority, toward which the general public may have strongly ambivalent feelings. Rastafarianism can be seen as one lower-class Jamaican response to poverty, alienation, the legacy of slavery, and a neo-colonial world order dominated by American and European financial and strategic interests. As Hebdige illustrates, Rastafarianism integrates two essential Jamaican symbolic clusters—Black Africa and the white man's Bible—inverting the message of the latter to place God in Ethiopia and the black sufferer in Babylon.[168] Rasta music incorporating neo-African Burru drumming constituted a peripheral, if significant element of fifties slum subculture and, to some extent, an influence on subsequent ska and reggae.[169] More importantly, reggae owes to Rastafarianism its "dread," its celebration of marijuana, its black nationalism, and above all, the Messianic fervor that lends reggae a sincerity and conviction so different from the sentimental puppy love and stylized nihilism of most North American popular music since the early seventies.

Reggae's Rastafarianism and its proletarian origins made it an important socio-political as well as cultural phenomenon. As Garth White notes, "Rastafarian theology and black nationalism set in motion a process that demolished the cultural dominence (sic) and psychological control of the foreign and local middle class."[170] Hence reggae's rise became an integral part of the idealism and mass political mobilization—especially among the young—that propelled the PNP to power in 1972. Reggae lyrics' call for social justice and black power and their denunciation of Euro-American imperialism complemented the PNP's platform of national autonomy, redistribution of wealth, and socialist reform. Hence Michael Manley, recognizing the influence of popular singers, praised reggae and courted Rastafarian support by bringing Haile Selassie to Jamaica in 1966. In turn, Bob Marley lent his support to Manley's re-election campaign in 1976, even after narrowly surviving an asassination attempt. For his part, Manley rival Edward Seaga, who became prime minister in 1980, claims his own grassroots connections with Jamaican popular music, recalling his earlier career in the national recording business.[171]

Reggae is generally regarded as having declined in vitality and popularity since the late 1970s. Live reggae is seldom heard in Jamaica outside the tourist hotels and the annual Sunsplash festival, and American pop dominates the airwaves. More popular than reggae are sentimental "lovers' rock" and the new generations of aforementioned dub deejays who recite topical, rhythmic raps over pre-recorded instrumental backings.[172] At the 1987 Sunsplash Festival, for example, the dub "toasters" drew crowds several times as large as those attracted by the live reggae bands.

On one level, reggae's decline commenced with the death, in 1981, of the genre's most charismatic performer, Bob Marley, whose musical talent and vision of social justice blended in a creative synthesis that reggae has since been unable to recreate. The murder of veteran bandleader Peter Tosh in 1987 was a further blow. Yet broader phenomena seem to be involved in reggae's waning. For just as the ebb and flow of Argentine tango coincided with periods of populist political mobilization, so did reggae's zenith seem to be linked to the ferment, activism, and idealism of the Manley years. When oil prices, red-baiting, and hostility from the International Monetary Fund and the USA led to Manley's defeat in 1980, so did reggae's enervation seem to commence, as if connected to the mood of popular disillusionment. Moreover, insofar as reggae's vitality was linked to the activist aspect of Rastafarianism, the surfacing of contradictions within the cult itself may have sapped the genre. From the perspective of one North American journalist:

> At its peak, Rasta seemed to be pitting its black nationalist, anticapitalist ethos against that of bourgeois Creole society. But Rasta's atavisms—its disdain for politics and collective action, its religious obscurantism and its sometimes virulent sexism—prevented it from becoming the force for radical reform many hoped it would be.[173]

Reggae had, by this time, won substantial audiences in Great Britain, the USA, and especially Africa, becoming an integral part of the international popular music scene; in England—since the early 1960s a refuge for Jamaicans fleeing poverty and anti-Rasta repression at home—local musicians, emigrant West Indians, and racially mixed "two-tone" bands popularized fusions of reggae with punk and hard rock. Meanwhile, in Jamaica, the rap music of dub poets like Mutabaruka has assumed reggae's legacy of grassroots protest and Messianic Rastafarianism.

Trinidad and Tobago

Trinidad and neighboring Tobago, claimed by Spain in 1498, were neglected cultural and economic backwaters until the late eighteenth century. The arrival of French planters with their slaves in the 1780s provided an initial impetus to development, which was furthered by British conquest of the islands in 1797. Following the abolition of slavery in 1837, the substantial black population was supplemented by a roughly equal number of East Indians. Since independence in 1962, blacks have tended to dominate economic life in the islands.

Free blacks and slaves had been developing acculturated as well as neo-African forms of music since the early 1800s. These included the *calinda* stick-fighting dance, and a more lyrical, text-oriented type of song called *belair* (*bele*), whose verses, like those of related West African genres, consisted of praise, satire, insults, or topical commentary.[174] Performance of such music came to be associated in particular with pre-Lenten Carnival. The central event of Carnival, in its early stages, was the procession called *cambouley* (*canboulay*, from French *cannes brulées*), in which groups of torch-bearing blacks would reenact plantation fire-drills to the accompaniment of drums. The use of drums in Carnival was abolished in 1883, giving greater importance to the acculturated topical songs which evidently evolved from the *belair*.

By 1900 these songs had come to be called calypso. The origin of this term has been the subject of much conjecture; the two most likely candidates for its source are the West African-derived word *kaiso* and the Venezuelan Spanish *caliso*, which denoted a mestizo song form of the nineteenth century. From the 1880s, Venezuelan influence—particularly of the *paseo* (*pasillo*)—also contributed to the adoption of the guitar and *cuatro* as basic instruments in calypso. In subsequent decades, English came to replace French patois in calypso texts, minor keys gave way to major tonalities, and *ad hoc* calypso ensembles came to include clarinet, cornet, and other instruments borrowed from New Orleans jazz.[175]

In 1914, the first records of calypso were produced, and competitions began between tents where spectators would pay a small fee to hear groups of rival calypsonians attempt to outdo each other in singing topical or sarcastic texts. As the expenses of the increasingly formal and elaborate tents grew, so did their rivalry become more pronounced, leading to official state management of the competitions. Calypsonians of the twenties and thirties—especially Chieftan Walter Douglas and Roaring Lion—established higher standards of textual and melodic creativity and sophistication. The number and importance of recordings (produced in New York) increased markedly in the mid-thirties, and from the forties, calypso-derived songs like "Rum and Coca-Cola" and "Banana Boat Song" became great hits in the USA. Meanwhile, the state-run radio stations broadcasted calypsos daily, many of which were topical songs set to stock tunes, commenting on the events of the previous day.

By the 1950s, Trinidad Carnival had become the most important cultural event of the island, annually attracting much renown as well as contingents of tourists. Carnival festivities centered around increasingly elaborate parades, the steel drum bands that had arisen in the late thirties, and, above all, the calypso competitions. The latter formally commence two or three months prior to Carnival, when singers release records of the newly composed songs that will hopefully earn them the annual crown and the recording contracts that generally ensue. In Carnival proper, the calypsonians perform with house back-up bands in halls and theaters (still called "tents"); visiting judges select finalists and, eventually, prizewinners, basing their decisions primarily on text, melody, and stage presentation. The public, meanwhile, chooses its own favorite for the "road march" to be played by steel bands in the final processions.

As a popular music genre, calypso is quite unique in several ways. Its association with Carnival is reminiscent of street *samba* in Rio de Janeiro; but whereas pop *samba* has shed its ties to Brazilian Carnival, calypso composition, live performance, and record output remain a largely seasonal affair, booming in January, February, and March and subsiding markedly during the rest of the year. In Trinidad during the extended yearly lull, calypso accounts for only a quarter of the music broadcast on the radio.[176] (The other English-speaking islands of the Lesser Antilles celebrate their own Carnivals, with calypso contests, at different times during the year.)

Calypso is also remarkable for its emphasis on text content. Calypsonians (as opposed to mere calypso singers) are generally expected to compose their own repertoire. In recording, instruments are traditionally seldom allowed to interfere with comprehension of the words. Accordingly, calypso texts, as expressions of popular sentiment, often acquire the nature of important political statements to be discussed in Parliament and the news media. The best calypsonians combine a keen sense of imagery, rhythm, wit, and socio-political insight with a flair for the extravagant and outrageous.

Calypso's topical contemporaneity is a notable feature distinguishing it from most other pop genres. We have mentioned the custom of broadcasting songs commenting on events of the preceding days. While an increasing number of calypso texts are of the "hey hey, let's dance" variety, a substantial portion remain devoted to diverse topics. As such, they constitute a rich source of urban folklore and have been the subjects of numerous studies.[177] A significant number of calypsos are socio-political. Traditionally, like Mexican *corridos*, these could serve as informal news sources, educating listeners on domestic and international events. With the advent of radio and near-universal literacy, calypso texts serve more to comment upon and interpret news rather than to merely inform. They continue, however, to sharpen political consciousness and to serve as mouthpieces for popular sentiments. Many songs lambast government policies; a large number have been supportive, particularly during the extended leadership of Prime Minister Eric Williams ("the Doctor"), who was widely respected and admired. Contemporary events like the Grenada invasion of 1983 have inspired innumerable calypsos.

Along with topical songs, the other main category of calypsos comprises those that deal, directly or indirectly, with male-female relations. Many of these songs are explicitly obscene and are the only ones to be censored on the radio. Others praise the sexual prowess of the singer, in accordance with the traditionally bombastic sobriquets calypsonians assume, such as Attila the Hun, Black Stalin, and the Mighty Bomber.

The sexism of calypso songs is remarkable even by traditional standards, leading some observers to opine that humiliation of women appears to be part of the national ethos. The emasculating effects of slavery and of the American GI presence during World War II may be partially responsible for this chauvinism.[178] Women are seen as sexual playthings for the calypsonian, while at the same time vilified if they are promiscuous. Physical imperfections are mocked, marriage and commitment are renounced, and in general, the calypsonian "is assured of heartfelt, howling approval when he devotes his talent to the degradation of woman."[179] (The few women that have achieved renown as calypsonians are, of course, exceptions to this norm.)

Calypso's topical contemporaneity and the explicitness with which it voices popular (male) sentiment distinguish it from most modern popular musics, and these features are themselves closely tied to the way in which the mass media have developed in Trinidad and Tobago. Modern calypso, like any popular genre, has evolved in close connection with the radio and the recording industry. Radio airplay is essential for achieving the record sales for which calypsonians strive. Yet the recording industry, as described in Wallis and Malm's *Big sounds from small peoples*, is relatively underdeveloped. Multinationals are not active in Trinidad, such that most recording firms are small, local affairs often run by the calypsonians themselves. International distribution is extremely limited, generally reaching only the neighboring islands and West Indian communities in the USA and Great Britain. Local distribution is often highly informal, such that even a top star like the Mighty Sparrow may be seen selling his records from the trunk of his car. The domestic record industry itself has been perpetually hampered by onerous tariffs and, more recently, cassette piracy. It remains a small, highly diverse, and local industry; thus, while limited in its reach and relatively unremunerative for most of its artists, it can constitute a grassroots *vox populi* in a manner quite uncharacteristic of a large corporate music industry.[180]

The topical contemporaneity of calypso songs is at once a cause and an effect of the exclusively local control and reach of the record industry. Songs addressing particular domestic political affairs may have little attraction or meaning to outsiders; at the same time, the indigenous control and orientation of the record industry *enable* calypsonians to continue the tradition of singing topical songs within the new context of the mass media. Hence, Wallis and Malm aptly point out the contrast between calypso's continued contemporaneity and the complete absence of social or political commentary in the Eurovision song contest.[181]

Calypso has, however, changed markedly since the early 1970s in the process of adapting to further development of the music industry environment. As investments in record production and sound systems increase, calypsonians produce only a few songs per season. While many of these may still be topical, they cannot be so specific and limited as the radio-sponsored songs of earlier decades, which, as mentioned above, often commented on events immediately preceding broadcasting. In live performance improvisation is negligible as performers strive to reproduce the sound of their own records. Moreover, disc jockeys and sound systems are frequently being substituted for live musicians.[182]

Soca

Calypso style has also changed under the impact of modernization and technology. Modern calypsos still adhere to strophic song format, quadratic meter, alternating verses (often of irregular length) and chorus, and predominantly major keys. Harmonies are simple and melodies diatonic. The adoption of the electric guitar and bass in the early 1970s changed the sound of the ensemble, and by 1980 most groups incorporated synthesizers as well.

From the mid-1970s increasing musical sophistication, continued growth of the record industry, and the intervention of the music arranger and producer have gone hand-in-hand with a greater emphasis on the musical aspect of calypso. To be successful, a calypsonian can no longer simply set his verses to a stock tune with conventional guitar, bass, and drums accompaniment. Higher standards of studio production and arrangement have come to prevail, and the suitability of calypso for dancing has acquired a new importance. In many new songs the catchy musical setting and driving rhythms assume much greater import than the lyrics, which may be trivial and barely audible.

Around 1977 the term "soca," for "soul-calypso" was coined— allegedly by Lord Shorty—to describe the energetic, disco-influenced style of commercial calypso party music coming into vogue; while the rubric is often applied to modern calypso in general, others reserve it for songs using a particular syncopated, dance-oriented rhythm. While this rhythm is not entirely standardized, the bass and drums parts shown in the following excerpt are typical.[183]

As in reggae, the bass plays an important role in the composite rhythm, and in live performance it can be deafeningly loud. Meanwhile, under the pressure of competition, showmanship has increased in extravagance, and performers incorporate all manner of gimmicks, costumes, and stage effects in order to stand out among their rivals. This trend, not surprisingly, has itself been the subject of at least one soca song:[184]

> I know we may have an argument
> As long as it's great entertainment
> But many artists really overdo
> Won't you listen to my point of view
> Just imagine you singin' about a jackass
> You gotta dress up with a bridle den eat some grass . . .
> You sing about a lamppost well tote de pole
> To sing about a donut, well hold a hole . . .
> To sing about a smoked herring bring the tail
> To sing about Jonah well tote the whale. . . .

In a word, calypso's instrumentation, rhythm, studio production, and stage presentation have changed considerably under the impact of modernity. Modern soca, however, continues to uphold the tradition of rich topical text content that has proven to be its most vital and distinctive asset.

CHAPTER 3

Africa

The field of African popular music is as diverse as the African people themselves. Several books and dozens of articles have already been published on the subject, and yet these only begin to describe the breadth and variety of modern African urban musics. Not only do entire areas remain relatively undocumented (such as Angola, Sudan, Mozambique) but published research invariably lags well behind the new styles and genres which constantly proliferate. A short chapter such as this one cannot substitute for the substantial extant literature and can at best outline broad trends and major national genres.

Despite the great diversity of traditional musics in sub-Saharan Africa, the region does lend itself to certain broad generalizations which to some extent distinguish it from other cultural areas, including North Africa (which, due to its predominantly Arab cultural orientation, is considered separately in Chapter 5). As mentioned in the preceding chapter, scholars have noted certain general tendencies of traditional African music, including: an emphasis on percussion and complex rhythms and polyrhythms; an association of music with dance; a high degree of collective participation; a strong connection between music and its social function (such as work, ceremony, worship); structuring of songs around repetition and variation of short segments; steady tempo; call-and-response vocal format; relaxed (rather than harsh or constricted) vocal timbre; polyphony; roughly diatonic tone systems; and, in the case of tonal languages, a close correspondence between melody and linguistic contour.

Most of these characteristics have persisted in modern popular musics along with other features associated with specific regional genres. A few such characteristics have changed or been forsaken. Most notable, for example, are the functional contexts in which music is performed. Modern popular musics like West African *juju* can be played in traditional contexts like births, weddings, funerals, and installations of tribal royalty,[1] but, most typically, *juju* and other pop forms are played for recreation and entertainment, lacking any other explicit social purpose. Uses of music (and dance) for simple diversion were common in most African societies, but that was but one context for musical activity; not surprisingly, many African popular musics have derived primarily from entertainment genres, rather than from those associated with specific traditional occasions or functions.

Aside from the widespread incorporation of Western musical elements, another departure from the characteristics cited above involves the simplification of rhythms. Traditional African music is celebrated for its complex polyrhythms and layered syncopations. Such polyrhythms are found in some modern commercial styles, but far more common is a simple, unvarying quadratic pulse over which relatively straightforward, albeit syncopated lines are added. As we have seen, the formation of hybrid pop forms can in many cases be likened to that of pidgin languages, in which elements of the parent languages are simplified in the process of mixing. Thus, Western harmony and African melody and rhythm become less complex as they are incorporated into syncretic urban forms like highlife. Yet the result, as Coplan stresses, should not be regarded as inept imitation of parent models but as "creative selection and integration of culture on the part of [African] musicians in response to a new situation."[2]

The "new situation," invariably, is the modern city, constituting a social, cultural, and economic environment that has little in common with the tribal village whence most Africans or their ancestors ultimately came. Urbanization entails a process of formidable adaptation and reorientation of cultural values, both on individual and group levels. For most urban Africans the process is accompanied by considerable poverty, insecurity, and alienation; moreover, many emigrants from the countryside leave their homes out of duress rather than choice.

Artistic creation, including music, plays an important role in facilitating and mediating adaptation to the new environment. Most traditional African music forms evolved in pre-capitalist, tribal, rural milieus, and do not completely fulfill the cultural needs of modern city-dwellers. Nor, for that matter, would indiscriminate borrowing of Western models. The need, as Coplan states, is for the creation of syncretic models that are "at once authentic and modern, indigenous but not isolated or provincial, African but not ethnically exclusive."[3]

In fact, much African popular music remains ethnically exclusive in terms of language and associations with specific tribes. Not surprisingly, imported musics—from reggae and rock to foreign African genres—tend to enjoy the most clearly pan-ethnic appeal. While most urban dwellers may come to share certain aspects of social identity, marked "de-tribalization" tends to occur only in special conditions, as when diverse ethnicities mix in a neutral context like a mining town. In such cases, the new popular music may develop as both an agent and an effect of the formation of a new social identity. Thus, Kazadi wa Mukuna describes the birth of modern Zairian music as a common denominator expression of the proletarian society emerging in the mines and urban work camps where members of different tribes lived and worked side by side.[4] Similar phenomena are described by researchers of music in West and South Africa.[5] Appropriately, song texts often employ the local lingua franca (such as English, French, or Swahili) or, in some cases—including highlife—they may even combine several languages within a single song.[6]

This process of creating such new musical forms is a complex one. It involves, on one level, the reinterpretation and remolding of features inherited from traditional musics, in such a manner as to reflect the new patterns of urban social organization. Hence, the persistence, albeit in frequently modified form, of most of the pan-Africanisms noted above. Equally conspicuous, however, is the incorporation of elements borrowed from other musical areas. The advent of the mass media in Africa created a new awareness of foreign musical styles and made syncretic adaptation possible on an unprecedented level. Three major sources of external influence and cross-fertilization can be noted: (1) various styles of European music; (2) Afro-American and Afro-Latin musics, particularly from Cuba; and (3) regional styles within Africa itself, especially Congo music, which became widely popular and influential throughout much of the continent.

Christian hymns, especially as taught by British missionaries, were the first form of Western music to be introduced in Africa on a wide scale. The churches became vehicles for the introduction of Western harmony and melody, which were in many cases readily grasped by Africans who had their own traditions of polyphonic choral singing. Hymnals tended to promote rigid homophonic settings and bland bourgeois conceptions of taste, and the ministers' attempts to set tonal African languages to extant Western melodies often produced ludicrous results.[7] Nevertheless, missionary hymns remained an important influence; as Coplan observes, many highlife melodies are very reminiscent of hymns, with their simple harmonies and diatonic scalar bases.[8]

An equally important source of Western influence was brass band music introduced by the colonists for military functions. As with church music, the British were the most zealous exporters and teachers of military music. Regimental bands were introduced in West Africa as early as the seventeenth century, and by 1750 a number of British-style bands with native musicians were extant. Significantly, as early as the 1840s the native bands were playing contemporary popular songs as well as marches.[9] A gradual process of Africanization subsequently transpired in the brass bands. In the early decades of this century, the European marches and dance songs were enlivened with indigenous syncopations, giving birth to hybrid dance forms like the Ghanaian *adaha* and the East African *beni*. As fondness for colonial music waned, especially after World War II, musicians trained in European brass music joined civilian ensembles specializing in dance music; in East Africa they tended to join Cuban-style *rumba* bands, while elsewhere, the brass musicians contributed to more indigenous hybrids, like West African *konkomba*.[10]

While the compatibilities between Western and African musics have often been noted, it is not surprising that Africans exposed to foreign musics developed a special fondness for styles that already incorporated familiar Africanisms. Hence, Afro-American and Afro-Latin musics became even more influential and popular than the pure Western church and military musics. The Afro-American impact started with the importation of ragtime and blackface ministrelsy in the late nineteenth century. These genres, ironically introduced by white colonists, soon became widely popular in various parts of Africa (especially the British colonies) and were disseminated by dance bands, sheet music, and cylinder recordings. By the 1920s, Africans had formed their own blackface Vaudeville troupes, whose ragtime and minstrel songs contributed to the evolution of hybrid African forms.[11]

The Afro-Caribbean influence, however, was even more profound and pervasive. By 1940, Cuban music—especially the *rumba* and *son*—had become the rage throughout much of Africa, even more so than in Europe and the USA, where the *"mambo* craze" was in full swing. Cuban styles became particularly popular after World War II, as many African soldiers in the colonial armies were exposed to them and recognized "something new in a familiar garment," in Kubik's words. The *chachachá, rumba,* and the Dominican *merengue* became dominant popular musics in much of East, South, and West Africa, but their impact was greatest in the French-speaking Congo region.[12] Cuban music, like other imported styles, generated its own set of hybrid, re-Africanized derivatives, which dominated Zairian music until *soukous,* rock, and disco emerged in the sixties and seventies.

From the 1940s, calypso enjoyed a particular appeal in the English-speaking West African countries and exerted considerable influence on highlife. Around this time the electric guitar was introduced, and its subsequent spread became one of the most important developments in the course of modern African music. Throughout Africa, guitar-based styles emerged, building on Cuban, Western, or traditional African sources. In the latter category, particularly noteworthy are the retentions of traditional thumb-piano patterns in Congolese and Zimbabwe guitar musics. As Roberts observes, the guitar-based styles tended to fall into two categories: amplified dance bands using a variety of traditional and imported instruments, and more intimate "listening" formats typically featuring one or two guitars and an unobtrusive percussion accompaniment, such as a knife tapped on a bottle.[13]

The emergence of soul music and the Black Power movement in the 1960s had prodigous impact in Africa, where James Brown and other American artists soon became models for local bands.[14] Perhaps even more influential, however, was Jamaican reggae, with its anti-imperialist "back to Africa" message. African reggae bands proliferated, and the genre continues to enjoy appeal, although not on the level of its mid-seventies heyday. It has since been rivaled by contemporary disco, which was heavily promoted by multinational recording companies. At present, rock remains the single most pervasive musical influence on African music, and most current styles can be regarded as fusions of traditional characteristics with heavy rock rhythms and instrumentation. Needless to say, rock elements are not imported indiscriminately; for example, rock's frequently harsh, strained vocal timbres and passionate intensity are not widely characteristic of African pop, wherein, despite the emphasis on percussion, more of a "cool" aesthetic prevails.

Western pop influence has contributed to an increase of song texts dealing with sentimental love. Nevertheless, the tradition of topical songs persists in modern urban music. Praise songs—an important genre in traditional African society—are not uncommon in *juju*.[15] Many guitar-band highlife songs continue the custom of commenting, often with sarcasm, on contemporary social life, serving as forums for the conceptualization and articulation of moral positions on social problems arising from modern urban life. The persuasive influence of highlife commentaries and narratives has led politicians like Kwame Nkrumah to cultivate musicians' support (through judicious use of the stick as well as the carrot).[16] On the whole, however, social commentary is far more common than explicit political criticism, as the authoritarian governments prevalent in much of Africa tend not to tolerate open dissent. Nigeria's provocative Fela Anikulapo Kuti is one of the very few who have persistently inveighed against their governments, and he has been persecuted harshly for his criticism.

Political song, nevertheless, has been an important category of modern popular music in various contexts. During the period of struggle against colonial exploitation, nationalistic songs played a significant role in sustaining morale. In many cases such songs were modeled after Western marches, hymns, and anthems, reflecting the European bourgeois education of the early nationalist leaders.[17] Not all propaganda music has been Western in character, however. The *chimurenga* songs of revolution against the white Rhodesian government derived primarily from traditional Shona music. In South Africa, political songs have reflected the complex contradictions and interaction between different classes of Africans involved in the liberation struggle. In the early stages of the resistance movement (late nineteenth through early twentieth century), the assimilationist black petty bourgeoisie, with its profound ambivalence toward the dominant white culture, tended to promote Westernized musical expressions. Syncretic forms subsequently arose, notably *makwaya* choral music, which combined European and traditional Xhosa elements. The use of traditional tribal styles, while persisting in protest music, has posed problems in its relation to the leaders' goals of transcending ethnicity and forming a pan-tribal, modernist solidarity movement. Hence, the liberation cause has continued to use hybrid and imported forms, from ragtime to reggae and "Zulu jazz-rock."[18]

Radio and the recording industry have played crucial roles in the development of African popular music, with the competition between multinational and local control as a recurrent theme. Records were marketed in Africa as early as 1907, and foreign and African popular musics were being widely disseminated by the thirties. In the following decade, multinational companies (especially HMV, Odeon, Columbia, and Pathé-Marconi) set up subsidiaries throughout the continent, producing local music for the African market. The West African record industry has been particularly active, especially in Nigeria and the other English-speaking countries.

In Africa as elsewhere, a large portion of the record industry is controlled by a few multinationals, while the remainder is divided among innumerable small record companies. Nationalist pressure against foreign domination has led to various government responses. In Nigeria, protests from the Musicians' Union in the late seventies persuaded the state to break up monopolies in record pressing.[19] In Tanzania the state has shut out multinationals in order to combat the domination of imported Western and Zairian music, but the shortage of indigenous investment in the music business has resulted in the complete absence of any record industry. While foreign cassettes are popular, the radio stations' promotion of local music and the weakness of foreign competition have created an unusually buoyant live music scene. East African music in neighboring Kenya, by contrast, has profited from the local recording industry, but has faced continual competition from imported Zairian and Western music.[20]

As in much of the developing world, copyright protection is minimal. Cassette piracy is rampant and may be formalized, as in Ghana, where innumerable music stores routinely sell pirate tapes of LPs for roughly a quarter of the cost of the record itself.[21] Such piracy produces its own mixed effects, undermining multinational profits but at the same time crippling smaller local industries and denying royalties not only to foreign superstars but also to struggling local artists.

Despite the variety and widespread popularity of African popular musics, it should be remembered that in many areas, modern syncretic musics continue to play only a limited role in musical life. Thus, for example, even in Ghana—a small country with a lively pop music scene—a large percentage of the population has only limited access to radios or cassettes, not to mention live performances of popular musics; this is true especially in the less developed northern regions. For such peoples, while popular music styles may not be unfamiliar, it is the traditional, communally performed songs and dances which constitute musical culture.[22]

West Africa

While syncretic popular music forms have developed throughout Africa, they flourished particularly early in West Africa, partly because of the relatively flexible British colonial policy which tolerated or even promoted racial interaction and acculturation.[23] As we have seen, the process of fusion had begun well before the twentieth century, as nineteenth-century brass bands routinely incorporated popular tunes into their repertoires. The development of modern commercial urban musics ensued in a complex interweaving of European, Caribbean, and indigenous elements, all playing their role in the evolution of new forms of urban social identity.

We have mentioned above the tendency for much African popular music to fall into two categories: guitar-based songs played by small ensembles, with extended texts containing social commentary and narrative, and, on the other hand, dance music played by larger bands, often with brass instruments, and with lesser emphasis on the text. In the evolution of highlife these two traditions developed in more or less parallel fashion, influencing each other while retaining their own individuality.

The roots of guitar-based highlife lie in the hybrid musics of the lower-class coast dwellers of West Africa in the early twentieth century; as in several other cultures, sailors—in this case, Liberian Krus—were an important catalyst in the development of the new music. The guitar had already become popular among Kru sailors, and their interaction with Caribbeans, Afro-Americans, and other Africans soon began to produce syncretic musical styles. The Akan and Fanti were especially influential in this process, no doubt because of the compatibilities between the imported folksongs and traditional Akan/Fanti musics; in particular, the techniques and styles of playing the Akan *seprewa* (a harp-lute resembling the *kora*) were easily adapted to the guitar.[24] Prototypical highlife genres soon emerged, including Fanti *osibisaba* music and various other now obscure forms (such as *ashiko, dagomba,* and mainline). Interacting with other syncretic forms such as the hymn-influenced, pidgin English *gombe,* the guitar-based styles came to be generically referred to as "palm-wine" music.

"Palm-wine" was a distinctively popular and non-aristocratic music associated, as its name suggests, with unpretentious seaport taverns offering cheap liquor and informal music. From the 1930s to the early 1950s, palm-wine highlife groups proliferated, gradually extending their popularity inland, occasionally by being incorporated into minstrel and dramatic troupes. The "E.K. Band" of Ghanaian musician E.K. Nyame was the most influential in the fifties.

The typical palm-wine highlife ensemble consists of vocals accompanied by one or two guitars, bass, and one or more percussion instruments—usually a *clave,* a knife tapped on a bottle, and a conga, bongo, or similar drum. The average song is built around a repeated harmonic ostinato—such as I-I-IV-V—set to a straightforward quadratic rhythm. The bass stresses the downbeat in straight quarter-notes or with more active patterns. The drum and guitar improvise loosely throughout, the latter alternating chordal strumming with arpeggios and short single-note phrases. The *clave* (or bottle) plays a repeated pattern, functioning more or less as a time-line; the standard Cuban *clave* pattern (usually in "reverse" 3-2 form) is quite common, although more typical is the pattern below, derived from the Akan *sikyi* dance music:[25]

Solo (generally male) vocal fragments alternate with choral responses; the latter are in two- or three-part polyphony, generally reflecting the Western harmonies of the string instruments but often employing distinctively indigenous parallel fourths and fifths.

Palm-wine highlife, with its proletarian origins and inexpensive instruments, still plays a marginal role in Ghanaian cultural life in the music of Ko Nimo (Daniel Amponsah), a composer-guitarist with some Western training who enhances the genre with jazz, bossa nova, and even classical influences. While Ko Nimo enjoys considerable respect among Ghanaians seeking syntheses of traditional and modern musics, on the whole, most young people with more modern tastes tend to regard palm-wine music as quaint and dated.[26]

The development of brass-dominated dance bands has paralleled that of guitar-based highlife, but relied on elite rather than working-class patronage. The earliest entertainment dance bands developed out of military and church bands and specialized in playing European waltzes and quicksteps for British and native elite social affairs. (The term "highlife" was coined by the lower-class spectators who gazed at such events from outside.) By 1920 some dance bands were routinely incorporating Akan tunes, suitably harmonized, in their repertoires.[27] The brass bands had already generated Africanized hybrids, especially the complex, polyrhythmic Fanti *adaha* and the choral and percussion *konkomba*. Yet until the forties, Western ballroom music (swing, *rumbas*, polkas, waltzes, quadrilles, and the like) had continued to dominate dance-band repertoires. The full emergence of dance-band highlife occurred in the forties, when most dance bands finally forsook these "colo" (colonial) genres for orchestrated songs based on indigenous rhythms and melodies. Bandleader E. T. Mensah (b. 1919) was the most influential figure in this development. Under his inspiration local music—sung in vernacular rather than English—soon came to replace imported ballroom genres throughout West Africa.

It may be more accurate to regard the evolution of dance-band highlife not so much as an Africanization of brass ensemble music but rather as a Westernization of African music. Mensah's innovation was aided by the aforementioned exposure of hundreds of Africans to Western music during the Second World War; as these soldiers returned to civilian life after becoming familiar with and often skilled at Western and Caribbean musics, they took to modernizing their own music by rendering it in orchestrated style with Western instruments.

Mensah's band, the Tempos, was smaller than most pre-war dance bands, patterned as they were after swing era big bands. The Tempos featured only three horns, guitar, and Latin percussion. Subsequent highlife bands frequently came to incorporate more brass and winds, although many were even smaller than Mensah's group, especially with the added amplification of the electric guitar.

Horn arrangements in dance-band highlife tended to derive from American and British "sweet" dance-band music (such as that of band-leader Paul Whiteman). The jazz influence was clear in voicings, instrumentation, and solos, but in other respects highlife remained distinct. The average dance-band highlife song used a straight quadratic rhythm (rather than triplet-divided swing rhythm) with Latin percussion; the *clave* was generally present, playing, as with guitar-based highlife, either the standard Cuban pattern or else the aforementioned *sikyi* ostinato. Similarly, vocal harmonies often contained distinctly non-Western voice leadings. Many dance bands also include in their repertoire songs based on traditional polyrhythmic patterns, such as the Calabari *akwete* and the Ewe *agbadza*. Both of these rhythms feature the standard West African time-line:[28]

Such songs illustrate the existence of what has been called a "highlife-bush continuum," with Westernized, "sweet" arrangements at one end and *konkomba* and traditional musics at the other.

Highlife lyrics range in subject matter from social commentary to sentimental love. Whether deliberately or not, many deal in some way with the changes wrought by urbanization and modernization. As mentioned, some groups reflect a pan-ethnic orientation in the use of several languages, occasionally within the same song.[29]

In the late fifties, the electric guitar came to dominate highlife, and horn-based bands either added guitars or else gradually declined. Brass bands performed highlife at various outdoor events, and traditional dances like the Akan *adowa* were increasingly incorporated into guitar and brass band highlife.[30] Calypso also became popular among highlife audiences at this time.

Highlife continues to be played, however, in a variety of hybrid forms and contexts; funerals in Ghana, for example, often conclude with dancing to live highlife. Nevertheless, since the mid-1960s highlife's popularity has been on the defensive against the vogue of soul, disco, reggae, Congolese music, and other imported forms, and the genre has never quite recovered. At present, musicians like George Darko are to some extent reinvigorating the genre by diluting it with Western soul and disco; such fusions, referred to as "burgher highlife," are to some extent associated with musicians living in or touring frequently in Europe. But despite highlife's frequent message of pan-African solidarity, Coplan states that younger Africans tend to regard the genre as too old-fashioned to be a meaningful contemporary vehicle of social commentary.[31] It is not surprising, then, that reggae and Western pop (especially black American and country-western music) appear to constitute as much as two-thirds of the product in an average Ghanaian music store.[32] Opinions and tastes regarding contemporary music in Ghana, as in the rest of Africa, are diverse and often polemical, representing the competing ideologies of tradition, modernity, and nationalism.

While highlife itself continues a somewhat attenuated existence, it has contributed to the evolution of several regional forms that continue to be popular. These include the *makossa* of Cameroon, "milo jazz" of Sierra Leone, Fela's "Afro-beat," and the Congolese-influenced "rokafil jazz" of eastern Nigeria, all of which, in keeping with the times, have a stronger rock and disco orientation than highlife. Also worthy of mention here is the music of the eclectic Ghanaian group Wulomei, which incorporates more traditional Ga rhythms and instruments.[33]

By far the most important relative of highlife, however, is Nigerian *juju*. *Juju's* roots, although obscure, are said to lie in the guitar, banjo, and ukulele music emerging in Nigeria since the 1920s, and in a more traditional genre called *kokoma*, which employed chorus, *mbira*-type hand-piano, and drums.[34] Waterman has further summarized *juju's* subsequent development as a syncretic genre embodying the evolving working-class identity of Yoruba city-dwellers. Until the late forties, *juju* was typically played in male-dominated bars or for neo-traditional life-cycle ceremonies by a quartet consisting of two singers with banjo and percussion accompaniment. Its audience consisted primarily of recently urbanized Yoruba and other non-Yoruba transients working in Lagos and other West African ports. By the early fifties, *juju* was changing markedly under the influence of nationalism, the spread of amplification and the electric guitar, and the innovations of bandleader I. K. Dairo and other musicians. Amplification (especially for voices) facilitated the introduction of traditional Yoruba percussion instruments, including the hourglass-shaped pressure drum that functioned as a "talking drum," commenting, as it were, on the song texts. Accompanying this re-Africanization of the instrumental style was a renewed emphasis on choral call-and-response vocals, which, thanks to amplification, could be easily heard over the expanded instrumental accompaniment. These developments further enhanced *juju's* role as a specifically Yoruba idiom.[35]

I. K. Dairo's re-Africanization of *juju* was so thorough that the only Western element in his music, the guitar, seems to play a limited and expendable role; songs like "Kaiye mase lenini ni," using the polymetric *agbadza*-type rhythm, strike the ear as purely Yoruba, with desultory, ornamental guitar phrases added. *Juju* does not use horns, which tend to be associated with the highlife dance bands that went out of style in Nigeria in the disruptive period of the civil war (1967–1970). The tempo of *juju* songs is somewhat slower than highlife, and it continues to be performed in traditional Nigerian contexts, such as tribal royalty installations and funerals. Older *juju* songs were frequently written in praise of some patron or public figure, but since the early seventies, social commentary has become more standard in texts. Religious songs abound, as many *juju* musicians are fervent Christians.

In the 1970s *juju* was further modernized and commercialized under the leadership of Ebenezer Obey and King Sunny Ade, both of whom have since developed international audiences. Under their influence *juju* has drawn closer to rock and lost some of its distinctive Yoruba flavor. Obey and Ade popularized the use of the pedal steel guitar and as many as six electric guitars. Some of the guitarists may serve more of a visual function than a musical one. In Obey's format, for example, one guitar may play a repeated background ostinato, another strikes percussive chordal patterns, a third improvises melodies throughout, while the remaining guitars are more or less inaudible. Ade strives for a balanced, layered interweaving of guitar lines and percussion patterns. Traditional Yoruba rhythms are mixed with rock and, occasionally, Afro-Cuban elements.[36]

Juju is not the only current Nigerian pop genre, and, indeed, it may seem that every prominent West African musician has coined some label for his particular fusion of traditional and modern sounds. Much of this contemporary music differs little from disco or rock in terms of style, and is thus outside the subject matter of this text. A few genres, however, are worthy of attention.

Fuji materialized in the early 1980s as an interesting derivative of *juju;* in a word, it consists of *juju* without any guitars, that is, it employs only percussion instruments. In this sense it represents a return to tradition, but its texts are vitally contemporary, and as such it has become extremely popular among the Lagos lower classes.[37]

Another related genre is *apala,* which emerged in the 1940s, integrating Yoruba elements with influences from the Muslim northern area of Nigeria.[38] Stylistically, *apala* differs from *juju* in its faster tempo, greater emphasis on percussion, and a generally more intense and "hot" character. While some modern *apala* ensembles include guitar or steel guitar, they, as well as early recordings (such as those by Haruna Ishola), are thoroughly percussion-dominated, with the talking drum adding a thundering, bubbling drive throughout.

Finally, no discussion of modern Nigerian music can ignore Fela Anikulapo Kuti (b. 1938). Fela's music is derived primarily from Afro-American soul—especially James Brown—and has little of the Yoruba flavor of *juju* or *apala.* Fela is a charismatic performer and his music is dynamic and original enough that its distinctive label—"Afro-beat"—has become generally accepted. The biting sarcasm and pungency of his lyrics, and his dramatic vocal style mark him as one of the most vital African performers of the century. Much of his notoriety stems from his flamboyant life style and the provocative socio-political criticisms in his lyrics. Fela himself is a paragon of contradiction. His texts denounce exploitative businesses and rail against government corruption and oppression. At the same time, he owns dozens of luxury cars and retained until recently a harem of twenty-odd wives, who can be seen arrayed bare-breasted on one of his album covers. Liberal Western audiences impressed by his criticism of economic and political injustice might well have difficulty with his views on female subordination, which he justifies with a thoroughly idiosyncratic interpretation of Yoruba customs.[39] Because of his outspoken criticism of the Nigerian government, he has been imprisoned repeatedly.

In the late 1970s a distinctive set of popular music styles emerged in the Sudanic desert countries, especially Mali and Senegal. Previously, Congolese music and other imported forms had tended to dominate dance repertoires in these regions, but as demand for music in local languages grew, the area developed its own popular genres. These were heavily influenced by the music of the *griots*, hereditary singers who traditionally performed in the service of Mandingo tribal patrons. The *griot* instrument *par excellence* is the *kora* harp. The new popular music styles frequently incorporate the *kora* itself, or else they imitate *kora* patterns on electric guitars. Another influential instrument is the *balafon* xylophone, often included along with the *kora*. As with other African popular musics, there is a clear continuum between the traditional-sounding styles and the more acculturated rock fusions of musicians like Toure Kunda and Foday Musa Suso.[40] One style currently gaining special popularity is the Sahelian Senegalese pop of Youssou N'Dour and others, with its distinctive Islamic-influenced melismatic vocal style.

Cape Verde

An interesting peripheral musical region is Cape Verde, a small archipelago nation off the coast of West Africa. A Portuguese colony for five centuries, Cape Verde developed a distinctive musical culture under a blend of African, Lusitanian, and Brazilian influences. Most of Cape Verde's inhabitants are descendents of West African slaves brought by the Portuguese to the previously uninhabited islands; accordingly, Cape Verdeans retain many Africanisms in their culture and language (an Afro-Portuguese creole). At the same time, the significant colonial presence and the islands' importance as a mercantile and whaling port contributed to the development of a particularly cosmopolitan blend of musical and cultural influences. Acculturation has been further promoted by the growth of overseas communities (especially in New England), whose population now exceeds that of Cape Verde itself (around 300,000).[41]

Music in Cape Verde can be said to comprise a continuum of African-derived and more European genres, some of which have developed into modern popular musics. The most important European-derived genre is the *morna*, which is regarded as a quintessential expression of national culture. The typical *morna* consists of a poem—often of high literary calibre—sung in medium-tempo quadratic meter by a solo vocalist, accompanied by an ensemble of stringed instruments including the violin (*rabeca*), guitar (*violão*), twelve-stringed *viola*, and the ukulele-like *cavaquinho*. The *morna* is believed to have emerged in the early nineteenth century, possibly influenced by the Luso-Brazilian *modinha*. At present it continues to be popular among all classes and age groups in Cape Verde, and is often performed in modernized style using electronic instruments.

In the 1960s the *coladera* emerged as a more lively, upbeat counterpart to the *morna*. The *coladera* is performed in fast duple meter, accompanying informal pop-style couple dancing. Its primary influences appear to be an obscure folk processional music by the same name, Afro-American commercial music, the *morna*, and, most important, modern French Caribbean pop. Its harmonies are simpler than those of the *morna*, often involving a simple oscillation between two chords. *Coladera* is occasionally performed by a traditional *morna*-style ensemble, but more often it is played by a modern dance band, that is, with drums, bass, electric guitars, and the like.

More pronounced commercial acculturation has marked the popularization of two African-derived forms, *batuco* (*batuque*) and *funana*. Both of these genres are associated with the *badius*, a poor, relatively unacculturated underclass living in the interior of the island of Santiago. The traditional *batuco* is a women's music and dance genre, in which a lead singer improvises topical verses while several other women sing choral responses and execute rhythms by clapping hands and slapping cushions held between their legs. The rhythms are fast and polyrhythmic, superimposing (in Western terms) 6/8 and 3/4 in a manner similar to West African genres like *agbadza*.

Funana is another *badius* genre, sung in fast quadratic meter and accompanying couple dancing. Instrumental accompaniment is provided on the *gaita* (concertina), on which are played two alternating chords, and the *ferrinho*, a strip of metal scraped with a peg in a rhythm similar to that produced by the *güiro* in the Dominican *merengue*.

Batuco and *funana* have traditionally been denounced by the Catholic Church for their suggestive dancing, and during the liberation struggle the Portuguese colonists attempted to repress the genres for their obliquely militant texts; moreover, middle-class Cape Verdeans have traditionally tended to disparge them as crude. Since independence in 1974, however, *badius* musics have been undergoing a folkloric revival, and, more significantly for the purposes of this text, they have been incorporated into the repertoires of modern Cape Verdean dance bands (especially Bulimundo) in stylized forms. Modern pop *batuco* retains the polyrhythms, responsorial singing, and occasionally nationalistic texts of its forbear while adding electronic instrumentation, sectional arrangement, and harmony. Pop *funana* has changed in similar ways and resembles its antecedent primarily in its particular harmonies, fast quadratic meters, and melodic contours.

Central Africa

The music of Central Africa, particularly the Congo region, has been more influential within Africa than any other regional style. Since the early 1960s Congo music has inundated West, East, and even South-Central Africa, often at the expense of local musics. It is ironic that such influential music should emerge from this most impoverished and exploited region, especially since the Belgian and French colonial rulers tended to discourage the sort of cultural interaction that in West Africa fostered the early rise of acculturated music forms.[42] In the first half of the twentieth century the relatively flexible British colonial policies had promoted the evolution of syncretic forms like *juju* and highlife. By contrast, in the Congo region development of local popular music was negligible.[43] In the early fifties, however, Congo music styles suddenly blossomed and soon began to exert influence throughout neighboring regions as well. As in West Africa, the new musics tended to fall into parallel categories of intimate, guitar-based "listening" music, and large-ensemble dance-band music.

By far the most influential guitarist was Mwenda Jean Bosco, by profession a petty clerk from Katanga. From 1951 Bosco made several recordings which became widely popular. David Rycroft's thorough analysis of Bosco's music reveals it to be an individual synthesis of indigenous and imported elements.[44] Unlike many early African guitarists, Bosco was no "mere strummer" but instead developed a complex and highly individual finger-picking style. Bosco's songs are generally set over a simple recurring harmonic ostinato, but his melodic patterns reflect elements of the *mbira* music of his Sanga tribe. Also of evident African derivation are his use of short, descending phrases and freely displaced melodies over a regular metric scheme. Bosco often accompanied his guitar playing with simple vocal melodies sung in Kingwana (a local "Congo Swahili" lingua franca). Bosco's creative muse appeared to wane somewhat after his earliest recordings, but some of those—especially "Masanga"—are enshrined as classics of modern African music.

At the same time, other Congolese guitarists were playing music that varied, in Roberts's words, from "imitation Western" to "traditional-on-a-new instrument."[45] The prevailing Western influence, however, was not European but Cuban; as Roberts notes, Cuban groups like the Trio Matamoros and Sexteto Habanero had been popular from the thirties—well before the development of any sort of popular music in the Congo.[46] Out of these diverse sources—traditional music, imitations of Cuban horn and guitar lines, and idiosyncratic styles like Bosco's— gradually developed a distinctive Congolese guitar style. In the late fifties the electric guitar came into vogue throughout Africa, further promoting the instrument and its incorporation into dance bands. Congolese guitarists, as in the rest of the continent, use a clear, trebly, bell-like tone (unlike, for example, the distorted sound of "heavy metal" rock); other features such as the penchant for parallel sixths and thirds further distinguish their style.

Cuban influence, especially what was internationally called *rumba*, pervaded the Congolese dance band music of the 1950s and early 1960s. Roberts points out that because of its generically neo-African sound, the *rumba* (and its Congolese derivatives) easily became popular throughout much of the continent, unlike such forms as highlife or *juju*, which sound too distinctively regional to gain pan-African appeal.[47]

From the early sixties, Congolese music began to break out of the Cuban mold. The use of Lingala or French lyrics was the first step. The spread of the electric guitar facilitated the introduction of local *mbira*-derived patterns into dance-band music. Zaire's independence in 1960, strife-torn as it was, also promoted the development of local music. In the late sixties, *soukous*—one of several regional dance rhythms—emerged as the dominant Congolese style, especially under the leadership of Tabu Ley Rocherau (b. 1940) and Luambo Makiadi Franco. Influence of North American soul can also be detected in the saxophone riffs and the occasional use of traps. Under the influence of disco in the late seventies, a steady quarter-note thumping bass drum also replaced the more subtle conga percussion of earlier *soukous;* still, the style's rhythmic momentum continued to derive more from the interlocking guitar ostinati than from percussion instruments.

Soukous style merits some further discussion here. The typical *soukous* song consists of vocal melodies and instrumental solos set over one or two simple, repeated harmonic ostinati. A single ostinato and unvarying rhythm may persist through an entire song, which may last over twenty minutes. Many songs have a bipartite form. In the first section, long vocal melodies are sung in three-part harmony over a medium tempo (M.M.130–140) vamp, which tends to have a composite syncopated feel somewhat like:

After five or ten minutes there is a distinct break, leading to a second section of indefinite length. The tempo here is technically slower (♩=90-115), but the bass drum plays a disco-style quarter-note thump which gives the impression of an acceleration and intensification. The high hat typically produces the following isorhythm:

This may be regarded as the familiar African 3+3+2, with an elision of the first beat (which is instead stressed by the bass drum and the electric bass). Vocal parts in this second section are often responsorial, although the calls and responses may each last several bars and thus could be regarded as verses and refrains. Guitar solos may be introduced here as well.

The modern dance band consists of bass, traps, and other percussion, and from two to five horns and electric guitars. The horns (saxes and trumpets) play occasional orchestrated riffs; much of the time they are silent. The guitars are more prominent and structurally important; indeed, many songs have the character of extended guitar jams with brief vocal and horn sections added for variety. Aside from the improvised solos which may occur, the guitars perform repeated ostinatos over the reiterated chord progressions; these ostinatos lend individual songs much of their distinct character. A few typical patterns are shown below:[48]

Congolese vocal style is also quite distinctive. The melodies tend to be high, such that vocalists sing in the upper part of their ranges. Syllabic settings in eighth-notes are a hallmark of the style. Diatonic major scales predominate. The melodic lines are harmonized in two or three parts, with parallel fourths and fifths occurring freely and, indeed, lending much charm to the style. The excerpt below is typical.[49]

1) TO-KO-MI MO-KA-YO KA-KA BE-PWE KI-TI   BAZ-WA LE VER-TE A MI

2) JEAN SE LAN-GA YE LAN-GA FO-LO LO YA BEM-BE   NA-OU-TI NA MU-SIKA-NA

NGNAI NA GEN-TIL NA-KO- LA-LA WA-PI-   KI   BO-ME-NA

VO-YA-GER NA   PO-TO NA-ZON-GI MBO-KA CHE-RI   NA BAN-GI

NGAI RE- SI-   DENCE MA-RI-NA

NA RE- SI-   DENCE MA-RI-NA

A pronounced feature of Congolese dance-band music is its gentle, lyrical quality, reflecting the oft-noted prevailing "cool" aesthetic of much modern African music. In spite of the dominance of percussion and electric guitars, the clean instrumental and vocal timbres and the tuneful melodies lend the music a gentleness which, upon hearing, contrasts markedly with genres like rock, *apala*, or Cuban *rumba*.

Most *soukous* songs are sung in Lingala, which, although unintelligible to a large percentage of Zaire's population, is a dominant language in the capital city Kinshasa, where the recording studios are located. Song texts are topical, frequently with light social commentary; political repression makes outspoken criticism of the government rare and dangerous.[50]

Soukous is the predominant popular music throughout Zaire; many groups, however, have also sought inspiration in other regional traditional genres, which they subsequently adapt to modern instrumentation. Musicians pay close attention to traditional dance steps in effecting such adaptations. Western pop does not appear to have made significant inroads.

Aside from dissemination via the mass media, live performances are common in clubs, which are frequently owned by the bands themselves. In the 1980s, Cameroonian *makossa* music (especially by Sam Fan Thomas) and Haitian *compas* have also become quite popular. The appeal of *compas* is not surprising given the Zairian influence thereupon, and the frequent use of lyrics in French, which is understood by substantial numbers of the residents of both Port-au-Prince and Kinshasa.

East Africa

The term "East Africa" generally denotes Kenya, Tanzania, Uganda, Rwanda, and Malawi. The area's population of some 70 million is ethnically and culturally diverse, although sharing a common British colonial heritage and, to some extent, the use of English and Swahili on lingua franca bases. Musically, the most conspicuous shared feature has been the popularity of Congolese urban styles.

Most of the basic categories of East African popular musics correspond to Central and West African counterparts. Military brass bands inspired a derivative brass genre called *beni*, which enjoyed popularity until the sixties, when it came to be regarded as archaic and colonial. Missionary and political songs also constituted an early influence on national musics. More important, however, have been the guitar musics and dance-band styles that emerged after 1945.

As Gerhard Kubik has noted, 1945 marked the real beginning of popular music development in East Africa. The relative economic boom following the Second World War led to the growth of radio and recording industries, especially in Kenya. As elsewhere in the continent, urbanization, availability of Western instruments, and the growth of a pan-ethnic social identity contributed to the rise of new hybrid musics. The earliest musics heard on imported wind-up gramophones tended to be Indian, but by the forties the most popular sounds were Cuban, and Cuban-derived African music (Afro-Afro-Cuban, as it were). After the war many locals trained in military brass playing joined the emerging dance bands, applying their instrumental skills and the fondness for *rumba* they developed in the service.[51]

Congolese music, from Bosco to Franco, continued to be a prevailing influence in both guitar and dance-band musics. Uganda, Kenya, and Tanzania were inundated with Zairian refugees fleeing the Congolese war of the early sixties. Many of these were musicians who settled in East Africa and tended to dominate urban music scenes. Nevertheless, distinctive regional styles did emerge, informed both by local traditions and idiosyncratic syntheses of outside influences. In Kenya a variety of guitar styles developed. As discussed by Kubik, some of these reflected retentions of traditional lyre musics (*nyatiti* and *litungo* among the Luo and Abaluhya, respectively). Influence of Congo musicians, especially Bosco and Losta Abelo, is more overt in the finger-picking styles, although the interlocking *soukous* patterns are less characteristic of Kenyan guitar music. Another style was inspired by the Hawaiian slide guitar, which enjoyed a worldwide vogue in the forties and fifties. In Zimbabwe, Malawi, and Zambia, traditions of playing monochords with slides (such as a knife or bottle shard) were revitalized and adapted to guitar styles, which subsequently came to be known as *hauyani*. Meanwhile, Malawi musician Daniel Kachamba (b. 1955) became renowned for his idiosyncratic guitar style and renditions of *kwela* and

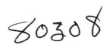

other South African styles; Kachamba frequently performed in a one-man-band format (playing guitar and harmonica while tapping his foot on a box), and he recorded in a solo "montage" process of over-dubbing, using two or more tape recorders.[52]

Roberts groups Kenyan guitar styles into two categories:

> One, vaguely Latin, was introduced via the Congo but was given idiosyncrasy by the Kenyan two-voice, two-guitar formula and by the use of a form consisting of three verses, each of a couplet repeated, and then the whole thing repeated. The other beat, the so-called twist, was a version of the South African kwela, which a European producer who had worked in South Africa introduced to certain bands in Kenya at the time of the twist craze. . . . Since around 1966, the hipper bands have all gone Congo.[53]

East African song texts, especially the more "listening-oriented" Kenyan styles, often deal with contemporary social issues, as elsewhere in Africa. Lyrics may praise political leaders or movements, or they may comment on phenomena like unemployment or changing social mores.[54]

As we have mentioned, the recording industry has been very active in Kenya, such that both locally produced music and imported pop are widely distributed. While the local music scene is lively, the concentration of the industry in a few areas, the competition from foreign pop, the ambivalent attitude of the state, and the fickleness of the market combine to produce an adverse environment for the musician.

In neighboring Uganda conditions have been even less conducive for the development and vitality of national popular musics. Roberts has noted that through the 1960s the dominance of Congolese music and musicians was particularly pronounced in Uganda; moreover, the country lacked any recording studios.[55] The Amin period (1971–1979) and its violent and chaotic aftermath have not proved much more fruitful for popular music.

Tanzania, under the leadership of Julius Nyerere, pursued a course of socialist development, with a goal of freeing itself from the capitalist world market. The government has attempted in various ways to promote national culture, including music. Traditional *ngoma*, incorporating music, dance, and drama, has been encouraged. The government-run radio and television broadcast only Tanzanian music. In the mid-seventies the state supported an attempt to oust Zairian bands. More significantly, it barred the import of records and blank tapes and has effectively prohibited multinationals from setting up record businesses in the country. Tanzania, then, has no record industry. Such conditions have prevented Tanzanian music from gaining an international audience, but they have contributed to a lively local music scene in which national music is far better prepared to compete with imported music than, for example, in neighboring Kenya. (Kenyan recording artists, indeed, face a stiff challenge from pirate tapes of Tanzanian music.)[56]

Tanzanian dance-band music remains heavily influenced by Congolese music but has its own distinctive sound, resulting largely from the different vocal and guitar styles, and from the use of Swahili rather than Lingala. Another important genre is *tarabu,* a syncretic form popular along the east coast and in Zanzibar. *Tarabu,* which has been documented by Roberts, is heavily influenced by Indian and Arab musics. It lacks the intense percussive character of most sub-Saharan African music, consisting instead of monophonic vocal lines sung in medium tempo with heterophonic and semi-harmonic instrumental accompaniment. In the thirties, Arab instruments—*^cud, darbuka, ghanun (qanun),* and the *gambuz* lute—were standard, but Indian-style instruments now predominate, especially harmonium, *tabla,* and *taisho koto,* the plucked zither which was invented as a Japanese toy; in India and Tanzania it is known, respectively, as banjo and *tuntunia. Tarabu* comprises a range of styles. In some songs, the melismatic, strained vocal style and the use of *^cud* and unison violins reflect Arab influence. In other cases, vocal style is clearly derived from Indian popular music. Rhythms often resemble the North Indian *kaherva* and *dādra,* of eight and six beats, respectively. A few songs reveal Cuban influence. The texts, written mostly in Swahili, are an important aspect of *tarabu.*[57]

Ethiopia

Although Westerners may be accustomed to associating Ethiopia primarily with images of famine and civil war, in fact, Ethiopia possesses one of Africa's richest cultural heritages, which includes a distinctive and vital contemporary music scene. At present Ethiopia comprises a prodigious variety of ethnic groups, speaking over a hundred languages. Musics of the western and southern regions bear affinities with black sub-Saharan styles, while those of the northeast reflect considerable Arab influence. However, most Ethiopian music—especially that of the Amharic peoples—shares certain distinctive stylistic features deriving primarily from the nation's own musical heritage which, indeed, constitutes one of the world's most ancient continuous musical traditions. This degree of stylistic unity within linguistic diversity is particularly visible in the realm of modern popular music; hence, while the following comments are based primarily on Amharic contemporary music, they are not wholly inapplicable to other Ethiopian popular styles.[58]

Ethiopian popular music, as in many other countries, developed as a stylization of traditional secular dance music. Particularly important as a source was the music sung at weddings and other festivities to the accompaniment of the *krar* lyre and *kebero* drum. The most distinctive features of this music include: extensive use of what Westerners would label a 6/8 meter; a tense, constricted vocal timbre, and a melismatic, intricately ornamented vocal style; wide-ranged melodies, which characteristically ascend to a high pitch and then descend to a low pitch, often the tonic; heterophonic instrumental accompaniment; and the use of a variety of modes, among which anhemitonic pentatonic scales are particularly common.

By the early 1960s an urban popular style based on this traditional dance music had emerged, performed in nightclubs, private parties, and weddings, and further disseminated on the radio and eventually on records. Such music has been loosely referred to as *zemenawi*—"modern"—as opposed to *bahlawi* or traditional.[59] *Zemenawi* music of this period retains all of the characteristic dance music features mentioned, but replacing the *krar* with Western instruments such as accordion, saxophones, and trumpet. In subsequent years the accordion has become less common, and the standard ensemble now comprises an organ, one or two saxophones, bass, Western drum set, and often a trumpet. The saxes generally play pre-composed passages between the vocal verses while the organ accompanies the vocal melody heterophonically or with chords. The electric guitar is sometimes used, occasionally to add chordal harmonies derived from the melodies. The solo vocal style, with its virtuosic rapid ornamentation, remains the most distinctive feature of the music. Song texts cover a wide variety of topics, and top vocalists like Tilahun are celebrated as much for their intelligent lyrics as for their melodies and style. A number of informal dance styles are performed to *zemenawi*.

Since the early 1970s, cassettes have replaced records as the primary mass medium of dissemination. The cassette producers are private rather than state enterprises; many groups record and produce their own cassettes, distributing them informally through neighborhood vendors. Copyright protection is negligible, and live performance at urban nightclubs and social events remains the most important source of musicians' income.

The socialist government that has ruled since 1974 has tended to promote traditional musics rather than *zemenawi*, which flourishes only in the private sector. The state radio stations, however, do broadcast revolutionary songs in *zemenawi* style. International pop styles—especially reggae—enjoy some popularity among the urban youth, and several groups have recorded songs combining reggae rhythm with Ethiopian vocal style.

South-Central Africa

Documentation of urban popular music in Mozambique, Angola, Zambia, and Zimbabwe is relatively scanty. Kubik notes that the development of popular music in Mozambique has been limited due to extreme poverty, shortage of radios and other media facilities, and, under Portuguese rule, political and cultural suppression and isolation.[60] Since independence, the South African-financed rebellion in Mozambique has further disrupted economic and social life and continued to hinder the evolution of a modern music industry. A distinctive national guitar style has nevertheless arisen, which combines imported Congolese, *hauyani,* South African, Portuguese, and possibly Brazilian elements. Angolan popular music has been subject to the same economic and cultural adversities as Mozambique, and reflects some of the same stylistic influences; one popular genre is the *merengue,* which bears only a superficial resemblance to its Dominican namesake. Brazilian influence is conspicuous in some modern Angolan recordings.[61]

Zimbabwe has not been immune to Congolese, South African, and Afro-American influences but has nevertheless fostered a unique national popular music style. Until the 1970s imported music dominated the media, in accordance with the tastes of the white Rhodesian government. By the mid-seventies an indigenous popular music had emerged under the familiar impact of urbanization and acculturation. This music constituted part of a spectrum of styles ranging from imitation of foreign hits to purely traditional music. Much of the distinctively indigenous music was closely allied with the war of liberation and thus came to be known as *chimurenga*—"songs of struggle." *Chimurenga* songs derive primarily from the music of the Shona tribe, who constitute three-quarters of the nation's population.[62] Throughout the liberation war such songs, especially those of Thomas Mapfumo, became widely popular and were broadcast on the "Voice of Zimbabwe" from Maputo, Mozambique.

Dance bands in Zimbabwe—which achieved independence in 1980—often perform successive sets in a wide variety of styles from swing and reggae to indigenous music.[63] The modernized indigenous forms are of most interest here. These tend to be based on Shona *mbira* music. Groups may employ *mbiras* and other traditional instruments, or, more frequently in dance-band formats, they imitate *mbira* patterns on electric guitars. In this respect the music bears close resemblance to Congolese *soukous,* although the vocal style might be described as more vigorous than that of Zairian pop. The instrumental excerpt below is typical and bears comparison with the *soukous* examples above. Note the polyrhythmic structure and the presence of the standard time-line.[64]

Other commercial popular musics in Zimbabwe are *makwaya*, a synco-pated choral genre derived from South Africa, and *jiti* dance music, which combines imported harmony with indigenous drumming and responsorial singing.[65]

South Africa

Popular music in South Africa is quite distinct from that of the rest of Africa, having evolved under a unique set of socio-historical conditions. The complexity of these conditions, especially in the broader context of their ongoing political ramifications, cannot be adequately dealt with in the space of a short sub-chapter such as this one. Fortunately, South African urban music has been the subject of several fine studies—most notably David Coplan's *In Township Tonight! South Africa's Black City Music and Theatre*—which are recommended for further study.

The most notable distinction between South African and other African popular musics is that the external models in the former have been predominantly Afro-American rather than Cuban or Congolese. Three reasons for this difference may be suggested. First, Cuban music is less compatible with southern African music than is Afro-American music. Traditional music in the south is predominantly vocal, characterized by choral singing in complex, overlapping responsorial patterns. Instrumental music is less developed, partly owing to the scarcity of trees from which drums and other instruments could be made. Accordingly, the complex polyrhythms that characterize other African musics are less prominent in South Africa. South Africans, then, felt less affinity toward the intricate, percussive, often polyrhythmic *rumba* and *son* than they did for the rhythmically simpler Afro-American popular styles, especially since such genres as swing-era jazz occasionally used familiar-sounding overlapping responsorial patterns.

Second, the fondness of the Afrikaans and English settlers for ragtime and other Afro-American styles exerted considerable influence on the native population; this influence was particularly strong due to the fact that the white settlers were more numerous than in other African countries.

Third, in the course of the protracted liberation struggle, South African blacks have tended to identify strongly with their black brethren in the United States, who have waged a similar struggle against discrimination, albeit under somewhat different conditions. This ideological affinity has served to enhance the interest in Afro-American musical expressions on the part of South African blacks.

Although European and African musics had been mixing in southern Africa since the eighteenth century, acculturation began in earnest in the mid-nineteenth century with the growth of the diamond-mining town of Kimberley; the process intensified markedly with the discovery of gold in 1886 and the systematic dispossession of the native population in order to exploit its labor in the mines near Johannesburg. As imported workers and members of the region's diverse tribal groups came to live and work together in the new cities, the processes of urbanization, proletarianization, racial segregation, cultural syncretism, and harsh white political domination began, which continue to govern the socio-cultural evolution of black South African life.

Musical syncretism was a natural and inevitable product of these conditions. European musics brought by settlers and missionaries, together with minstrel songs introduced by American white and black prospectors, generated transculturated hybrids in the hands of resident Africans whose own socio-cultural traditions were rapidly being disrupted by forces beyond their control.

One early syncretic genre which emerged in the late nineteenth century among the more acculturated, middle-class Africans was the aforementioned *makwaya*. *Makwaya* was a vocal style variously integrating hymn-derived European harmonies or ragtime elements with traditional (predominantly Xhosa) rhythms and overlapping choral formats. Indigenous instruments such as the *uhadi* musical bow could also be used. Despite its significance for assimilationist blacks, *makwaya* also came to be associated with the African nationalist movement, which had already gained momentum. As Erlmann observes, *makwaya* manifested the contradictions of the early nationalist struggle, for its combination of European and native features reflected the middle class's simultaneous opposition to and gravitation toward the dominant culture. *Makwaya* also represented an early attempt to find a form of musical expression that could be pan-tribal, "civilized," and yet African.[66]

Proletarian South African musical culture evolved under different, if related conditions, and with distinct functions. As blacks were forced into squalid slumyards and townships, new forms of social and cultural organization replaced the pastoral traditions. Urban recreation, social life, and cultural activity came to be centered around the *shebeens*, extra-legal beer gardens where African men and women from diverse tribes could gather and socialize freely. Coplan notes that in the *shebeens*, music played an important role both in attracting clientele and, on a more abstract level, in contributing to the development of a pan-ethnic, urban social identity.[67] Other contexts for urban music-making were *stokfels*, urban credit associations that held entertainment functions, and *ndunduma*, rowdy Zulu proletarian dances. As in several other cultures, lumpen proletarian elements—the *abaqhafi* "cultural driftwood" of South African black society—played a particularly important role in generating the new popular styles, especially since middle-class blacks tended to scorn the *shebeens*.[68]

The music that emerged in the *shebeens*, as well as the accompanying dance and social occasion when it was performed, came to be known in the 1920s as *marabi*. Most *marabi* musicians were urbanized Xhosa and mulatto "coloureds" who felt little affinity toward traditional tribal culture. *Marabi* drew upon a variety of models. Most prominent among these was ragtime, which had been popularized in the second decade of the century by recordings, sheet music, and visiting performers. Other sources included Pedi and Tswana tribe brass music, *tula n'divile*, or keyboard adaptations of Xhosa folk melodies, and *tickey draai*, itself a syncretic acculturated dance style played on guitars or small string and concertina ensembles by Xhosa and "coloureds."[69] Particularly important was the contribution of composer, performer, and bandleader Reuben Caluza. Under Caluza's inspiration there emerged in the twenties a *marabi* style—oriented toward the black petty bourgeoisie rather than the proletarian *shebeens*—which combined ragtime keyboard style with melodic phrase displacements typical of Zulu music. On the whole, however, the Westernized black middle class tended to deplore *shebeen*-style *marabi* culture, preferring spirituals, Europeanized *makwaya*, and other genres for expressions of their own ambivalent nationalism. Thus *marabi* came to represent more unambiguously the new proletarian social identity, becoming the dominant working-class musical form in the twenties and thirties.[70]

Marabi was archetypically a keyboard style, generally played on a pump organ. String, brass, and percussion could also be added, however. *Marabi* songs are invarably based upon what Rycroft has aptly called "the merciless two- or three-chord vamp." Most *marabi* songs use a simple I-IV-I$_4^6$-V progression that has persisted as the basis for successive South African genres like *kwela*, *mbube*, *mbaqanga*, and much "township jazz." The use of this progression, constituting more than the simplistic adoption of a Western cliché, may be seen as providing an effective vehicle for the projection into a Westernized style of a traditional South African musical practice, namely, the process of "root progression" described by Blacking, wherein a bass melody moves in reiterated patterns amongst a higher, multipart tonal structure.[71]

In the 1930s South African popular music continued to be influenced by current American trends, especially as records and the radio increased dissemination of Afro-American musics. Ragtime and minstrelsy thus gave way to swing jazz as models. The black middle class, while deploring *marabi* culture and tiring of sit-down *makwaya* concerts, also developed a taste for dance-band music. Thus, in urban South Africa, "township jazz" arose as a dance-band style, derived primarily from Count Basie-style big band swing. Township jazz bands like the Merry Blackbirds played in a pure swing idiom, often for white audiences. Those playing for African audiences, however, often retained elements of *marabi* in their arrangements, especially a propensity for simple vamps like the familiar I-IV-I$_4^6$-V progression.

Most blacks, of course, could not afford expensive brass instruments, and many could not afford to attend functions where the dance bands played. Hence, in the forties and fifties a more grassroots version of township jazz developed which came to be known as *kwela*. *Kwela* could be performed in a variety of instrumental and vocal formats. In its original and most humble version, *kwela* was performed in the streets and at informal dances by youths playing penny whistles. As the recording industry took interest in the genre, studio producers added guitars (acoustic or electric), bass, saxophone, piano, and other instruments to accompany the penny whistlers.[72] *Kwela's* popularity spread to neighboring countries and, indeed, as far as Kenya; the genre, for example, forms the basis for much of the music of Malawi guitarist Donald Kachamba. The music of popular singers like Miriam Makeba retains much influence of *kwela*.

In the workers' hostels of Durban, the traditional Zulu fondness for choral music generated vocal styles closely related to *kwela*. In the 1940s these were known as "bombing styles," but they eventually came to fall under the rubric of *mbube* in the wake of the international success of Solomon Linda's hit by the same name (meaning "lion"), popularized abroad by the Weavers and Pete Seeger. *Mbube* is typically sung by a group of eight or nine male vocalists without instrumental accompaniment, often in the context of a night-long competition with other groups in the all-male hostels. *Mbube* arrangements retain Zulu practices of rich overlapping antiphonal harmonies in distinct ranges; most are based on simple harmonies, sung in medium to slow tempi. In recent decades the high-pitched bombing style has given way to a more polished style called *iscathamiya* ("stalking approach"), popularized in particular by Joseph Shabalala's Ladysmith Black Mambazo.

Somewhat more popular and commercially successful than *mbube* is "jive," which denotes the music of a vocal group backed by a rhythm section. Jive has often consisted of versions of American swing hits sung in African languages, modeled after American groups like the Ink Spots and the Mills Brothers.[73] Jive, unlike *mbube*, may be sung by female groups, which may, however, incorporate male "groaners."

Coplan portrays the Johannesburg suburb of Sophiatown as the focus of black urban cultural life in the 1940s and 1950s.[74] Here the black struggle for cultural autonomy and identity generated a flowering of syncretic *mbube, kwela,* and jive, disseminated on the media, by the *stokfels,* and in concert halls. Theatrical productions such as "King Kong," although more reflective of the tastes of their white producers than of authentic township music, became renowned among white South African and international audiences. But such a cultural heyday was not to last. Aside from the disruptions of violent gangs, it was the deliberate policy of the racist government to prevent the consolidation of black urban social identity, even as the state eradicated rural traditions by dispossessing natives from their ancestral lands. This policy led to the destruction of Sophiatown and its replacement by the prison-like barracks of Soweto. With the circumscription of public musical and theatrical life, several of the most prominent black musicians (such as

Miriam Makeba and Hugh Masakela) went into exile. Thus, in the early sixties, while the rest of Africa was gaining independence, South Africa moved in the opposite direction, intensifying apartheid with draconian pass laws, artificial "homelands," and massacres of protestors.

While the vitality of Sophiatown culture was not to be regained, black South African musical and theatrical life continued to develop, although within more sharply circumscribed parameters. From the late 1950s the term *mbaqanga*—denoting commercialized syncretic pop musics—came to be applied to various forms of jazz- (and later) rock-derived jive. Much of modern *mbaqanga* consists of choral vocals accompanied by rock-style rhythms and instruments. The traditional $I-IV-I^6_4-V$ progression remains common; in some cases, the interlocking electric guitar patterns seem to reflect Congolese influence. Some syncretic *mbaqanga* groups (such as Malomba Jazz Men) have self-consciously combined jazz elements with traditional tribal rhythms and instruments.[75] Top *mbaqanga* groups like Abafani Basheqhudini feature a group of all-male vocalists, clad in white, who combine choreography, theatrics, and singing to the accompaniment of a dance band.

White domination of commercial aspects of popular music life in South Africa has constituted a formidable constraint on both the form and content of musical evolution. Even in the heyday of Sophiatown, African musicians were helplessly exploited by the white promoters who controlled the lively scene of variety shows and musicals; the South African record industry has been notorious for its corruption.[76] Since the early sixties, the South African Broadcasting Corporation, which controls the air-waves, has tended to promote apolitical pop/rock/jive/*mbaqanga* styles and Western popular music. In order to get airplay, groups tend to censor their own lyrics, singing of love and peaceful rural life and avoiding use of township slang. Performance and recording of socio-political songs, moreover, can entail not only media censorship but banning, torture, and imprisonment as well. Strictly prohibited on the media is a great corpus of music deemed politically objectionable, such as recordings of Bob Marley, Pete Seeger, Pink Floyd, and, needless to say, dissident expatriates like Hugh Masakela and Miriam Makeba.[77]

Commercial recording companies have given some promotion to a few outspoken groups like Juluka and Harare, which incorporate traditional and modern sounds in a *mbaqanga*-derived rock idiom. But the only overt musical expressions of African solidarity are the songs sung in syncretic choral style at rallies and funerals, and the expatriate music broadcast from the African National Congress's "Radio Freedom"; these genres, needless to say, operate entirely outside the realm of the commercial South African media.

South African popular music, from *marabi* to *mbaqanga*, has always drawn heavily on Afro-American music for inspiration and musical materials. This dependency has provided a partial solution to the problem of finding a popular musical expression that could be in some sense African and modern without being ethnically exclusive. At the same time it illustrates the black South Africans' profound ambivalence toward the dominant culture; observers have well questioned whether the reliance on "an imported solution for the problems of modernization" may ultimately have inhibited the development of a truly indigenous expression of solidarity and a more active metaphor for social mobilization.[78] At the same time, the use of traditional elements in contemporary music runs the risk of reinforcing the tribalism that is promoted by the apartheid media in the state's effort to weaken inter-ethnic solidarity. Thus, in the South African context the racial dimension of socio-political conditions have added a special visibility and urgency to the dialectic between ruling class and dominated class musical styles.

Madagascar and the Mascarene Islands

Madagascar (Malagasy Republic) is populated primarily by people of Indonesian and African descent. Its musical traditions have long been distinct from those of its neighbors on the African mainland, most notably in the prominence of chordophones such as the *valiha* tube zither. Although diverse, much of Malagasy music is markedly more lyrical and melodic than, for example, the intense, percussive Chopi xylophone music of nearby Mozambique. French colonization of the island in 1896 contributed to the development of acculturated forms of music. Use of the violin and accordion became standardized in the *mpilalao* ensemble. In the fifties and sixties, urban musician Maurice Halison became known for his compositions combining Western harmony, violin, bass, and guitar with indigenous additive meters and instruments.

Malagasy melodic, chordophone-oriented musics have blended particularly well with imported African musics as well as European music; drawing from these sources, a distinctive and rich syncretic popular music has emerged in recent decades, disseminated on the radio, through recordings, and, to a limited extent, in urban nightclubs.

Modern Malagasy urban music retains several features of traditional local music, most notably, the preference for fast 6/8 meter and a non-percussive, chordophone-dominated texture. Several modern groups use acoustic or electric *valiha*, generally in combination with guitar; alternately, guitars may be used to play *valiha*-style patterns. Congolese as well as French influence is clear in the adaptation of these patterns to simple chord progressions, and in the two- and three-part vocal harmonies.

Ben Mandelson, in his documentation of the leading Malagasy syncretic musicians, observes that they consciously draw from traditional dance rhythms, including: the *basese* (from Diego Suarez), the *salegy* (of the Sakalava ethnic group), the *watsa-watsa* (derived from Mozambique and Zaire), the *sigaoma* (a modernized *salegy* influenced by South African pop), and the *sega* (of the nearby Reunion Islands).[79] Nevertheless, the nearly invariable use of a fast 6/8 meter lends the modernized versions of most of these dances a relative homogeneity. As elsewhere in Africa, one may discern a continuum of styles from traditional acculturated songs with acoustic instruments, to more modernized hybrids with electric instruments, and finally, to further Westernized syntheses like *sova*, which seeks to incorporate features from all the island's six provinces. These musics coexist with imported styles like *soukous, mbaqanga,* and rock, popularized via the media and local bands which perform cover versions.[80]

The Mascarene Islands comprise Mauritius, Reunion, Rodrigues, and a few smaller atolls, with a present combined population of around 1.5 million. In the eighteenth century the islands were colonized by the French, who imported slaves from East Africa and Madagascar to work on sugar plantations. The British subsequently occupied Mauritius, and under their rule substantial numbers of Indians immigrated, contributing to the island's mixed racial, demographic, and cultural character. Mauritius became an independent country in 1968, while Reunion has remained a French colony.

Western and Indian popular music are widely enjoyed, but equally popular is the islands' own indigenous music, called *sega,* which exists in both acculturated and traditional forms. *Sega* was the predominant secular and ritual musical form among Mascarene slave society in the nineteenth century; discouraged by colonial authorities, it appears to have gone underground in the first half of the twentieth century, only to resurface around mid-century with renewed vigor. *Sega* now enjoys the status of a "national" music, closely allied with the use of the local Franco-African creole language. Presently, *sega* is a secular entertainment genre, accompanying dance in a variety of recreation contexts. As in other neo-African dances like the Cuban *rumba,* the *sega* dance consists of highly erotic movements performed by couples who nevertheless do not touch.[81]

The most important instrument used in traditional *sega* is the hand-struck *ravanne (ravane),* a shallow circular frame drum with a diameter of some two or three feet. Accompanying the *ravanne* are the *maravanne* (a maraca-type rattle) and a metal triangle struck with a short rod. One or more vocalists sing topical texts, occasionally in responsorial fashion. The creole texts often contain suggestive puns, insults, and onomatopoeic innuendos. Melodies typically incorporate triadic structure, sung in a wide range exceeding one octave.

Musically, the most distinctive aspect of *sega* is its rhythm. In Western terms, the basic *sega* meter would be approximated as a fast 6/8, with the *ravanne* adding a distinctive syncopation by playing a loud, open stroke on the second and fifth beats:

first *ravanne:*

second *ravanne:*

maravanne:

The *sega* of the small island of Rodrigues is believed to represent an older, more purely African tradition, distinguished by the use of the *tambour* drum and, most notably, the considerably faster tempi.

A number of elements make the *sega* rhythm considerably more complex than a simple $\frac{6}{8}$. In the Rodrigues style another percussion instrument may play steady quarter-notes, affording a variant of the familiar $\frac{6}{8}$-$\frac{3}{4}$ polyrhythm. In most cases, however, rhythmic complexity is achieved by other means, in particular, by suggesting the superimposition of a quadratic meter over the prevailing triple framework. This suggestion is achieved in two ways. First, the triangle often plays a Cuban style three-two *clave* pattern, fitting this quadratic phrase into the space of two cycles of the *ravanne* pattern:

ravanne: $\frac{6}{8}$

triangle: $\frac{4}{4}$

Secondly, the *ravanne* pattern itself is syncopated in a distinctive manner, by elongating the first and third beats such that they approach the quadratic pattern:

The result is a unique sort of polyrhythm, which at times seems to conform properly neither to Western $\frac{6}{8}$ nor $\frac{4}{4}$, but rather to lie somewhere in between. Listening to *sega* rhythm thus poses a particular sort of challenge to the foreign ear, as it often seems to resist classification as a triple or quadratic meter. *Sega* rhythm, indeed, illustrates the inherent problems in applying Western analytical concepts to non-Western musical practices. *Sega* rhythm defies Western analysis not only by virtue of its very structure, but also because its own performers do not conceptualize it in Western terms. Hence the reader should be aware of the potential distortions and ethnocentricities inherent in the analyses above (including the previous discussions of other African rhythms).

Acculturation, urbanization, the advent of the tourist industry, and the electric guitar have contributed to the evolution of modernized syncretic forms of *sega* since the 1950s. The modern commercial *sega*, heard on the media, in hotels, and at local dances, retains the rhythms and some of the instrumentation of the traditional style. These, however, are supplemented by Western instruments and harmonies; the vocal style is more relaxed and "polished." Typically, the electric guitar strums chords on the second and fifth beats (normally stressed by the *ravanne*); the bass can play a variety of patterns, most typically either quarter notes ($\frac{3}{4}$) or dotted quarter-notes ($\frac{6}{8}$). Most songs are in major keys; the harmonies are simple, although they generally involve more than a repeated vamp. Vocal parts tend to follow a simple verse-refrain pattern, rather than the loose responsorial style of traditional *sega*.

CHAPTER 4

Europe

Portugal

Portugal is host to a wide variety of regional folk musics, many of which continue to be lively performance traditions in spite of the increasing popularity of Western commercial musics. *Fado* is perhaps the single most visible and well-known Portuguese genre. In its traditional form, it is a sophisticated urban folk music primarily of Lisbon and Coimbra, which continues to be heard in *tavernas* in those cities and elsewhere. In this century, however, *fado* has also adapted to mass media dissemination, and a commercialized form of the genre has established itself as an indigenous popular music which competes with imported mainstream European and American pop styles. Since little has been written in English about traditional *fado*, it merits some discussion by way of background to its contemporary evolution as a popular music.

Fado is primarily a vocal form, sung by a solo vocalist accompanied, traditionally, by a *viola*, which resembles the Spanish guitar, and a Portuguese *guitarra*, a mandolin-like instrument with a pear-shaped soundboard and six double courses of steel strings. In recent years, an acoustic bass guitar, the *baixo* (with four strings tuned like the lower strings on a guitar), has come into use. While *fado* is now widely heard on radio, television, and recordings, its most characteristic performance context continues to be the urban cafe, where listeners may participate by singing, expressing approval, and, occasionally, dancing. *Fado* texts may be romantic, topical, or historical, but the recurring trait is the poignant expression of *saudade*—a quintessentially Lusitanian melancholy mixed with nostalgia and yearning; in this century the vague, wistful longing of *saudade* has acquired an added poignancy from the memory of Portugal's vast colonial empire and the humble reality of the present.

There are two distinct traditions of *fado:* the Lisbon *fado* and the Coimbra *fado.* The two differ not only in place of origin, but also in social background, style, and current status. The Coimbra style is said to have roots in the troubador music which entered Portugal from Aragon,[1] but its true development occured among the students of the University of

Coimbra, which dates from the thirteenth century. The Coimbra *fado* was traditionally sung, then, not by professionals but by amateurs— primarily affluent students; accordingly, the style is more light, lyrical, restrained, understated, and aristocratic, in contrast to the often melo-dramatic Lisbon style. The Coimbra *guitarra* differs slightly from its Lisbon counterpart, and it and the *viola* are tuned lower; the repertoire and performance style are also somewhat distinct.[2]

The Lisbon *fado* has been predominant, and is of greater interest here since it is that style that has played a larger role in the emergence of modern commercial *fado*. The style was nurtured not by elite university students, but in an urban underworld of sailors, prostitutes, pimps, underemployed tavern-goers, and other lumpen social outcasts. Many of its prominent exponents were professionals, but the style owes much to the melodramatic, *castiço* (lit., "heavy") singing of impassioned ama-teurs who would spontaneously rise from their cafe tables to sing a few verses.

The origin of *fado* is a subject of much controversy. Portuguese scholar Mascarenhas Barreto has illustrated the development of *fado* texts from Provencal Portuguese troubador poetry dating from the twelfth century. Noting certain similarities in form and content between modern *fado* and medieval *cantigas de amor*, Barreto postulates a gradual evolution of the genre from such genteel musical forms. Moorish rule of Portugal (eighth to thirteenth centuries) is also argued to have influ-enced *fado's saudade*, for much of Arab poetry is itself characterized by a fatalistic and wistful melancholy.[3] Scholars claim the existence of *fados* dating back to the sixteenth century.[4] Nevertheless, there appears to be no documentation or mention of *fado* as a *musical* genre prior to 1833, and it is clear that *fado* was not widely popular until the nineteenth century. This period saw the emergence of the first famous *fadista*, the half-gypsy Maria Severa, whose renown and affairs have been cele-brated in innumerable songs, poems, and paintings. Moreover, it was in the nineteenth century that the classic *fado* stock forms of the *castiço* style crystallized, and a more aristocratic, literary *fado* emerged as a counter-part to the spontaneous, informal *típico* style.[5]

While the epoch of *fado's* emergence can be roughly ascertained, the musical sources of the genre remain ambiguous. Portuguese rural folk music, although quite distinct from *fado*, may have exerted some influ-ence. Moorish musical influence, although asserted by some authors, is dubious. More plausible is the hypothesis, advanced by Gallop and others, that the incipient *fado* absorbed elements from the Afro-Brazilian *modinha* and *lundu*. These genres enjoyed considerable popularity in eighteenth- and nineteenth-century Lisbon, where they were re-Euro-peanized with Italian *bel canto* vocal influence.[6]

Sailors appear to have played an important role in the early evolu-tion of *fado*, and thus the genre is one of the several prototypical popular musics whose development is linked with cosmopolitan, racially mixed, maritime laborers. Many *fado* texts describe the sailor's yearning for his lost and remote homeland. The Lisbon *fado* came to be associated with lumpen rogues, freed blacks, and rowdy sailors. Not surprisingly, the genre was condemned by many of the aristocracy, one of whom, for example, decried the "immoral melodies . . . to be understood and felt only by those who vegetate in the mire of crapulence."[7]

By the mid-nineteenth century, *fado's* audience had grown in diversity and numbers. New forms of fado subsequently developed, with refrains and melodies that departed from the *castiço* forms (which continued to be upheld as most authentic by the purists). *Fado* continues to find its primary home in restaurants and cafes called *típicos,* especially in the old quarter of Lisbon, where after-dinner performances, usually by four or five singers in succession, last until early morning.

With the advent of the recording industry in Portugal, *fado* began to achieve broader popularity among all classes and regions of the country. Mass media exposure led to the emergence of recording stars like Amália Rodrigues and Carlos do Carmo, although *fado* is still performed, even by such recognized singers, in small cafes.

The Traditional Lisbon *Fado* Style

Fado may be regarded as a regional sub-style of Western popular music, "ethnic" in terms of its exclusively Portuguese audience and evolution. The use of the Portuguese *guitarra* and *viola,* Portuguese language and topical texts, the unique song repertoire and, to some extent, the style distinguish *fado* as a discrete genre.[8]

A *fado* comprises the vocal text and the instrumental accompaniment. In traditional *fado,* the texts are set to a finite number of conventional stock forms (analogous to flamenco *cantes*). These distinct types, themselves called *fados,* are distinguished by such criteria as harmonic progressions, vocal melodies, verse form, tempo, and accompaniment patterns; the latter criteria are especially important in the numerous *fados* that share the same chordal progression. The names of the *fados* derive from places of origin (such as Mouraria), from the *fadistas* who invented them (for example, Vianinha, Lopes), or from other factors.[9] Many modern *fados* are not set to the classic forms.

Other aspects of *fado* are quite stereotypical; formally, for example, most songs consist of four-bar vocal passages set strophically to recurring harmonic patterns, with instrumental interludes punctuating the verses. Harmonies tend to be simple, consisting mostly of tonic, subdominant, dominant, and secondary dominant chords. The harmonic-melodic forms themselves are stereotyped, with a large number of fados being set to the following scheme:

```
harmony:    //: I V V I  :// //: I V V I  ://
text line:      1  2            3  4
rhyme:          a  b            a  b
```

Typically, major and minor tonalities may alternate in repetitions of the above pattern; this may occur while remaining in the same tonic key—such as juxtaposing A major and A minor—or by modulating to a relative key. Other *fados* are set entirely to one tonality, although modulations to closely related keys do occur. "Andalusian" harmony—in particular, the familiar Am-G-F-E progression—occurs in some fados (for example, *Victoria*). Some *fados* (*corrido*, for example) can be performed in either major or minor throughout.

Vocal style is predominantly syllabic, and, in the traditional Lisbon style, use of rubato is limited. The dramatic *castiço* style acquires a particular impetuous intensity by the use of a fast, shallow vibrato (also characteristic of *guitarra* playing), stylized pronunciation, and dramatic crescendos and decrescendos.

As in flamenco, the instrumental accompaniment, while subsidiary to the voice, provides much of the genre's charm. The *viola* supplies chordal harmonic support, while the *guitarra* plays melodic passages and occasional chords and arpeggios, complementing the vocal line and coming to the fore in the passages between verses and in the preceding introduction. The *guitarra* parts, while not formally pre-composed, follow stock stereotypical patterns and thus cannot really be called improvisatory. *Fado Mouraria*, for example, is usually recognizable by the following opening *guitarra* pattern:

Fado corrido uses the same harmonic progression, but has a distinct set of *guitarra* patterns, which typically commence:

Some *fados* (for example, *Victoria*) have more complex, through-composed harmonic progressions.[10]

The *fado* repertoire is divided into *fado maior* and *fado menor*, denoting fast (M.M.90–130) and slow (M.M. ca. 45) tempo, respectively. Certain *fados* are performed only in one tempo or the other; *fado triste* (lit., "sad") is sung only in slow tempo, in accordance with its melancholy character, while Lisbon-style *fado corrido* (lit., "running") is generally in fast tempo.[11] *Fado* is invariably set to 4/4 meter.

The most distinctive feature of *fado* texts is their melancholy *saudade*, which is said have roots in Islamic fatalism, sailors' loneliness, and the unrequited love which was the perennial theme of troubador poetry. *Saudade* has been described as "a vague and constant desire for something that does not and probably cannot exist, for something other than the present, a turning towards the future; not an active discontent or poignant sadness, but an indolent dreaming wistfulness."[12] Many *fado* texts "extol the joys of being unhappy and of expressing one's wretchedness through the medium of *fado* and the guitar."[13] This well-known *fado Hilario* (named after nineteenth-century Coimbra composer Augusto Hilario) is typical:

My worn cape has the color of dark night,
Herein I want to be buried when I go to the grave;

As I cannot speak, my cape will tell the worms
the obscure secrets of my sobbing soul;

I desire that my coffin should have a peculiar form—
the shape of a heart, the shape of a viola.[14]

Other *fados* deal with a wide range of topics, including bullfights, descriptions of beloved places, political satire, life at sea, and the vicissitudes of inexorable fate. The word "*fado*," in fact, derives from Latin *fatum*, or fate.[15] "Love passes, everything passes! The years pass by as well; But *saudade*—only that never passes, not for anyone."[16] *Fado* lyrics have been a highly cultivated form of poetry at least since the mid-nineteenth century, and possibly from a much earlier time. The texts, indeed, may be considered at least as important as the music itself, as is reflected in the use of stock melodic forms.

Fado composition continues to be a lively and popular art, encouraged particularly by annual competitions. Many *fados* are written about contemporary events and issues, although sentimental love predominates as a subject. Several of the topical texts succeed in transcending the prosaic and particular, and critics are quick to disparage those that do not.[17]

Contemporary *Fado*

The advent of the recording industry promoted the popularity of *fado* beyond the underworld of Lisbon and the student taverns of Coimbra. It also contributed to the adulteration and commercialization of the genre, as *fado* adopted features of mainstream European music in an evident effort to reach a wider audience.

Given the tradition of topical song-texts, *fado* was influenced profoundly by the 1974 revolution, when progressive elements within the military staged a coup, instituted land reform, and renounced colonialism and the repressive African wars which were bankrupting the country and decimating Portuguese (not to mention African) youth. Many of the new *fados* dealt with the country's new, post-colonial nationhood. At the same time, the genre began to undergo stylistic changes accompanying its growing mass dissemination. The most noticeable feature of the new style was the vocal rubato, in which phrases were rendered in a spontaneous, irregular, almost conversational fashion, often over a steady rhythmic accompaniment. This development is associated in particular with singer Carlos do Carmo. Some listeners, while greatly admiring his singing, attribute his style to the relative weakness of his voice, which, especially in his old age, was not strong enough to sustain the long vocal lines of the old style[18]. Nevertheless, the rubato, affording greater scope for sentimentality and individual styles, seems a natural concomitant of the increasing commercialization of the genre.

In do Carmo's wake emerged the modern *fado canção* (lit., "fado song"), which incorporated more features of the contemporary mainstream pop ballad style, supplementing or replacing traditional instrumentation with bass guitar, additional strings, and slick orchestral background. The instrumental passages dividing the verses in this style occasionally seem to borrow from traditional motives played on the *guitarra*, but on the whole they tend to be distinct, through-composed bridge sections which lend the song a progressive rather than strophic structure. Foxtrot rhythm is particularly popular.

The orchestrated *fado canção* serves a distinct function from the recorded versions of traditional *fado*, for, whereas the latter served primarily to supplement the primary experience of *fado* in cafes or at home, the modern *fados* can generally be accessed only through the mass media and are thus alienated from personal performance contexts, whether in local taverns or by amateurs at home.[19] The vocal style of the *fado canção* is more sentimental and idiosyncratic, and album covers promote singers as fashionable stars.

In this context, the *fado canção* imitates and competes with the mainstream pop ballad, while more traditional *fado* survives in the cafes. Contemporary *fadistas*, noting the preference of the Portuguese youth for imported pop, are not optimistic about the future of *fado*, and the genre continues to suffer from negative association with the pre-1974 fascist dictatorship, which attempted to promote *fado* as a "national" music.

As mentioned above, competitions (including the Eurovision song contest) have become a lively part of the Portuguese *fado* scene. Originality in text and music is an important criterion for success in these contests, and, as a result, many of the modern *fados* no longer conform to the classic stock forms.

Pinto de Carvalho opines that *fado* will always persist because it is such a quintessential expression of Portuguese nostalgia for its faded glory.[20] But as Portugal's colonial past recedes from the memory of new generations, and *fado* incorporates more and more features of the mainstream pop ballad, it seems questionable whether the genre can resist being adulterated out of existence. Nevertheless, it is not inconceivable that a *fado* revival might take place, as has happened in recent years with Greek *rebetika*.

Spain

Through the first half of the twentieth century, Spain remained an economically and politically backward appendage of Western Europe, having little to show for its former colonial glory. The puritanical Franco dictatorship (1939–75) attempted to repress many forms of contemporary cultural expression, including, for example, rock music, which tended to be shunned by the state-run mass media.[21] Nevertheless, industrialization, general economic development, and the restoration of democracy and socio-cultural freedom have since brought Spain effectively into the twentieth century and into the cultural and economic orbit of the West. Hence, for a majority of Spaniards today, popular music taste tends to correspond to mainstream European and American styles—especially rock and the sentimental ballad, whether performed by foreigners or locals.

Popular mass culture, however, has by no means erased Spain's rich panorama of folk music traditions, many of which enjoy a contemporaneity and vitality incomparable to the marginal or artificially preserved folk cultures of other advanced industrial countries; in recent years, the unprecedented boom of *sevillanas*—a folk dance and music genre of Seville—throughout much of the country is but one example of the healthy coexistence of tradition and modernity. But while folk music and dances continue to influence modern culture in much of Spain, it is only the music of the southern state of Andalusia that has adapted to modernity in such a way as to form a complex of popular music styles that are at once contemporary and uniquely Spanish.

Andalusia's distinctiveness as a cultural area, although not unrelated to its particular economic underdevelopment, is a product primarily of the region's cosmopolitan artistic heritage, which has incorporated Arab, Berber, gypsy, Sephardic Jewish, and black African as well as European traditions. Hence, the regional varieties of Andalusian folk music occupy a special place in Spanish culture.

The most renowned of these musics, of course, is flamenco, which was nurtured in the last two centuries primarily by assimilated, settled gypsies in the cities and large towns of Seville and Cádiz provinces. While the informal gypsy *juerga* ("spree") remained an ideal and archetypical flamenco performance context, since the mid-nineteenth century the genre became increasingly professionalized and, whether in a pejorative or neutral sense of the word, commercialized. During the period 1850–1950, flamenco, and diluted forms thereof, were frequently performed in cabarets called *cafés-cantantes;* more "pure" varieties of the art survived in the *juergas* and in private parties held by non-gypsy (*payo*) aristocrats. The period 1920–60 constituted a nadir for flamenco, with declining public interest in traditional gypsy flamenco—especially *cante jondo* ("deep song")—and further bastardization of the genre in the context of theatrical flamenco opera. By this time, flamenco had ceased to be an exclusively gypsy art, as several Andalusian *payos* had become recognized as leading performers. Correspondingly, aside from the now-forgotten eccentricities of flamenco opera, the genre came to incorporate Andalusian non-gypsy folk musics (especially the regional varieties of *fandango*) and Latin American (especially Cuban) influences alongside the basic gypsy *cantes* (*soleares, bulerías, tientos, tangos, siguiriyas,* etc.)—all rendered with characteristic flamenco improvisation and guitar and vocal styles.

Nothwithstanding the vitriol of purists, flamenco has been since its very inception an eclectic, if not omnivorous genre, adapting in stylized versions diverse other musics into its repertoire. In this sense, the various flamenco-pop fusions that emerged from the late sixties do not constitute a dramatic break with tradition. At the same time, these hybrids have been products of—and active participants in—a set of interrelated, broader cultural, economic, and political developments, which must be at least mentioned here.

Of primary importance has been the unprecedented vogue of flamenco itself, which commencing in the sixties, must be regarded as one of the major cultural developments in modern Spain. For various reasons which we need not discuss here, flamenco has not only recovered from its erstwhile slump but has indeed come to thrive as never before. Clubs, night-long festivals, cabaret-like *tablaos,* books, recordings, media coverage, and a new scholarly field of "flamencology" have all flowered in recent decades, and musicians who were formerly living in penury now find themselves lionized as cultural heroes. Correspondingly, a new generation of brilliant young musicians—both gypsy and *payo*— has emerged, many of whose members have experimented freely with eclectic fusions while continuing to perform traditional flamenco. Foremost among these have been guitarist Paco de Lucía and vocalist Camarón de la Isla—of whom more will be said below.

Foreign musical influences have played an important role in the development of pop flamenco (as in that of traditional flamenco itself). The first external catalyst of a populist flamenco fusion was the Cuban *rumba* (or more properly, the *son*), which in the early twentieth century was incorporated in stylized form into flamenco as a light *cante chico.* The flamenco-style *rumba,* while generally lacking the "song"-*montuno* structure and complex composite rhythms of the Cuban *rumba,* did retain the characteristic melodies and lively, syncopated, quadratic meter of its Caribbean parent. During traditional flamenco's lean decades of the forties and fifties, the lighter *rumba* and *fandango* become the genre's most popular substyles. While more serious *cantes* (including a more refined *fandango*) have since come back into vogue, the flamenco-style *rumba*—often performed in Andalusian restaurants by gypsy duos—continues to be popular. More important, however, is the pop commercial *rumba* which emerged in the sixties—a development we shall discuss below.

Contemporary with the flamenco boom itself has been the advent of rock music. Franco's cultural xenophobia notwithstanding, rock has enjoyed roughly as much popularity in Spain as in the rest of Europe, and it has been an essential ingredient in the hybrid varieties of pop flamenco that have emerged in recent decades. The rock era has coincided with an expansion of the Spanish recording industry (both records and cassettes) and, for that matter, of an affluent middle class with money to spend on music.

Ultimately, however, the most important catalysts in the emergence of modern Andalusian popular music have not been purely stylistic innovations or influences, but the dramatically altered demography of southern Spanish society—specifically, the processes of urbanization and mass migration. Andalusian urbanization accelerated considerably in the mid-twentieth century, under the pressures of population growth, inflation, the simultaneous mechanization and stagnation of agriculture, and the continued concentration of land ownership in the hands of a tiny elite of absentee landlords. But the Andalusian cities—quaint provincial towns with negligible industry or commerce—could absorb only a small fraction of the hordes of unemployed southerners. Instead, well over two million laborers have been obliged to seek work in the industrial cities of France, Germany, Madrid, and, above all, Barcelona. This massive migration is significant less for the innumerable songs dealing with the vicissitudes of exile than for the emergence of an entire proletarian subculture in Barcelona and Madrid, consisting of first- and second-generation transplanted Andalusians, engendering a new musical and cultural aesthetic that reflects their new social environment.

A final extra-musical development to be considered is the return of political freedom and democracy within a few years of Franco's death. Repression of cultural activities had eased somewhat in the last decade of the *dictadura*, but Spain under Franco remained a country where, for example, rock and hippiedom were discouraged, and the Mexican *corrido* "La Cucaracha" was banned because of its whimsical reference to marijuana (smoking of which has since been legalized). The advent of democracy opened the way for a torrent of previously repressed cultural expressions and socio-political movements—including Andalusian autonomy and gypsy identity mobilizations—which found expression in popular music forms.

The emergence of Andalusian popular music was an inevitable concurrent of the developments outlined above. Its most immediate precedent was the aforementioned flamenco-style *rumba*, which, despite its popularity, should better be regarded as an urban folk form rather than a mass-mediated popular music per se. The first true incarnations of Spanish *rumba* as a commercial entity appeared in the sixties in the music of Peret (Pedro Pubill Calaf), a Catalonian gypsy who popularized a somewhat crude fusion of rock, Cuban music, and, to some extent, the flamenco *rumba*, and in the *tango-rumba* of the Madrid-based singer-guitarist Manzanitas. By the early seventies, the *rumba catalan* had taken a more definitive form with the flowering of dozens of combos—including Las Grecas, Los Chunguitos, Los Chichos, and others—whose members consisted mostly of young first- or second-generation gypsy migrants from the south, living in the slums of Barcelona and Madrid. Such proletarianized gypsies, together with lower-class *payo* youths in general, also constituted the audience for this new *sonido andaluz*.

The *rumba* (*rumbita*) *catalan* is in fact much closer in rhythm and instrumentation to rock than to *rumba;* moreover, despite its name, it is devoid of any influence of Catalonian music. Only in its relatively simple instrumental arrangements, frequent use of Andalusian harmonic progressions (e.g., Am-G-F-E) and vocal style does it bear affinities with the flamenco *rumba*. As in most popular musics, the majority of its song texts concern romance; but a significant portion of them deal with themes of barrio life: unemployment, drugs, crime, and, in general, the vicissitudes of trying to adapt to an insecure and impersonal urban environment. Given the high numbers of gypsies among both performers and audiences, a gypsy orientation pervades many, if not most songs; the beloved is usually a *gitana* (gypsy), and traditional gypsy values of freedom and antinomianism are explicitly celebrated.

By the mid-seventies, Paco de Lucía (b. 1947) was already becoming recognized as the leading flamenco guitarist and, in the eyes of many, as the most outstanding genius in the recorded history of the genre as a whole. Alongside his pure flamenco concerts and recordings, Paco began experimenting with a number of eclectic innovations, which inspired many imitators and became established as a *sui generis* pop style. His 1974 instrumental *rumba* "Entre dos aguas," combining virtuoso guitar improvisations over a lively percussion background, saturated Spanish radio, elevators, airplanes, and supermarkets for several years. His collaborations with foreign musicians like John McLaughlin won him international and jazz-oriented audiences. Meanwhile, Lucía and star vocalist Camarón de la Isla continue to record and perform both traditional and modernized flamenco, together with tasteful pop-flavored hits like the *tango* "Como el agua" (1985).

In Paco de Lucía's wake, there flowered a host of eclectic fusions of flamenco with rock, sentimental ballad (*canción*), and even Arab music. Like Lucía and Camarón, most of the leading exponents of these hybrids come from flamenco backgrounds, and several continue to perform pure flamenco while experimenting—and greatly augmenting their incomes—with more marketable innovations.[22] Since the mid-eighties, vocalist Tijeritas has been the most popular exponent of flamenco-rock (also referred to, depending on text content and the ethnicity of the performer, as *rock gitano* or *poder* (power) *gitano*). These substyles tend to depart from the more unprepossessing *rumba catalan*. On the one hand, they reflect modern rock influence in the more complex and sophisticated ensemble arrangements, the disco rhythms and instrumentation, and virtuoso "heavy metal" guitar playing; on the other hand, harmonic vocabulary and the intense, passionate solo vocal style are much more closely rooted in flamenco than are those of the *rumba catalan*, which is archetypically sung in unison by two vocalists, in a relatively straightforward style. Flamenco-rock songs, however, do tend to treat the same themes as those of *rumba catalan*, and their most concentrated audiences remain the Andalusian migrants in Barcelona and Madrid. Not atypical is the mid-eighties' hit of Cordoban singer Queco, "Caballo Maldito" ("Cursed Horse"), whose text deals with the now-familiar theme of heroin addiction:[23]

Llevo por mis venas un caballo galopando
caballo maldito, tú me estás matando

Yo veía la vida felíz hasta el día te conocí
Hoy ya no puedo engañarme, mi sangre es veneno . . .
Ya no puedo luchar contra ti, pues tú siempre me ganas.

Creí que eras amigo mio que daño me estas haciendo!
Ahora sin ti no puedo vivir, te llevo y formas parte de mí . . .

I carry in my veins a galloping horse
Cursed horse, you are killing me.

I knew a happy life until the day I met you
Now I can't fool myself any longer, my blood is poison . . .
I can't fight you any more, because you always win over me.

I thought you were my friend—but how you hurt me!
Now I can't live without you
I carry you and you form part of me . . .

An interesting and not insignificant footnote in the array of eclectic flamenco hybrids has been the variety of fusions with Arab popular and traditional musics, representing, in part, an attempt to reforge Andalusia's bonds with the Arab world that were forcibly sundered, with ruinous results, during the fifteenth-century *reconquista*. Flamenco duo Lole and Manuel (separated in 1986) have enjoyed prodigious commercial success with their Andalusianized renditions of Umm Kulthum songs, and in 1987, Lole (Montoya) was performing, among other hybrids, a blues, accompanied by flamenco guitars, with Arabic text and vocal style!

Another contemporary genre to emerge from the south has been *nueva canción andaluza* (Andalusian new song). Like the Catalonian *canto novo* which flourished in the sixties and early seventies, Andalusian *nueva canción* is a product and expression of regional socio-political consciousness. But whereas Catalonia's main demand—regional autonomy—has since been satisfied, Andalusia's endemic problems of underdevelopment, unemployment, and consequent migration have in many respects intensified in recent decades. *Nueva canción* texts tend to address these issues, attempting to raise socio-political consciousness; such themes are, of course, common in several other genres, from *sevillanas*, and the aforementioned pop styles, to the *tangos* and *pasadobles* of the Cádiz carnival. *Nueva canción* may be said to differ in its audience—a relatively small group of students and activists—and in the styles that it encompasses. These latter span a continuum of text-oriented European pop styles, while often including a distinctive Andalusian flavor in harmony, guitar style, and the like. Miguel López, Carlos Cano, Pepe Suero, and Miguel Rios have been leading exponents of this genre.[24]

Finally, worthy of mention here are the pop versions of *pasadobles*, *columbianas*, and generic sentimental ballads sung by flamenco vocalists like Chiquitete, Ana Reverte, and Remedios Amaya. These tend to resemble mainstream commercial *canciones*, with the exception of the flamenco vocal idiosyncracies introduced by the singers.

Greece

Greece has one of the most distinctively national popular musics of any European country. The vitality and uniqueness of this tradition derives from several factors, including the richness and diversity of Greek folk music, the strength of Near Eastern musical influences, and the peripheral nature of Greece's geographical and cultural relationship with Western Europe.

The remarkable diversity of Greek folk music (*demotiki*) is a product of ethnic heterogeneity (the presence of Ulachs, Greeks, Turks, gypsies, and Sephardim) and more importantly, regional diversity deriving from mountainous terrain and the scattering of much of the population over many islands. Highly developed musical traditions date back over two millenia, and regional practices have been in turn strongly influenced by neighboring Balkan cultures, immigrant ethnic groups (including gypsies), four centuries of Ottoman Turkish rule, and the massive migration to Greece in 1922 of Greeks who had been living in Asia Minor. Finally, of course, Western European culture has exercised an ongoing influence on Greek culture; since the early nineteenth century this influence has intensified as Greek society, especially the bourgeoisie, has become tied to Western commercial, political, and military interests.

The diversity of Greek folk music is paralleled by that of its Balkan neighbors. At the same time, however, prolonged Turkish domination and shared gypsy cultures have promoted certain similarities between musical traditions in these areas, particularly in the case of urban professional musics. Turkish and other Near Eastern influences on Greek music are most evident in the use of improvised *taxim* (*taqsim*), additive meters and specific dance rhythms like the *çifte telli* (*tsifte teli*) and *zebekiko*, and instruments like the *outi, santouri,* and *bouzouki,* which derive from Middle Eastern counterparts. Since gypsies have traditionally constituted a significant portion of mainland professional musicians (especially wind instrumentalists),[25] gypsy influence has similarly contributed to the presence of certain modal and stylistic affinities with related traditions in Eastern Europe and Asia Minor.

Rebetika

The development of urbanization, nationalism, modern classes, and national music in Greece may be said to commence with the Greek war of independence, which triumphed in 1827. This was also the beginning of an unprecedented and continuing wave of Western European influence; modern Greek working class music, or *laiki,* developed in a synthetic, dialectical, and in many respects competitive relation to these foreign cultural influences.[26]

Rebetika (*rembetika*) is the name for the Greek urban popular music that arose, primarily in Athens and Piraeus, in the first decades of the twentieth century.[27] Like several other popular musics, its origin is associated with a lumpen proletariat, an urban underworld of bohemian vagrants, petty criminals, addicts, and unemployed or underemployed "street people." Many were dispossessed peasants from the countryside who had come to Athens looking for work on the docks and in the growing industries. Others were among the 1.5 million Greeks who, in 1922, were forcibly repatriated to Greece from their homes in Asia Minor. As the population of Athens grew from 167,000 in 1907 to over 3 million in the 1960s, the inability of the city to digest and employ so many refugees created a distinctive subculture among the lower classes.

The members of this subculture were called *rebetes* or *manges.*[28] Despised by the upper and middle classes, the *manges* gathered in bars, brothels, and dope dens, smoking hashish, smuggling, fighting amongst themselves, and trafficking in stolen goods. Hashish smoking was central to *rebetiko* culture; *rebetes* tended to prefer the introspective euphoria of the hashish high to drunkenness, especially because of the violence that often broke out in cafes that served liquor.[29] Nevertheless, many *rebetes* prided themselves on their fighting ability, along with their independence, their distinctive and often vulgar slang, and their eccentric dress—typically, tight trousers, a fedora hat (with a black band showing mourning for their own victims), and a jacket worn with only the left arm in the sleeve so that it could be readily flipped around the forearm for use as a shield against a knife-wielding attacker.[30] Because of their iconoclastic habits, and especially because of official persecution of hashish smoking, many *rebetes* spent much time in jail, where numerous *rebetika* songs originated.

As in the case of tango and jazz, the development of modern Greek popular music out of lumpen proletarian subculture was not a matter of coincidence. As Angeliki Keil has illustrated, the *rebetiko* class was the only social group able to generate a dynamic new urban music, by virtue of its freedom from Western European musical aesthetics, its alienation from bourgeois values, its access to the mass media, and its strong roots in local culture. As Keil explains, while the Greek countryside became increasingly denuded, acculturated, and incapable of generating new art forms to express its plight, "In the city the middle class and those who aspire to it [could not] create art. The bourgeois does not have roots in the culture that he admires and he is trying to kill his own true cultural roots with his hate for his 'ex-peasant' self."[31]

Perhaps the most distinctive, prized, and integral expression of *mangas* subculture was its music, *rebetika*. *Rebetika* consisted of songs performed informally in cafes, taverns, and jails, usually by amateurs or semi-professionals. The texts are rich sources of urban folklore, relating the everyday concerns of the *manges*—poverty, drugs, prison life, contemporary socio-political affairs, and especially, unrequited love. They tend to be despondent laments, reflecting the indigence and social alienation of their authors.

> I'm a junkie, see, and wherever I go
> they shit on me, I don't know what to do.
>
> My clothes are rags, nothing but holes,
> junk completely wrecked me.
>
> I live in a freight car and don't remember home,
> a burlap sack is where I sleep . . .
>
> The police are coming when I die, my friend,
> with a garbage cart for a hearse.[32]

Some songs portray the narrator—like the archetypal tango singer—nursing a drink while brooding over his lost love.

> . . . In the corner of the tavern it's for you I drink,
> for your love I shed rivers of tears;
> pity me, baby, and don't leave me lonely
> since you see I'm wasting because of you . . .[33]

The sources of *rebetika* are mixed. Its earliest origins may lie in Byzantine church music and certain general Mediterranean musical practices shared by Middle Eastern Jews, Greeks, Turks, and Arabs. As Athens began to grow in size and importance, an urban folk music developed among the *rebete* class, synthesizing Italian-derived *cantades* with elements from the folk music of the surrounding mainland and the nearby Cyclades Islands.

Perhaps the single most important source was the musical heritage brought by the refugees from Asia Minor in 1922. A large portion of these were urban expatriate Greeks who had played important roles in cultural as well as commercial life in Turkish cities, especially Smyrna (Izmir) and Istanbul; as such they represented the dynamic synthesis of Turkish and Greek musical cultures which had been flourishing for centuries.[34] Turkish-derived traditions already had taken root in Greece during the long Ottoman occupation, and in the late nineteenth century cafes abounded in Greek communities in Greece and Turkey where singers would informally improvise verses and melodies in free-rhythmic *amané* songs, named after the practice of singing florid melismas to the exclamation "aman."[35] This Middle-Eastern heritage also accounts for the use of modes resembling the Turkish and Arab *Rast, Hijaz,* and *Nihavent (Nahawand)*.

While the musical traditions of the refugees exerted prodigious influence on the development of *rebetika*, the immigrants from Asia Minor also continued to play their own more purely Middle Eastern cafe music, conveniently designated as "Smyrna" style after the port whence so many refugee musicians came. Smyrna-style cafe music was generally sung by women, who might dance as they sang, and it tended to emphasize the more Oriental *amané* songs, the Turkish *çifte telli* dance form, and improvised, melismatic *taxim* played on the violin or *santouri* (a struck zither resembling the Persian *santur*). Moreover, the Smryna cafe music lacked *rebetika's* associations with the underworld of hashish and prison life.[36]

Rebetika emerged as a major popular genre in the first decades of the twentieth century. Some early recordings are almost completely modal in character, with extensive improvised passages.[37] On the whole, however, *rebetika* soon came to incorporate more Western influences than the Smryna style, particularly in the use of chord progressions, instruments like the piano and accordion, and the increasing adoption of major and minor scales rather than the Middle Eastern modes.[38] The neutral intervals so essential to Arab and Turkish music became less common in *rebetika*. Early *rebetika* songs might be accompanied by a solo *bouzouki* or *baglamas*, a diminutive *bouzouki* popular especially in jails because it could be hidden easily. However, the typical instrumental ensemble soon grew to include free combinations of accordion, violin, *santouri*, guitar, and *outi* (a Greek counterpart of the Middle Eastern *ᶜud*).[39]

In the 1930s—the "classical" period of *rebetika*—the *bouzouki* came to dominate the ensemble, particularly under the influence of composer and performer Markos Vamvakaris; often it replaced the older instruments altogether. Lutes resembling the *bouzouki* were extant in Greece at least as early as the nineteenth century, but the instrument is clearly a close relative of the Turkish *saz*—one variety of which is called *bozuk saz*—and the Levantine *bouzouq*.[40] Until the 1950s, the *bouzouki* had three double courses of steel strings, for which four or five tunings were in common use, the most typical being D-A-D'.[41] In the 1950s, *bouzouki* virtuoso Hiotis added a fourth pair of strings, increasing the range and enabling the musician to play Western-style chords. From the 1940s on, it became customary to use two *bouzoukis*, typically playing precomposed melodic lines in parallel thirds.

Unlike Greek church music, narrative ballads, and funeral laments, *rebetika* was conceived of primarily as dance music; as such it drew most heavily from dance music traditions of the Greek communities in Greece and Asia Minor. Two folk dance-songs were of particular importance: the *zebekiko* (*zeybekiko, zembekiko*) and the *khasapiko* (*hassapiko*). Of these, the *zebekiko*, originating in eastern Anatolia[42] is by far the most popular; while it may still be encountered as a rural folk dance in such places as the island of Syra, its urban form has developed somewhat independently in the last century. The *zebekiko* is commonly performed in medium or slow tempo (M.M.ca. 70), generally in one of two varieties of 9/4—better regarded as 2+2+2+3 or 4/4 + 5/4:

zebekiko kophto: ♫ ⅄ ♪ ♩ ♩ ♫ ⅄ ♪ ♩ ♩ ♩

            1 2 3 4 5 6 7 8 9

zebekiko syriano: ♩ ♫ ♩ ♩ ♩ ♫ ♩ ♩ ♩

Within both forms, the first four beats of the 5/4 section are rhythmically identical to the commencing 4/4 section; as a result, the addition of a cadential fifth beat to the last section gives the meter the character of two sections in antecedent-consequent relationship.

The urban *zebekiko* dance may be performed by a couple, but in *rebetika* subculture it was archetypically a solo male dance, performed in a tavern. Ted Petrides describes it thusly:

> Envision a small smoke-filled room late at night, the neighborhood hangout, a dozen or more *manges* and perhaps some of their women seated at tables around a small space for dancing. At one end of the room, or at one of the tables, are seated the musicians, apparently tuning their instruments: a *bouzouki*, a guitar, and a *baglamas*. The aimless strumming and picking gradually leads into something more recognizable—a *taxim*, an arhythmical instrumental introduction which draws the *manges'* attention. They try to follow the course of the improvised melody in their minds, murmuring satisfaction at an unexpected turn, or disappointment at the insufficient development of a theme. Gradually the *taxim* builds to a climax and the tension mounts as the rhythm of the *zeybekiko* is introduced. Now one of the *manges* pushes back his chair and gets up. Putting his lit cigarette

between his lips, eyes on the floor, body tense and slightly crouched, arms loosely out to the sides, he begins to move slowly, deliberately around some fixed imaginary point on the floor. Snapping his finger to the rhythm, he elaborates his steps, occasionally doubling a step or holding a step for two beats, always circling round the point on the floor which is the unwavering focal center of his intense concentration, now and then breaking the heavy tension of the dance with explosive outbursts of energy as in sudden leaps, hops, turns, squats. No one else gets up to dance; it would be an insult and a trespass on his impending emotional release. Oddly enough this moment may come at any time, and he may decide to sit down again in the middle of the song; he is satisfied, he is released.[43]

The *khasapiko* (the "butchers' dance") is a more social dance, bearing some affinities with the Yugoslav *koro*, Levantine *dabkah*, and the *hora;* set to a slow or medium tempo duple meter, it is danced by two or three men side by side with their hands on each other's shoulders. Traditionally one man would lead the others through intricate, sometimes informally rehearsed variations on basic steps; at present *khasapiko* is often rendered in a simplified *syrtaki* form.[44]

Two other dance/metrical forms used in *rebetika* are the *çifte telli* and the *karsilama*. Both originated as solo or couple dances in Asia Minor; in Greek contexts they lacked the popularity of the *zebekiko* and *khasapiko*, and in the early *rebetika* period they tended to be danced mostly by female entertainers, or by males in a similarly suggestive, hip-swaying style. *Çifte telli* vocal style is distinctively melismatic, soloistic, and improvisatory. The *karsilama*, like the *zebekiko*, has a nine-beat meter, but it can usually be distinguished by its faster tempo and its internal structure:[45]

The *çifte telli* may be rendered in various forms, the last of which shown below most clearly shows its Turko-Arab derivation:

The folk *sirto* (*syrtos*) rhythm (with its characteristic 3+3+2 syncopation) occasionally appears in *rebetika* but is more characteristic of later *bouzouki* music.

The typical *rebetika* song begins with an improvised *taxim* rendered on the *bouzouki*, introducing the mode in free rhythm, often with fast melodic runs. The ensemble then plays a short instrumental refrain leading to and subsequently punctuating the vocal sections, which may be performed by one or more singers. Often the vocal verse is sung solo, the other vocalists joining in the refrain, which may be rendered in parallel thirds or even triads. An improvised *taxim* may also appear in the course of the song itself.

A variety of modes are used in *rebetika*, corresponding to modes used in Greek folk music, Byzantine church music, and, in several cases, to Middle Eastern art and popular music. Early *rebetika* musicians used the Arab-Turkish word *makam* (*maqam*) to denote these modes, but that term was eventually replaced by the Greek word *dromoi* (*thromi*), literally meaning "road." Some of the dozen or so *dromoi* in use resemble Western major and minor scales, or the Mixolydian and Dorian modes. The Greek *minoré* (occasionally referred to as the "altered dorian" scale) appears to be of Rumanian gypsy origin, while the Turkish- derived *Hijāzkār* or *Hijāz* is used by gypsy musicians throughout Eastern Europe. In songs with major tonic chords, the *Hijāz*-type mode is particularly common, while minor key songs often employ the *Ussak* mode, loosely corresponding to the Phrygian scale.[46] The *Hijāz*-derived scale is roughly as follows, with free use of both raised and lowered sixth and seventh degrees:

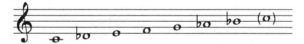

Some Greek musicians call this scale *piraiotiko*.[47] The "altered dorian" *minoré* scale, with its distinctive raised fourth degree, is as follows:

While practicing musicians may be fluent improvisers and be familiar with the names and characteristics of the most important modes, modal theory does not appear to be an important concern for most, nor are pedagogy and usage standardized. Melodic lines, whether improvised or pre-composed, need not adhere rigidly to any one mode; instead, alternate notes and accidentals are freely introduced.

Harmony is also an important component of the music. The chords, although major and minor triads, do not follow Western common practice; instead, they are adapted to, or, in Angeliki Keil's words, "in tension with" the modal resources. In the example below, the chord vocabulary—including major triads on Ab and the "tonic" G, and a minor triad on F—derives from the tones of the *Hijāz*-type scale: G Ab B C D Eb (and E) F. The following example uses a similar scale, built on A; here, the very tonality may be ambiguous to the Western ear, which may tend to hear the Dm triad as a tonic rather than a subdominant, even though the piece ends with a clear cadence on the A (with the Bb major triad functioning as a sort of upper-neighbor chord, as in Andalusian harmony).

Ornamentation style is another characteristic feature of *rebetika*. Although some aspects of its usage are distinctively Greek, it has much in common with ornamentation practices in the urban and gypsy musics of neighboring Balkan countries and Anatolia. *Rebetika* vocal style, indeed, is less distinguished by its ornamentation than by its rough, gravelly, almost intentional crudity which gives it its unique earthiness and saves it from the sentimentality of later *bouzouki* music.[48] Perhaps the most characteristic ornament is the decoration of a note or sequence of notes with their upper neighbors, which, in *bouzouki* playing would be "hammered-on" rather than plucked independently. The following excerpt is typical:[49]

This sort of ornamentation gives Greek clarinet music much of its distinctive, "laughing" sound.

The following simplified transcription of the first verse of "True Sunset," a popular *zebekiko syriano* recorded in 1949, illustrates some of the features discussed.[50] The formal structure is as follows:

//: instrumental passage (2 mm., played twice)
    solo verse (2 mm.)
    choral verse (2 mm., sung twice) :// entire sequence three times

The melody is in the *Hijāz-piraiotiko* mode, and the chord vocabulary derives mostly from its pitch resources. The harmonies accompanying the instrumental bridge and solo verse sections alternate between the tonic A major, its upper neighbor Bb major, and the subdominant (or secondary tonic) D minor. The choral verse section modulates via D major to G minor—in this harmonic system, a key closely related to A major, to which it then returns directly.

Il-yo-va-si-le-ma so-   sto   ti-no-ra pu-nikh-to   ni   tra

vo skif-tos to dro-mo-mu sto-dro-mo-mu kai-mos me ma-ra zo-ni

While *rebetika* was most characteristically performed live in a tavern or cafe, from the early 1930s it was disseminated extensively on records. In this context, the length of the songs had to be artificially shortened, and song texts referring to drugs and sex were subject to some censorship. Nonetheless, the recordings of artists like Markos Vamvakaris, Papaioanou ("The Tall"), and Stratos ("The Lazy") were highly influential and exerted a significant influence on the genre's development. They also increased public exposure to and familiarity with the composers themselves, such that most recorded *rebetika* songs are not anonymous, but rather are the works of known musicians.

World War II caused a temporary hiatus in the *rebetika* recording industry, but music continued in several urban clubs, and many songs were sung throughout the country as expressions of the hardships of war and foreign rule.[51] The decade following the war is spoken of as the last vital period of *rebetika*. The outstanding figure was Vassilis Tsitsanis, and his music and background characterize the transformations of the genre. Tsitsanis did not grow up in the bohemian *mangas* underworld, and his song-texts generally concern love rather than hashish, prison life, or the *rebete* life-style. Tsitsanis largely abandoned the *dromoi* in order to incorporate simple Western harmonies, which henceforth played an intrinsic rather than incidental role. He compensated for the modal simplification, however, with his innovative melodies, refrains, and poetic structures.[52] Tsitsanis preferred female vocalists, especially Sotiria Bellou—called the "Bessie Smith of *rebetika*"—and the more sentimental Marika "Ninou" Nikolaidou. Tsitsanis's music, with its fuller orchestration, Westernized melodies, and more romantic styles and texts, was more commercially accessible in style than the pre-war *rebetika*, and it brought *rebetika* firmly into the realm of mediated popular music.[53]

By 1955 the prime of *rebetika* was over, and purists regard subsequent developments as decadent. *Rebetika's* eclipse resulted from the absorption of many of the *manges* into middle-class society, and from the commercialization that ensued when *rebetika* became the source for a national popular music. At present, *rebetika's* status is ambiguous. On the one hand, it retains some of its association with the underworld and lumpen life. Hence, for example, one club owner informed me that he discouraged his house band from playing *rebetika* because while it generated substantial tips from wealthy underworld kingpins, it often seemed to promote violent behavior, ranging from smashing of bottles to gunfights. At the same time, some educated middle-class youths have cultivated an interest in *rebetika* as an urban folkloric genre. In the last decade, *rebetika* has been to some extent revived as an earthy, bluesy alternative to commercial *bouzouki* music. Yet, as with the persistence of Dixieland jazz, many of the modern performers of groups like the Rebetika Compania of Athens are from middle-class backgrounds, for whom the genre cannot possibly have the same social significance as for the outcast *manges* of the 1930s Greek underworld. Moreover, most young Greeks tend to prefer more modern-sounding music—whether rock derivatives or the contemporary ballad styles of composers like Theodorakis and Hadjidakis (of "Zorba the Greek" and "Never on Sunday" fame, respectively).

Modern *Bouzouki* Music

In the 1950s *rebetika* evolved into an urban pop form that had broader appeal across class boundaries than did its lower-class predecessor. The new *bouzouki* music was part of the sophisticated urban popular culture which had been emerging in Greece.

Modern *bouzouki* music retains many features of *rebetika*, including the *bouzouki* itself, the traditional dance-rhythm forms, some flavor of the *dromoi*, and the distinctive ornamentation and improvisation styles. It differs, however, in several respects. The *bouzoukis* are electrified and now have eight strings instead of six, and the ensemble is expanded to incorporate electric bass and standard Western drum set, while *baglamas*, accordion, electric guitar, electric organ, clarinet, and, in studio settings, orchestrated violins may also be used; the instruments are all loudly amplified in performance. *Bouzouki* technique has reached new levels of virtuosity, pioneered especially by Hiotis, such that the instrument often tends to upstage the singer and dancers—hence the common Greek parlance of going "*sta bouzoukia*"—to hear the *bouzoukis*—rather than going to listen to *rebetika*.[54] Intricate melodies played in parallel thirds by paired *bouzoukis* have become trademarks of the new style.

The song repertoire is new, and the *dromoi* must accommodate increased use of Western major and minor scale settings. Imported dance rhythms like the waltz are also used, such that distinctions between *rebetika*, *bouzouki* music, and mainstream pop are often ambiguous—hence the utility of the more general term *laiki* to denote pre-war rather than modern urban popular music.[55]

Bouzouki music has lost its associations with the underworld culture, instead being widely disseminated in clubs, in the media, and, most typically, at festivals and private functions like weddings.[56] With expanded mass media production, singers and groups are marketed and idolized as in other pop cultures. Moreover, as in many other pop musics, texts have become more sentimental, dwelling almost exclusively on love. Vocal style exhibits more rubato and effeminate polish, and avoids the languid roughness that lent *rebetika* so much of its distinctive appeal.

A continuum exists between commercial *bouzouki* music and the more intellectual, sophisticated songs of composers like Theodorakis, Hadjidakis, and Xarhakos. *Zebekikos* of such modern composers often lack the somewhat ponderous rhythmic intensity of their antecedents, allowing greater emphasis to be placed on the texts. Accordingly, many of the texts are of high literary content, including, for instance, verses of Nobel Prize winner George Seferis (1900–1971) which have been set to music. A large portion of such texts express progressive socio-political themes. Many songs of this type are sectional, juxtaposing different traditional additive meters. Such songs are often referred to as "ballads"—that is, through-composed songs—and are especially popular among the left-of-center youth. The new ballads could be said to constitute a sort of Greek "new song," with its own distinctive clientele, content, and self-conscious fusion of old and new elements.

Modern commercial *bouzouki* music tends to be performed more often in expensive nightclubs than in humble lower-class cafes. Expressions of approval are now ritualized into extravagant smashing of plates and glasses. While solo and line dances continue to predominate over couple dances, purists complain that the cathartic, introspective *rebetika* dance style has become stylized into acrobatic displays of technique— often more for the benefit of tourists than that of the dancers themselves. The up-tempo Serbian *hasaposerviko* has been revived to accommodate the flashy new dance styles,[57] and musicians in the sixties have popularized the *syrtaki*, "a synthetic dance pieced together from various styles and popularized by paid dancers in tourist night spots."[58]

To purist *rebetika* lovers, modern *bouzouki* music is decadent, sugary, commercial, and lacking in the "soul" that *rebetika* had.[59] To most Greeks, however, it is a vital and lively expression of Greek culture. Moreover, the evolution of *bouzouki* music and its continued rivalry with imported pop are best seen as inevitable developments paralleling the emergence of modern Greek society.

Yugoslavia

Yugoslavia, like Greece, is host to a rich variety of traditional rural and urban folk musics, several of which bear the clear imprint of the centuries of Ottoman Turkish rule. In the twentieth century, these genres, while themselves remaining vital, have been important sources for a set of modernized popular musics, which are stylistically quite distinct from Western pop. Yugoslavia's six republics retain a keen sense of pride in their distinct cultural traditions, and their cultural nationalism, supported both at grassroots and bureaucratic levels, has tended to reinforce and enhance the uniqueness of its musics, both traditional and modern.[60]

In Yugoslavia as in many other countries, contemporary musics span a continuum from traditional styles to locally produced rock and pop in mainstream Western idioms. Of interest here are the intermediate musics on this continuum, that is, the modernized versions of traditional musics which have evolved in close connection with the mass media, whether commercial recordings or the state-operated radio network.

While Yugoslavia's republics are quite distinct in their musical cultures, the southern (or eastern) areas of Macedonia, Serbia, Montenegro, and Bosnia-Hercegovina share a common heritage dating from the extended Ottoman rule; as a result, the republics in this area exhibit to some extent the same kinds of relationships between traditional musics, modernized adaptations of these musics, and imported styles. A look at traditional music genres in Macedonia may illustrate the range of musics which dominated provincial musical life until World War II, and which remain important both in a folkloric capacity and as sources for syncretic urban popular music.

Southern Yugoslavia inherited a set of acculturated music genres from the Ottoman period, which ended in 1912. Aside from traditional, predominantly indigenous rural musics, a variety of musics existed which reflected varying sorts and degrees of Turkish and Western influence. Small brass bands played Europeanized military music as well as Turkish-informed dance music. Urban *čalgija* ensembles (from Turkish *çalgi*), consisting of *kanun*, violin, clarinet, *darabuka*, *ud*, and/or *džumbuš*, played *makam*-based music of primarily Turkish derivation. Turkish theater melodies were widely popular (at least until 1912), as was a large repertoire of urban secular songs, played by Christian musicians, combining Turkish elements (especially, *makam* and ornamentation) with Slavic-language texts and Western harmony and instrumentation.

Musical life in Yugoslavia changed considerably after World War II, with the advent of socialism, economic development, urbanization, the spread of the mass media, and enhanced contact with Western Europe (especially through emigrant workers). Mainstream Western popular music (referred to as *zabavna muzika*) has become widely popular among the young throughout the country. Nevertheless, musics in indigenous styles continue to thrive, albeit on attenuated levels. These musics are generically referred to as *narodna muzika* ("national," "people's," or "folk" music). Macedonian *narodna muzika* comprises a variety of traditional styles. Village musics often employ a distinctive vocal style, drone polyphony and, occasionally, glottal ornamentation. Urban vocal styles are characterized more by melismatic ornamentation and vibrato; songs may be free-rhythmic or set to traditional meters like the familiar 2+2+2+3 so popular in Turkey. Western instruments—accordion, guitar, violin, clarinet, bass, and drums—may be combined with indigenous or *čalgija* instruments in urban *narodna muzika*. The radio is perhaps the most important means of dissemination, and musics broadcast are thus influenced by the cultural policies of the regional mass-media bureaucracy.

While traditional *narodna muzika* is promoted by the state media, far more popular in southern Yugoslavia (especially among the young) are modernized, stylized versions of this music, which often incorporate some features imported from the West or elsewhere. Such musics, while still in the category of *narodna muzika*, are occasionally referred to as *nove narodne pesme*—"new folk songs"—or *novokomponirana* music—"newly composed folk music"; we shall henceforth designate them as pop *narodna* music. Critics and cultural bureaucrats tend to regard this music as a vulgarization of folklore into mass culture; nevertheless, it is best seen as a product of the transformation of Yugoslav society since 1945 and, in particular, the mass migration of peasants to the cities and the consequent emergence of a new class of urban dwellers with a distinct social identity and musical aesthetic. Pop *narodna muzika*, with its folk roots and general lack of pretention, is most popular among the working class, especially first- or second-generation migrants from the countryside. Its status—including the condescension with which urban sophisticates regard it—has been compared to that of country-western music in the USA.

Stylistically, pop *narodna* songs vary somewhat in accordance with regional characteristics. Most songs, however, consist of three or four verses, set strophically, with refrains and instrumental interludes. Traditional additive meters are common, as is a wide melodic range often exceeding one octave. The vocal style is particularly distinctive, with its rich ornamentation, melisma, vibrato, and use of augmented seconds and other Turkish-derived features. As Ljerka Vidić has illustrated, embellishment and extension of the skeletal melodic line play a structural rather than merely decorative function.[61]

Pop *narodna* songs, as the term *novokomponirana* suggests, differ from their folk antecedents in that they are newly composed; moreover, they make a free usage of imported (primarily Western) elements. Harmony is quite common, although the chord vocabulary often draws more from the modal tonal resources than from Western common practice. In recording, songs are frequently modernized by addition of reverb to the vocal part, and song texts tend to be concerned almost exclusively with romantic love. Pop *narodna muzika* may thus share characteristics of both popular and "urban folk" musics, in terms of style, image, and its association with recordings. According to Jane Sugarman,

> *Novokomponirani* songs are the most popular music in southern Yugoslavia, especially among the young and the less well-educated. They are heard on television and at live concerts. . . . At least in Macedonia the new songs are given almost no radio play except for request shows, which they dominate. They have been condemned repeatedly by commentators on culture.[62]

While pop *narodna* music often reflects specific regional stylistic features, at the same time, commentators have accused it, in conjunction with the "omnipotent pressure of [the] media," of contributing to the homogenization of musical culture and, by implication, the weakening of regional distinctions in music.[63] As Vidić observes,

> The regionalism expressed [in pop *narodna muzika*] absorbs the disparate audiences while fostering the quintessential idea of promoting amorphous 'folk values' which unify the singers' personalities and the composers' creative and marketing strategies.[64]

In this sense, the syncretic *narodna* songs appear to be playing an important role in the formation, throughout southern Yugoslavia, of a pan-ethnic super-regional identity which is at once modern and broad in its appeal, while retaining ties to traditional culture.

Also straddling the folk and pop realms are various kinds of contemporary music performed by the Gypsies, who constitute an important ethnic minority in Yugoslavia, and one that has traditionally dominated performance of secular entertainment musics in certain regions. Sugarman notes that in Macedonia, aside from the traditional *zurla* (oboe) and *tupan* (barrel drum) wedding music, Gypsies play dance music for themselves, using sax, *džumbuš*, accordion, and drum, and for others, using accordion, clarinet and/or sax, bass drum (or *tupan*), and occasionally trumpet and/or violin; more modern Gypsy bands employ electric guitar and bass, organ or accordion, and other amplified melody instruments. The music of such ensembles is markedly Turkish in its modal basis, melismatic vocal style, improvised *taksim,* duple and 9/8 *čoček* meters (cf. Turkish *küçek*), and use of the *čalgija* repertoire.

Vidić's study of gypsy musical culture in Bosnia and Hercegovina further reveals the extent to which pop *narodna* music has permeated Gypsy musical practices; at the same time, Gypsy musicians—especially stars like Šaban Bajramovič—have been able to respond fruitfully to the current popular demand for pop *narodna* music with a distinct Gypsy flavor.[65] Similarly, several Macedonian Gypsy musicians—especially those who sing in Serbian rather than Romany—have enjoyed prodigious commercial success among non-Gypsy audiences. Indeed, Gypsy music, with its lively rhythms, spirited improvisations, instrumental virtuosity, and its exotic subculture ethos, has many of the key features usually associated with popular youth musics.[66]

Also worthy of brief mention is the current vogue, within the Gypsy community itself, of Hindi film music and Gypsy imitations thereof. This trend is closely related to the Gypsies' own renewed sense of ethnic pride, which has stimulated their interest in their former homeland, India.

In Yugoslavia, as in other socialist countries, official cultural policy plays an important role in popular music dissemination. These policies, determining such matters as assessment of entertainment taxes, are formulated by committees of bureaucrats, including folklorists and musicologists.[67] On the one hand, the media attempt to satisfy popular demand for modern pop styles, and the state, for example, will also provide dance-band instruments for adolescent musicians in youth clubs. On the other hand, the media promote traditional *narodna muzika,* which is further exempted from entertainment taxes levied on imported music and pop *narodna muzika* recordings. The latter are regarded by many critics as *"kič"* (kitsch) or, even worse, *šund* ("trash"). Spirited polemics take place regarding the assessment of these taxes and media broadcast policy. Despite the ambivalence toward pop *narodna muzika*, the decentralization and self-management which distinguish Yugoslavian socialism do enable the media and entertainment industries to respond to the grassroots popular taste in ways quite atypical of the centralized, corporate, capitalist music industry.

CHAPTER 5

The Arab Middle East
by Virginia Danielson

Music in the Arab world has a long history, documented by scholarly treatises, historical accounts, and more recently, by notations and recordings.[1] The Arab musical heritage includes diverse regional folk and religious musics, as well as a classical music tradition with a sophisticated written theory originally formulated between the ninth and thirteenth centuries. Insofar as the various forms of Arab classical music share a basis in this theory—especially the use of melodic modes (*maqā-māt*, s. *maqām*)—they can be regarded as a "Great Tradition" common to many Arab countries. However, regional variants do differ somewhat in terms of intonation, *maqām* names, preferred instruments and meters, and, to some extent, style, such that one can distinguish Moroccan, Tunisian, Egyptian, and Iraqi art musics.

Although instrumental improvisation (*taqsīm*, pl., *taqāsīm*) is considered to be one of the most important aspects of Arab musical culture, historically it is vocal music, the sung poetry, which has occupied the more prominent place in musical life as a whole. As an Arab musicologist recently observed, "Today, after over a thousand years of Arab history, musical life is . . . still centered on the person of the singer"[2]

A common assumption is that the teachings of Islam strongly discourage the practice of music in the Arab world. Among a minority of Muslims, such has been the case. However, songs and singing have found advocates among religious Muslims as well, notably the philosopher and theologian, al-Ghazāli (d. 1111), who distinguished the singing of worthy texts from other undesirable activities associated with public entertainment, such as drunkenness, gambling, and immoral behavior. Music plays an important role in the rituals of Sufi groups and in religious celebrations. The low social status sometimes accorded public entertainers is certainly not peculiar to Islam and can be overcome in the Arab world, as in other societies, by success and stardom.[3]

Among the variety of musics supported by Arab society in the twentieth century one may count *taqāsīm*, Turkish instrumental pieces for small ensembles, folk dances and songs, Arabic musical theater, Western popular dance music, Islamic and Christian religious music, classical Arabic song, jazz, and rock music. Modernity has been an important goal for musicians. While great respect is shown for the music and musicians of the past, performers have been more often rewarded for their innovations than their reproductions of past models. Innovation has frequently yielded hybrid musics, drawn from a variety of styles and genres, indigenous and foreign. One result of this persistent cross-fertilization of varied repertoires is that classification of Arabic musics as "folk," "popular" or "classical," "religious" or "secular," or even "Eastern" or "Western" is often difficult. One may speak of "popular" music as music that is widely disseminated by the media and well liked by many people. In the twentieth-century Arab world, that category includes music having religious, folk, classical, and Western traits, among others. This large corpus of primarily vocal music of varying styles has been called the "central domain" of modern Arabic music.[4]

Egypt, the focus of the following discussion, has been a principal center for the development and dissemination of Arab popular music throughout the nineteenth and twentieth century. Long a center of trade, political leadership, scholarship, and cultural expression, Cairo gained early ascendancy in the development of the mass media and the musics associated with them. The opportunities offered in Cairo attracted performers from throughout the Arab world.[5] Thanks to relative political and social stability, Cairo consistently supported the creation of music which was marketed and broadcast throughout the Middle East. Thus modern Egyptian music has become well known and influential throughout the Arab world in the twentieth century, constituting, in effect, a pan-Arab popular music.[6] Mass media of all types enjoyed early, substantial and continuous support in Egypt, beginning with commercial recordings around 1904. Modern Egyptian popular music has developed as a product of the complex relationships among musicians, audiences, and those who owned and controlled the various media.

At the turn of the century, wealthy elites and the growing middle class, frequently interested in Western innovations, supported the Cairo opera house and performances of ballets and musical plays, some of which were adapted directly from European models and others based on indigenous comic figures and situations. However, most of the population could not afford these diversions and instead listened to singers and story-tellers who performed in coffee houses or at weddings, saints' day celebrations, and similar occasions to which entire neighborhoods or villages were customarily invited. Virtually everyone was familiar with indigenous music heard at such occasions. Even elite families celebrated traditional holidays with traditional music. Many regularly patronized both local and Western music, especially those among the influential landowners of rural Egypt who moved to Cairo at the turn of the century to assume greater roles in Egyptian political and economic life. In some cases, patronage of local musicians may have represented a condescending interest in the rustic or a search for a quaint novelty to display to one's friends. However, sources indicate that singers, especially the educated performers of religious and neo-classical repertoires, provided a link with what was viewed as authentically Egyptian culture. This became especially important in times of growing resistance to foreign domination.[7]

Early in the 20th century, the most pervasive type of musical performance (and one which has retained strength throughout the century), was that of the singer of religious and classical texts who performed at weddings and saints' days, for community gatherings and in coffee houses. Such a singer was commonly referred to as *shaykh* (pl., *mashāyikh*), a title accorded a learned man, suggesting that he is an educated, mature, observant Muslim.[8] The *shaykh* appeared in wealthy salons as well as at village occasions, depending on his reputation and prestige. According to a Cairo journalist:

> The *mashāyikh* had a big role in village life . . . The voices which charmed the people for the saints' days and other religious holidays were the voices of the *mashāyikh* . . . The *mashāyikh* used to present all kinds of religious songs during evenings which were the most beautiful and the sweetest in the Egyptian village.[9]

These performers manifested a relatively high degree of learning. Most had been initially trained to recite the *Qur'ān*. A few were faculty members at the old and venerated Azhar University in Cairo. They usually studied and performed religious and secular classical poetry such as *qasā'id* (s., *qasīdah*) and *muwashshahāt* (s., *muwashshah*) and sometimes popular, colloquial *mawāwīl* (s., *mawwāl*).[10] Familiarity with these texts was thought to be responsible for the *mashāyikh's* superior skill in composing settings for new texts and effectively performing old ones. Some of these singers were affiliated with Sufi organizations, especially the al-Laythi order in Cairo, renowned for the musicality of its rituals.[11] The *qasā'id* and *muwashshahāt* performed by the *mashāyikh* were musically more complicated than other genres in their repertoire, demanding a thorough command of the *maqāmāt*. Mastery of the repertory, in turn, provided the singer with well-developed skills in composition and improvisation. The repertory has served as pedagogical foundation for many singers' careers.[12] Collectively, the *mashāyikh* came to be regarded as important custodians of Egyptian Arabic culture:

> The *shaykh* who would read the *Qur'ān* with a beautiful voice was at the same time the professor of the science of the Arabic melodic modes, the poetic meters and the rhythmic modes of music. Thus the traditional school of musical training in Egypt was the school of the *mashayikh*.[13]

The careers of Darwish al-Hariri (1881–1957) and Ali Mahmud (1881–1946) are representative. Both lived and worked in the lower-middle-class quarters of Cairo. As children, both learned to read the *Qur'ān* and later entered the program of religious study at al-Azhar University. They pursued the customary courses in grammar, religion, the rules of Qur'anic recitation, and Islamic law and jurisprudence. Both supported themselves as *Qur'ān* readers. Al-Hariri went on to study principles of music with a composer of musical plays, Syrian Ahmad Khalil al-Qabbani al-Dimashqi, and then embarked on his greatest success, the composition of religious *muwashshahāt*. According to a contemporary source, "All of the modern singers know Darwish al-Hariri's music." He became the principal teacher of Zakariya Ahmad, one of Egypt's most popular composers of musical plays, films, and commercially recorded songs. Ali Mahmud continued as a *Qur'ān* reader and also became a famous singer of religious songs as well as amorous *qaṣā'id*, many of which he recorded and performed on the radio before his death in 1943.[14] The ranks of the musical *mashāyikh* included a few women as well, notably al-Hajjah al-Suwaysiyyah, Sakinah Hasan, and the young Umm Kulthum.

Musical theater in Egypt received its greatest impetus from one who had studied with the *mashāyikh*, al-Shaykh Salamah Hijazi. As a composer, singing star, and impresario in his own company, Hijazi was celebrated for his skillful integration of songs into the plots of plays and for his text-sensitive composition and delivery. Taking as its original models the plays written and staged in the Levant, musical theater became extremely popular among the middle and upper-middle classes in Egypt. Support for theater drew many Levantine actors, singers, and writers to Cairo.[15] Troupes toured annually, typically spending a month or more in the provincial cities of Egypt and several months in Baghdad, Mosul, the cities of the Levant, and, occasionally, North Africa. Many musicians claimed to have learned new musical techniques and styles during these tours abroad, which they also incorporated into their performances at home.[16] Urban musical life also included solo song performances in theaters and music halls. The singers, male and female, usually performed modern songs accompanied by a small ensemble of Arabic instruments including *ʿūd* (lute), *qānūn* (plucked zither), violin, and *riqq* (tambourine). The repertory varied with the competence and preference of the singer and the nature of the audience. Performances typically included popular songs from musical plays; light-hearted, strophic songs called *ṭaqāṭīq* (s., *ṭaqṭūqah*) which were often musically and textually simple; and the more demanding *qaṣā'id*. During the early 1920s, newspapers carried frequent criticism of the occasionally vapid *ṭaqāṭīq* and public outcry against some of the lyrics which were considered to be morally objectionable, such as "Lower the Curtains so the Neighbors Won't See," and "Who Among You Is My Father?"[17]

The life of Naʿimah al-Masriyah offers another illustration of a successful singing career. Born (ca. 1898) and raised in a lower-middle class neighborhood in Cairo, al-Masriyah turned to professional singing to support herself following a divorce. She began by performing at weddings with two neighborhood women. As her reputation spread, she moved on to Cairo's music halls, appearing nightly prior to the main singing star. She worked in clubs in the provincial cities of Egypt as well as in Cairo, and finally at prestigious establishments in the main theater district. By 1927, she had purchased her own casino, which she managed herself, appearing as the star singer and programming the other entertainment.[18]

Ever popular among the middle and lower classes were songs and dances referred to as "country," "rustic," or "folk." These included colloquial songs featuring elaborate plays on words and sometimes stinging social criticism (*mawwāl* and *zajal*), men's stick dance music, and other dance music played on drums and reed instruments. The dialects of the songs and the musical styles were particular to regions of the country and served to invoke memories of "home" for the thousands of immigrant city-dwellers in the neighborhoods of Cairo.

The Mass Media: Commercial Recordings

The recording industry enjoyed early success in Egypt.[19] In 1890, local newspapers carried advertisements for phonographs and recordings available to Egyptians via mail order from London. Recordings of Egyptian music were being made by 1904, and, in its 1913–1914 catalog the Odeon Company advertised over 450 locally recorded discs, including Qur'anic recitation.[20] By World War I, Gramophone, Pathé, Odeon, and as many as six smaller foreign companies were marketing recordings of Arabic music in Egypt. After the war Columbia, Polyphon, and others entered the Egyptian market. They recorded popular music in Cairo and manufactured the discs in European or American factories for export to Egypt and other Arab lands. In 1929, the number of foreign-made discs marketed in Egypt (most of which were of Arabic music) totaled over 725,000 records.[21]

Locally owned recording companies in the Middle East were rare. However, a Lebanese family established its own company, Baidaphon Records, in Beirut during the first decade of the twentieth century. By 1914, the company had expanded its enterprises to Egypt where it had released recordings of major Egyptian singers. This label enjoyed a long life, with Muhammad Abd al-Wahhab joining the company as an Egyptian partner during the 1930s. The Egyptian branch of Baidaphon became Cairophon Records in the 1940s, while Baidaphon continued its own operations in the Levant and North Africa.

In Egypt itself, a locally owned company was established by Armenian-Egyptian Setrak Mechian and remained in business from about 1910 until the 1940s. While the recording quality and the pecuniary rewards of his business failed to attract the most popular Egyptian stars, Mechian's company played a unique role:

> Because it was self-sufficient during the years of World War l, when recording engineers of foreign companies were no longer available in Cairo, Mechian's factory became a refuge for Egyptian recording artists. Many believe it salvaged and popularized music which might otherwise have been forgotten.[22]

The price of phonographs and records gradually dropped so that by about 1925 they were generally accessible to middle-class Egyptians. According to a popular magazine, "the phonograph spread among all classes of people after its price went down and it became possible for any family of medium means to acquire one along with with some records to fill the home with music."[23] More important, phonographs appeared in public places, such as coffee houses, and were shared throughout Egypt so that much of the population could hear and enjoy the new records. Singing star Umm Kulthum reported that, as a child in about 1910, in her small Delta village she listened to records at the home of the mayor, the wealthiest man in town, who had purchased a phonograph and regularly invited his neighbors to listen.[24] In the early twentieth-century Levant, mobile disk jockeys often carried phonographs throughout towns and villages playing records for a small fee.[25] Thus, the public phonograph existed throughout the Middle East in one way or another.

As a business, the recording industry was profit-oriented, generally conservative, and unlikely to take risks by recording unknown performers. However, in the early years in Egypt, most companies adopted the tactic of soliciting a wide variety of musics in the hopes of reaching the largest possible market.[26] Although usually foreign-owned, by the early 1920s the companies had hired Egyptian managers and artistic directors whose job it was to select and contract the most popular artists and to successfully market their discs. Record companies also kept accompanists and occasionally composers, lyricists, and singers on retainer to produce songs on demand. Other types of contracts specified a number of songs to be recorded for a single, one-time fee. The most popular artists could obtain royalties ranging between 3 and 10 percent of record sales. In order to gain greater control over the recording process and profits than was usually available from contracts, a few artists, including Muhammad Abd al-Wahhab and Abd al-Halim Hafiz, bought interests in recording firms or established their own companies. For popular artists who successfully negotiated recording contracts, the business was extremely lucrative—much more so than any other performing opportunity. The outstanding example is Umm Kulthum, although she was not the first singer to amass wealth through record sales.[27]

Thus, the recording industry became extremely attractive to musicians on the basis of its potentially high financial rewards and broad public exposure. It widened the gap between the famous stars and younger or not-so-famous performers. Commercial recording also had a palpable effect on musical styles and repertories. The six-minute time limit per recording restricted improvisation, which was essential to such genres as the *dawr* and the *qaṣīdah*. As demand for new records increased, recording companies promoted the *ṭaqṭūqah*, which could be quickly composed and learned, and easily tailored to the six-minute limit. Singers were required to record at any hour of the day, according to the schedule of the visiting recording engineer, in a studio with no audience. Some singers could not adapt to these circumstances at all and fell by the wayside.

The fortunes of the recording industry and its artists declined after the 1920s. The Great Depression adversely affected record sales in the Middle East, and, as the economy was slowly recovering, the establishment of a strong Egyptian National Radio station with eight hours of broadcasting daily and a commitment to music programming made it possible to hear songs, old and new, by requesting them from the station rather than buying the record. This practice dramatically altered the recording business. Annual retainers disappeared, and contracts became limited to a specific, named group of songs that had been popularized in films before being marketed as records. Material shortages during World War II marked the end of much recording activity in Egypt and the consequent demise of most companies. Cairophon was one of the few recording firms to survive the war. It was joined in the late 1940s by Misriphon, founded by the actor-singer Muhammad Fawzi. In 1964, Misriphon was taken over by the Egyptian government. Under a new name, Sawt al-Qahirah, this company continues to market new recordings and re-releases of tapes from the archives of Egyptian Radio, thus offering a wealth of inexpensive entertainment to its public.

In the 1970s, cassette tapes offered new life to the recording business in Cairo. Small companies proliferated, bringing new opportunities for aspiring young musicians and veterans alike. But Egyptian musicians have, of course, suffered from the attendant problems of poor sound quality and piracy.

Radio

The first small, Egyptian privately owned radio stations were established in the 1920s. The medium had little impact, however, until the Egyptian National Radio station opened in 1934. After a relatively inconspicuous beginning, almost completely overshadowed by the new musical films, radio became extremely popular throughout the Arab world, easily replacing the phonograph as the predominant medium of popular culture.

During the 1930s, Egyptian radio broadcast approximately eight hours daily. Programs included sequences of popular recordings, lasting 3 to 15 minutes, as well as daily live concerts by singing stars, in which 20 to 40 minutes were allotted per song. Established stars Umm Kulthum and Abd al-Wahhab were offered first choice in scheduling, and each performed once a week. Thus a considerable amount of time was available for other singers, and broadcasting featured a variety of performers throughout the 1930s and 1940s, ranging from film stars to folk singers and young newcomers. Egyptian radio became a principal patron of musicians.[28] With continued governmental support its facilities were expanded, especially during the 1950s.[29] Like musical theater and recording, it attracted musicians from other parts of the Arab world who believed their careers would advance through broadcasting.

Perhaps more than any other artist, Umm Kulthum (1904?–1975) made the broadcasting medium her own. The daughter of a *Qur'ān* reader from rural Egypt, she had performed with her father in the countryside for weddings and celebrations before moving to Cairo in 1922. She learned to read the *Qur'ān* as a child, absorbing the value of clear, correct text articulation which was essential to recitation. These skills were honed by her principal teachers in Cairo, who also taught her to shape musical phrases so as to enhance the meaning of the text. By 1928 she had surpassed the popularity of the city's theatrical and singing stars. In 1934, she was able to negotiate the best contract Egyptian radio offered to any star, and she consistently used her influence to improve the technical quality of her broadcasts. As early as 1937, she arranged for her performances to be broadcast live from the concert hall, thereby putting full-length song performances on the air. As a singing star and chairman of the board of selectors for radio, she used her considerable influence to persuade Egyptian radio to constantly upgrade its studios and broadcasting equipment. Her concerts on the first Thursday night of every month were legendary for having "brought life in the Arab world to a stop." Hundreds of people would fill a Cairo theater to attend such events, but thousands more routinely gathered with friends and family near the radio to listen to the concerts over the airwaves. "Umm Kulthum night" became an institutionalized media and social event.

After its first few years, Egyptian Radio settled into a pattern of music programming which has remained essentially the same to the present day—a feature favoring the stars who were able to entrench themselves in broadcasting during the 1930s and 1940s. Several musicians whose works were played on radio became members of the board of selectors for music. Subsequently, other aspiring performers complained that the board members, especially Umm Kulthum and Abd al-Wahhab, chose music according to personal interests.[30] Another complaint has been that undue emphasis is given to urban stars at the expense of such indigenous arts as the singing of epic poetry and *mawwāl*. A music programmer remarked in 1982 that many young singers no longer attempted to break into radio because the process of selection

Salsa superstar Ruben Blades (*Fran Vogel*)

Indefatigable *timbalero* and bandleader Tito Puente (*Fran Vogel*)

Merengue idol Wilfrido Vargas
(*Fran Vogel*)

Jamaican dub poet Mutabaruka
(*Donna Cline, Alligator Records*)

Steel band playing in Brooklyn's 1986 road march

Tex-Mex accordion virtuosos Santiago Jimenez and his son Flaco (right, with *bajo sexto*). Center: Juan Viesca (*Chris Strachwitz, Arhoolie Records*)

Juju's reigning monarch, King Sunny Ade (*Claudia Thompson*)

Fela Anikulapo Kuti (*Claudia Thompson*)

Nigerian *fuji* star Ayinde Barrister

Ghanaian highlife poet and composer
Ko Nimo (*Courtesy of Andrew Kaye*)

Afro-Brazil meets Afro-Cuba meets Africa: Brazilian Airto Moreira, Nigerian Baba Olatunji, and Cuban Patato Valdez (*Claudia Thompson*)

Record/cassette dubbing kiosk in Ghana; reggae, soul, and Indian film music dominate the merchandise. (*Courtesy of Andrew Kaye*)

Gypsy vocalist Lole Montoya performing *flamenco arabe*

Innovative flamenco singer Camarón de la Isla
(*PolyGram Iberica*)

Transnational cinema: Hindi film poster, with Hebrew translation,
in Israel

Singer-prostitutes performing film songs in Bombay's red-light and courtesan entertainment district

Logo on CBS cassette boxes in India

Disco comes to old China

Hawaiian guitarists at the beach (*Burl Burlingame*)

Gabby Pahinui in his later years (*Burl Burlingame*)

Genoa Keawe and a youthful hula dancer (*Burl Burlingame*)

was too time-consuming and difficult, and they preferred instead to perform at private functions and in night clubs, and to sell their own video and audio cassettes. Nevertheless, radio easily retained its popularity until the advent of the cassette tape player. Radios quickly replaced phonographs in public places and the appearance of the transistor greatly increased the number of listeners. In the 1960s, radio was considered the best way of reaching the Egyptian public, as the following description of a village indicates:

> Anyone visiting Kafr el-Elow for the first time is impressed by the large number of villagers listening to music and news on their transistor radios. Everywhere I went in the village—to the grocery store, to private homes, to the barber shop, to the vegetable peddler sitting in the street—I encountered a transistor radio operating at full volume. Many factory workers and field hands in the village carry transistor radios to work.[31]

By the sixties, "the mass media [had become] a part of the everyday life of all but a few of the citizens of Egypt."[32]

Film, Television, and Video

Beginning in 1932 with the release of a song film starring the Syrian singer Nadirah, it was the aim of virtually every aspiring commercial singer to star in a musical film. In addition to exposure, cinema offered great financial rewards. Many singers subsequently built careers mainly on films, as Umm Kulthum had done in radio. Among them were Druze composer, ⁽ūd virtuoso, and singer Farid al-Atrash, his sister Asmahan, and matinee idol Abd al-Halim Hafiz. Egyptian businessmen, led by nationalistic banker Talaᶜat Harb, were quick to invest in the new medium. Locally-owned Egyptian companies established in the 1920s and 1930s soon produced their own song films.

The arrangement of songs in films, as in musical plays, tended to further alter older conceptions of proper performance. Songs tended to be short, cast in a variety of *maqāmāt*, accompanied by large orchestras modeled on those of the Hollywood studios, and sung once through with little or no improvisation. Background music was often borrowed from Western sources ranging from nineteenth-century symphonic works to recently popular Western dance tunes. Although this varied collection of styles drew negative comment from critics, it persisted for years.

A substantial change in popular music brought about in films was the growth of the accompanying ensemble. New instruments were added and the numbers of instruments, particularly violins, increased to form ensembles of twenty to thirty pieces, rather than five or fewer. Choral singing was also included in the films. Large ensembles, vocal and instrumental, were then adopted by composers for songs outside the realm of films, affecting the color and occasionally the structure of the resulting compositions.

Egyptian song films were in many respects an outgrowth of musical theater. As cinema came to overshadow the stage, many theatrical stars moved directly into film. Such was not the case in Lebanon, however, where the productions of the Rahbani Brothers, starring a clique of accomplished and popular singers led by Fayrouz, moved both musical theater and film into contemporary settings. Linking plots and music to current issues, notably the plight of the Palestinians, the Rahbanis drew upon Arabic legends and heroes for characters and stories. Songs ranged from virtuosic solos to simpler strophic pieces learned by thousands of audience members.

Television, established in 1960, became increasingly popular, but did not rival radio in widespread usage until the 1980s. Television broadcasts included live concerts by Umm Kulthum and other stars and variety shows featuring instrumental and vocal performances. The medium has become a prestigious source of patronage and exposure for popular musicians. Older song films and video tapes of concert performances are regularly aired on television. Productions made for television have been aided by the governments of Kuwait and other Gulf States which, before they had developed their own production studios and technical personnel, commissioned works from Egyptian television. Recently, television serials—evening programs in ten or more parts—have featured musicians in starring roles, often portraying aspiring musicians. Stars such as ᶜUmar Fathi and ᶜAli al-Hajjar have appeared in these night-time dramas, for which they have also composed and performed theme songs, marketed separately on audio cassettes.

Characteristics of Popular Music

It is difficult to generalize about a repertory as large as that of Arabic popular music, but one can identify a few trends which have an important place. One of these is the growing role of instrumentalists and instrumental music. In the early twentieth century, a substantial quantity of vocal music, notably that of the *mashāyikh*, was sung with no instrumental accompaniment at all. Except in musical theater, instrumental ensembles were typically small, consisting of one to five players accompanying a singer and performing improvisations and precomposed pieces, usually of Turkish origin. During the 1920s, composers saw the adoption of new instruments and new combinations of instruments, frequently from Europe or the United States, as an important means of innovation and modernization. While virtually every composer in Egypt experimented with new instruments, Muhammad Abd al-Wahhab probably provided the greatest inspiration to the composition of instrumental music, beginning with his addition of the cello, string bass, accordion, clarinet, and castanets in song accompaniments during the 1920s and 1930s. The new sounds had great appeal. In fact, even the *mashāyikh* adopted their own accompanying ensembles.

Owing to the widespread popularity of the large orchestras in films, almost every commercial singer enlarged his accompanimental ensemble during the 1930s to include several violins, a string bass, cello, and, often, a variety of percussion instruments, electric guitars and keyboards, saxophones, and instruments for special effects such as the Hawaiian guitar. The traditional Arabic instruments which remained in these ensembles were rarely audible. However, they did not disappear from the scene. In his many films, Farid al-Atrash played ʿud taqāsīm which did much to reinforce the place of that instrument in the modern Arab world. *Nay* virtuoso Mahmud ʿIffat recorded a number of successful cassette tapes featuring himself as a soloist accompanied by a quartet or quintet of various other Arabic and Western instruments. Composers Zakariya Ahmad and Sayyid Makawi used Arabic folk instruments such as the double-reed *urghul* (not usually a part of song accompaniments) for special effects and to add the flavor of folk music to particular songs. Recently the young Muhammad Munir has used combinations of percussion instruments to give his compositions a Nubian flavor.

Instrumental introductions and interludes have assumed greater dimensions in songs. Whereas previously, a short, well-known piece composed in the appropriate *maqām* would serve to introduce a song, beginning in the 1920s newly composed introductions appeared, consisting in part of musical phrases from the song itself. In compositions of the 1960s, these introductions might last as long as twenty minutes. Muhammad Abd al-Wahhab, among others, composed a number of independent instrumental pieces which attained great popularity. They are frequently performed by ensembles such as that of Mahmud ʿIffat or, when possible, used as pedagogical pieces for students.

Musical modernization in the Arab world has consistently involved the borrowing of musical styles and features from a variety of sources. Turkish music inspired stylistic innovation in the nineteenth century. As public attention turned to Europe and the United States, Western musical styles of all sorts were adopted by Arab composers. As a result, triadic passages have appeared in melodic lines, where previously such lines tended to move in a stepwise fashion. Triadic bass lines and harmonizations have emerged alongside the older heterophonic accompanimental style. Rhythmic innovations captured the fancy of many composers. Zakariya Ahmad renovated the popular *taqtūqah* using triple meter, common to Turkish and Arabic instrumental pieces but new to the strophic song. Latin American dance rhythms appeared frequently in instrumental passages for songs and in film music.

The large ensemble with its new and varied instrumentation occasionally overwhelmed the solo singer. Previously, small groups of instrumentalists would merely provide heterophonic accompaniment embellished with melodic ornaments which did not interrupt or obscure the singer's rendition. Often, the accompanists lagged slightly behind the singer, allowing him to set and alter the tempo or to repeat a phrase that was particularly well received by the audience. The new larger ensembles, however, were often led by one of the instrumentalists or by a conductor, who established a tempo which the singer followed. The new compositions, with multiple instrumental lines, often did not lend themselves well to extemporaneous repetitions or variations. The frequent criticism generated by this innovation suggests that a particular balance of vocal and accompanimental lines may be an essential property of Arabic music.

At the same time, musicians borrowed from indigenous styles, searching for little-used *maqāmāt* or interpolating folk dance rhythms from Upper Egypt in modern songs. Audiences came to expect successful integration of new materials into a recognizably Arabic framework. Negative criticism followed a new piece if it was perceived as a *mélange* of unrelated styles or as being simply a copy of a foreign model.

Tone color has played an important role in popular Arabic music, as the ready acceptance of new instruments may indicate, and timbre in vocal lines is equally appreciated. Perhaps most noticeable to the Western ear is the apparent nasality of Arabic singing. Not all singers utilize nasal resonance, but it is essential to certain styles. The rules of Qur'anic recitation mandate nasalization of consonants in specified contexts. Nasal resonance has become associated with Muslim religious repertories and more loosely with the *mashāyikh* and the communal celebrations in which they performed. Nasality may be used to invoke traditionalism or religiosity in the rendition of a song. It is also common to the rendition of the *mawwāl*. In the view of some critics, undifferentiated nasality marks a singer as old fashioned or countrified in a negative way. A singer who would prefer to be viewed as modern might avoid this color. On the other hand, populist performers who assert links with the middle and lower classes of Egypt, such as Sayyid Makawi, may deliberately nasalize large portions of their renditions to underline this relationship. Generally, an Egyptian singer would use "full voice" throughout his entire range, introducing head resonance or falsetto as a color with which to ornament a high-pitched passage. Similarly, *baḥḥah*, a quality of hoarseness, is considered to be expressive when deftly incorporated into a melodic line, usually in the upper ranges. In a man's voice, huskiness may be appreciated as lending character to a voice, although it is not considered to be a beautiful quality per se.

In much of Arabic music, the sound of the language itself is important. The distinctive, emphatic Arabic consonants may break an otherwise sustained melodic line in much the same manner as German consonant clusters do in a rendition of classical *lieder*. Pitches may be sustained or melismas sung on the consonants m, n, or the liquid l. Clear articulation of a text is highly valued, and command of the necessary skills is usually attributed to training in the recitation of the *Qur'ān*.

Of course, musical nuances such as tone colors, as well as tunings and intonations, differ from place to place in the Arab world. The fluid, open-throated singing of the Lebanese Fayrouz differs markedly from most Egyptian singers, although Egyptian audiences have come to appreciate this style, and the young Egyptian Afaf Radi has successfully adopted it. Most competent vocalists are adept at choosing qualities to fit a song or context of performance in order to present themselves as traditional, modern, countrified, or international, or to appeal to a specific audience.

A Syncretic Genre: The *Ughnīyah*

As composers experimented with rhythmic, melodic, and harmonic innovations, they also developed new formats for their pieces. The "monologue," created in the 1920s, was one such genre. Designed for musical plays, it was a through-composed solo song, intended as a virtuosic, emotive expression for a leading character. Monologues were soon written independently of musical plays. They offered to the composer a high degree of flexibility, and to the singer a chance for expressive and virtuosic display.

The life span of the monologue was less than twenty years. A more resilient song type was the *ughnīyah*, or simply "song." Although the *ughnīyah* (pl. *aghānī*) frequently included some sort of internal repetition, its shape depended upon the design of the composer. Most frequently the texts were love songs in colloquial Arabic. Musically, they were cast in the style of the composer's choice.

The following exerpts from three *aghānī*, all performed by Umm Kulthum, and all very popular in Egypt, might suggest the range of popular song styles and their musical sources, and illustrate a number of their salient characteristics:[33]

A. "Sahrān li-Wahdī" ("Alone at Night")

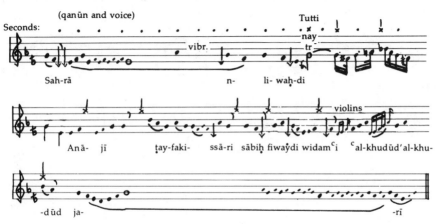

B. "Amāl Hayātī" ("Hope of My Life")

1.

2.

(Strings, qānūn, and voice)

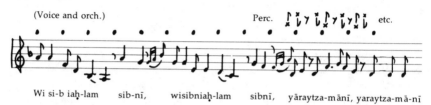

A-malhayā-ti   ya hub-bi   ghā-li   mā-yin-ti-hish

3.

(Voice and orch.)

Wi si-b iah-lam   sib-nī,   wisibniah-lam   sibnī,   yāraytza-mānī, yaraytza-mā-nī

4.

C. "al-Awwilah fīl-Gharām" ("The First Thing in Love")

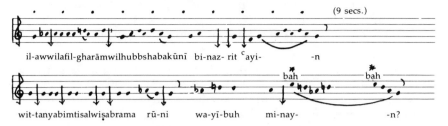

il-awwilafil-gharāmwilhubbshabakūnī bi-naz- rit ʿayi-   -n

wit-tanyabimtisalwiṣabrama   rū-ni   wa-yī-buh   mi-nay-   -n?

The *ughnīyah* of Riyad al-Sunbati, "Sahrān li-Waḥdī" (Example A), closely follows classical models of Arabic composition; it begins in the lower ranges of the mode *Huzām*, gradually ascends, modulates to various other modes, returns to the initial mode, and descends to close. The overall shape of the piece is that of an arch. The accompanying ensemble, consisting of about eight violins, two cellos, a string bass, an *ʿūd*, a *nay*, a *qānūn*, and a *riqq*, plays a composed introduction of about three minutes in length, and accompanies the singer heterophonically, with an occasional *nay* obligato or independent bass line. The singer controls the tempo of the piece. Much time is given to varied repetitions of the more poignant phrases, especially when the audience response is enthusiastic.

The accompanying ensemble for "Amāl Ḥayātī" (Example B) by Muhammad Abd al-Wahhab is much larger, featuring well over thirty members playing acoustic and electronic instruments. The introduction lasts twenty minutes and features solos such as that notated in Example B, 1. The introduction and instrumental interludes draw upon American fiddle-tune style (Example B, 4) and jazz (Example B, 1). The voice enters (Example B, 2) in the manner of a traditional Arabic song, in the lower register of *maqām Kurd*, with sparse accompaniment. However, only a few phrases later (Example 16-B, 3) the vocal line has already moved into the upper register and includes a passage descending by leaps, uncommon in traditional music. Instrumental accompaniment remains heavy throughout most of the piece, and reiterations of single phrases *ex tempore* are few.

"al-Awwilah fīl-Gharām" (Example C) by Zakariya Ahmad is markedly different. Taking its inspiration from Egyptian folk music, it closely resembles a *mawwāl* in text and music. Bayram al-Tunsi, the lyricist, uses the formulaic "al-awwilah" ("first"), "al-tānyā" ("second"), and "al-talta" ("third") to introduce phrases which are then augmented in successive appearances:

First, passion and love entangled me
Second, they commanded me to be compliant and patient.
Third, they went and left me without warning . . .

First, passion and love entangled me with the glance of an eye
Second, they commanded me to be compliant and patient, and how am I
    supposed to do that?
And third, they went and left me without warning, oh tell me where?

The melody is relatively simple. Phrases are short, syllabic, narrow in range and free of intricate flourishes, wide leaps, and difficult modulations. The artistry lies in the initial clear delivery of the text and the subsequent variation of its melody in accordance with the meaning of the text. Instrumental accompaniment is kept to a minimum (about eight players), leaving the emphasis upon the text and the vocalist's rendition, in the traditional manner of a *mawwāl*.

These examples, composed and performed by some of the most accomplished musicians in the Middle East, are perhaps more sophisticated than the average popular song. However, they exhibit the type of borrowing, combining, and integrating of new and old, and foreign and indigenous musical sources which mark the work of many successful Arab popular musicians.

Issues Bearing on Popular Music

Cultural expression in twentieth-century Egypt falls into the context of the society's concern for modernization and its resistance to foreign domination. On the one hand, musicians and critics have been attracted to the cultural and technological resources of the West. Some Egyptians genuinely enjoy Western genres of opera, symphony, and popular music. A few have suggested abandonment of Arabic music with its microtones and heterophonic texture in favor of Western harmony and equal temperament. Most critics, however, including those who enjoy Western music, urge the modernization of Arabic music along culturally authentic lines, proceeding from indigenous models and using Arabic compositional principles. According to Umm Kulthum:

> We must respect ourselves and our art. The Indians have set a good
> example for us—they show great respect for themselves and their arts.
> Wherever they are, they wear their native dress and their music is known
> throughout the world. This is the right way.[34]

Opinions have differed concerning exactly what constitutes authentically Egyptian Arabic art, and, of course, there are also those who prefer Arabic rock music or jazz to modern music based on any sort of neo-classical Arab model. However, the overwhelming support for musicians and other entertainers considered to be authentically Arab, such as Umm Kulthum, composers Riyad al-Sunbati, Zakariya Ahmad, and Sayyid Darwish, comedian Najib al-Rihani, poets Bayram al-Tunsi and Badi^c Khayri, and the approbation of recent critics for the musical *mashāyikh* strongly suggest that cultural authenticity in musical expression is a matter of importance to Egyptians.

Historically, popular colloquial Arabic song has been a vehicle for social commentary, whether of one's enemy or of faults in one's social group or political leadership, or complaint of one's condition. This type of song persists in the Arab world, although not at the forefront of musical life. Algeria, for instance, has a long history of protest songs aimed at the French colonial government. Songs in support of nationalistic leadership were noted as early as 1830 and seem to have consistently served as vehicles for the expression of protest until the withdrawal of the French.[35] Songs critical of society or the government have not been encouraged where the state has controlled the media for dissemination of popular songs.

In Egypt, socio-political commentary has occasionally appeared in the context of *zajal*, as in the lyrics of Bayram al-Tunsi. Criticism of political leadership still appears in the poetry of a few local singers.[36] In the national arena, the outspoken texts of Ahmad Fu'ad Najm sung by al-Shaykh Imam during the 1970s and 1980s addressed to Egyptian and Western political leaders resulted in jail sentences for both. Egyptians continue to enjoy clever, barbed commentary. In some cases, though, the protest song has been perceived as belonging to the culture of the intellectual elite and is in that sense even further removed from grassroots culture than is commercially marketed music.

Music in Other Arab Countries

International mainstream Arab popular music has been produced as well as enjoyed in virtually all Arab countries. From Morocco to Iraq, radio and television broadcast music in this "central domain" lingua franca style, whether performed by local or foreign artists. Nevertheless, insofar as regional folk musics and socio-cultural backgrounds can indeed color the "central domain" styles, distinctive regional characteristic styles have emerged. This, of course, is hardly surprising in so large a geographical region, which includes seventeen independent states and over one hundred million people. The desire for modern music in local Arabic dialects has given further impetus to regional differentiation of musical styles. The Saudi singer, Muhammad Abduh, stressed his desire to perform the colloquial poetry of his native dialect. Umm Kulthum and Fayrouz have also performed in local dialects to great popular acclaim.[37]

Modern Western instrumental styles, especially rock music, have penetrated most Arab lands through commercial recordings, films, and concert tours. Local musicians have learned these styles, sometimes singing popular Western tunes in their original languages. They have also generated their own syncretic popular styles which appear on the surface to be highly Westernized but which also manifest important

indigenous musical and textual features.³⁸ Before the chaos and violence
ensuing from the 1970s, Beirut had rivaled, if not surpassed Cairo as the
cosmopolitan center of modern Arab culture, including music. Nevertheless, much popular music in Lebanon has been shaped by cultural
and historical conditions distinct to that country. The general trends that
influenced musical life in Beirut, as described by Jihad Racy, were not
markedly different from those in Cairo, but they did produce distinctive
musical sounds. The population of Beirut, like that of Cairo, included
influential families proud of their region's cultural heritage, as well as
more Eurocentric elements, who found local cultural expression
"unscientific" and unsuited to the technologically-oriented world.

> The city of Beirut in particular had absorbed a substantial number of
> people whose ethnic and social roots went back to various Lebanese vil-
> lages, especially those in the mountainous regions of central and northern
> Lebanon. Politically and socially influential, this segment provided fertile
> ground for the rise of a new artistic tradition—music, dance, poetry, fash-
> ions, handicrafts—whose context was unmistakably urban but whose
> inspiration was folk and rural.
> Beirut was also experiencing the growing impact of modernization and
> Westernization . . . Beirut was becoming a highly cosmopolitan communi-
> ty. A significant number of the city residents had non-village and even non-
> Lebanese and non-Arab backgrounds. These developments and the exten-
> sive role of the modern entertainment media—radio, television, concert
> halls, public theatre—were conducive to the rise of an urban mass audi-
> ence. They were also prerequisites for the development of the kind of
> modern musical language of wide appeal that is superbly manifested in
> Fayrouz' songs.³⁹

Since the late 1950s, Fayrouz has ranked with Umm Kulthum as a
favored singer of modern Arabic music. In collaboration with lyricist
Mansour Rahbani and his brother, composer-arranger Assi Rahbani, she
performed stylized harmonizations of Lebanese folk songs. Her texts,
usually colloquial Arabic despite the tendency of many urban Lebanese
singers to perform in French, dealt with matters of interest and concern
to the indigenous population and frequently expressed support for the
Palestinian cause. Fayrouz also performed classical *muwashshaḥāt* and
pieces by Egyptian composer Sayyid Darwish, widely considered to be
indigenously Arab in style. Many of her songs in the sixties were originally performed in musical plays and films which combined Lebanese
traditions such as the *dabkah* line dance with orchestral suites of European, Russian, or Arab inspiration. Her music thus incorporates various
Western, Russian, and even Balkan elements, making extensive use, for
example, of European instrumentation, harmony, polyphonic melodies,
and major and minor tonalities. At the same time, her songs remain
rooted, however idiosyncratically, in indigenous styles. Fayrouz, like
Umm Kulthum (whose musical style is very different), has become "an
emblem of modernity and an exemplar of the self-respecting, dignified

Arab artist."[40] New musical plays, especially those featuring Fayrouz, the Rahbani brothers, Nasri Shamseddine, and Wadi^c al-Safi, were well supported by the Lebanese government and formed a prominent part of the annual Baalbak Music Festival. This festival also sponsored reinterpretations of folkloric music and dance along the lines of Soviet national ensembles. These styles formed the basis for a new Lebanese music idiom which subsequently became popular throughout the Arab world.[41]

Fayrouz's renditions of *muwashshahāt* and Umm Kulthum's renditions of *qasā'id* exemplify the neo-classicism which has constituted a trend in popular Arabic music throughout the twentieth century, in which complicated poetic texts have been set by modern composers, and classical melodies have been arranged by the Rahbanis and others. These pieces, although constituting only a small percentage of popular music, have become quite popular and have been marketed on commercial recordings and broadcasts along with film songs, folk songs, and indigenous jazz. Syrian Sabah Fakhri, for instance, regularly performs ^c *ūd taqāsīm* and *muwashshahāt* along with harmonized folksongs at large concerts and on recordings.

Until recently, the production capacity for commercial recordings in Beirut certainly equalled that of Cairo, although the development of Egypt's broadcasting facilities has been greater. These two centers supplied most of the Arabic recordings, and their broadcasts permeated the Arab world, especially after the invention of the transistor.[42] One result has been that less is known about popular music of Iraq and the Arabian peninsula. Muhammad Hussein Mar'i and Mai'da Nez'hat have recorded and performed locally in Iraq to great success. Several performers of mainstream modern music from Saudi Arabia and the Gulf states, among whom the best-known may be Muhammad Abduh, have gained wide audiences by means of Egyptian mass media.

Indigenous popular musics of the Arabian peninsula exhibit complex rhythms not usually present in Arabic music. According to Poul Røvsing Olsen, these were learned from the musics of peoples with whom local populations have historically been in contact: Indians, Persians, and especially Indonesians and Africans.[43]

In recent years the national governments in the Arabian peninsula have greatly expanded their capacities for broadcasting, but these countries have been relatively slow to develop their own networks and have devoted most of their efforts to television rather than radio. Urban television broadcasting was established by 1965 and expanded to serve most of the peninsula by 1975, broadcasting about seven hours daily. In Saudi Arabia and the Yemen Arab Republic, by the late seventies over 50 percent of television programming was locally produced.[44] Whereas during the sixties the Kuwaiti government commissioned Egyptian artists and production staff to film special variety television programs for its own national holidays, it is now increasingly able to produce these programs itself, featuring locally popular as well as international artists.

Mass media and the recording industry developed earlier in North Africa. By 1910, Gramophone had made over 400 records in Algeria and Tunisia. By 1912, Pathé offered several hundred recordings of North African artists advertised in special catalogues for Morocco, Algeria, and Tunisia. By 1930, French exports to Algeria, including French and international music, reached about 500,000 records.[45] Radio Algiers began its locally broadcast Arabic program as early as 1929; by 1976 four television channels had been established by the Algerian government and most programs were locally produced.[46]

In 1971, a new and uniquely Moroccan syncretic popular style arose. The trend was initiated by urban educated youth who sought to modernize traditional regional styles in a way which would reflect the new social identity of urban Moroccans—an identity which was national rather than regional, and modern while retaining ties to traditional culture.[47] The groups Nass el-Ghiwane and Jil Jilala were the first and most influential exponents of the new style. They and their imitators self-consciously blended Western and regional traditional elements. Song texts, melodies, drum patterns, and instruments (such as the *gnibri* lute and *bendir* frame drum) were freely adapted from urban secular musics, rural communal dance styles, and, above all, musics associated with the religious brotherhoods like the Aissawa and the Gnawa. These fraternities, which have historically played essential cohesive roles in Moroccan society, were an important source of inspiration for the new syncretic bands. The groups often combined elements and instruments from disparate sources in a mosaic that would suggest a national rather than strictly regional orientation.

The Moroccan features were also blended with other features of Western derivation. The latter were by this time not unfamiliar to urban Moroccans, as tourists and visits by rock groups like the Rolling Stones had made considerable impact on Moroccan youth. Stage attire and presentation, album cover art, chordal harmony, and the use of instruments like the guitar, *bouzouki*, and banjo all reflected Western influence. This folk-pop revival has since become a significant cultural phenomenon, promoted by a large number of eclectic performing groups. These play at various functions, including traditional contexts like weddings, and further disseminate their music on inexpensive cassettes. Despite the considerable diversity of the various eclectic groups, all of them "convey the message that it is possible to be modern and maintain traditions at the same time."[48]

Throughout the Arab world one notes the tendency of Arab peoples to assimilate new musical styles from neighboring peoples or from exposure to the musics of distant peoples through the mass media.[49] At the same time, communities strive to maintain their own authentic musical identity and place high value on what they believe to be indigenously theirs: the emergent repertoires which are at once eclectic and distinctively Arabic.

CHAPTER 6

The Non-Arab Middle East

Turkey

Turkey's musical heritage—one of the richest of the non-Western world—is remarkable for its diversity and for the influence it has exerted on the cultures of its neighbors. The legacy of extended Ottoman rule is clear in the urban musics of Greece, Yugoslavia, and other Balkan countries, as in the art music of the Arab world, which developed hand-in-hand with Turkish classical music during the several centuries of Turkish rule. At present, Turkish popular music, although little known in the West, finds substantial audiences in Greece, Israel, and elsewhere, and flourishes with great vitality in West Germany as well as Turkey.

The evolution of Turkish popular music, although intimately related to modern phenomena like urbanization and the mass media, should be considered in a larger historical perspective encompassing the important changes in Turkish urban musical life during the nineteenth and twentieth centuries.[1] As of the late eighteenth century, the most important forms of urban secular music were art music, musics associated with professional dancing boys, and various types of entertainment musics provided by the court for the public on festival days. Secular art music, patronized by the court and the aristocracy, ranged from pure classical forms like vocal *fasil* and instrumental *semaî* and *peşrev* to light-classical *şarkı* songs. Entertainment musicians were organized in guilds, many of which were subsidiary to or, in the case of the *mehter* military bands, incorporated in the Janissary (*yeni çeri*) corps. The Janissaries were perhaps best known as the once elite fighting corps which had degenerated into an unruly and archaic nuisance ("a menace to all but the enemy"); they also, however, comprised large numbers of professional musicians who were influential in urban secular as well as Bektashi Sufi music in Istanbul and other cities.

In the first half of the nineteenth century, urban secular musical life was dramatically disrupted. According to Walter Feldman, by 1840 the musicians guilds appear to have degenerated (perhaps due partly to the increasing bankruptcy of the court) and the dancing boys had been

161

officially outlawed. More importantly, in 1826 the reformist Sultan Mahmud II massacred most of the Janissaries and scattered the remainder, abruptly terminating, in the process, their role in urban musical activities. While Mahmud and his successor, Abdul Aziz, retained some interest in Turkish music, they nevertheless imported European bandmasters to replace the Janissaries for court and military musical functions. Court patronage of Turkish music further declined during the rule of Abdul Hamid II (1876–1909).

The breakdown of urban music patronage led to several related developments in the latter half of the nineteenth century. Much music patronage shifted to the increasingly affluent non-Muslim merchant class, including Greeks, Armenians, and Jews, who established nightclubs and casinos offering live music in the Pera section of Istanbul and elsewhere. Particularly popular in such venues, according to Feldman, were the light classical *şarkı*, imported forms like the *sirto* and *longa*, and, above all, improvised gypsy dance musics like the instrumental *çifte telli* and *karsilama*, and the vocal *çifte telli gazeli*. *Çifte telli* and *karsilama* are lively dance-oriented genres—also referred to in Turkey as *koçekçe* ("dancing boy music")—which have been mentioned above for their role in Greek *rebetika*. *Şarkı* is a metered, pre-composed vocal song, with instrumental accompaniment, solidly grounded in *makam* (mode); *sirto* is a dance and music form derived from Greek island folk music, with a lively 3+3+2 meter; the *longa* is an urban genre adopted from Rumanian gypsy music related to, although distinct from Turkish urban music in style and modal repertoire. With the advent of recording technology in the early twentieth century, the nightclub-oriented *şarkı, sirto, longa,* and gypsy musics came to be widely recorded on 78s, both for domestic consumption and for expatriate Anatolian Armenian, Jewish, and Greek communities. While the popularity of these musics has declined somewhat in recent decades, they continue to form an important component of the urban music scene. A related development was the rise of gypsy musicians, who emerged to fill some of the vacuum left by the extermination of the Janissaries. Since this period, gypsies have constituted a substantial and much-appreciated portion of urban musicians.

In Turkey, as in the Arab world, while "art," "folk," and "popular" musics can often be clearly distinguished, much modern urban music may incorporate aspects of two or more of such categories and hence resists such neat categorization. Consequently, it may be more fruitful to employ the approach used by Racy in regard to Arab urban music, that is, to conceptualize Turkish urban music in terms of a mainstream "central domain," whose elements may derive from or reflect affinities with various other musics, specifically, art music, rural folk music, gypsy urban styles, Arab pop, and Western rock.

Turkish classical music, like its Arab counterpart, enjoys a rather limited popularity—especially in comparison, for example, to India. Public concerts are irregular, and the state extends only a moderate amount of support; in general, art music continues to suffer from its association with the decadent Ottoman court and with the Sufi (especially Mevlevi and Bektashi) orders, whose role in civil society is circumscribed by a government commited to a rigid and principled separation of church and state.

Perhaps as a result of the attenuation of pure classical music, features of art music continue to play an important role in mainstream popular music—again, in contrast to India, where classical and film music have little in common. Semi-classical sources constituted an important component of early Turkish popular music, as is demonstrated by singers such as Müzeyyen Senar, who popularized middlebrow versions of *şarkı* and other urban traditional genres for predominantly bourgeois listeners. Recordings of Senar and her followers (such as Zeki Muren and Muazzez Abaci) continue to sell, although mainstream Turkish popular music has changed considerably in the last fifty years. Aside from such dated styles, classical influence remains evident in the extent to which much popular music remains based, whether loosely or strictly, on *makam;* moreover, it is not at all unusual for a pop cassette as well as a nightclub performance to include a *taksim*—a classical-type instrumental improvisation in free-rhythmic style, based on one or more *makam.* The Indian counterpart—*ālāp*—would seldom be heard in mainstream pop music, which avoids improvisation. Thus, while most Turkish pop singers may have only a limited understanding of theory, a knowledge of *makam* is a prerequisite for most professional melodic instrumentalists.

Despite the continued classical influence in Turkish urban music, the major trend in mainstream Turkish popular music since mid-century has been an increasing orientation toward rural folk music. The reason for this, not surprisingly, is the unprecedented flood of rural migrants to Turkish cities since 1950, effectively "ruralizing" urban society as never before. This migration, which has accompanied the processes of industrialization, population growth, and land alienation, has altered the culture and demography as well as the size of Turkish cities—especially, of course, Istanbul, whose population has grown from less than one million in 1950 to nearly seven million at present. As a result, mainstream Turkish popular music now draws primarily from the country's rich heritage of rural folk music, reinterpreting this heritage in a manner reflecting the new social character of Anatolian cities.

While the diverse regional varieties of Turkish folk music are too numerous to be reviewed here, a few general features may be noted. Additive meters are common in some areas. Modal monophony predominates, although polyphony is essential to some regional traditions, such as the *kemençe* (fiddle) music of the Black Sea coast. Neutral intervals are common; the *Huseni*-type mode, with its characteristic flatted third and half-flat second degree, is particularly common. Melodies frequently take the form of descending sequences, wherein a phrase will be

rendered, perhaps with some variation, at three successively lower levels. Vocal style in some genres is marked by the use of a yodeling-like
ornamentation resembling the Persian *tahrir*.

Many Turkish folk music genres, such as the free-metered *uzun
hava*, do not lend themselves well to incorporation into pop format.
Most prominent among those that do admit modernization are the *türkü*
category of songs. The term *türkü*, in a general sense, denotes any Turkish rural folk music but is used more specifically to describe a set of
strophic, traditional, secular songs, with text lines set to particular numbers of syllables (that is, as opposed to genres like *şarkı* based on *uruz*,
the quantitative, Arabic-derived system of metrical prosody). The generally romantic *türkü* texts are serious in nature and are valued for their
poetic merit. A variety of meters may be used in *türkü*, but simple meters
of four or eight beats are especially common. Many "central domain"
songs (by singers like Belkis Akkale and Nurhan Savas) are simply traditional *türkü* pieces, wherein the traditional instrumentation (such as *saz*
and *ney*) may be supplemented by Western instruments; frequently the
saz is electronically amplified and played through a phase-shifter, which
modulates its timbre. Other central domain songs may consist of newly
composed pieces in *türkü* style.[2]

The example below is a traditional *türkü* song, modernized for dissemination on commercial cassette by the electronically altered *saz*; the
modal, sequentially descending melody, the neutral second degree, the
verse form (11+5 syllables in each line), and the melismatic vocal ornamentation are typical of the genre. Not shown in this transcription are
the accompanying drum part and the *ney* and *saz* duplication of the vocal
melody.[3]

BIR GÜ-ZE-LIN HASCE TIN-DEN A-HIN-DEN
TU HERYA-NIMYAN HAYAN-DI
OL-DUM O-NUNMAH CE-ME-LI- NE

CA-NAN A-HIN- DEN   TU-TUŞ- AS-KIN-DEN HER-YE-   NIM-   DE
YAN-DI   HA YAN-DI   AŞIK   ÜÇ YÖZ ALT-MIŞ BES GÜ-NÜM DE
MAH CE- ME-LI- NE

YAN-DI HA YAN-DI   YAN-DI HA   YAN

DI   YAN-DI HA   YAN-   DI

A distinguishing feature of modern Turkish popular music is that it may combine, in a single song, folk instruments and styles which would never be heard together in traditional contexts. Thus, for example, instrumental interludes to a pop song may feature a *zurna* (oboe)—used for outdoor festivities like weddings—in alternation with a *saz*, a *ney*, and a *duduk* (indigenous single-reed aerophone).

Regardless of the ambivalence many Turks may feel for gypsies in general, Turks hold gypsy musicians in great esteem. Aside from performing in various Turkish music genres, gypsies specialize in a number of genres in their own musical domain. These include, on an informal level, groups of from two to seven instrumentalists, playing clarinet, violin, *djumbus*, *ud*, and *dombak*, who perform for tips at urban cafes (for example, in Istanbul's Cicek Paisaje).[4] Other groups, which may also incorporate *kanun*, *ney*, and other instruments, play at nightclubs and private parties. The repertoire of such groups may include regional folk dances, urban popular songs, and an occasional classical *semaî*. Gypsy violinists, *kanun* players, and clarinetists (such as Mustafa Kandirali) are especially renowned for their expressive *taksim;* gypsy clarinet playing, which is particularly enjoyed, is remarkable for having attained such sophistication in the short period since World War I when the instrument was adopted in Turkey and Greece. A third, not unrelated category of gypsy urban music is that which accompanies dancing-girls in the Sulukuleh gypsy entertainment district of Istanbul; unlike the other musics mentioned, these are primarily vocal songs with instrumental accompaniment.

In themselves, these gypsy styles are better regarded as urban folk rather than popular musics. However, they exert a strong influence on mainstream popular music. Many of the instrumentalists in popular music recordings and concerts are gypsies, who play in their own distinctive style. Moreover, pop musicians may consciously imitate gypsy musics in choice of text and melody. The following example—a mid-1980s hit of Cengiz Coşkuner—recalls gypsy dancing-girl music in its catchy melody and its light, colloquial text. It also demonstrates the syncretism of much Turkish popular music, in its combination of, on the one hand, gypsy *karsilama* meter, modal melody, and ornamented vocal style, with, on the other hand, chordal (although distinctly non-Western) harmony, and instrumentation which, aside from the electric bass pattern shown here, includes synthesizer and electric guitar—the latter played through the obligatory phase-shifter.[5]

A fourth influence on Turkish modern music is Arab popular music. The evolutions of Arab and Turkish art musics were closely linked throughout the Ottoman period, and it is not surprising that despite the language barrier, their popular musics now exert considerable mutual influence. Arab-influenced Turkish pop, which has come into vogue since the early seventies, is referred to as "Arabesk." Arabesk, like Arab pop, often employs the simple quadratic meter (Arab *baladi*) which would be rendered on the dombak as *dum dum - tek dum - tek -*; certain less tangible melodic similarities with Arab pop music can also be observed. Arabesk is regarded as lighter in character than much Turkish mainstream music; musicians tend to speak of it with condescension, and the state-run radio and television shun it. The public, nevertheless, enjoys it greatly.

Finally, some mention is due to Western-oriented pop music, whose most respected exponent since the 1960s has been Baris Manca.

Given the diverse sources from which Turkish mainstream music draws, it is not surprising that its exponents are of varied backgrounds. Instrumentalists range from conservatory-trained classical musicians to gypsies and semi-professionals who have learned music informally from friends and relatives. A look at the two most popular vocalists of the seventies and eighties—Orhan Gencebay and Ibrahim Tatlises—presents interesting and representative contrasts.

Orhan Gencebay emerged on the popular music scene in the late 1960s. Like other top popular singers, he is photogenic and fashionable, and his music is solidly within the "central domain" category. He is unusual in that, unlike most leading pop vocalists, he is also a talented composer and arranger, and a performer on *saz, bağlama,* and other instruments. He is credited with being the first to record modern pop songs with sophisticated, pre-composed arrangements, as opposed, for example, to recording simple strophic *türkü* songs with modernized instrumentation. His evocative song texts, according to informants, make grown men weep. At the same time, he seldom, if ever, performs in public, preferring to disseminate his music entirely through the mass media.

Since the early seventies, Gencebay has shared stardom with Ibrahim Tatlises, a singer of quite different background. Tatlises, a native of the provincial southeastern town of Urfa, has had little formal education in either music or general schooling. Like most pop singers, he does not compose his music and may have only a limited under-standing of *makam.* His roots, rather, are in folk music—especially *türkü, uzun hava,* and, accordingly to informants, Sufi devotional *ilahiler* songs. His early cassettes of the sixties were devoted almost entirely to such genres, and he continues to record them alongside more standard pop songs. Musicians respect the integrity of his folk roots, and the public enjoys his fine voice.

Turkish popular music arose in close connection with the mass media. While records, radio, and television were initially predominant, cassettes have become the most popular means of dissemination since the mid-1970s. Top vocalists like Ibrahim Tatlises and Ferdi Tayfur also star in cinematic musicals and produce music videos as well. Audio cassette production appears to be in the hands of a large number of small firms, including several based in West Germany. The strength and ubiquity of the cassette industry illustrate that regardless of the limited interest in classical music and some folk genres, Turkish popular music is flourishing as never before and shows no signs of declining or of being overwhelmed by Western inroads.

Iran

Persian popular music has not attained the international visibility or audience that, for example, Arab or Indian popular musics have, and it has attracted little attention from scholars; even cities such as Los Angeles and New York, with their substantial Iranian communities, have sustained very few venues offering live Persian music. Also, Persian popular music itself has become increasingly more Westernized in recent years, such that the more distinctively national-sounding styles appear to be growing ever more peripheral. To date, the only accessible study of Persian popular music is a succinct article of Nettl, which, although brief, does present an overview of the subject as of 1969.[6]

One may generalize at the outset that Persian music has not fared well in its confrontation with Western music. Art music suffered from neglect, if not censure, during the Safavid period (sixteenth to early eighteenth century), and the already low status of the musician reached a new nadir. The trend toward Westernization was established in the latter nineteenth century and continued in the twentieth in spite of some government patronage of traditional art music.[7] The absence of a standard, accepted body of theory, the tendency to regard traditional music as backward, the low prestige of professional performers, and the orthodox Islamic disapproval of music all evidently combined to render Persian art music vulnerable to marginalization in the twentieth century. The same factors appear to have limited the sustained development of a popular music scene comparable to that in, for instance, neighboring Turkey or the Arab world.

Nevertheless, a dynamic set of popular music styles did flourish in Iran, especially in the three or four decades prior to the fall of the Shah. These musics were performed in urban nightclubs and disseminated on the radio, in films, and on 45-rpm records, coexisting with music in purely Western idiom. Nettl, grouping the variants according to stylistic orientation, discerns first a "mainstream" style, whose characteristics would include: solo singing, generally by a woman; absence of improvisation, or its confinement to ornamentation or heterophonic variation; accompaniment by an ensemble of mixed Persian and Western instruments, frequently dominated by violins playing in unison or octaves; use of simple rhythms—especially 6/8; prevailing modal conception of melody, but accommodating simple chord progressions; use of both traditional Persian intonation, with its distinctive neutral intervals as well as Western scales; and occasional use of elements derived from classical or regional folk musics. One might add that despite the clear Arab influence in the ensemble playing, the vocal style in such music is thoroughly Persian, especially in the occasional use of light *tahrir* ornamentation.[8] Further, chord progressions, when present, tend to follow simple Western conventions to a greater extent than in Turkish or Arab pop styles, perhaps because the favored Persian modes are more diatonic than the *Hijāz*-type modes common in other Middle Eastern musics. In addition to the singers mentioned by Nettl, recordings of Marziyi and Ahdiyi well illustrate these features.

Nettl's second category is the more Westernized popular music which nevertheless retains some distinctively Persian character. Here, the harmonies, rhythms, and instrumentation (especially the use of bass and traps) are predominantly Western; although *tahrir* is not used, the vocal style reflects some indigenous flavor in subtle nuances of ornamentation and contour. Pop star Gougoush, cited by Nettl, remains perhaps the best-known exponent of this style.

A third sub-style of Persian popular music reflects greater affinities with Persian classical music. Recordings of Golpayegani, for example, feature predominantly Persian instrumentation, improvised solos, and free-rhythmic *āvāz* singing with some use of *tahrir*. A song in this style could be classed, either as a light *tarāne*, or as a *tasnif*, that is, a metered classical vocal piece with a largely pre-composed melody, set to a particular *maqām*.

Finally, Persian popular music comprises modernized versions of regional folk styles (such as those of Khurasan or Azerbaijan), and pieces which are overwhelmingly Arab in style (referred to as *raqs-e-arabi*—"Arab dance"), popular especially in Khuzestan. Even more popular have been cover versions of Turkish pop songs (with new texts in Persian) and Afghani-style music, popularized in particular by singers such as Gougoush and Suli.

Since 1979, the orthodox Islamic regime led by Ayatollah Khomeini, while promoting religious and classical music, has endeavored to eliminate popular music because of its perceived sensuality and decadent Western elements.[9] Women, who had dominated popular music singing, are now forbidden to sing in public. Cassette sales are illegal, and offenders are harshly punished. The once-lively nightclubs on Tehran's Laleh Zar Avenue have been closed, and the government-run radio stations play only traditional music. Such conditions, while not conducive to the continued flowering of Persian pop culture, have not destroyed modern music, but rather forced it into exile. Thus, leading pop musicians have either joined or emerged anew amongst the expatriate communities in France, the USA, and elsewhere. Cassette production is now based in Los Angeles and Paris; many cassettes, naturally, find their way back into Iran.

Israel

A particularly interesting sub-genre of Middle Eastern popular music has arisen in Israel since the early 1970s. Prior to that period, popular music in Israel consisted primarily of songs in Western styles or pieces blending Western features with elements of Israeli folk music—that is, the self-consciously syncretic music, predominantly Eastern European in derivation, which earlier generations of Ashkenazi Israelis had fashioned and promoted as part of a new national folk culture. These musics did not entirely satisfy the tastes of the Oriental Jews, who by now outnumber the politically and economically dominant Ashkenazi Jews. The Jews of Middle Eastern origin, indeed, retained strong predilections for the musics of their former homelands, despite attempts on the part of the Israeli government to integrate them into a new, more Europeanized national culture.[10] The complex dialectic of the social, political, and cultural interaction between Ashkenazi and Oriental Jews in Israel is too involved to examine here; however, its musical ramifications, as summarized by Erik Cohen and Amnon Shiloah, are of interest in reference to the emergence of Oriental Jewish pop in recent decades.[11]

While mainstream Western styles remain the most widespread idiom for popular music in Israel, they do not entirely dominate contemporary musical culture. The early 1970s saw the emergence of a syncretic pop style which, whether deliberately or not, turns away both from Western pop and Israeli folk styles. The new Oriental pop—sometimes referred to as rock *misrahi* (*mizraḥi*)—has borrowed instead from Mediterranean musics, especially Greek and Arab; its audience consists primarily of Oriental Jews. In the initial stages, many songs in this style were simply cover versions of Greek or Arab songs, often using Hebrew translations for texts; Israeli singer Ruby Chen's Hebrew version of Farid al-Atrash's "Laila" was one such hit.[12] More common are original songs in Hebrew using borrowed styles. Thus, songs based on the Greek model use *bouzoukis* or electric guitars in Greek style, with characteristic ornamentation and intricate melodies in parallel thirds.[13] Groups playing such musics have proliferated among the Oriental Jewish communities in Israel; they play frequently at clubs, lavish weddings, and other family festivities. Eurocentric Ashkenazi Israelis and cultural bureaucrats in general have tended to regard Oriental pop with condescension. Accordingly, until the mid-eighties the Israeli radio relegated it to short, discrete programs (which detractors have referred to as "ghettoes"). The music, however, became widely disseminated on cassettes, completely independent of the state-controlled media.

Oriental pop appears to be establishing some audience among young Arabs, not only in Israel but in several Muslim countries as well.[14] Recognizing the potential for fostering goodwill through the medium of music, state radio stations in the mid-eighties belatedly began broadcasting more "rock *misrahi*," especially on the Israeli radio's Arabic service.

Also worthy of mention here are the more intellectually oriented Israeli groups which have produced self-consciously eclectic combinations of Western styles with elements derived from Arab countries. The army radio station has been particularly influential in promoting such "avant-garde" innovations.

Given the socio-political complexities involved, the manner in which musical taste can overlap ethnic and national boundaries is significant. Regional and ethnic distinctions notwithstanding, the affinities between the musics discussed in this chapter and the preceding one also serve to illustrate the degree to which the Mediterranean cultures—Arab, Turkish, Greek, Armenian, and Oriental Jewish—may be regarded as constituting a relatively unified musical area. Moreover, the emergence and social role of Oriental Jewish pop music illustrate once again how popular music is not a mere passive product of its socio-cultural environment, but how it constitutes an active participant in that milieu mediating and negotiating complex dialectics of power, race, class, and even religion in a manner unique to musical expression.

CHAPTER 7

South Asia

India

The South Asian subcontinent, comprising India, Pakistan, Bangladesh, Nepal, Bhutan, and Sri Lanka, encompasses a great diversity of musical cultures and styles. The multitude of folk music traditions reflect the linguistic, ethnic, class, regional, and religious diversity of the South Asian population, now surpassing one billion. The South Asian aristocracies sustain two "Great Traditions" of art music, the Hindustani, or North Indian, and the Karnatak, or South Indian. South Asian popular music has incorporated elements from these two art music systems and manifests some of the variety of the idiosyncratic tastes and traditional folk musics of its regional audiences.[1] Nevertheless, the commercial nature of this pop music, and the deliberate attempts of producers to reach broader audiences have also led to the rise of a mainstream musical lingua franca which to a large extent transcends the heterogeneity of its audience.

South Asia's linguistic diversity has been perhaps the most formidable barrier to the development of a subcontinental pop music. Over fifteen major languages are spoken in the area, each having their own sophisticated traditional poetic and musical idioms; in some cases, native speakers of a given language are reluctant to patronize music sung in a different tongue. As a result, popular musics using these various languages have arisen, and indeed, such regional diversity seems to be increasing with the advent of cassette technology. Throughout North India and Pakistan, however, the sister languages Hindi and Urdu are widely understood, and pop music using these tongues now coexists throughout the North alongside commercial musics in regional languages.

Since the introduction of the record industry in India in 1902, commercial producers have attempted to tap all possible regional markets, leading to the growth of several pop stylizations of regional folk musics. This trend has increased in the 1980s, as the spread of cassettes has made recording production and consumption cheaper and thus more conducive to regional control. But given the extreme diversity of South Asian peoples, the relative homogeneity of Indian pop music style is more striking than its variety. Melodies tend to be in diatonic scales, to which Western harmonies can be added as background. Indian instruments—especially, for example, the *tabla* drum pair and *dholak* barrel drum—are often combined with Western ones, particularly congas and orchestrated violins. The folk-derived *kaherva* and *dādra tāls,* in eight and six beats, respectively, are the predominant meters. Vocal timbre—particularly among female singers—is remarkably stereotyped, and a large percentage of North Indian film songs of the last thirty years are sung not only in the same vocal style, but by the same woman—Lata Mangeshkar, who holds the distinction of having the most-recorded voice in the world.

This relative homogeneity derives in part from the music industry's natural desire to tap and, if need be, create a mass audience with relatively homogeneous taste. Indian cinema and commercial film music do reach the countryside, but their primary audience is in the cities and towns, where dissemination is easier and greater profits are to be made. Many city-dwellers may be immigrants from the countryside, but their regional ethnic consciousness tends to be diluted when they enter urban society and become acclimatized to the new "Great Tradition" of pop culture. Thus, the musical tastes of the clerk in Karachi and the factory worker in distant Calcutta may have much more in common than those of peasants in neighboring Sindh and Gujerat.

The degree of homogeneity of Indian pop music also stems from the traditional concentration of the largest sector of the popular music industry—that associated with the cinema—in a few large cities—especially, Bombay and Madras—such that to a large extent, musical style has been superimposed on its audience by urban commercial producers, rather than growing naturally from regional roots. The vast capital required to produce a feature film has entrusted the production and marketing of film music to the moneyed business class, whose tastes cannot be expected to reflect the variety of South Asian traditions.

Film Music

Film music is by far the single largest category of popular music in South Asia, and it provides the model for much of the popular music that exists outside the cinematic world. In many other cultures, pop music has evolved in close connection with its use in cinema; Indonesian *dangdut,* Argentine tango, and modern Egyptian urban music all matured in the context of cinematic musicals. Yet the association between cinema and music is particularly strong in South Asia, where film music constitutes a majority of all the popular music disseminated by the mass media.

The weakness of the print-based media in India has contributed to the vastness of the Indian cinema industry, which, generating over seven hundred feature films yearly, is the world's second largest.[2] Every day an average of 12.5 million Indians see films; but, as Pradip Krishen observes:

> Even the figures do not express the extent of the popular cinema's dominance as a channel for the transmission of ideas and information. [Indian] urban environments are cluttered with its signs, filled with its sounds. Its tastes and values spill out to define the very texture of contemporary mass and middle-class culture.[3]

Film music is itself an essential component of this mass culture, and it enjoys a wider and more diverse audience than any other music in South Asia.

As cinema developed first in the West, it is not surprising that Indian cinema borrowed extensively from Hollywood and European productions; several Indian films, especially in the early stages, were simply adaptations of Western hits. But anyone who has seen a commercial Indian film can attest to the distinctive character of Indian cinema, which since 1912 has developed not as an ersatz imitation of Western cinema but as a home-grown domestic entertainment form guided by indigenous aesthetics and conditions.

Some characteristics of Indian cinema appear to have origins in traditional entertainment forms found in the subcontinent. During dance scenes, enthusiastic Indian film audiences have been known to fling coins at the screen, just as they might shower rupees on folk dancers or courtesans. The very length of the films—usually three hours—may derive from the various traditions of folk theater that exist throughout India; in such genres, like the Bengali *jātra* and the Kanpur-region *nautanki*, episodes from the *Purānas* or the Hindu epics are dramatized in night-long presentations, often incorporating music, dance, battle-scenes, and digressive comedy.[4] The stories themselves are often fantastic rather than realistic, relating the mighty feats of the gods, the boundless wealth of kings, and the cosmic repercussions of mortal escapades; such narrative extravagance seems to have contributed to Indian cinema's oft-noted aesthetic of excess rather than economy, not only in the films' length but in their delight in spectacle, implausible coincidences, and the heroes' superhuman acts.[5]

In terms of subject matter, Indian films can be grouped in five general categories: (1) mythological stories, drawn from the epics (the *Rāmāyana* and *Mahābharata*), the *Purānas*, or from oral folklore; (2) family melodramas, portraying domestic complications; (3) "costume dramas," based on historical themes involving the lives of saints, princes, or other well-known figures; (4) Indian equivalents of Westerns or spy films, stressing action rather than sentiment or character development; and, finally, (5) "social" films, weaving a melodrama around some contemporary public issue.[6]

The category of "social" films encompasses the largest number of movies. Themes treated may include problems relating to untouchability, prostitution, arranged marriages, crime and corruption, religious dogmatism, oppression of women, and—most common of all—conflicts between the rich and the poor; these last often center around a love affair between two people of different classes. The message of the "social" films is usually liberal: romantic love is exalted over matters like caste, dowry, and parental preferences, and, most consistently, the rich are shown as venal and corrupt while the poor are upheld as moral and good. The explicit "moral" celebrating the poor, however, is often contradicted by the ideology implicit in the cinematic language, which may ultimately be more persuasive than the message of the plot or the closing soliloquys. Regardless of the overt message, films seldom portray actual poverty, but instead generally take place in mansions, palaces, chic cabarets, and immaculate gardens. The vast majority of heroes and heroines are themselves rich. Even if one of them is poor, the plot will generally be so construed as to take place mostly in sumptuous settings.[7] A heroine in the role of a simple village lass will appear dressed and manicured like a princess.[8] In many films, poor characters may appear only as menial ciphers, often to be ridiculed.[9] At this level, it is not the poor that are celebrated but rather synthetic, urban, Westernized luxury. In this sense the films can be seen as responses to a mass desire for escapism, and as reflections of the rampant consumerism of the Indian bourgeoisie and the ideology of the affluent corporate producers. A typical lower-class cinema viewer explained his love of Indian films: "Watching films is a lovely way to pass the time. . . . I love to sit in the dark and dream about what I can never possibly have. I can listen to the music, learn all the songs, and that way I can forget about my troubles."[10] The ultimate effect of such a cinema, given its refusal to confront Indian reality, can only be alienating.

Music is essential to Indian cinema. Commercial films without songs are rarities—from 1931 to 1954 there were only two.[11] Music directors and composers are often better paid than actors or film directors, and billboards and credit titles highlight their names accordingly. Film singers are as famous as the actors themselves. Sarkar notes:

> Often a film is judged solely on its catchy tunes, even when it is essentially a dramatic film. Sometimes a film-goer goes repeatedly to see the same film, because the songs appealed to him in the first place. He could easily hear them individually at leisure on the radio, tape or records, but he still prefers to *see* them sung. This is a distinctive feature of the Indian audience . . .[12]

In the early stages of Indian cinema, songs were sung on screen by actors who were themselves vocalists, such as K. L. Saigal. Since the forties, by convention the songs have been recorded separately by "playback singers," and the actors pretend to sing by mouthing the words in lip-sync. Thus an actor might break into song at any time or place. A couple cavorting in a park sing accompanied by an invisible string orchestra; or in the course of a single song an actor is shown singing in an apartment in Bombay, and then by a waterfall in Kashmir. Two lovers at opposite ends of the country communicate by singing the same tune in juxtaposed cuts; a man being flogged bursts into impassioned song.[13] Such uses of music seem implausible to some educated Indians, not to mention Westerners accustomed to greater cinematic versimilitude. But for most Indian spectators, the effect is not unnatural. Rather, it is a continuation of the traditions of the aforementioned folk theater forms, where speech, song, and dance are tightly integrated into a unified dramatic style. In traditional genres like Orissi *leela*, Punjabi *swang*, Keralan *kathakali*, Kashmiri *jashan*, and Bengali *jātra*, speech, poetic recitation, chanted speech, and song form elements of a continuum between conversation and music. Thus, as Beeman notes:

> For Indian spectators the psychological distance between speech and song is considerably narrower than for Western spectators. The artificial "break" which is felt in the West when an actor bursts into song is thus less apparent to the Indian viewer.[14]

Aside from their own musical entertainment value, songs have other conventional uses in India cinema. The music may broaden a film's audience beyond language barriers; the catchy tunes of the film *Pyasa*, for example, drew prodigious audiences in South India, where the film's sophisticated Urdu was little understood.The songs also provide convenient vehicles for the expression of otherwise unarticulated sentiments; a song sequence may compress the depiction of "falling in love" into four or five minutes. Often, however, the musical interludes are little more than digressions gratuitously inserted into the plot.

The typical song scene occurs in a garden, mansion, or cabaret, notwithstanding the paucity of such nightclubs in India. The hero and heroine (perhaps accompanied by a chorus) often dance as they mouth the text. The dance style, like much of the music, is a hybrid of Indian classical, folk, and Western elements. At times it seems to be a maudlin version of the mimetic *abhināya* used in classical *kathak* and *bharat nātyam*. Western pop styles, especially disco, are also clearly influential. Overhead shots of choreographed group effects appear to derive their original inspiration from the dance sequences of Busby Berkeley films of the early 1930s. Much of the movement cannot be said to derive from any style at all, and has been aptly described as "a lot of unknown jerky callesthenics" (sic).[16] The overt eroticism of much film dance may be seen as an attempt on the part of the producers to compensate for the strict censorship restricting sex and kissing on screen.[17]

The film dance style has taken root among courtesan performers and, at a less formal level, among middle-class girls who dance for each other at household parties; but, on the whole, film dance is not a widely popular participatory art, especially since in much of South Asia there are few occasions when dancing (especially by women) is socially acceptable. Its comparative weakness as an art may also be attributed to its relative lack of roots in popular or folk dance styles, and to the fact that the actors and actresses who perform it on the screen are not specialists in dance. In this sense, film dances contrast with film songs, which are generally sung by highly competent professionals, while the actors need only mouth the words.

Film Music until 1940

Cinema, like the recording industry, enjoyed a remarkably early start in India, where a growing urban bourgeoisie had developed a taste for Western technological innovations. By 1899 films were being shown in India, and a few short Indian films had been produced. In 1912 appeared the first feature film, *Pundalik,* a dramatization of a Maharashtran saint's life. Other narrative features soon followed, and the silent era of Indian cinema was soon in full swing. Films in the first decade were mostly historical or mythological in subject, often portraying episodes from the *Rāmāyana* and the *Mahābharata.* In the 1920s, contemporary melodramas, often with reformist and nationalistic messages, began to appear, and these gradually came to dominate output. The silent cinema was at its peak in 1931, when 207 films were produced. That year, the production of the first sound film, *Alam Ara,* inaugurated the era of the "talkie" and the decline of the silent film; by the end of the year, twenty-seven other talkies in four languages had succeeded *Alam Ara.*[18] Most of these films incorporated musical interludes, often with dance, and thus was born film music, a new and distinct genre of Indian music.

After the success of the 1931 musical *Shirin Farhad,* music was accepted as an essential component of every commercial Indian film. Indeed, some films, such as *Indrasabha* (1932), which contained 72 songs, were little more than sequences of verses and songs woven into a familiar plot.[19] Many of the "songs" were simply short musical renderings of couplets rather than extended compositions. The advent of the talkie brought with it the rise of the singing actor and the music director. Kunda Lal Saigal (1904–1946) soon emerged as the most famous singing actor of the early talkie period, especially with the success of *Devdas* (1935), in which he played the tragic (and somewhat autobiographical) role of a tormented alcoholic. Saigal was not a formally trained singer and had limited knowledge of classical music. Nevertheless, his recordings were often more classical in style than most modern film songs, in that they incorporated fluent improvisations and traditional semi-classical instrumental accompaniment (*tabla*, *tānpūra*, and harmonium). Many were in the light-classical *ghazal* form, using free strophic renditions of verses by classical or contemporary Urdu poets. His version of the semi-classical *thumri* "Bābul morā naihar chūto hi jāe" acquainted millions of listeners with this venerable nineteenth-century composition. The classical orientation of the music of this period was a reflection of the fact that most music directors in the prewar period were themselves trained in art music. Saigal's recordings sold widely, and they continue to have an audience today, even if most young listeners find his style dated.

Film music in the early period tended to derive more from traditional Indian sources than did the eclectic hybrid music of the postwar years. One important source was the music of the Parsi and Marathi theater, which had been flourishing Bombay entertainment genres until bankrupted by the cinema. Many songs were in the light-classical *ghazal* form, with loose improvisation in the first line of each couplet. Another important light-classical source was *dādra*, which has a Hindi (Braj Bhasha) text and a greater emphasis on rhythmic lilt. Pankaj Mullick, a renowned screen actor, singer, and composer, introduced melodies of Rabindranath Tagore, the Nobel Prize-winning Bengali composer, writer, and painter. Some songs, especially in regional films, reflected folk origins, but on the whole the production and orientation of Indian cinema and music remained primarily urban. The eight-beat *kaherva* and six-beat *dādra* meters have predominated in film music since its inception. They presumably derived originally from folk music, as they are common throughout North India, but they have long since been incorporated into light-classical music.

Most films in the prewar years were produced by a handful of major studios. The largest of these were the Bombay-based New Theatres, Prabhat Studios, and Bombay Talkies; smaller studios could easily go bankrupt from a single box-office failure. In other aspects, however, the early film industry was more decentralized than in the postwar period. Regional cinema—using diverse languages and, often, regional music—was an important part of the industry, and, Bombay's preeminence notwithstanding, films were produced in several urban centers in the country. Moreover, the studios themselves were not involved in related sectors of the industry like distribution and theater ownership.

Film Music from 1940 to 1970

In the 1940s the Indian film industry underwent a dramatic reorganization. Some problems ensued from a shortage of raw film, and from the colonial government's censorship of any material interpreted as promoting Indian nationalism. But the real causes of the shakeup related to the industry's growth from a handful of family-run businesses to a vast corporate field involving huge expenditures of capital for each film. High taxes, both by the British colonial government and the new independent administration, promoted financing by black market sources. Cinema became recognized as an ideal sheltered investment for "black" money, and the infusion of massive amounts of underground currency changed the character as well as the size and sources of film financing. Bombay and Madras came to dominate film production, as studios in Calcutta and other regional cities declined.

As the old studios folded or were broken up, the studio system itself was replaced by the "star" system. Fear of box-office failure led producers to rely on a standardized formula: a star, six songs, and three dances. Social relevance, ideological integrity, and high-quality production, editing, and plot could help a film, but they were seen as secondary in importance. A few smash hits eschewed the formula, and many films following it failed ignominiously; but on the whole, producers, aware that 70 percent of films lost money, preferred not to risk failure by departing from the norm.[20]

The films of the 1940s and 1950s reflected the values of the middle class in their sentimentality and their concern with the fate of the family in a rapidly Westernizing and modernizing urban milieu.[21] Equally noticeable was a trend toward melodramatic escapism, and away from the treatment of controversial contemporary issues. A parallel could be drawn with the light musicals of Busby Berkeley that were in vogue in the Depression years in the United States; India, indeed, could be said to be in a state of indefinite depression. The handful of realistic portrayals of poverty and exploitation have always been exceptions to the standard entertainment fare produced by the Bombay "dream factories."

The reorganization of the film industry brought with it a new era in film music production and style. With Saigal's death in 1946, the age of the singer-actor gave way to the "playback" system, where the actors would mouth songs already recorded by playback singers. Thus, the actors did not need to be able to sing, and, conversely, the songs could be recorded by skilled vocalists who were not required to act (or dance) as well. The "star" system subsequently became a feature of music production as well as acting. The demand for star vocalists and music directors remains just as strong today, and producers go to great expenses to secure the services of top singers and music directors, believing them as important as the star actors and actresses. Delays in production are not uncommon when the music director is involved in several films at once.[22]

One result of the domination of the music "stars" is that despite the vastness of the film industry, since the war most of the music emanating from the Bombay film industry has been directed and sung by a mere handful of artists. The two most popular directors have been Naushad and S. D. Burman. The major male singers have been Mohammad Rafi, Mukesh, and Kishore Kumar, while Lata Mangeshkar (b. 1928) and her sister Asha Bhosle have continued to dominate female vocal music in the North. Between 1948 and 1984, Lata, with her shrill, girlish voice, made over 30,000 recordings for more than 2,000 films, earning her the distinction in the *Guinness Book of World Records* of having the most-recorded voice worldwide. In the Madras-based South Indian film world the current favorites are Yeshudas and Janaki. These artists are all extremely gifted, but in a country so diverse as India, it is difficult to believe that the domination of *one* vocal style, as performed by half a dozen singers, could be simply the result of popular demand. Rather, their popularity can be seen as reflecting one trend in post-war film music—a tendency for common-denominator mass music styles to be created in corporate urban studios and subsequently promoted and superimposed upon a heterogeneous listening audience; this audience has no active role in the creation of this music, and can exercise only indirect influence by choosing among the songs and styles proffered by the industry.[23]

A countervailing trend has been the continued growth of regional film music styles, incorporated either into the lingua franca Hindi cinema or, more noticeably, into regional cinema itself. An early trendsetter was *Khazanchi* (1941), produced in the Punjab and featuring songs based on the lively folk music of that region.[24] In the late forties, *Sangtye Aika, Lakshahir Ramjoshi,* and a Hindi version of the latter, *Matwala Shair Ramjoshi* popularized *lāvni (lāvani)*, a folk music genre of Maharashtra; ever since, an important genre of Marathi cinema has been the so-called "tamāsha" film—*tamāsha* being the folk entertainment event in which *lāvni* is traditionally heard.[25] The folk dance-music forms of Gujerat—*rās* and *garba*—have been widely used in Gujerati cinema, especially since the Gujerat state government provides subsidies to films promoting such elements of local culture. Rabindranath Tagore's melodies have appeared in several Bengali movies, and some South Indian film music has a distinct Karnatak flavor. In the forties and fifties, three of the leading Hindi film directors—Hemant Kumar, S. D. Burman, and Salil Choudhrey—drew considerably on the folk music of their native Bengal. This Bengali dominance was moderated only after the late fifties with the emergence of the more eclectic Naushad.[26]

Such uses of folk musics may take the form of composition of new melodies in folk style, or popularization of existing tunes. Generally, when folk forms are incorporated in film music, they are "modernized" with the addition of pre-composed orchestral accompaniment, employing Western and/or Indian instruments. Improvisation is eliminated, songs are shortened to last under ten minutes, and chordal instrumental harmonies may be added to the modal melody. Dances are also formally choreographed and often enlivened with Western-influenced "bumps" and gyrations. The results include hybrids like "disco *garba*," which subsequently influence traditional performance styles outside of the cinema. Often, the "folk dance" scenes in Indian cinema represent little more than producers' naive conceptions of rural styles.

The postwar period also saw an increased use of Western musical elements, despite efforts by the government to reverse this trend. The most visible borrowed elements were: (1) instruments like the violin, clarinet, conga, and saxophone; (2) rhythms like the foxtrot and polka[27], and (3) chordal harmony. These and other aspects of mainstream film music style are worth examining in greater depth.

Modern Film Music Style and Structure

In spite of the variety of regional film music styles and changes over the last forty years, postwar Indian film music exhibits enough homogeneity and continuity to enable one to speak of a "mainstream" style, particularly in North India. The following discussion focusses on this style, many features of which may also prevail in regional and South Indian styles.

The majority of North Indian films are in the Hindi-Urdu language. On the levels of simple colloquial speech, the two languages are interchangeable and mutually intelligible. They serve as a lingua franca throughout the North, and are widely understood by educated as well as many uneducated speakers of regional languages. In literature and more complex speech, the languages become more distinct: Urdu, the language of the Muslims of North India and Pakistan, uses a variety of the Arabic script, and its vocabulary borrows heavily from Persian and Arabic. Hindi is written in the Devnagari script and derives its literary vocabulary from Sanskrit.

While it is commonplace to speak of "Hindi films," in fact, both the dialogue as well as song texts tend to be based more on Urdu. At times the speech and the lyrics may be in such Persianized "high Urdu" that they are unintelligible to some Hindi speakers. The preference for Urdu seems to derive from the rich poetic tradition of that language, and its subsequent reputation as a "sweet" and romantic tongue. Urdu poetry, especially the *ghazal*, enjoys wide popularity throughout North India, even among Hindi speakers unable to read Urdu script. By contrast, the dialect of Hindi used as a lingua franca (*khari boli*, based on the dialect originally spoken in the Delhi area) has a limited poetic and literary tradition. Most song texts, therefore, incline more towards Urdu than Hindi in their diction. The content is generally amatory, and is more sentimental in character than classical Urdu poetry, which treats lover and beloved more as archetypes.

Use of the *ghazal* form is extremely common. *Ghazal* is primarily a poetic form, consisting of rhymed Urdu couplets in the scheme *aa ba ca da* and so forth. A *ghazal* may be set strophically to music in different styles. The simplest form is *tarannum*, wherein a poet will chant his verses in a stock melody at a poetry reading (*musha'ira*). *Ghazal* is often used in *qawwāli*, the lively Sufi devotional music performed in shrines by a group of singers with instrumental accompaniment. *Ghazal* is also a sophisticated light-classical genre, where a solo singer, accompanied by *tabla* and harmonium or *sārangi* (fiddle), performs interpretative improvisations on the first line of each couplet, returning to a melodic refrain with the subsequent rhyming line; each couplet is followed by a short *laggi* section, where the *tabla* player improvises in fast tempo.[28]

The film *ghazal* bears some resemblance to the light-classical *ghazal*. As in most film music, however, improvisation is minimal or non-existent. The *laggi* sections between couplets are replaced by orchestrated instrumental passages, which are generally distinct from one another in melody and instrumentation. Other techniques may be used to lend the song a more progressive structure; for example, the male and female singers might alternate singing successive couplets, and join on the final verse. Thus the film *ghazal* often loses its traditional, simple, open-ended strophic structure, acquiring a closed, "song"-like structure more in accordance with bourgeois aesthetics.

Qawwāli is occasionally used in films. In its traditional form, *qawwāli* is performed by one or two lead singers with accompanying chorus and instrumentalists. *Dholak* (a folk barrel drum), harmonium, and *tabla* are the most typical instruments used, and hand-clapping is essential. The lead singers may indulge in virtuoso coloratura improvisations, which alternate with a group refrain. The texts, usually in Urdu, are devotional; they may be mystical love poetry—often in *ghazal* form—or elegies in praise of a particular holy personage. *Qawwāli* is traditionally performed at Muslim shrines, with considerable interaction between performers and audience. In this century, *qawwāli* is often heard in a concert format and on recordings, removed from direct associations with Muslim shrines.

Film *qawwālis* generally maintain the genre's collective character by showing the entire performing group on screen (even if the sound track is actually recorded separately); thus, the presence of the group is generally worked into the plot. In this sense the film *qawwāli* differs from most other film songs, wherein the musicians usually are not visible, such that the hero can burst into song in any locale, from a Kashmiri glade to a crowded bus.[29] The film *qawwāli* also retains the traditional *qawwāli's* solo coloratura passages, hand clapping, solo-chorus alternation, and the use of Urdu texts and traditional instrumentation. It differs, however, in several respects. The accompanying ensemble usually includes Western string and wind instruments. Female singers are common, unlike in the traditional *qawwāli*. The coloratura passages, although in improvisatory *style*, are generally pre-composed. Finally, the erotic rather than the devotional aspect of the text is stressed; very often, the text is explicitly concerned with personal love relationships and admits no devotional interpretation.

A large number of film songs do not adhere to any traditional form structure like that of *ghazal* or *qawwāli*. A variety of forms may be used, most of them alternating two- or four-line phrases with refrains and orchestral interludes. Many songs feature sections with contrasting orchestration, alternation of different meters (mostly *kaherva* and *dādra*), and juxtaposition of solo and choral lines.

The melodies of Indian film songs are predominantly modal. Often they are clearly based on a particular classical *rāg*. In other cases, a song may resemble a *rāg* but contain individual phrases which would be unacceptable in a classical rendition of that *rāg*. For example, the opening phrases of the excerpt below ("Āp ki nazroṅ," from *Anpadh*) resemble the *kānṛha* group of *rāgs* (*darbāri, aḍāna,* and others) in their scalar material and the oblique passage E♭ F D C (bracketed). The melody to the line "hameṅ manzūr hai", however, freely departs from the *kānṛha* pattern with its direct descent E♭ D C.

In many cases, the melody bears no more than a fortuitous relationship to any *rāg*. Most of the melodies are diatonic. By this we mean to say that, first of all, the scales are predominantly heptatonic, although alternate forms of notes may appear (for example, raised or lowered seventh degrees). Secondly, scales incorporating augmented intervals are generally avoided. Augmented intervals are found in some of the most important Indian *rāgs*. Yet film music melodies—like those of most North Indian folk songs—generally conform to modes resembling Western minor, lydian, dorian, aeolian, and especially major scales.

Chordal harmony has long been common in Indian film music. The instrumental accompaniment in Saigal's prewar recordings tended to be purely modal and heterophonic, but by the early 1940s, Western harmony was being used in many songs of Pankaj Mullick and others. Since then it has been a feature of a large percentage of songs. The chordal progressions in film music tend to be simple, generally consisting of primary major and minor triads built on the scale tones of the melody. Harmonic accompaniment is particularly prevalent in songs using "major"-sounding scales. The study of the use of such harmony in Indian pop music is problematic. Analysis of the chordal progressions may be simple enough from a Western perspective, but it may not explain their function in the Indian context. In order genuinely to understand the function of harmony in Indian music, we must be able to comprehend how Indians themselves perceive it. A chordal accompaniment to a melodic line may not influence an Indian's apprehension of the melody in the same manner as it would a Western ear. It may be difficult to ascertain whether harmony is perceived as a structural element, fundamentally altering dissonances and consonances, or as a superfluous ornament which does not alter the fundamentally modal character of the music.

The diversity of the South Asian listening audience renders impossible any broad generalizations about harmonic perception. Naturally, an acculturated, educated urban listener will perceive harmony in a different manner from a villager who has little or no exposure to it. Moreover, it is conceivable that very few listeners apprehend harmony from the perspective of the Westernized studio musicians who employ it in recordings. However, the frequent use of harmony suggests that it must serve some musical function for its listeners.[30]

The role of harmony in a song may ultimately derive from the nature of the melody, especially since almost all film songs consist of a solo vocal melody with accompaniment. In most songs using harmony, the conception of the melody is clearly modal, such that the chordal accompaniment functions in an ornamental rather than structural manner. Typically, a sustained fourth or sixth degree in the melody is supplemented by a subdominant chord, or a sustained seventh degree by a dominant chord. Simple plagal (IV-I) cadences may appear over tonic notes.

In other cases, however, it is clear that the melody has been composed in conjunction with the harmony (as in Western music), and that the structure of the melody renders it either implicit or indispensable. Some melodies explicitly suggest chords by means of arpeggios, such as the early 1970s hit "Duniya men":

In many songs, the role of harmony is ambiguous. "Āp ki nazroṅ" (page 182) has a complex modal melody which, as we have seen, roughly conforms to that of the *kānṛha* group of *rāgs*. The melody itself does not clearly suggest any harmony. Throughout the song, however, accompanying chords are strummed on a guitar. In the passages marked with asterisks in that example, the melody comes to rest on the fifth degree, G; this would be a stable resting point from a modal perspective, but at these points the guitar is playing not a tonic triad, but a minor dominant chord (G-Bb-D). For a Westerner this accompaniment renders that pitch unstable and unresolved; but it is difficult to say whether that accompanying harmony has a similar effect on Indian listeners.

Western influence is also evident in film music instrumentation. Many songs employ only traditional instruments, and the *tabla* and *dholak* (or *nāl*) remain the most popular percussion instruments. But clarinet, violin, saxophone, xylophone, piano, conga, and other instruments are widely used. Moreover, the juxtaposition of sections in contrasting instrumental timbres is clearly a concept imported from the West, as the practice is not characteristic of traditional classical or folk music.

Aside from language, the one feature that remains most distinctively Indian in virtually all film music is vocal style. Indian ornamentation and melodic nuances are quite distinct from the characteristic styles of, for example, Greece, Southeast Asia, or the Arab world. One distinguishing element is *gamak,* a technique in which every note in a passage is approached from its lower neighbor, such that a simple scalar phrase might be notated as follows:

The ear can soon learn to distinguish Indian vocal style from that of other non-Western cultures, but written description of such microscopic although essential minutiae will have to be sought in future studies, ideally incorporating electronic transcriptions.

Regional Cinema

As mentioned above, regional cinema—produced in languages other than Hindi-Urdu—has been an important feature of Indian film since its conception. By the late 1940s, cinema production came to be dominated by Bombay and Madras, but a large portion of this output has always been aimed at regional markets. Much of regional cinema consists of imitations of glittery Bombay films, distinguished only by language and less slick production. Music directors for such films tend to be based in

Bombay and Madras and may have little knowledge of or interest in regional musics. Other regional films reflect a greater orientation toward local life and culture, and are of interest here for their frequent use of stylized regional folk musics. This aspect, however, is perhaps least evident in Tamil cinema, which comprises the largest category of films in South India. Much of Tamil film music differs from Hindi film music only in subtle Karnatak vocal nuances; the North Indian *tabla* and *nāl* seem to be preferred to the Karnatak *mrḍangam*, whose tone is lower and less ringing.

More distinctive in musical style are the commercialized versions of folk musics in other regions. Often these inclusions of local culture are promoted by state governments. We have mentioned, for example, how the Gujerati government provides tax subsidies to films highlighting Gujerati culture. The result is a profusion in cinema of Gujerati traditional music—particularly two dance-music genres, *garba* and *rās*. These are socio-religious folk dances which are extremely popular not only among rural peasants, but also among the urban middle classes. Indeed, in no other state does the urbanized bourgeoisie participate with such spontaneity and enthusiasm in a traditional dance form. In *garba*, men and women dance in concentric circles around an altar; in *rās*, smaller groups clap hand-held sticks against each other. A traditional choreography may predominate, but avid, competing neighborhood and school groups may devise more complex and challenging steps. Music is provided by one or more singers, with *dholak* and harmonium accompaniment. Film *garba* and *rās* may either use traditional or newly composed pieces. As is the case with other film genres, they are shortened to less than six minutes, improvisation is curtailed and orchestration is enhanced. Similar processes are evident in Punjabi cinema, where the most important music form is *bhāngra*, another lively social dance. In Marathi films, the *lāvni* song form is most common.

Recent Developments

Since 1970 Indian cinema has continued to evolve, and the cinema scene has become more complex and varied. One development has been a degree of overlap between the commercial exploitation films and the art films of directors like Satyajit Ray and Mrinal Sen. A few new filmmakers—especially Shyam Benegal—have endeavored to produce movies that combine box office appeal with artistic integrity. Stars like Sharmila Tagore and Waheeda Rahman have performed in both categories of films. Filmmakers like Govind Nihalani, Mani Kaul, and Mrinal Sen have produced art films in regional languages, ending the Bengali monopoly in that category. Regional cinema in general has become more diverse and extensive than before. Meanwhile, the commercial Bombay formula has tended to stress more *masāla*, literally, "spice," in increasing the amount of violence and eroticism; the new heroes are "angry young men" whose peripheral or antagonistic relationship to society seems to reflect an increasing social disillusionment and alienation.[31]

Modern Indian film music continues to incorporate elements from contemporary Western pop; hence, the influence of disco is strong. Synthesizer, traps, bass, and electric guitar (often with wah-wah or other effects) are common. Cabaret scenes often portray rock bands.[32] In such songs, the only Indian feature may be the characteristically ornamented vocal style. Other songs, meanwhile, may adhere to a more mainstream Indian sound. Predominance of LP and cassette rather than 78-rpm format has led to a lengthening of film songs to an average duration of five minutes.

The most popular film music directors in the 1980s have been Laxmikant and Pyarelal, whose demand is such that they are reputed to work on as many as thirty films at once, resulting in what has been called a "conveyor-belt" approach to composition. The relatively highbrow artistic goals professed by former directors like Naushad tend to give way to those voiced by music director Kalyanji: "We try to write songs so simple that they can be hummed by everybody. Every song should be as simple as a nursery rhyme."[33]

Film Music Outside the Cinema

Film music is widely disseminated by radio and recordings as well as by cinema itself. With the spread of cheap Japanese phonographs after 1928, film-style music soon came to dominate record output.[34] The advent of cassettes is further spreading film music to areas previously uninfluenced by the mass media. The most common medium of dissemination, however, is the radio. Radio broadcasting is state-controlled in South Asia, and official policy has included attempts to promote musics other than commercial film music. In the fifties and sixties, for example, under the direction of Dr. B. V. Keskar, All-India Radio curtailed the broadcasting of film music in an effort to promote traditional musics, but the policy was abandoned after it was discovered that listeners were simply tuning to Pakistani and Ceylonese stations.[35] Since then, All-India Radio has offered a steady fare of film music on selected stations, alongside channels promoting art and folk musics.

In urban environments film music is ubiquitous, blaring from overloaded speakers in tea stalls, shops, homes, restaurants, buses, and elevators. In the villages, dissemination may be limited to a few radios or to one or two shops that have cassette players. Recorded film music often replaces performance of live music in traditional contexts; in other cases, it may merely supplement live performance, as in weddings in Banaras, where recordings are played during intervals between women's songs and sets performed by professional musicians.[36]

Film music is performed live in a variety of contexts and styles. Top vocalists like Lata occasionally perform in large public halls or stadiums.

Somewhat more common are formal concerts by "orchestras," which, like the star concerts, reproduce the orchestral timbres of the original recordings with ensembles using bongos, congas, *nāl*, harmonium, Casio keyboard, and other instruments. Film *lāvnis*, for instance are frequently played in Bombay auditoriums in this format, especially in the context of Marathi theater. In the eighties, the number and sophistication of such concerts appears to be increasing.

Film music now dominates the repertoires of most courtesans, who perform in urban red-light districts throughout India. These women—often generically called *tawā'if*, *bāi-ji*, or *nāch-wāli* ("dancing-girl")—traditionally specialized in light-classical music with accompanying dance. Thus, in North India they concentrated on *thumri* and *ghazal*, which could be sung seated, with interpretative *abhināya* (mime). With the growth of bourgeois fine arts patronage, the semi-classical *thumri* and *ghazal* moved from the courtesan salon to the public concert-hall, and the *tawā'ifs* who were still able to support themselves by singing have been obliged to cater to the tastes of their new patrons, who are primarily of lower-middle-class rather than elite backgrounds. Hence, courtesans now seldom perform *thumri*, but rather pop *ghazal* and other film songs, generally in a pre-composed fashion with *tabla* and harmonium accompaniment.[37]

A more conspicuous performance context of film music involves the incorporation of film music melodies into regional folk music. Indeed, except in isolated areas, there are very few folk genres in which this phenomenon does not occur. It is most evident in urban folk musics; in Banaras, for example, such use of film melodies (often with new texts) is widespread in nearly all folk music forms, including *biraha* (a narrative tale sung to a long suite of melodies from disparate sources), *nautanki* (a music drama sung with harmonium and *naqqāra* drum pair), Muslim devotional *nāt* sung in the streets by groups of males on the occasion of Mohammad's birthday, *bhajan* (Hindu devotional song), *qawwāli*, and many other genres.[38] A song from the film *Nagin* has long since been the standard melody for *bīn*-playing snake-charmers throughout North India. Weddings and festivals often incorporate film songs played on ensembles of drums, harmonium, amplified *taisho koto* ("banjo") zithers, and Casio keyboard. These incorporations of film melodies thus disseminate film music even beyond the mass media.

Finally, the prodigious spread of Indian film music beyond South Asia itself merits mention, for *filmi gīt* has become an international phenomenon with an audience rivalling that of Western popular music styles. Indian film music is widely disseminated throughout Eastern and Southeast Asia, the Middle East, Africa, and Eastern Europe; not only are the films and songs themselves popular, but throughout these areas Indian film music may be performed in local variants. A commercial cassette from Kashgar, Xinxiang province, features a singer with lute accompaniment performing "Āwāra Hūṅ"; Indonesian *dangdut* emerges as a Malay-Javanese offspring of Indian film music, with its characteristic *kaherva* rhythm; pop music in Gulf states like Oman combines Arab vocal style with Indian film-style orchestration; and a Vietnamese national music and dance troupe features Indian film music as one third of its repertoire on a 1980 Indian tour. And, needless to say, Indian film music enjoys great popularity among South Asian immigrant communities in the Middle East, Fiji, the Caribbean, and elsewhere. The popularity of Indian film music in these countries and elsewhere obviously derives from both the glitter and the glamor of the films as well as the appeal of the music itself.

It is clear that in South Asia, film music has become a "people's music" insofar as it is consumed by such a broad and diverse portion of the populace, and in the sense that it is so widely incorporated into performance of regional folk musics. However, imitation, reproduction, and passive consumption are distinct from actual production of music, and it is the latter process that would distinguish a true grassroots "people's music" from a corporate-created mass music. Indian music is clearly a popular creation to the extent that it incorporates folk elements, and the influence between folk and film music is certainly mutual. Yet it may remain questionable to what degree film music responds to or manipulates taste, with its homogeneous vocal style, lush orchestration, corporate origin, avoidance of topical contemporaneity, and the entire glittery and unreal world of the cinema. Thus, the diversity of South Asian popular tastes may ultimately be better reflected in the popular musics which have emerged independently of the cinema.

Popular Music Outside the Realm of Cinema

Film music comprises the largest single category of South Asian popular music, but it is by no means the only category. Indeed, recorded popular music predates Indian sound cinema by some thirty years, and today, with the dramatic spread of cassette technology, the amount of popular music independent of the film world is increasing exponentially, as new regional pop forms spring from traditional folk genres and new audiences previously unexposed to the media are reached.

Recording technology reached India relatively early and soon became an important part of musical life. By 1910 the Gramophone Company of London had produced over four thousand recordings, which were being marketed in cities throughout the country. As the producers were attempting to tap all possible musical markets, the diversity of these recordings was remarkable. Many were short classical pieces—condensed versions of free-rhythmic *ālāp* or, more often, segments of improvisation in fast tempo, displaying the artist's virtuosity. At the opposite end of the musical spectrum were a number of recordings of different regional folk genres. Yet perhaps a plurality of the early 78s were light-classical pieces, sung, more often than not, by renowned courtesans. In North India, *thumri, ghazal,* and *dādra* were the most common forms. Their semi-classical style affiliated them with the Great Tradition of Hindustani music practiced throughout the urban north, and their use of texts in Hindi and Urdu enabled them to reach a broader audience than genres sung to regional languages.

Within the realm of these light-classical forms, there soon developed a sort of stylistic continuum, having at one end the more classicized pieces emphasizing sophisticated improvisation, and at the other end, more accessible, singable numbers that constituted an incipient popular music. At the former end of the spectrum would fall the recordings of *thumri,* with its rhapsodic, improvised interpretation of text within the framework of a *rāg. Ghazals* and *dādras* might also be recorded in this more classicized style, often with virtuoso coloratura runs and intense, complex exploration of *rāg* even within the condensed time format.

A market gradually developed for *ghazals* and *dādras* rendered in a more popular style. In this approach, improvisation would be limited to ornamentation and short flourishes, such that the appeal of the piece would be not the singer's skill at text interpretation, but rather the tunefulness of the pre-composed and generally strophic melody. The music, instead of representing a *process* or an elaboration (of a mode, for example) became more like a *song*—a catchy, singable piece which the listener could *possess* not only in the material sense but also in the conceptual sense, insofar as he could hum or sing the tune himself. At the same time, in such recordings, the sparse, loosely improvised accompaniment of *tabla* and harmonium would often be augmented with a larger ensemble including violins, clarinets, and other instruments. As with many popular musics, the use of such accompanying ensembles indicated that the recording no longer was meant to complement the live performance experience of the listener but rather to constitute a new realm of musical experience, generally available only through the recorded media and in that sense alienated from the listener's own immediate life.

Many of the most popular and widely selling *ghazals* and *dādras* of the thirties and forties remained predominantly improvisatory in character, such as the still-popular hits of Saigal and Begum Akhtar (d. 1974). Nevertheless, the trend toward orchestration and limited improvisation is evident in recordings such as the *ghazals* of Pankaj Mullick. In the sixties and seventies this tendency increased, as did the number of pop crooners.

On the whole, the record-based popular music industry led a parallel existence alongside the film music industry. The record format was more hospitable to improvisation, since there was no need to worry about the difficulty of lip-syncing on the screen. But in general, the record industry popular style derived largely from the film style. Occasionally, a record would become such a hit that it would subsequently be incorporated into a movie. For example, after the success of Begum Akhtar's *ghazal* "Divāna banānā," the songstress re-recorded the haunting melody (with a new text to avoid copyright conflicts) for the 1958 film *Roti*.[39] More recently, Ghulam Ali's *ghazal* "Chupke chupke" enjoyed several years of wide popularity and media dissemination before being worked into the film *Nikah*. Interestingly, both of these hits contained some improvisation, the skillful rendering of which was clearly as appealing as the melodies of the pre-composed refrains.

The 1980s have seen an extraordinary boom of the cassette-based pop *ghazal;* this vogue has been largely at the expense of film music, which is regarded by some as being in a state of decline, accounting for barely half of all cassette sales as of 1986.[40] The first *ghazal* superstars of the modern period were two Pakistanis, Mehdi Hasan and Ghulam Ali. Both can be regarded as "crossover" singers in that they record both in light-classical style (with fluid and extensive improvisation, backed only by harmonium and *tabla*), as well as in more *filmi* format. In the early eighties they have been overshadowed by a new group of singers, especially Anup Jalota, Pankaj Udhas, and the duo Jagjit and Chitra Singh. In the music of these artists, the distinctions between light-classical and pop, or between tasteful and kitsch, become even more blurred. While they often eschew film-style orchestration, their simplistic *ghazal* settings and tame improvisations at times seem to approach the nursery-rhyme aesthetic of the film composers.

The modern crossover *ghazal*, with its sophisticated-sounding lyrics, relaxed, urbane vocal style, and history of elite patronage, has a pseudo-aristocratic ethos which distinguishes it from the stylized syncretic folk musics emerging with the cassette vogue. Its primary audience is the new Indian bourgeoisie—especially those who lack understanding of art music and high Urdu but who nevertheless seek in their music an affirmation of their socio-economic position. Given the predominantly Hindu and, to some extent, Sikh composition of the North Indian bourgeoisie, it is significant that none of the new crop of *ghazal* stars is Muslim.

Cassettes and Indian Popular Music

The amount and variety of non-cinematic popular music has sky-rocketed since the advent of cheap cassette technology in the late 1970s, which was further promoted by the reduction of import tariffs in the early 1980s. The low price of cassettes and players, their durability and portability, and, above all, the ease with which they can be mass-produced have extended cassette technology to regions and musical genres where recordings previously had little or no impact. Thus, throughout the subcontinent, pop versions of regional folk musics are developing out of local traditions, often promoted by small, local "cottage" cassette producers for local audiences. Cassette players have become ubiquitous in the cities and commonplace in many villages. While many are Indian-produced, the best ones are imported, often being brought by workers returning from the Middle East. They are used to provide music at tea-stalls, restaurants, social festivities, religious contexts, and at various informal listening occasions. The cassettes marketed commercially include both film music and so-called "private" cassettes of popular musics which have no direct connection with cinema.

Owners of recorders have also become avid collectors; audiences at classical music performances have become used to the clicking and clacking that occurs 45 minutes into a concert as listeners change sides on their cassettes. Relatively new is the vogue of recording folk performances, as cheaper cassette players become accessible to the lower-middle classes.

Due to the unwillingness or inability of South Asian governments to enforce copyright restrictions, pirate cassettes dominate the market. These may consist of bootleg recordings of concerts, but more often they are simply *naqli* versions—copies—of previously released legitimate commercial recordings. The pirate industry bankrupts many legitimate cassette companies, or obliges them to join in the production of *naqli* tapes. Artists themselves receive no royalties from the sale of *naqli* cassettes, and the piracy has greatly undermined the production of records. In 1985, legitimate recording companies established an anti-piracy foundation to lobby for enforcement of copyright laws, and artists have united to publicly denounce the parasitism. But tape piracy is flourishing as never before, accounting for 95 percent of all cassette sales in 1985.[41]

The development of the recording industry in the city of Banaras has been typical and illustrates many of the problems and blessings of the cassette boom.[42] Before the 1970s, the most visible mass media in the Banaras region were radio, cinema, and phonograph records. There were many records of local folk genres like *biraha;* since relatively few people owned phonographs or records, the discs would typically be owned by travelling professionals who would play them on their own portable systems for a fee at various social occasions. Most of these records were produced by a Calcutta-based firm, but in 1971 a Banaras-based company was formed under the name of Madan Machinery Mart. Madan concentrated on regional folk and popular genres like *biraha, nautanki,* wedding songs, and abuse songs (*gāli*). Record production was soon replaced by cassettes, and a number of "legitimate" competitors soon entered the market, producing and marketing their own recordings of local musicians. In the wake of these competitors arrived the bootleg companies, who duplicate and market the original releases with such speed and efficiency that as soon as a legitimate recording appears, within a week, five or six bootleg versions of it may be on sale, generally for slightly more than half the retail price of the original. Indeed, in some cases involving internal connivance, the bootleg version may actually appear *before* the legitimate one. In such an atmosphere, most of the legitimate companies either have folded or have taken to piracy themselves.

Many of the commercial cassettes of local music in Banaras are live recordings, with traditional instrumentation (such as harmonium and *dholak*), generally made without the consent or knowledge of the artists. The legitimate originals, however, are usually "enhanced" with instrumental background added in the studio. This background generally consists of orchestrated, pre-composed passages played on combinations of instruments such as the violin, *shahnāi*, clarinet, guitar, or piano. Improvisation is eliminated, and songs are shortened to less than six minutes. The new "enhanced" versions may be subsequently imitated by live performers.

The new, cassette-based grassroots popular genres differ from the Bombay- and Madras-based film music in their responsiveness to local demand. They are performed in regional dialects, using stylizations of regional folk genres. Songs often concern contemporary socio-political events, unlike film songs, which generally deal only with sentimental romance. And, parasitic as the pirate cassettes may be, they have at most an indirect relation to the advertising promotion and the unreal cinema world which clearly manipulates demand for film music. In this sense, it is these cassette-based pop styles, rather than film music that can claim to be "people's music" in that these new genres are *produced* by the same ethnic group and class that consumes them.

Some of the most popular cassettes do achieve pan-regional popularity without being associated with advertising or cinema. In North India, such hits naturally tend to be in the lingua franca Hindi-Urdu, like the *ghazals* of singers like Mehdi Hasan and Ghulam Ali. Equally popular in the 1980s have been the recordings of Tulsidas's Hindi (Awadhi dialect) version of the *Rāmāyana* epic, as set to music by the late vocalist Mukesh. Like some of the most popular *ghazals* of Ghulam Ali and Mehdi Hasan, these recordings eschew the shortened duration, heavy orchestration, and pre-composed settings of the film style. Mukesh instead sings with sparse and tasteful instrumental accompaniment, using only harmonium and traditional instruments. The verses are sung in a free and often improvised style, without Western harmonies. The frequent changes in instrumental timbre are the only reflections of modern commercial aesthetics; aside from them, the extraordinary popularity of these cassettes must be attributed to Mukesh's rich voice, fine taste, and brilliant gift of melody.

The flowering of cassette-based popular musics has greatly enriched South Asian cultural life. Prior to the advent of cassettes, folk musics were in many cases waging losing battles for survival against film music. But the new stylized versions of folk musics, while different from their rustic models, are growing in strength and vitality, and are presenting an unprecedented challenge to Bombay's mass-produced bubble-gum music. The relationship between the corporate film style and the new grass-roots products is complex and contradictory, for it is at once antagonistic and symbiotic. Unless the situation changes dramatical in the future, it also ensures the inability of any single class to exercise complete hegemony over the field of South Asian popular music.

Sri Lanka

Geographically, Sri Lanka is overshadowed by the Indian subcontinent, and it is not surprising that the origins of much of its music and culture can be traced to Indian sources. Some of these features, including the Theravada Buddhism practiced by the Sinhalese majority, constitute continuations of traditions which have since expired in India itself. Further, over the millenia, the imported cultural forms have acquired their own, distinctively Sri Lankan character. While the culture of the Tamil minority (about 18 percent of the population) remains closely tied to that of the Indian Tamils, Sinhalese culture is more distinct, and the ongoing influences from the mainland have been inspiring ever more defensive or chauvinistic measures to preserve the integrity of Sinhalese language, religion, and culture in general.

Musical life on the island illustrates some of the complex and conflicting ideologies and ethnicities involved. Sri Lanka's most distinctive musical forms are the percussion-dominated ensembles used in traditional religious ceremonies (now regarded as elements of "folk religion" by the middle class) and in such secular arts as Kandy dancing. These, however, have not developed into recognized "classical" or popular music forms. Instead, art music in Sri Lanka consists of South Indian (Karnatak) music popular among the Tamils, and a certain amount of North Indian (Hindustani) music, patronized to a limited extent by the Sinhalese. Hindustani music has also been promoted by the Sinhalese-dominated government, as a counter-balance against Tamil musical domination, and in accordance with the alleged Aryan, North Indian origins of the Sinhalese race.

Indian music and Sinhalese music in Indian style tend to dominate the pop scene as well. This trend became especially marked in the 1950s, when Radio Ceylon capitalized on All-India Radio's boycott of Indian film music by broadcasting that music to India, thereby obtaining substantial commercial sponsorship from Indian advertisers (particularly film companies). A Sinhalese critic wrote that this promotion of Indian film music, while balancing Radio Ceylon's budget,

> . . . was like the great Banyan tree under which no other plant would grow. Sinhala films were remakes of successful Hindi and Tamil films. Sinhala film music was merely the substituting of inappropriate Sinhala words to Hindi tunes. Lyric-writing was a dignified name given to Hindi-Sinhala translations.[43]

In the seventies and eighties, some Sinhala film producers have attempted to create a more distinctively national film music, but on the whole, the prevalence of Indian music, along with imported Western forms (especially reggae) has continued.

Nevertheless, independently of both cinema and radio, Sri Lanka has developed its own distinctive forms of popular music, called *baila* and *kaffrinna*. These genres, like Indonesian *kroncong*, are themselves hybrid derivatives of music brought by the Portuguese, who controlled much of the coastal areas of Ceylon from the early sixteenth to mid-seventeenth century. Curiously, as in Indonesia and Malaysia, it was the Portuguese rather than the colonial Dutch and British who were to leave a lasting musical imprint. The early Portuguese seafarers, whether they came as traders, conquerors, or both, seem to have regarded the peoples they encountered with a familiarity and openness which was uncharacteristic of the arrogant Northern Europeans. The British and Dutch, unlike the Mediterranean cultures, had no prolonged experience of contact and trade with diverse African, Arab, and Semitic peoples; as a result, they tended to shun personal contact with those whom they dismissed as inferior due to the color of their skin. Although the Portuguese colonists could hardly be called enlightened, in Ceylon and elsewhere their relative sociability appears to have contributed to significant musical acculturation, not to mention widespread miscegenation.

Baila and *kaffrinna* are still referred to by Sri Lankans as "Portuguese music," and most of the leading performers have been and continue to be "burghers," that is, people of European descent. But the genres may date back four centuries to the early colonial period, and, moreover, they are not Portuguese music per se but rather Sri Lankan hybrids which, although European in character and originally derived from Lusitanian styles, no longer resemble any European genre except in the most general sense.

Baila is Portuguese for "dance," while the word *kaffrinna* (*kaffrinha*) would be the Portuguese diminutive for *kafir* (from Arabic, "pagan," or, by extension, "negro"). The latter term thus reflects the African influence from Portuguese colonies in that continent, and indeed, both *baila* and *kaffrinna*, properly speaking, are Afro-Portuguese-Sri Lankan forms. Both forms employ simple harmonic progressions, often I-IV-V-I, or simply I-V-I-V repeated *ad infinitum*. Stock, stereotypical melodies are sung over these. Most songs are in major keys. Vocal quadratic verses alternate with instrumental passages. The meter is a fast 6/8, and while this rhythm is hardly unique to Sri Lanka, it seems clear that its popularity derives in part from its widespread usage in traditional Sinhalese percussion music.

Kaffrinna and *baila* do not differ markedly from each other. *Kaffrinna* is regarded as older and more traditional. Its instrumental ensemble usually incorporates acoustic stringed instruments like violins (often playing passages in parallel thirds or sixths) and guitars. An essential element of *kaffrinna* is the *rabana* tambourine. *Baila* has developed into a more modernized, commercial version of *kaffrinna,* particularly since the sixties with the influence of singers like Wali Bastian. It is typically played on electric guitar and bass, with drums, synthesizer, horns, and other instruments freely added. *Baila* is usually slightly faster than *kaffrinna.* Both are dance genres, but, as might be expected where stock melodies and simple harmonies are used, much of the emphasis is on the text. As in the case of calypso and other genres, the lyrics may deal with a wide range of topics, from love to contemporary socio-political events. Anton Johns, of the older generation of *baila* singers, is particularly popular for his topical songs. One sub-genre is *wada baila,* in which two singers engage in a verbal duel, matching wits in improvised, often insulting exchanges.

Baila and *kaffrinna* have traditionally received only limited air play on Sri Lankan radio, which is state-controlled. Instead, they are disseminated primarily via cassettes. New releases are popularized to a large extent by taxi drivers, who have come to assume that aspect of promotion normally performed by the radio.

Afghanistan

Afghanistan, aside from having been a traditional buffer state between rival political powers, has also long constituted a meeting ground for South Asian, Central Asian, and Middle Eastern cultural influences. In spite of the strength of orthodox Islam, Afghanistan hosts a variety of musical traditions; some of these, such as the urban art music, synthesize imported elements, while folk musics tend to emerge more from local traditions. Afghanistan is not an industrialized nation in the Western sense, but the increasing influence of the mass media—particularly radio and cassettes—has promoted the development of a distinctive popular music.

Afghans have traditionally distinguished between art music, semi-classical *ghazal*-singing, and folk or "local" music. A modern urban style of *ghazal*-singing and a new category of urban popular music, called *kiliwāli,* have arisen in close association with the Kabul radio station. Radio broadcasting in Afghanistan started late and progressed slowly, but by the early 1950s improved reception, increase in radio ownership, and the spread of loudspeaker systems were beginning to have an impact on musical life. On a general level, the spread of radio music increased the amount of musical activity, stimulated popular interest in music, and weakened the influence of religious discouragement of music. Media orientation has been markedly more secular since the coup of 1978. More specifically, the radio has served to promote the development of the new *kiliwāli* style.[44]

The most influential medium for *kiliwāli* has been the Kabul radio station, which employs several musicians and frequently records and broadcasts visiting regional artists. Prominent musicians, some of whom have acquired "star" identities, tour the provinces regularly (or did so before the turbulence of the post-coup period). Thus, a typical evening concert in the Herat theater in the mid-seventies might consist of *ghazal* recitation, a short theatrical skit, and *kiliwāli*, with male and female singers.

Kiliwāli traditionally denoted the regional music of the Pashtun people. Pashtun traditional music constituted the basis for the new popular style, which now is heard, performed, and imitated throughout the country. In that sense, it has become a sort of national style, promoting an unprecedented degree of musical homogeneity in Afghanistan.[45] Accordingly, the language used in *kiliwāli* is Persian (*dāri* dialect), the lingua franca of the country.

The modern urban popular styles have incorporated elements from several different traditions. The South Asian influence is most conspicuous in the use of the harmonium and *tabla* drum pair. Hindi film music, which is widely popular in Afghanistan, is one source for song melodies, and a few songs reflect some Indian influence in the realm of orchestration or style. Urban music derives many elements from traditional Afghan art music, in particular the modal repertoire and the use of traditional Afghan instruments like the *tambur* and *rabāb*. Finally, regional folk (*mahali*) musics and, to a lesser extent, Iranian popular musics are additional sources for songs.[46]

In the 1970s, cassettes became increasingly important in popular music dissemination. Cassettes are sold in local bazaars, and are played in shops and teahouses. The recorders are easily available, whether brought by workers returning from the Middle East, or imported (legally or not) through the country's porous borders.

The instruments most commonly used in the urban radio style are the *tabla*, harmonium, *dhol* barrel drum, *delroba* (Indian fretted fiddle), and the lutes *tambur*, *dotār*, and *rabāb*. A small ensemble might consist only of *tabla*, *tambur*, and harmonium. Three melodic modes (called *rāg*) predominate: *Bairami, Kesturi,* and *Pāri. Bairami* and *Pāri* loosely correspond to Hindustani light *rāgs Bhairvi* and *Pahāri*, respectively. The scales of these *rāgs* are roughly as follows:

Bairami

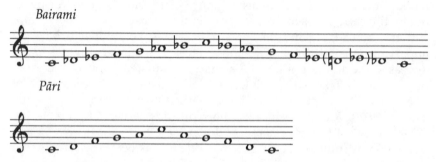

Pāri

Kesturi

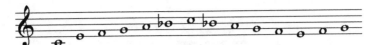

In *Pāri* (as in Hindustani *Pahārī*), the fourth degree (here, F), functions as a tonal center; in *Kesturi*, the fifth (G) is the ground note. The most common rhythms are *gedu*, *dādra*, and *mogholi*, of four, six, and seven beats, respectively.[48] *Gedu* is often played in a manner resembling the Indian *kaherva*, with a strong anacrusis on the final beat. Most of the texts are in the *ghazal*, *ruba'i* (quatrain), *do baiti* ("two lines"), or *char baiti* ("four lines") form. In performance, strophic sung passages (*khāndān*) alternate with instrumental interludes. The latter may consist of two successive melodic lines (*duni, naghme*), each of which progress to a cadence,[49] or the instrumental passage may consist of a single line. During the *khāndān*, the melodic instruments heterophonically accompany the vocal line.

CHAPTER 8

Southeast Asia

Vietnam

Vietnam, with a present population of over 60 million, has one of the richest musical cultures of Southeast Asia. Aside from the wealth of folk and religious musics, Vietnam possesses a sophisticated art music tradition which, although heavily influenced by that of China, has a distinct flavor and theoretical basis of its own. In the realm of popular music, Vietnam enjoys a vitality and individuality unrivaled by contemporary musics in smaller, war-ravaged Laos and Cambodia, as well as in Thailand and Malaysia, where, with the exception of the Malay-Indonesian *dangdut* and Thai *luk tung*, Western-style pop predominates. In spite of over a century of colonial rule and neo-colonial occupation, Vietnam succeeded in fostering a truly national, dynamic, indigenous popular music which borrows little from Western styles.

The predominant Vietnamese popular styles developed from urban professional musics associated with theater, in particular, the *cải lương* music drama of the southern region. A variety of musical theater traditions existed in Vietnam, from classical *hát tuong* of the ruling courts to the numerous forms of folk theater (*hát chèo*). In the period of French colonial rule (ca. 1860–1954), rural poverty, population growth, and superimposition of a capitalist economy contributed to an unprecedented urbanization in Vietnam. A new urban bourgeoisie of merchants and civil servants developed in the cities, and this class in turn sponsored the rise of new musical and theatrical forms.

Cải lương, or "reformed" theater, emerged in the years 1917–1920 as a popular entertainment form for the new middle class of the Saigon-Cholon area.[1] *Cải lương* incorporated elements from the Chinese-derived *tuong tau* classical theater, including some use of traditional Chinese plots, costumes, formalized gestures, and theatrical effects. One main source of music was the chamber music of the South (referred to as "amateur music"), played on traditional Vietnamese instruments. But *cải lương* was "reformed" in its free addition of new scripts, modernized costumes, more natural gesture styles, and an increasingly eclectic use

198

of Western and contemporary indigenous musics. French scripts and newly-written national stories with social themes became especially popular in the experimental period 1928–1937, as did Western music— particularly the tango and Cuban-style *bolero*. Chinese "swashbuckler romances" incorporating all manner of action, fights, and extravagant stage effects continued to be in vogue.[2] Most distinctively national and modern, however, were the *cải lương* plays stressing individualism and freedom rather than the Confucian obedience and loyalty lauded in the traditional theater.[3] During the revolution against the French, many of these plays celebrated, however obliquely, the patriotic national struggle. In the post-colonial war period, both North and South Vietnamese governments used theater extensively to promote their causes.

Broadly speaking, *cải lương* uses two kinds of music: Western and Vietnamese. These are juxtaposed rather than combined, and thus, while some Vietnamese elements are evident in the Western songs, the indigenous music used is free of Western stylistic borrowings. The musical interludes may range in length from one to five minutes; in the modern style, most are relatively short and are interpolated between spoken passages.

The songs in Western style are played on Western instruments such as piano, traps, bass, and organ. As mentioned above, Latin American tango and *bolero* rhythms, introduced via France, are extremely common, as are songs in polka and slow rock-ballad tempi. The vocal style in these songs, however, is often distinctively indigenous, partly, no doubt, because of the tonal structure of the language and the necessity of replicating it in song.[4] The anhemitonic pentatonic melodies favored in these songs are also congruent with modes used in Vietnamese folk and art musics, particularly the *sa mac* mode of northern Vietnam. The most distinctive national trait in the Western songs, however, is the use of the characteristic Vietnamese vibrato, which occurs on unstable leading tones and is so fast as to resemble a trill. These idiosyncrasies are evident in the example below.[5]

Most of the music used in *cải lương* consists of pieces in purely Vietnamese style. These songs are played on traditional instruments, including woodblock or clappers, the two-stringed "moon-lute" *nguyệt*, the spike fiddle *nhi* or *co*, and the zither *tranh*. The latter two instruments resemble and are presumably derived from the Chinese *erh-hu* and *cheng*, respectively. Other Chinese instruments may be used in more Sinicized drama. One imported instrument that has become virtually ubiquitous is the Western guitar, preferably electric, with steel strings. It may be tuned in Western style or in octaves or fifths.[6] In order to play the neutral intervals and fast vibrato essential to the style, the spaces between the frets are scalloped out to form concavities. These greatly increase the guitarist's ability to bend notes by deflecting the string; a variety of techniques and effects are used to produce slides and vibrato, including depressing the plucked string with the first finger of the left hand, while the second or third finger holds the string down on the fret.[7] Vietnamese refer to the altered guitar as an *octaviana*. (Rock guitarists could certainly learn some new techniques from *cải lương* musicians.)

Cải lương vocal melodies are modal and predominantly monophonic, although the instrumental accompaniment is freely heterophonic. Vietnamese modes are classified in terms of two basic modes and six or seven subsidiary "nuances," whose usage is to some extent based on regional preferences. The modal practice and theory are quite complex, involving frequent modulation and transposition.[8] The most common mode in *cải lương* is the southern Vietnamese *oán* nuance of the *nam* mode. This sub-mode is commonly referred to as the *vọng cổ* mode, and is based on the following pentatonic skeletal structure:

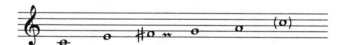

The neutral, half-sharp fourth degree is invariably performed with the distinctive fast vibrato, which heightens its instability. This pitch usually resolves upward to the fifth or, even more characteristically, downward to the tonic (see page 203). Other pitches may also be introduced in this mode, and the heterophonic instrumental accompaniment to a vocal melody may include gapped pentatonic and diatonic "dorian"-type scales. The mode itself may use passing tones as follows:[9]

In *cải lương* performance style, much of the melodic interest derives from the use of sudden, wide interval leaps, as on page 203. Pitches are sung with extreme accuracy and evenness, vibrato being used only on specific tones like the neutral fourth. Rhythms, marked at intervals by the clappers, are predominantly duple. Songs are generally preceded by *nói loi* introductions, sung solo without instrumental accompaniment.

Typically, a *cải lương* composer will choose from a stock melodic repertoire of tunes, to which new texts can be freely set.[10] These melodies may be in different modes, including the aforementioned *vọng cổ* mode. Often male and female singers will alternate singing extended sections; the modes may be transposed up or down a fourth in order to accommodate the singers' different voice ranges.

By far the most important pieces in *cải lương* are those based on the song entitled *vọng cổ* ("Nostalgia for the Past"). The original *vọng cổ* was a piece composed, or formally recomposed, around 1919 in the southern Bac Lieu province. It was set to the gapped *bac* scale of central and northern Vietnam (roughly, CDFGA) but soon came to be performed in the *oán* nuance of the *nam* mode; as the popularity of the song spread, this nuance came to be commonly referred to as the *vọng cổ* mode, as shown above.

The *vọng cổ* aria is seldom, if ever, performed in its original form. Rather, the song is subjected to an expansion technique whereby phrases (whether improvised or pre-composed) are inserted between each note of the original melody; the original notes are then used as structural cadential pitches. These inserted phrases grew progressively longer over the decades. As a result, in order to keep the rendition of a piece from growing unmanageably long, the original *vọng cổ* melody was shortened by deleting pitches at the end. This process continued to the point that in the last few decades the performance of a *vọng cổ* would seldom go past the first six pitches of the original piece.[11] The opening phrase of the original (*oán* nuance) melody is roughly as follows:

The structural pitches of this melody—marked with accents in the above example—changed slightly to become:

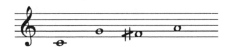

In chamber music and *cải lương,* a passage lasting as long as two minutes or more might be performed after the definitive commencement on the tonic; this passage would eventually cadence on the second pitch (the fifth degree), after which point, in vocal *cải lương,* a short instrumental interlude would follow. Another extended passage would then ensue, eventually cadencing on the third structural pitch (the neutral, shaken fourth, usually resolving to another more stable pitch. Such a piece would be referred to as *vọng cổ',* even though the original *vọng cổ'* melody is stretched out and truncated to the extent that it is unrecognizable. Moreover, only professionals and afficionados would be able to distinguish such a *vọng cổ'* from another piece set to the *vọng cổ'* mode, but lacking this recondite internal structure.

The use of this expansion technique resembles similar compositional and improvisational practices of other Southeast Asian musics—notably, Thai art music, and Javanese *gamelan* music. In the latter, a given melody may be drastically decelerated and expanded in a modulation to a different rhythmic density level (*irama*); at this level the original melody and its accompanying colotomic structure progress at a half or quarter of the original tempo, and new melodies moving at the original tempo are superimposed on the expanded structure.

Thus, the term *vọng cổ'* denotes: (1) a particular mode, equivalent to the *óan* naunce of the *nam* mode; (2) a particular song, dating from around 1919; and (3) any piece in the *vọng cổ'* mode which employs the pitches of the original *vọng cổ'* song as structural cadential points. The last and most general sense of the term is perhaps the most common; commercial cassette labels, for example, generally cite the two composers of Western music (*tân nhạc*) and *vọng cổ',* that is, Vietnamese music.

In most cases the *vọng cổ'* is preceded by a *nói loi.* Although unmetered, this is usually sung in even note values, in a syllabic style. Often it begins in a different mode—most typically, an anhemitonic pentatonic scale—and then modulates to the *vọng cổ'* mode just before cadencing on the tonic. The tonic is usually approached via the "leading tone" of the neutral, shaken fourth degree; the arrival at the tonic—the first structural pitch of the original melody—marks the beginning of the *vọng cổ'* proper. The instruments enter, playing a stereotyped phrase usually resembling that marked "a" in the example below. The syllabic vocal melody commences, while the instruments are free to improvise; all will pause at given lesser cadential intervals and, of course, at the important structural cadences. Often, the piece ends upon reaching the first structural cadence. The excerpt below is typical:[12]

Stephen Addiss has described *cải lương* and the role of *vọng cổ'* therein:

A writer making up a new *cải lương* operetta, for that is what the form most resembles, can select from at least 100 melody types or tune-formulas already known to the performers and audience. He will write a new set of lyrics for each piece, and some spoken passages as well as stage action. Actors in the larger troups learn their parts word for word, while smaller troupes improvise many of the actual lines from a rough draft of the plot. Most important is that the leading players will have a chance at a spectacular *vọng cổ'* at climactic movements, and that each of the main performers has both musical and dramatic exploits to perform. A successful *cải lương* star is the one kind of Vietnamese traditional musician [able] to earn more than a decent living nowadays. . . . Singing is the most important feature of the *cải lương,* as 70% to 80% of a performance may be devoted to song. . . .[13]

Cải lương has for decades been disseminated widely on the media, especially records, radio, and cassettes. As elsewhere in the developing world, urbanization has been a dramatic factor, especially in the case of Ho Chi Minh City, whose population has more than quadrupled since 1950.

While *cải lương* is most closely associated with the south, it has become widely popular throughout the country. Cassettes of old and new operettas abound. Since reunification of the country in 1975, *cải lương* continues to be popular, and musical standards are maintained. The state has zealously promoted national forms of culture like *cải lương,* giving special encouragement to socially relevant themes which, in the words of Party Secretary General Le Duan, "assert the new system, the new way of life, the new morality and develop the fine national traditions and revolutionary traditions of our people."[14] Thus, in *cải lương*, socio-political themes have become more common. One particularly popular operetta of 1986, for example, dealt with the opportunistic machinations of a woman from Ho Chi Minh City who attempted to emigrate to the USA by means of her neglected son, whom she had sired with an American GI.[15]

Meanwhile, state policy toward Western music continues to be ambivalent. After 1975, the government made some attempts to curtail the popularity of the "poisonous weeds" of bourgeois culture, limiting, for example, the amount of Western music on the radio and television.[16] Recent reports indicate, however, that Western music and dancing—from the tango to disco—continue to be popular in the cities and are even taught in youth clubs.[17]

Cải lương recordings are also produced by Vietnamese communities in Paris and Southern California, although it is clear that the younger generations of emigrants are losing interest, preferring Western-style pop music.

Finally, a discussion of Vietnamese popular music should mention the revolutionary mass music produced by the communist governments over the last several decades. Much of this music bears certain resemblances to Chinese mass music in its martial style, patriotic texts, choral vocal parts, heavy orchestration, and mixture of national and European elements.

Thailand

Popular music in Thailand is, on the whole, far more Westernized than that of Vietnam or neighboring Burma. The relatively limited development of indigenous popular musics is surprising in view of the fact that the country underwent no colonial period that could have weakened its own traditions; the explanation for the prevailing musical acculturation, then, may lie partly in such factors as the limited popular base of Thai art music, and the American influence prevalent especially during the Vietnam War.

Sakon, the most widespread Thai popular music, is predominantly Western in style, consisting of disco, rock, and rock ballads sung in Thai, with sentimental love as the invariable topic. Radios, cassette players, and even VCRs are common throughout most of the country and serve to disseminate *sakon* well beyond the cities. *Luk tung*, a somewhat more indigenous genre, is popular among rural audiences and urban immigrants from the countryside. *Luk tung*, like *sakon*, uses simple harmonies and standard rock instrumentation and rhythms. Many *luk tung* melodies, however, derive from rural folk songs; as such, they tend to be anhemitonic pentatonic in structure. In the least acculturated styles, the vocal melodies are extended, loosely melismatic, and ornamented in the style of northern Thai and Lao song.[18] In such cases, especially when the instrumental accompaniment is sparse, *luk tung* retains an earthy, rustic character that is quite distinct from the synthetic *sakon* music. Although most song texts are romantic, they often deal with rural life or the hardships of adapting to city life, as in the following excerpt:

> This year it's very cold and the rice has failed,
> The rice is dead and there is no rain.
> The sky is red like a fever,
> My love, you must be crying, and so am I.
> You starve for rice and the buffalo starves for grass.
> There is no money to spend.[19]

Luk tung singers distinguish their lyrics from the sentimental escapism of *sakon* texts. One star vocalist explained:

> Mostly our songs are about love, melancholy and grief, but they are not sentimental. They are too realistic for that. When there is a flood and the crops are destroyed, there is nothing left. People starve and have to go to Bangkok to find work. Tens of thousands do this every year. So our luk tung songs tell their story: about how people live and work in the countryside.[20]

Luk tung singers tour extensively in the countryside, presenting their music in the context of what Marre describes as "a brash, extraordinary, show-biz circus complete with midgets, clowns, fat men, superstars and nymphet chorus girls."[21] *Luk tung*, then, is one component of modern rural entertainment, and may be said to serve a mediating function between urban and rural cultures.

Indonesia

Indonesia, an archipelago nation of over 170 million people, encompasses a great diversity of musical cultures, from the complex *gamelan* traditions of Java and Bali to the diverse musics of Borneo, Sulawesi, and the other eastern islands. The "Great Traditions" of Java and Bali have tended to receive the most attention, and similarly, it is in these densely populated islands, and to a lesser extent, Sumatra, that modern popular musics have arisen. Imported and locally produced versions of Western pop enjoy considerable popularity, and indigenous syncretic forms have not gained the international visibility that Indian or Arab popular musics have. Nevertheless, the popular music scene in Indonesia must be regarded as one of the most vital in the developing world, encompassing a range of dynamic modern forms, from acculturated, Westernized rock hybrids to genres which are purely indigenous in origin and style.

The most characteristic traditional musics in Java and Bali are those performed by *gamelan* ensembles. A variety of regional *gamelan* styles exists, but all tend to share certain fundamental musical principles. These include: polyphonic stratification, cyclical time structures, predominance of metallophones and knobbed gongs, complex elaboration of skeletal melodies, close association with poetry (*tembang*), prevalence of *slendro* and *pelog* scalar systems, and a collective approach to music making, in which individual parts of varying difficulty combine to form complex aggregate structures. *Gamelan* musics continue to be popular and meaningful to a broad spectrum of Indonesians, and they still evolve and adapt and are in no danger of becoming ossified "museum pieces." The flowering of the Balinese *kebyar* style in this century is only one of the more visible signs of creative evolution within the framework of traditional *gamelan*.

As Martin Hatch notes, the continued vitality and contemporaneity of *gamelan* musics and their changing social context and function render problematic any categorization of Indonesian music as either "traditional" or "modern."[22] At the same time, dramatic changes in Indonesian society in the twentieth century have, as elsewhere, generated new forms of popular music which display fundamental divergences from traditional patterns of dissemination, evolution, social meaning, and style. The rise of modern cities—especially Jakarta—has created new classes of urban dwellers with new aesthetic standards and needs; the introduction of bourgeois capitalism has eroded the pre-capitalist communal values of the traditional village, contributing to the rise of an individualistic, superstar ethos absent from previous *gamelan* musics; and, most notably, the spread of the mass media has engendered new forms of acculturated, and even indigenous-derived popular musics which did not exist a century ago. In this sense, regardless of the ambiguity of the "traditional-modern" categories, one can identify a set of popular musics which are distinct from other forms of Indonesian music. Aside from modern imitations of Western pop, the most important indigenous genres are *kroncong, jaipongan,* and *dangdut.*

The impact of the mass media, and especially cassettes, has been particularly visible in Indonesia. Hatch has summarized the phenomenal growth of the local recording industry and its effect upon popular music. Record companies—particularly Lokananta—were active prior to the cassette vogue of the late 1960s, but their impact was limited due to the high expense of phonographs, the shortage of electric power, and the deleterious effect of the moist tropical climate upon vinyl. Radios were common throughout much of the populous western islands, but the state-controlled programming policies tended to restrict and direct popular music broadcasts.

In the 1960s and 1970s oil revenues and the relatively unrestricted import of cheap tape and recorders led to an extraordinary boom of the Indonesian cassette industry. As elsewhere in the developing world, cassettes, because of their durability, portability, low cost, and minimal power requirements, came into use throughout the country, extending mass media influence to regions and classes previously unexposed to phonographs.[23] The impact upon musical life has been considerable and mixed. In the realm of traditional musics, Sutton has noted several effects, including: increased imitation of recorded performances, widespread use of cassettes in pedagogy, enhanced popularity of certain styles, a greater tendency toward secularization of some genres, replacement of live performances with cassettes in certain regional contexts, and the emergence of new criteria of musician status based on who has and who has not recorded.[24]

The impact upon popular music has been even more remarkable. Cassettes have extended the appeal of regional popular styles throughout the country, and contributed to the emergence of new syncretic genres. On a socio-economic level, the cassette boom has extended control of mass media music production to small, backyard outfits throughout the country which, although often owned by Chinese entrepreneurs, have been capable of responding to diverse class and regional tastes in a manner uncharacteristic of large music industries. (Happily, the spread of new popular musics does not seem to have led to a serious decline of traditional styles, or to a homogenization of taste.)

Indonesian popular musics reflect varying degrees of acculturation. At one extreme lie locally produced versions of rock and pop whose styles do not differ markedly from Western pop and are thus outside the purview of this study.[25] At the other extreme are *jaipongan* and its various regional derivatives which are wholly indigenous in style.

Acculturated forms of music, of course, predate the advent of the mass media. The Dutch, who ruled most of the country from the mid-eighteenth to mid-twentieth century, did not attempt to foster a Europeanized middle class, as had British colonists in India. Nevertheless, the colonial settlers, rather than import musicians, expected native artists to provide Western music for various dances and functions. Hence Indonesian brass bands and string ensembles emerged which specialized in Western music. These in turn contributed to the evolution of hybrid forms like *tanjidor* brass band music,[26] and West Javanese *tarling*, which uses guitar in a more indigenous idiom and is marketed on commercial cassettes in Cirebon and Sunda.[27] Missionaries also promoted hymn singing in Christian enclaves. These syncretic musics, while interesting, have not evolved into modern popular genres.

Kroncong

Kroncong, the one acculturated traditional style that has become an important popular genre, is a legacy not of the Dutch, but of the Portuguese. *Kroncong*, whose evolution has been outlined by Judith Becker and Ernst Heins,[28] is one of several popular musics worldwide whose development has been associated with a maritime, racially and ethnically mixed, lumpen proletariat. Its roots lie in the trading communities developed by Portuguese seafarers in the sixteenth century. The Portuguese established trading outposts and settlements at various ports in the Malay peninsula, Sulawesi, the Moluccas, and elsewhere in modern-day Indonesia in order to secure mercantile monopolies. These settlements came to share less cultural affinities with their inland environs than with other Portuguese ports in Africa, South Asia, and Portugal itself. In Southeast Asia, the outposts developed as maritime enclaves distinguished by their Christianity, use of Portuguese or Portuguese-derived languages, and their racially-mixed populations which combined Indian, African, Chinese, and European as well as native Malay blood. Another distinction was their fondness for *kroncong*, a syncretic music of primarily Lusitanian flavor and derivation.

In the early seventeenth century, the Dutch ousted the Portuguese from Java and the Malay peninsula, and Malay/Indonesian gradually eclipsed Portuguese as a lingua franca. Jakarta emerged as the center not only of commerce and shipping, but of the cosmopolitan, lower class, hybrid society that the Portuguese had initially engendered.

By the nineteenth century, *kroncong* had become popular in the *kampungs* (lower-class neighborhoods) of Jakarta and the neighboring coastal towns. Becker describes how the genre was closely associated with the Javanese stereotype of a lumpen, roguish dandy variously referred to as *buaya* (crocodile), *jago* (rooster), or a variety of other epithets. The archetypical *jago* was hard-drinking, womanizing, belligerent, and seductive.[29] Like his counterparts in Piraeus and Buenos Aires, he was at once envied and despised by "respectable" society, and his creative energy, unbound by traditional or elite conventions, helped foster a dynamic incipient popular music genre.

As Indonesian cities grew, and the Indonesian language was adopted as the nation's official lingua franca, *kroncong* began to emerge from its lowly origins and gain popularity in numerous cities and among a wider social class spectrum. Indonesian films of the 1930s made use of *kroncong* as a vehicle for reaching the broad masses of Indonesians. Composers turned to *kroncong* style as a medium for nationalistic anthems. For patriotic Indonesians who resented Western and Chinese cultural intrusions in their country, *kroncong* came to be identified with an "earthy camaraderie" and a distinctively Malay/Indonesian grassroots urban culture.[30] The Japanese occupation further consolidated *kroncong's* appeal, for the Japanese banned foreign pop musics and contributed, albeit unwittingly, to the rise of Indonesian nationalism. After 1945, further experiments involved expansion of the *kroncong* ensemble and incorporation of Latin rhythms. With the advent of cassettes in the late sixties, *kroncong* became an important pop genre, and has since extended its popularity to nightclubs in Singapore, Bangkok, Manila, and Hong Kong.[31] With Indonesia, the genre has spawned several regional hybrids, sung in local languages with influences from local musical traditions.

The term *kroncong* denotes a five-stringed ukulele-like instrument, the larger musical ensemble containing that instrument, and the characteristic musical style itself. The ensemble consists mostly of European chordophones—typically, one or two *kroncongs*, guitars, violins, a flute, and occasionally a cello and light percussion. These accompany singing, usually by a solo female. The songs are set in a medium-tempo quadratic rhythm. The vocal lines have a languid, free-rhythmic character, with sentimental leaps and appoggiaturas; the vocal style resembles Western bel canto in its use of vibrato and relative absence of ornamentation.[32] In standard *kroncong asli* ("original" or "authentic" *kroncong*), the plucked instruments carry the harmonic progressions, while the violin(s) and flute play loosely improvised melodies, occasionally in a heterophonic relationship to the vocal line. Most of the songs employ diatonic major-minor scales and simple harmonies, although the chord progressions, as Heins observes, may not always follow Western expectations. Traditional *kroncong* texts, in Hatch's words, tell of "love lost and love found, yearning for someone far away, the felicitous effects of *kroncong* songs and rhythms on sad and lonesome hearts, [and] the beauty of the countryside. . . ."[33]

In its simple harmonies, string accompaniment, and languid, crooning vocal style, *kroncong* bears affinities with other acculturated Portuguese-derived genres and even, superficially, with modern *fado* itself.[34] The alleged maritime origins of *fado* further suggest that the evolutions of the two genres may be interrelated. Such acculturation notwithstanding, *kroncong* remains a distinctively Malayo-Indonesian genre, for it combines the aforementioned Westernized features with indigenous ones. Becker relates how *kroncong*, in spreading to inland areas, "became 'gamelanized' both musically and in its affective connotations and associative meanings, and it became respectable."[35] Thus, *kroncong* instruments are used in ways which correspond to *gamelan* instruments, giving *kroncong* a colotomic, polyphonic texture whose affinities to traditional Indonesian musics are readily apparent to the ear. Most conspicuous is the resemblance of the plucked cello punctuations to Javanese *kendhang* (drum) style. In many songs—especially those from the hinterland—the parallels extend to other instruments: thus, the violin recalls the *rebab* melodies, the melodic guitar imitates the perpetual "sixteenth-note" *celumpung* figurations, and the *kroncong*, striking stacatto chords on the "-and-" upbeats, functions like the *ketuk*. Moreover, some songs are set in modal (especially *pelog*) frameworks rather than harmonic ones.[36]

Kroncong is best regarded as a complex of styles and hybrids with certain broad similarities. Some of the older styles are the most Westernized, for the "gamelanization" occurred only after the genre spread to Central Java. Old Malaysian 78s document such sub-styles as *kroncong slowfox* (that is, the *kroncong*-style foxtrot). Chinese melodic influence is present in much of Jakarta *kroncong*. The style of *kroncong* used in the early twentieth-century *komedi stambul* urban folk theater came to be known as *stambul II*. *Langgam jawi* denotes *kroncong* using regional languages and local scales and rhythms (hence, for example, *kroncong madura*). Commercialized, rock-influenced styles of *kroncong* have also gained some international popularity. In Indonesia and Malaysia, young people may tend to regard *kroncong* as old-fashioned, but the genre nevertheless seems to enjoy a secure, albeit somewhat peripheral place in the local music world.

Dangdut

Dangdut is an acculturated modern music genre of vastly greater popularity than *kroncong*. Moreover, *dangdut* is more of a "pure" popular music, in the sense that its proper evolution does not predate the mass media. At the same time, while *dangdut* is Indonesian in origin and audience, it possesses few, if any, stylistic features which can be identified as distinctively Indonesian. Rather, in terms of style, it is a hybrid of imported features and acculturated Sumatran styles; still, it deserves some mention in this text because it does incorporate notable non-Western attributes, specifically, elements borrowed from Indian popular music.

In spite of *dangdut's* present absence of indigenous stylistic elements, the genre appears originally to have evolved out of local forms, in particular *kroncong* and *orkes melayu*.[37] The latter term is used to denote a variety of ensembles—including, to some extent, *kroncong* groups—which played syncretic musics combining Western and Malay elements. *Orkes melayu* had been flourishing and developing as a provincial hybrid in central and western Sumatra since the early decades of the twentieth century. *Orkes melayu* integrated elements from Indian film music and Arab urban music in a syncretic style with a more lively beat than the languid *kroncong*. Song texts were generally in Indonesian, but occasionally in Arabic.[38] Under Sukarno's rule (1949–1965), film composers responded to populist sentiment and resentment against foreign pop music by using modernized forms of *orkes melayu* in their musicals.

The coup and counter-coup of 1965 brought to power General Suharto, who renounced the progressive and nationalistic Sukarno policies and aligned Indonesia more closely to Western financial and political interests. Accordingly, restrictions on the import and broadcast of foreign pop were lifted, and Western music soon became the major influence in the world of Indonesian popular music. The newly refined forms of *melayu* music came to be regarded as quaint and even elitist, and young pop musicians turned increasingly to rock for inspiration. The introduction of cassettes and the vogue of social dancing also contributed to the rise of new musical tastes.

At the same time, some emerging musicians felt a need to foster some sort of style that could be popular among all national regions and social classes, that could spread a meaningful, populist message and be at once modern and somehow Indonesian. By far the most influential of these musicians was Rhoma Irama (b. Oma Irama, 1947), who has been the central figure in the evolution of modern *dangdut*. From the late sixties, Irama set out, with a combination of Messianic zeal, talent and business acumen, to create a synthesis of *orkes melayu* and imported musical styles that could constitute a new pan-Indonesian popular idiom. By 1975 a distinctive style had emerged, and the term *dangdut* had come into vogue to describe it.

In modernizing, *dangdut* forsook much of the *orkes melayu* style, although it continued to use Malay/Indonesian as its lingua franca. Partly under Irama's influence, the *dangdut* ensemble incorporated electric guitars, bass, traps, and synthesizer. While the music of artists like A. Rafik and Elvy Sukaesih retained a more indigenous flavor, Irama's *dangdut* came to resemble a home-grown rock variant. Arab influences decreased somewhat, but the Indian flavor remained in the use of *tabla*, in instrumental ornamentation styles, and, more noticeably, in the rhythm. The ubiquitous *dangdut* rhythm derives from the North Indian *kaherva*, itself the most popular meter in Indian film music. If regarded as a quadratic meter, its trademark is a low-pitched stroke on the fourth beat leading iambically to a high-pitched stroke on the first beat of the following bar. The term *dangdut* is an onomatopoetic realization of this rhythm as it is played on a drum and/or bass guitar.

Dangdut soon became widely popular as social dance music, and was often performed in large, outdoor concerts. The flamboyant theatrics indulged in by Irama's band soon came to be widely imitated, and the *dangdut* craze generated new modes of attire. Most importantly, Irama started producing *dangdut*-laden films, which inaugurated a new phase in Indonesian cinema. Irama's most celebrated films have been semi-autobiographical dramatizations of his rise from relative poverty to stardom. His films juxtapose *kampung* life with urban luxury, and celebrate honor, diligence, romantic love, and family devotion, while at the same time portraying the honest pursuit of wealth and fame as legitimate aspirations. Intended to instruct and inspire the lower classes, his movies convey a fervent populism and a sympathy for the underdog. At the same time, many of Irama's songs contain didactic Islamic messages. Most early *dangdut* texts concerned themselves with sentimental love or "hey, let's dance" themes, but Irama, after completing a pilgrimage to Mecca, turned to light social criticism and moralistic themes. Hence, his songs praise Allah, denounce excessive materialism, call for religious freedom, and exhort listeners not to stay up too late at night. All these developments culminated in his 1980 film *Perjuangan dan Do'a* ("Struggle and Prayer"), which, as Frederick notes, must surely be the first Islamic rock (*dangdut*) film. The cassette sound track is also representative of

Irama's mature style, with its tuneful songs, infectious rhythms, and texts denouncing alcohol, poverty, violence and other evils.[39] *Dangdut* seems to have reached a peak around this period, accounting for perhaps one half of all Indonesian cassette sales and dominating cinema production.[40] Some indications suggest that the fad has waned slightly in the mid-eighties.

Dangdut, then, represents much more than a musical style; it is a major socio-cultural phenomenon, involving cinema, fashion, youth culture, Islamic resurgence, and populism as well as the capitalist entertainment industry. As such it has been the subject of much controversy in Indonesia. Articulate supporters assert that its egalitarianism and inherent vitality impart to it a unique ability to respond to mass tastes and needs, and that its didacticism constitutes a healthy moral influence. Meanwhile, progressive critics denounce its commercialism, and elitist detractors dismiss it as *kampung* trash. Indeed, as Frederick observes,

> . . . nearly every aspect of dangdut has been attacked: the simplistic lyrics, the Islamic content, the often blatant but "laundered" sensuality, the "crazy vitality" and "phony dynamism," and even the pseudo-auto-biographical content of the films, which one enterprising critic portrayed as a kind of masturbation.[41]

Dangdut films invite comparison and contrast with commercial Indian cinema. Irama's populist movies address themselves directly to the poor—that is, the majority—in a manner which Indian films do not. Irama's goal seems to be to portray luxury and wealth not primarily for their escapist fantasy value, but as real goals to be achieved through perserverance. Moreover, *dangdut* films, unlike their Indian counterparts, do not shirk from depicting poverty and lower-class life. Most importantly, while Irama certainly enjoys box-office receipts as a measure of his popularity, his films reflect that conveyance of his didactic message is at least as important to him as commercial success;[42] the same cannot be said of commercial Indian filmmakers.

At the same time, *dangdut* films reflect the inevitable contradictions of a medium produced for lower-class masses by a corporate entertainment industry. Irama's rags-to-riches stories remain unrealistic fantasies in a country where poverty is the norm and socio-economic mobility is limited. Moreover, it is questionable whether his religious and didactic homilies (on, for example, going to bed on time) really address and confront the iniquities and adversities of lower-class Indonesian life. *Dangdut* music itself reflects these contradictions, for *orkes melayu* origins and nationalist ethos notwithstanding, much modern *dangdut* closely resembles rock, a genre imported from the capitalist West, to whom Indonesia's foreign and economic policies remain ultimately subservient.

Jaipongan

The realm of Indonesian popular music is not limited to acculturated forms or those dominated by corporate entertainment industries. Indeed, the country has fostered at least one dynamic popular music which is totally indigenous in style and origin. *Jaipongan* is a popular genre which emerged in the 1970s in Sunda (West Java) and has since gained audiences throughout Indonesia, spawning various regional hybrids in the process.[43]

Jaipongan, devoid as it is of foreign influences, can be seen as one of many regional varieties of the Indonesian gong-chime or *gamelan* performance continuum. *Jaipongan's* roots lie in a Sundanese folk entertainment form known as *ketuk tilu*. *Ketuk tilu* was archetypically performed in a village, as part of a ceremony related to a harvest ritual, or often to a circumcision or marriage. The typical ensemble, whose instruments are small enough to be carried about, consists of a solo female singer-dancer (*ronggeng*), accompanied by spike fiddle (*rebab*), a hanging gong, two iron plates (*kecrek*), two or three barrel drums, and three pot-gongs (*ketuk*).

Ketuk tilu songs, following a free-rhythmic introduction, are structured sectionally, juxtaposing segments of short gong-cycles (ca. 10″) with those of longer gong-cycles (ca. 30″), each section having a characteristic sequence of dance steps associated with it. As in many older Javanese musical genres, poetic meter corresponds with gong and melody structure.

The large hanging gong, and the smaller gongs *kempul* and *ketuk* serve colotomic functions, punctuating the time-cycles at regular fixed intervals. The *ketuks* play a standardized three-pitch figure (high-low-medium-low) from which the name *ketuk tilu*—"three *ketuks*"—derives. The spike fiddle may anticipate, imitate, or generally support the singer in a loosely heterophonic manner, or it may solo freely when the singer is silent. All the musicians, and especially the drummer, freely supplement the texture with rhythmic cries and yells (*senggak*), often in interlocking hocket style. The most important roles are those of the drummer and the singer-dancer. The drummer plays in a far more aggressive and assertive style than in most other Javanese and Sundanese ensembles, commanding particular attention just before the large gong stroke by playing a loud, variable cadential figure. The *ronggeng*, however, remains the central figure, carrying the vocal melody while dancing at the same time. The lively interplay between the drummer and the *ronggeng* is one of the more distinctive features of *ketuk tilu*, and one which has carried over into *jaipongan*. Typically, a male in the audience will dance with the *ronggeng*, circling her gracefully without touching, in a dance style whose vocabulary of gestures and postures derives in part from the traditional martial art *pencak silat*. The dance, like the music, is structured around the gong cycles, in which tension is built up to be

dispelled at the large gong stroke; often, just before the gong, the dancers, facing each other, will gracefully jerk their heads toward each other.

The figure of the *ronggeng* singer-dancer, who is generally assumed
to be a prostitute, is central to a number of Javanese and Sundanese
genres. The *ronggeng* as an institution has been metaphorically carried
over into *jaipongan*, divested of its disrepute. The female singer is the
most important personage in the *jaipongan* ensemble, and her name and
image are invariably featured on cassette covers.

The relatively recent and unprecedented rise to prominence of the
pesinden (singer) in Javanese gamelan parallels the rise of a *pesinden*-
centered genre like *jaipongan*, and the two phenomena seem to be related to broader socio-economic factors. The market demand for solo superstars is an obvious impetus, but this itself must be seen in the context
of the changes in Indonesian social economy. Traditional *gamelan* music
is a communal activity in which there is no concept of stardom. This
collective approach to music-making can be seen as a natural reflection
of the traditional village economy in which collective endeavors played a
large role. With the advent of free-market capitalism in the twentieth
century, stressing the role of the individual as the primary socio-economic unit, it is perhaps not entirely surprising that new popular
forms like *jaipongan* and *dangdut* are more individualistic and "star"-
oriented.[44]

In the late 1970s, *jaipongan* began to evolve as a more slick and
expanded version of *ketuk tilu*, largely free of any association with prostitution. *Jaipongan* is also less strictly associated with rustic ceremonial
functions like harvest rituals, although performances of the genre are
particularly common at annual festivals. While most performances may
still be loosely related to some life-cycle function, they now have the
character of secular social functions, attended by young and old, primarily for entertainment and socializing.

The rise of *jaipongan* is directly linked to the advent of cassettes in
Java. Competing groups—and especially drummers—take active interest in the innovations and musics of other groups as recorded on
cassettes. *Jaipongan* dance styles are generally taught with cassette rather
than live accompaniment. The rise of *jaipongan* social dancing has, indeed, led to the flowering of innumerable private dance instruction
schools where middle-class teenagers may attend classes in *jaipongan*
much as would Westerners amuse themselves learning the foxtrot and
the *chachachá* at an Arthur Murray studio. Thus, the traditional absence
of female social dancing in Sunda—or rather, its confinement to the
disreputable *ronggeng*—is quickly being altered by the rise of *jaipongan*
and the dance schools related to it.[45] The *jaipongan* dance style is less
acrobatic and martial than the male *ketuk tilu* style, although it has a
sophisticated polish which its rustic ancestor lacks. The female *jaipongan*
dance, moreover, is considerably more active than that of the *ketuk tilu
ronggeng*, whose main choreographic role is to coyly receive or parry the
male's stylized advances.

The instrumentation of *jaipongan* resembles that of *ketuk tilu*, with the difference that the drummer may use up to six drums (rather than two), and the idiophonic accompaniment may include a few *sarons* or a *degung* (an L-shaped row of inverted gongs) and often a *gambang* (xylophone). The *kecrek*, spike fiddle, *kempul*, and gong are retained, performing similar functions as in *ketuk tilu*. Instrumentation may vary somewhat, depending on the group or on the availability of instruments.

The sectional formal structure of *ketuk tilu* is one feature that has not been carried over to *jaipongan*; typically, a *jaipongan* piece opens with a few gong cycles (often in a different tempo from the rest of the piece) during which the *rebab* player improvises over the idiophone and drum accompaniment; the vocalist then enters, usually singing four *gongan* (gong-cycles) consecutively, then allowing the fiddler to improvise for two *gongan*. After alternating in this fashion for several minutes, the piece ends with a deceleration leading to the final gong.

Jaipongan has adopted certain aspects of the internal *ketuk tilu* colotomic structure; notable among these are the *kempul* patterns, whose stroke density characteristically doubles or quadruples as the final gong approaches, as shown below (p=*kempul*) and in Example 34:

```
   p      p      p      p      p      p       p   p   p   p  (gong)
 1  2  3  4  5  6  7  8  9  10  11  12  13  14      15      16
```

Jaipongan drumming, while clearly an extension of *ketuk tilu* style, is considerably more flamboyant and virtuosic, and accordingly, cassettes generally feature the drummer's name immediately below that of the singer. As in *ketuk tilu*, the drummer performs lively improvisations throughout, building up tension which culminates and is released at the gong stroke. A distinctively Sundanese feature is the variation of the pitch of the main drum, whose head tension is governed by the foot of the drummer. Another unique characteristic is the practice of concluding a drum cadential figure immediately before the gong, thus climaxing on the upbeat and allowing the downbeat to be stressed only by the gong, and by the listener's own learned *perception* of the inherent importance of that beat. Two typical examples of these cadences are shown here:

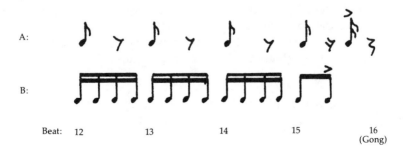

Beat:	12	13	14	15	16
					(Gong)

Jaipongan melodies invariably consist of four lines set within a single gong-cycle. The text is rendered strophically, and the rhythmic setting of the quatrain usually loosely resembles that of the example below.

The melodies are set either to heptatonic *pelog*, a Sundanese variant of *pelog* called *madenda*, or, less often, to pentatonic *salendro* (*slendro*) skeletal tunings. Precise intonation of these scales varies considerably; the *pelog* configuration may be vaguely approximated as: D Eb F (G) A Bb (C), with D generally functioning as what Westerners might call a tonic. In *madenda*, the second scalar degree would be closer to E natural.

Salendro intonation is even less consistent and the sense of a "tonic" much weaker; the configuration, however, usually approximates the familiar anhemitonic "black-key" pentatonic scale. Within this broad framework, however, Sundanese, and especially *jaipongan* treatment of mode is very distinctive and merits detailed study.[46]

Since *jaipongan* melodies are sometimes stereotypical, much of the charm and expressiveness of the singing comes from the introduction (whether improvised or pre-composed) of extraneous notes functioning as alternate scale degrees or establishing temporary modal modulations. Often the melody may alternate between *pelog/madenda* and *salendro*, or seem to be a free combination of the two, as, for example, when the sixth degree of the *madenda* scale (here, Bb) is raised and the normally weak fourth degree is stressed. Intonation may be further obscured by the characteristic vibrato, used especially on the unstable second and sixth *pelog* degrees.

An interesting feature of *jaipongan* (and other Sundanese genres like *ketuk tilu*) is that while the vocal (and fiddle) melodies are usually in the *pelog/madenda* scale, the fixed-pitch idiophonic accompaniment is strictly in *salendro*. This combination of *pelog* and *salendro* contrasts with most Javanese *gamelan* traditions, where *gamelans* usually consist of paired instruments in the two tuning systems. However, it is encountered in a few lesser Indonesian genres, especially archaic ones that seem to represent fusions of discrete vocal and instrumental traditions. *Jaipongan* may be an instance of this sort of confluence, since Sundanese gamelan, *calung* and bamboo *anklung* ensembles are strictly *salendro*, while the predominant Sundanese vocal genres *pantun* and *tembang* are mostly in *pelog* or *madenda*.

The apparent dissonance between the *salendro* idiophones and the *pelog* voice and fiddle is mitigated, first, by the frequent vibrato and microtonal alterations in the vocal line, and, more importantly, by the stressing of the common (or approximately common) notes in the two systems. The congruence between the two systems as used in Sunda is illustrated below (taking D as a *pelog* "tonic"; all pitches are approximate):

salendro (idiophones):	D		F	G	A		C
pelog (voice, fiddle):	D	Eb	F	(G)	A	Bb	(C)

This juxtaposition of the two tunings is also evident in the example below.

The song repertoire of *jaipongan* is quite varied, and hence, *jaipongan* is better understood as a performance style than as a distinct body of compositions. In Sunda, as elsewhere in Java, compositions, or *patokan*—denoting skeletal melodic structures—may be performed in different styles and contexts. To some extent, however, one may distinguish between the song repertoires of the *anklung* and *calung* ensembles (dominated by bamboo shaken rattles and xylophones, respectively), and that of the more professional *ketuk tilu, degung,* and *gamelan* traditions. *Jaipongan*, in accordance with its origins in *ketuk tilu*, derives its repertoire mostly from the traditions of the latter group, although it may occasionally employ songs from the *anklung/calung* repertoire. Much of the *jaipongan* repertoire, however, is not traditional, but consists of songs of recent origin (whether composed specifically for *jaipongan* style or not). Such a song is "Mat Peci," a *lagu alit* or "short song," one gong cycle of which is presented below. The melody of this song is so typical as to constitute almost a stock tune; the gong cycle accommodates one strophic quatrain, whose text concerns a famous urban bandit of the 1970s.[47]

Subject matter of song texts varies in accordance with the diverse sources of the repertoire, encompassing amatory, moralistic, bawdy, topical, and even spiritual subjects (as in the traditional invocation "Kidung").

Jaipongan is frequently performed during festivals, in clubs in Bandung, and in between acts of a *wayang* performance. However, the most typical setting for a *jaipongan* performance is a side street or alley, where a private host—for whatever special occasion—will have a canopy-covered stage constructed, extending from his front porch into the alley. The event follows a customary sequence, proceeding from an opening invocation, to one or two speeches by local bureaucrats, to the dance itself, which is commenced by children but gives way to couple dancing by adults.

Like several other popular music genres, *jaipongan* has evolved in association with a disreputable social group—in this case, the rustic *ketuk tilu*, with its singer/prostitute *ronggeng*. *Jaipongan*, however, differs from genres like *rebetika* and *kroncong* in that its origins were predominantly rural, and, perhaps more noticeably, in that it is totally indigenous in style. Unlike many syncretic popular forms, there is no addition of electric guitar or of Western harmonies over a modal melodic conception. *Jaipongan* is thus one of the relatively few mass media-based pop musics that has resisted any Western or foreign influence; moreover, it is one of many felicitous illustrations of the fact that where control of the media is not excessively concentrated, the mass media, rather than obliterating regional traditions in a cultural "grey-out," may in fact promote the rise of vital new regional styles.

Jaipongan has become perhaps the only regional Indonesian genre sung in a regional language to achieve great popularity outside its place of origin. Top names like Tati Saleh, Dede Winingsih, Karawang, and the Suwanda Group are now familiar to listeners throughout Java and Sumatra, and, moreover, the genre has spawned several hybrids, including *reog-jaipong* (using *anklung*), Chinese influenced *mandarin-jaipong*, *jaipongan*-style renditions of TV pop tunes, *calung-jaipong, jaipongan versi Banyumas*, and *jula-juli jaipongan*—the latter two being fusions with Banyumas and East Javanese styles, respectively.[48] While a few informants have opined that the *jaipongan* fad has already started to wane, these hybrids and the evident cultural vitality of Sunda would seem to assure its continuation in some form.

Pop

Around 20 percent of Indonesian cassette sales fall in the category known in that country as *pop*. *Pop* styles differ from the genres discussed above in that they are almost entirely Western in style and derivation. They constitute an important part of the Indonesian musical world, but are of only peripheral relevance here because of their relative absence of non-Western ingredients. Hatch has outlined the development of *pop* from Western music introduced in the colonial period and, more importantly, from recent rock influence. Various styles have since emerged: *pop ringin* (light pop) is accessible and simple; *pop tengah* (middle pop) has more sophisticated and occasionally slightly obscure lyrics; *pop country* derives primarily from Western folk and folk-rock. *Pop berat* (heavy pop) is the most sophisticated, highbrow, and intellectual of the styles. Its audience consists mostly of high school and university students. As Hatch states, *pop berat*

> . . . includes songs that have difficult or complex words; texts that contain social criticism or mix archaic language, regional ethnic dialects or obscure references with colloquial Indonesian; rhythms or meters that are complex, disjointed, interrupted or mixed; melodies with disjunct contours, mixed tunings, harsh timbres, mixed timbres or quotations from regional ethnic music.[49]

The occasional self-conscious use of regional musics in *pop berat* merits some mention here. Of greatest interest is the music of the genre's most distinguished exponent, Guruh Soekarnoputra (who is the youngest son of the late Indonesian populist leader). Most of Soekarnoputra's music is slick, highly professional, sophisticated pop, in an idiosyncratic rock/disco style. Several of his songs, however, incorporate indigenous musics, fusing old and new. His 1977 cassette "Guruh Gypsi," mixing *gamelan* music, various regional languages, prayers, social commentary, and Western pop styles, was hailed in Indonesia as the most important national music release of the decade.[50] Other songs (notably, "Janger Jakarta" on *Guruh and Swara Maharddhika*) blend rock with Balinese *gamelan*, which Soekarnoputra used to play as a youth in his father's palace.

Such innovations represent an interesting, albeit peripheral and intellectual development in Indonesian popular music. Were it not for government censorship of social commentary, such fusions might inspire others to form an indigenous "new song" movement, rather than constituting merely a footnote in modern Indonesian culture.

CHAPTER 9 ·

China

If the development and direction of popular music are reflections of socio-economic change and modernization, then the study of Chinese popular music should be of particular interest. China's dramatic social upheavals in this century—most notably, of course, the Communist Revolution—have indeed contributed to an accompanying revolution in the field of music; these musical developments are of interest not only because of their impact on the lives of one-fifth of the world's population, but also because of their illustration of the possible effects of socio-political changes upon music.

At the same time, the study of Chinese popular music is inherently problematic. The spectrum of Chinese music, both before and after 1949, does not lend itself to clear division into categories of folk, art, and popular music. Of course, one may label without hesitation *qin* (ch'in) music as "classical," Deng Li-Chun's sentimental crooning as "popular," and village wedding music played on gongs and oboes as "folk." But much of Chinese music lies in a continuum that resists such taxonomies. For example, the classification of opera music (both traditional and modern) would be ambiguous.[1] In the pre-revolutionary period, with the exception of film music and Shanghai cabaret music, it is difficult to regard any Chinese music as "popular" in the same sense as, for instance, Indian pop music; and since the revolution, much of Chinese mass music, regardless of its mass media dissemination and reproduction, may sound more like Rimsky-Korsakov in style and orchestration than any kind of popular music discussed in this volume.

The degree of Westernization in modern Chinese music renders the identification of a national pop style especially difficult. Chinese popular music has not evolved into such distinct non-Western forms as, say, Indian film music or Arab urban music. In much of Chinese music today, national elements may consist only of language and such features as a preference for pentatonic melodies. Yet national elements are in fact present in modern Chinese music, and the distinct ways in which Western music is incorporated are also governed ultimately by Chinese aesthetics and by broader socio-political developments within China. Thus, the adoption of Western elements has been neither arbitrary nor indiscriminate, but rather has tended to follow the guidelines of the prevailing aesthetic and socio-political climate (whether at the grassroots level or among a ruling clique).

Chinese Music and Westernization

When a culture confronts Western music, a variety of responses are possible. It may reject Western music, accept it in a compartmentalized fashion, incorporate selected features in an idiosyncratic manner, modernize in its own distinctively national ways in order to challenge Western music, or it may succumb to the onslaught in varying degrees. A genuine impoverishment of the native tradition may result when, as Nettl puts it, an increasing amount of the supply of musical "energy" is invested in Western styles.[2]

Several factors are involved in determining which response a culture may adopt. The presence of Western influence in much of modern Chinese music illustrates some of the complexities at work. In many respects the Westernization in Chinese music is paradoxical. China has a rich musical heritage, which includes one of the great non-Western classical traditions, with a well-developed theory and pedagogy. The Chinese have had for millennia a strong sense of cultural identity, regarding foreigners as barbarians and their own land as "the middle kingdom." China was never intensively colonized by Europe as were, for example, Latin America or even India. Moreover, Chinese nationalism has been a pervasive and intense force in shaping national destiny in the twentieth century.

Clearly, however, in other respects, Chinese music was ripe for remolding into a Western form, and its duple meters, emphasis on composition rather than improvisation, and the absence of neutral intervals must have facilitated incorporation of Western traits.[3] One important factor involved was the inroads made by Christian missionaries, who promoted choral hymn singing as a means of proselytization. The missionary presence in China by the turn of the century was considerably stronger than, for example, in India or Indonesia, and in many cases, the churches' dominance of village economies contributed to the adoption of Western devotional music along with conversion to Christianity.

Another factor was the weakened state of Chinese traditional music in the period of its confrontation with the West. On a general level, the vulnerability of Chinese music was part of the crisis facing Chinese traditional culture as a whole. The Qing (Ching) dynasty and its court culture had been in decline for centuries prior to contact with the West. After the colonial powers arrived, the dynasty was prostrated by the unequal treaties, the Opium Wars, and the failure of the Taiping Rebellion. Because of these humiliations and the corruption of the government itself, many Chinese—especially urban intellectuals—seemed to have lost faith in the integrity of their traditional culture. Indeed, it became difficult for Chinese to emulate the figure of the contemplative intellectual playing his *qin* by a waterfall at a time when the Chinese state, economy, and culture were in such an unprecedented crisis.[4]

As a result of these factors, in the cities on the east coast Western concepts of music—especially harmony, orchestration, vocal timbre, and homophonic rote-singing—began to make inroads in both the art and popular spheres. China, it was felt, could challenge the West only by learning from it and discarding the archaic native traditions encumbering modernization. Ultimately, many urban Chinese came to conceive of Western music not just as a foreign art which should be mastered, but as the new music of Chinese culture.[5] Moreover, the Communist Revolution, its nationalist fervor notwithstanding, further contributed to the adoption of Western music.

Chinese Popular Music before 1949

Distinctly Chinese popular musics (generically labeled *luixing gequ*) began to emerge in the 1930s. By this time, increasing urbanization had created new bourgeois and proletarian classes with new tastes and unprecedented access to mass media. Moreover, the growth of the communist movement, as a response both to the Japanese invasion and the corruption of the Chiang Kai-shek regime, constituted a vital new social force with its own new aesthetic.

The most characteristic popular music developed in Shanghai, which had emerged as the most important commercial city in the country. Aside from its economic activity, Shanghai was known for, on the one hand, its organized and militant labor unions, and, on the other, a seamy, albeit lively entertainment world of brothels and cabarets. The city, indeed, was the center for the financial and literal prostitution of the country at the hands of the imperialist powers and the native elite. In the Shanghai nightclubs, a distinct kind of popular music evolved which came to be known as "yellow music." "Yellow" was in this context analogous to "blue" in Western cinema; that is, it denoted the erotic associations of this music with the urban underworld of the brothels. (The term is pejorative, and the entire musical and social culture associated with it are regarded with embarrassment by many Chinese today.)

"Yellow music" generally consisted of Chinese melodies (mostly pentatonic) harmonized in Western fashion. Western instruments—especially strings—predominated in the orchestral accompaniment, although the Chinese *erh-hu* (fiddle) and the *ti* and *hsiao* flutes were often used. The music tended to be non-percussive and slow in tempo. Although many of the musicians involved were Filipino, the king of "yellow music" in the thirties was one Li Chin-hui, of whom one critic wrote in 1934:

> . . . a writer of popular songs, he has been called charlatan, impostor, and immoral. From the very beginning of his career until today he was shunned by society as a person vulgar and depraved beyond the hope of redemption. He has not only written songs that appeal especially to maidservants and cabaret girls, but has also had the bad taste to allow his wife and daughter to see the girl choruses trained by him. . . . Musicians have heaped abuse on Mr. Li and have found faults with his compositions, but in spite of all this Mr. Li is as popular as ever. Although he employs the technique of Western music, his tunes are essentially Chinese. He is not content with copying others, that is why he is called an upstart by other musicians in China.[6]

With the expansion of radio in the post-war years, "yellow music" reached a new level of popularity. Some songs from this period continue to enjoy popular appeal, such as the favorite "Ho ri jun zai lai" ("When Is My Lover Returning?").

As in India, another important variety of popular music developed in close association with cinema. The evolution of Chinese cinema was well under way by 1920, and by the mid-twenties over a hundred companies were producing films in Shanghai. When speculation in cinema investments subsided in the 1930s, the number shrunk to half a dozen but the cinema continued to gain in popularity.[7] Most of the films were melodramas dealing, directly or indirectly, with contemporary social issues, such as the position of women and, especially, the defense of the country against the Japanese invaders. Many films incorporated music, and the songs became widely popular among the urban middle and lower-middle classes.

While "yellow music" was associated with the most disreputable and lumpen aspects of society, the expression of nationalistic sentiments in cinema tied film music to the leftist social movement that was rising to challenge the Japanese and the corrupt and oppressive native ruling class. Because the Kuomintang (KMT) regime was unwilling to confront the Japanese until 1937, leadership of the nationalistic struggle passed to the communists, and the struggle thus fused with the socialist cause itself. The movement enjoyed considerable support among the urban proletariat, but because of state repression in the cities its real power base was the countryside, particularly the expanding liberated areas.

The communist/patriotic struggle gave birth to a vigorous movement in literature and the arts. Mass revolutionary song (*geming gequ*) played an important part in this movement. In the cities, such music was disseminated at rallies and through the mass media (mostly cinema and radio), while in the countryside, because of the limited access to the media, the songs were spread orally, by inexpensive mimeograph sheet music in cipher notation, and by professional performing teams. These teams promoted the new music throughout the country, teaching and performing songs in workers' night-schools, peasant literacy classes, and student rallies.[8]

The roots of *geming gequ* may be said to lie in Protestant hymns, the songs associated with the Taiping Rebellion, and the Westernized, didactic songs introduced in classrooms after the 1911 revolution.[9] By the 1920s, revolutionary songs, often based on Russian models, had become important vehicles for the expression of political sentiments and their usefulness came to be recognized by Mao Zedong himself.[10] Most of these song texts dealt with the contemporary struggle against foreign and native exploitation, celebrating heroes and martyrs, consoling the bereaved, instilling indignation over war crimes and KMT treachery, and everywhere inciting patriotic militancy.

The style of the new mass music reflected its broader goals. The Confucian aesthetic of moderation, poise, stability, and harmony was replaced by a martial and aggressive dynamism. March-like military rhythms in duple meter predominated. In accordance with the mass nature of the artistic and social movement, most songs were choral, both in performance and in recorded versions; in this respect they clearly resembled their antecedents, the Protestant hymns and didactic school songs. As in "yellow music," Western harmonies and orchestral effects were combined with Chinese melodies. The martial character of the music may have been adapted to some extent from the Western brass bands that had become common in urban China, although native precedents could be found in the raucous wedding and processional music traditionally played on oboes, drums, and gongs.

Composers made some usage of Chinese folk and traditional elements. Several songs were constructed on folk models, such as the well-known modern opera piece "The Northern Wind Blowing," whose modal melody allegedly derives from two folk songs of Hebei province ("Xiaobaicai" and "The Story of Qingyang"). Folk influence was particularly strong in the music based on *yangge* folk theater, which became an important propaganda medium of the revolutionary government in the forties.[11] Most songs, however, were predominantly Western in character, using four-bar phrases and closed, arched melodic structures rather than repetitive strophic form. A few songs were in the form of rounds.

Two composers achieved special renown: Nie Er (Er Nieh), a communist film composer, and Xian Xinghai (Hsien Hsing-hai). Nie Er (1912–1935) composed many film songs dedicated to the liberation cause. An excerpt of one such piece, "Graduate Song," is shown below in its modern Chinese notation form. This notation, based on the French Chevé system, is simple to use and well-suited to the prevailingly diatonic or pentatonic Chinese melodies. Thus, in the excerpt the numbers represent the pitches of the major scale (with zero denoting a rest); as the melody here is largely pentatonic, numbers two and seven are used sparingly. The notation does not, of course, represent the orchestral harmonic accompaniment of the song's most familiar recorded version.

Nie Er's most famous song is "The March of the Volunteers," penned in 1934 for a patriotic film. The song became popular in the war years and was later adopted as the national anthem of the People's Republic of China. As Malm has observed, the piece starts in Western fashion, with diatonic melody and four-bar phrases, but becomes progressively more Chinese in character, with pentatonic scale and irregular phrase and rhythmic patterns;[12] its opening phrase, like that of many other *geming gequ*, is patterned after that of "The Internationale."[13]

Nie Er's name is usually coupled with that of Xian Xinghai (1905–1945). Xian Xinghai grew up as an impoverished orphan, but managed with great difficulty to acquire an education in Western music at the Paris conservatory. After composing film songs for several years, he became involved in the liberation struggle and, moving in 1938 to the Communist headquarters at Yenan (Yan'an), was made director of the music academy there. Aside from popular songs, he composed symphonies and cantatas with patriotic themes, most notably the celebrated "Yellow River Cantata" (which was revised in the sixties to become a piano concerto). In 1940 he went to Moscow to continue his studies, and he died in the USSR in 1945.[14]

Music and Ideology in Communist China

Marxist ideology has played a crucial role in shaping the course of Chinese music evolution in the twentieth century. Since the early stages of the Communist Revolution, explicit formulations of cultural policy have directly influenced music development, encouraging certain kinds of music at the expense of others and attempting to regulate the role of music and art in daily life. Artistic policy has derived in a general sense from the writings of Marx and Lenin, but the Chinese revolutionaries have adapted and reinterpreted these seminal, and often ambiguous guidelines in their own manner.

The most fundamental premise of Marxist theories of art is the idea that all art reflects, actively mediates, and is to some extent conditioned by its class background. Marxists are not alone, of course, in stressing the close relationship between art and society, but their approach is characterized by the particular analytical framework emphasizing the economic substructure, and by a value system, whether explicit or implicit, which underlies concepts of socio-economic development. Ethnomusicologists may tend to locate music in ethnic rather than class backgrounds, while most traditional Western musicologists might argue that class analysis of, say, Western art music could yield only the most general insights which would not illuminate aesthetic processes on the level of detailed formal analysis.

Decoding aesthetic ideology and relating art to its social context are goals as important in bourgeois societies as they are in Communist ones. In the latter, however, the course of musical development may stem less from the commercial market than from bureaucratic factors, especially cultural policy (whether as practiced or as proclaimed).

The Chinese Communists frequently invoked Marx and Lenin in formulating and explaining their policies. Particularly influential, for example, was Lenin's dictum that revolutionary art should serve "not the bored upper ten thousand suffering from fatty degeneration, but the millions and tens of millions of working people."[15] However, on many subjects, including artistic freedom and the role of high art, Lenin and Marx were ambiguous or even contradictory, and nowhere did they outline guidelines for cultural policy.

In the 1937 "Talks at the Yenan Forum on Literature and Art," and in subsequent missives, Mao Zedong outlined what was to become official cultural policy for Communist China.[16] Artists were to strive to be responsive to the aesthetic and ideological needs of the common people; elements of foreign and traditional Chinese art could be used to serve the masses and the Revolution; slavish imitation of Soviet models was to be avoided; art should contain both aesthetic and political value.[17] Accordingly, many Chinese composers incorporated folk themes in their songs and sought inspiration in the struggles and experiences of the working classes.[18] Thus, for example, the committee of composers who created the aforementioned "Yellow River Concerto" claimed at one point to have been inspired by living and working for a time amongst boatmen on the river; one of the composers, Yin Cheng-Chung, described the concerto as "playing a militant part in uniting and educating the people and attacking the enemy."[19] At the same time, however, the concerto revision of Xianhai Xian's work is heavily influenced by European Romantic music; moreover, Yin Cheng-Chung has since defected to the USA and renounced his earlier statements on the composition of the concerto.[20]

Such contradictions as could be found in the concerto were also evident in Mao's own pronouncements. Although overtly nationalistic, they differed little in substance from Stalinist cultural policy as articulated and implemented by Andrei Zhdanov. And although they stressed the importance of both the artistic and political aspects, it became clear that ideological correctness was of greater importance to the state, for thousands of artists were persecuted for deviation from party guidelines.

The subordination of aesthetic concerns to political propaganda in art is generally regarded with scorn in Western culture, where Romantic conceptions of artistic freedom and individuality prevail. Nevertheless, music has long been used for persuasive ends in the West, whether in religious, military, or commercial contexts. The singer crooning an advertisement ditty certainly cannot claim any greater artistic integrity than one who, out of duress or opportunism, performs or composes a political song whose message he does not endorse. Still, it may be difficult for Westerners to regard songs such as "The Three Main Rules of Discipline and the Eight Points for Attention" as anything but prosaic sloganeering.

Arnold Perris has illustrated how such overtly didactic pieces of propaganda may seem less artificial to Chinese than to others.[21] First, bureaucratic guidelines for music did not originate with the communists, but have hoary historical precedents in the national music offices regulating ritual music during various periods in classical China. Second, Confucianism maintains that all music embodies inherent ethical powers which may incite the listener to concrete behavior and attitudes, and that music inspiring anti-social behavior is to be discouraged. Perris argues further that Chinese have traditionally expected some sort of verbal "message" to accompany most of their music. Aside from opera songs, whose content is explicit, most instrumental classical pieces have programmatic titles, often with ethical content; these titles generally evoke concrete or conceptual referents and discourage an abstract, formalistic perception of music. In contemporary China, the titles tend to suggest political themes. Listeners, moreover, may be intended to find even more programmatic messages than the titles might suggest; thus, for instance, the "Yellow River Concerto" was allegedly aimed at expressing "Chairman Mao's concept of people's war."[22]

Thus, the foreign observer of Chinese political mass music, before dismissing it as propaganda, should be aware of the extensive use of music as propaganda in his own culture, and should appreciate the degree of continuity and acceptability of ethical uses of music in the context of Chinese traditional culture. It may be instructive to contrast popular music's role in China with that in South Asia, where entertainers are not expected to confront contemporary social issues; the Chinese communists, indeed, should not be criticized for stressing the social responsibility of the artist.

Mass Music from 1949 to 1964

The Communist victory and establishment of the People's Republic of China in 1949 led to a complete reorganization of musical life in the country. With the termination of civil war and the expulsion of the discredited KMT, economic, social, and cultural reconstruction began under the guidance of the Communist Party. Capitalist forms of musical patronage were replaced by state ownership. The Ministry of Culture inaugurated a massive program designed to stimulate interest in performance and to make music accessible to everyone. Under state control, radio and television broadcasting and the production of films, records, and sheet music all increased dramatically. Local bureaus of culture promoted the production, study, and collection of music throughout the country. Traditional and modern songs were widely disseminated via the media and through amateur performances in festivals and informal occasions in schools, collectives, and other institutions. Conservatories teaching Western and Chinese music were established throughout the nation. Many students traveled to the Soviet Union and Eastern Europe for training. In short, the first fifteen years of the Revolution were a period of prodigious musical activity.[23]

The mass dissemination and accessibility of a broad spectrum of music styles gave a new and enhanced meaning to the concept of "popular music" in revolutionary China. Classical Chinese and Western musics, modified folk songs, and the new "mass music" styles all became "popular" in the sense that they were taught, disseminated, and performed in the context of a (relatively) classless society, and in that they were designed for consumption by the entire nation, not just by an elite class of educated intelligentsia. Finally, the recordings produced for individual purchase were not commodities in the capitalist sense, since they were produced by state ministries for public, not private profit.

The state has promoted a revival and revision of folk and traditional musics. It has continued to promote the composition and dissemination of songs for the masses, generally along the stylistic lines established by

Xian and Nie. Such pieces could be modern creations imitating tradi-tional style or they could be old tunes with new texts, often "enriched" with Western harmony. Some songs with Western harmonic accom-paniment were sung in traditional shrill, constricted vocal style with irregular phrase lengths;[24] often, however, traditional vocal style was replaced by a "modern and scientific," more Western vocal style.[25] Predominantly pentatonic melodies were often harmonized in idiosyn-cratic ways which were only vaguely functional in the Western sense.[26] Purists, Western observers, and some Chinese Party critics have tended to regard these synthetic folk songs as artificial and sterile.[27]

In order to promote mass participation in music production, amateur composition was encouraged, professionals were sent to live among workers and peasants, and collective composing techniques were cele-brated—generally with uneven results.[28]

In spite of the nationalistic fervor, Western influence continued unabated. The Chinese leadership looked to the Soviet Union for guid-ance and inspiration in the cultural as well as political and technological spheres. Moreover, cultural borrowings were justified by the proletarian internationalism of communist ideology. Hence, the revolutionary gov-ernment adopted the Soviet practice of forming large orchestras and choirs for the performance of traditional and modern musics, along the lines of the Soviet Army Ensembles and Cossack choirs.[29] Folk songs and contemporary mass music were recorded with symphonic accom-paniment in the style of Tchaikovsky or Rimsky-Korsakov. As in the civil war period, most of the songs tended to be militant march-like pieces expressing the revolutionary zeal of the new society.

The Cultural Revolution

The situation in our country is fine, with the great proletarian cultural revolution winning victory after victory.
Chinese journalist, 1967[30]

The Motherland's culture of several thousand years was thrown to the winds.
Guang Ming Daily assessment of the
Cultural Revolution, November 15, 1978

From 1966 to 1976 China experienced a traumatic upheaval which dras-tically disrupted and warped cultural, social, and economic life. The Cultural Revolution is now recognized as one of the darker periods in Chinese history, and it serves to illustrate the dangers of totalitarian bureaucratic control over art and culture in general.

The Cultural Revolution commenced as an attempt by Mao Zedong to re-establish his authority and to redirect socio-political life in accordance with his radical conception of democracy. Since 1960, Mao's political power had been in decline, due to his deteriorating health and, more importantly, the recognition of the extent of the damage wrought by his bungled Great Leap Forward of 1958–1959. Mao had since been watching with dismay as his radical collectivization policies were dismantled, moderate socialists like Liu Xiaoqi and Deng Xiaoping grew in power, and a landed bureaucracy emerged as a new privileged class. In 1966 Mao struck back, bypassing state and party apparati by launching the Red Guards in a campaign to destroy the existing power structure. The young, militant cadres, with the support of the army, proceeded to purge or execute hundreds of thousands of bureaucrats, intellectuals, and artists. Industrial and agricultural production stagnated throughout the country, and in many places, virtual civil war ensued as rival armed factions battled for power. By 1968 Mao seemed to have realized the nature of the catastrophe he had wrought, but was unable or unwilling to prevent the radical left, headed by the now-notorious "Gang of Four," from subjecting the nation to eight more years of repression in his name. The Cultural Revolution, which Mao had envisioned as a grassroots movement, became the most extreme totalitarian program.

The effect of the Cultural Revolution on the arts, including music, was especially disastrous. Western music and traditional Chinese music were discouraged or banned as counter-revolutionary. Conservatories, music schools, and many record companies and music publishing centers were closed. Local performing troupes were dissolved. The authorities closed the thousands of dance halls that had sprung up throughout the country, and they effectively prohibited the celebration of traditional events like the Lantern Festival and Dragon Boat Festival, which had brightened the lives of Chinese of all classes for centuries.[31] Relatively little music was composed or performed on the media or, for that matter, in public. The engineers of the Cultural Revolution sought to eradicate traditional culture because of its feudal origins, in order to create a "clean slate," a blank consciousness upon which a new, revolutionary culture could be inscribed.

Under the direction of Mao's wife, Jiang Qing, for nearly ten years, the only music actively promoted by the state was that drawn from the five "model operas" and three modern ballets.[32] Lyrical or amatory music of any kind was denounced as revisionist, for all forms of art were to be turned into weapons of class warfare. The range of emotions expressed in the new revolutionary works, in the words of a Western observer, was limited to "anger, militant resolve, hatred, triumph, and steely optimism."[33]

Most foreign observers and Chinese themselves seem to agree that the Cultural Revolution left China a cultural wasteland. The attempt to engineer by force a new consciousness succeeded only in embittering and wasting an entire generation, while retarding development and preservation of all that was beautiful in Chinese art.

The Contemporary Scene

Mao Zedong's death on September 9, 1976, paved the way for the eventual lifting, in 1978, of the repressive policies of the Cultural Revolution. The actual processes of restructuring power in a communist country like China may remain to a large extent hidden and inscrutable to the outside observer, since much of the negotiation and contention may take place behind closed doors and press censorship may obscure public events precipitating the change. But it is clear that both bureaucratic top-level jockeying and spontaneous public dissent (including strikes, slowdowns, and demonstrations) combined in ousting the radical left faction headed by Jiang Qing, who was arrested in October 1976. Deng Xiaoping, who had been purged during the previous decade, was reinstated in mid-1977 and by 1978 was in effective command of the central government. Deng launched a series of far-reaching economic and social reforms, dismantling communes, encouraging private enterprise, liberalizing foreign trade and investment, embracing the United States, and promoting tourism and cultural exchanges with the outside world, especially the West.

Cultural policy was liberalized, and the onerous restrictions of the previous decade were rescinded. Deng had been scathing in his criticism of the effect of the Cultural Revolution on the arts. "How can eight shows satisfy an audience of eight hundred million people?" he asked.[34] In his address to the Fourth Congress of Writers and Artists in October 1979, he condemned the persecution of artists and upheld their freedom of creation.

The effects of these developments on musical life have been dramatic. Traditional and Western music are again acceptable, and opera, both traditional and modern, has flourished anew. Mood music has replaced military marches in public places, and the music industry is more active than ever, promoted by a torrent of radios, televisions, and cassette players imported from Japan. Regional radio stations, replacing the centralized commune stations, now broadcast various sorts of local and foreign music (especially Western art music).

The core of Deng's reforms has been the emphasis on economic efficiency and production; revolutionary ideological concerns are not top priorities, although they continue to be the subject of much debate and conflict. Much musical production remains in the hands of state-owned enterprises, but their character has changed in accordance with market demands and the new acceptance of humanistic as well as political goals in art. One foreign journalist, bemoaning the spirit of private enterprise which has penetrated popular culture, writes:

> As a result of general economic policies, many cultural units have assumed responsibility for their own profits and losses, and have become more closely attuned to the box office and marketplace. The popular market for

entertainment in China appears to differ little from its counterparts elsewhere, and when now it demands violence, romance, fantasy or sex, it is duly served by the new style of cultural units which place profit above all else.[35]

In terms of musical style, the change is overwhelming. Seldom heard now are the martial choral pieces expressing the fiery optimism of militant cadres; instead, media programming now tends to offer a potpourri of local and imported rock, art music, modern orchestral compositions, Chinese opera, and lyrical love ballads. The latter are typically sung by a solo female vocalist, with light accompaniment by piano, bass, electric guitar, and other Western instruments. The style is predominantly Western, and it differs little from the sentimental popular music produced in Taiwan.[36] Such overseas Chinese music—especially that of Taiwanese songstress Deng Li-Chun (Theresa Deng)—has also come to enjoy great popularity in China.

Hand-in-hand with the commercialization and sentimentalization of Chinese mass music has come an unprecedented case of "disco fever" among the young. Dance bands and discotheques are now found in cities throughout much of China, from the heartlands to remote Inner Mongolia; they prosper even though the admission price may equal a month's wage for a soldier or an unskilled worker.[37] The entertainment in such clubs is called "disike," which, although a Sinicization of "disco," actually denotes any informal dance, especially where the partners do not touch. The music is Western, ranging from Glenn Miller, to contemporary rock hits, to such rousing numbers as "La Cucaracha."[38] In 1985 the New China News Agency announced that China had an estimated ten million guitarists.[39] These are among the most visible manifestations of a Westernized, apolitical *liumang* youth culture that has arisen. *Liumang* is an untranslatable term which can mean loafer, hoodlum, or punk, but now may be applied to the growing ranks of lumpen, uninhibited, denim-clad youths, whether they be unemployed, frustrated intellectuals, fashion-conscious students, or anti-social thugs. Together they constitute an embryonic alternative culture reminiscent of that in the USA of the sixties, and one which may become increasingly visible and influential in China in the next decades.

Foreign bourgeois observers have spoken with optimism about the *liumang* culture, and it certainly is a genuinely popular movement among many Chinese young people.[40] It is also clear, however, that many Chinese are ambivalent about the new forms of commercialism, vulgarity, and Westernization. Many of the older generation, who remember China's humiliating prostitution at the hands of the colonialists and the local elite, cannot help but associate the breathy, sensual crooning of singers like Theresa Deng with "yellow music" and its world of brothels and bullying, brawling foreign sailors. Critics have also pointed out that in many rural areas, cultural services have declined because they are not profitable; the number of amateur theater performers, for example, dwindled from seven million in the early 1960s to under two million in 1985.[41]

Motivated by such misgivings, authorities have put certain limits on freedom of artistic expression, although these do not compare in scope to those of the Cultural Revolution. A "Spiritual Pollution" campaign in 1983–1984 was one ineffective endeavor; more recent symptoms of a mild crackdown have included the arrest, for rape, of rock star Zhang Hang in November 1985 and the simultaneous closing of 84 of the 136 dance halls that had sprouted up in Shanghai.[42] Both Deng Xiaoping and former party General Secretary Hu Yaobang have expressed concern about the overemphasis on romantic themes, the inattention to patriotism, and the potentially pernicious influence of objectionable "capitalist and feudal ideas." But on the whole, the party seems to be at a loss as to how to contend with the new pop culture, especially since, with regard to music, most of the concert organizers and music companies are state-owned units now required to show profits.[43] As a result, the most likely course will be a continuation of the status quo, with occasional attempts to curb the most marked excesses of vulgarity and Westernization.

Since 1986 a new ideological-aesthetic dilemma has arisen in the form of disco adaptations of tunes from the eight model Revolutionary Operas, which have been gaining prodigious popularity among the young. Jiang Qing's model operas are anathema not only to most elements of Deng Xiaoping's reformist administration but also to the hundreds of millions of citizens who suffered bitterly under the Cultural Revolution; hence the operas themselves have been under an official ban, as well as a cloud of popular resentment, since 1977. Yet for a generation of Chinese teenagers too young to remember the persecution, the modernized, buoyant tunes from these operas pose a lively alternative to the shrill singing and irrelevant plots of traditional opera now being revived by the state. The disco versions of the model songs are also supported by some serious musicians, and they have the blessing of certain elements of the government who feel that cheap Taiwan and Hong Kong pop music is a far more serious cultural threat to the young. Consequently:

> One hears the disco opera music in Peking taxis, Hunan buses, at the Canton Railway Station and even in such far-flung locales as the Bakhor Market in Lhasa. And in coffeeshop discos throughout China, young people can be seen dancing to the twisted threnodies of pop Revolutionary Opera.[44]

It has been suggested that the enthusiasm of the young for the model opera music is a reaction against the tastes of their parents, and that even many Chinese in their twenties and thirties enjoy the disco opera tunes out of a sense of misplaced nostalgia for the songs that were the pop music of their teens.[45] At present, the government does not seem to have adopted an explicit policy toward this most unexpected ideological problem.

The development of Chinese popular culture in the last decade would seem to suggest that a certain degree of vulgarity as well as ideological contradiction may be an unavoidable concomitant of a free and dynamic culture. However, the traumas of the nineteenth century and the complexities of China's socio-cultural development render it a special case. One's verdict on the current scene is as likely to depend upon one's ideological perspective as on one's musical taste; what will continue to be most influential in China, of course, is the verdict of the ruling party cadres.

CHAPTER 10

The Pacific

The cultures of the Melanesian, Polynesian, and Micronesian Pacific represent a formidable diversity with respect to language, religion, history, and music, as well as racial origins. At the same time, a degree of cultural affinity and similar socio-historical developments in the twentieth century have contributed to the evolution of a set of popular music styles that can be accommodated into a relatively unified continuum of pan-Pacific styles. In the use of simple three-part vocal harmonies, most of these musics reflect the impact of the Protestant missionaries, who popularized hymn singing throughout much of the Pacific since the early nineteenth century. Acoustic guitars and ukuleles, introduced by sailors, have become the most popular accompanying instruments. Also notable in the standard Pacific styles are the marked preference for major keys, simple rhythms, and a non-percussive texture. In regard to the latter two characteristics, the modern popular musics stand in contrast to the complex, intensely percussive traditional musics found in much of Polynesia.

To some extent, the predominance of Hawaiian influence has been a unifying factor in the development of modern Pacific musics. In recent decades, derivative rock music has also become popular throughout much of the Pacific, especially in those areas incorporated in the American geopolitical sphere of influence.

It is beyond the scope of this volume to explore the vast number of regional expressions of the standard Pacific style. Hence we shall restrict our discussion to the two largest, and perhaps most distinctive musical cultures in the Pacific, namely, Hawaii and Papua New Guinea.

Hawaii

Hawaiian popular music is a heavily acculturated form which is perhaps only marginally non-Western. It does, however, merit some discussion because of its distinctiveness and its syncretic retention of certain features derived from ancient Hawaiian chant, which itself is entirely non-Western in origin and character.[1]

Pre-contact Hawaiian society bore significant affinities with Polynesian cultures in terms of language, social stratification, religion, and other aspects. Music and dance played important roles in Hawaiian daily life, transmitting mythology and genealogy, expressing praise for deities and nobles, and accompanying all manner of secular activities, such as games, social festivals, and the like. While lacking a term for "music" per se, the Hawaiian language contains extensive nomenclature for different types of chant, voice production, instruments, rhythms, performance styles, and other musical parameters. Although most chants appear to have been melodically and rhythmically simple, the poetry, accompanying mimetic dance (*hula*), and subtleties of vocal style are complex and rich even in the attenuated forms in which they survive today.

The European discovery of Hawaii in 1778 precipitated a decline of native cultural traditions. Infectious diseases decimated the local population, while the introduction of alcohol, firearms, and commercial capitalism subverted traditional social norms. In spite of such traumatization, however, the native population continued to embrace imported culture.[2]

Elizabeth Tatar's chronology divides the development of post-contact Hawaiian music into seven periods.[3] The first period (1820–1872) covers the initial period of acculturation, commencing with the arrival of missionaries who established choirs along Protestant models. Along with the hymns (*himeni*), Hawaiians were exposed to a variety of European secular musics, including those of Portuguese sailors and Mexican immigrant laborers (who worked primarily as cowboys). The latter introduced the guitar, which, together with the violin, was avidly adopted by the native population.

The second period (1872–1900) saw the initial flourishing of acculturated yet distinctively Hawaiian music, stimulated not only on the popular level but also by the avid interest of members of the royal family, and by the activities of composer, bandleader, and musicologist Henry Berger (1844–1929). Along with the continued spread of hymn singing and use of guitar, violin, and string bass, the ukulele (*'ukulele*), derived from the Portuguese *braguinha*, became widely popular.

In the third period (ca. 1900–1915), Hawaiian music became integrated into the realm of American popular music. On the one hand, contemporary popular genres like ragtime were introduced to the islands, while on the other hand, *hapa haole* ("half-white") songs with English lyrics and more or less adulterated Hawaiian style came into vogue on the mainland. From 1906, when the Victor Talking Machine Company made fifty-three records of Hawaiian music, the recording industry became an important feature of the island music scene. While initial recordings were produced exclusively for the local market, by

1912 the demand for Hawaiian and pseudo-Hawaiian music was orienting record marketing toward the mainland.[4] In the fourth period (1915–1930), the mainland craze for *hapa haole* songs reached a new peak. Indeed, by 1916, pseudo-Hawaiian songs produced by Tin Pan Alley were enjoying greater sales than any other American popular music. Americans were enchanted by the music's exotic and romantic imagery, its lush, sweet harmonies, and the sound of the ukulele and the steel guitar, which had by then become trademarks of the style.[5] *Hapa haole* music by this time had little to do with Hawaiian values and identity, and it was not without resentment that Hawaiian musicians found themselves obligated to play nonsense ditties like "Yacka Hula Hickey Dula" for tourists.[6] Meanwhile, Hawaiian music was also coming under the influence of the faster and rhythmically more intricate Tahitian and Samoan music.

Radio, cinema, and record production of Hawaiian music—both *hapa haole* and songs in Hawaiian—enjoyed a final "golden age" in the fifth period from 1930–1960. Mainland musicians adopted Hawaiian music to big band and orchestral formats; native entertainers like Sol Hoopii and Lani McIntire became national celebrities. Record production increased exponentially, with a small but significant portion of releases oriented toward the local market. Hawaiian music, in a word, had become big business.

In the sixties, during the sixth period, Hawaiian music suffered a marked decline, largely due to the hegemonic influence of rock. While the dilettantish mainland craze for Hawaiian music had ebbed, many Hawaiians themselves continued to regard their own traditional culture with ambivalence as quaint and backward. Radio programming of local music in Hawaii itself dwindled to a mere 5 percent. Roland Cazimero of the Cazimero Brothers (perhaps the most popular group of the eighties), related how, by the 1950s,

> It wasn't cool to be playing Hawaiian music. And for a long time no one was learning the language and it was a case of "You're playing Hawaiian music? You're playing what?" If you were playing [Hawaiian music] you were dead.[7]

By the early 1970s the rising nationwide interest in ethnic roots was stimulating a heightened sense of social identity and pride among Hawaiians, contributing to a marked revival of Hawaiian music, including ancient chant as well as modern acculturated styles. Established artists like Gabby (Phillip) Pahinui and the Sons of Hawaii were rediscovered, if not lionized, and media coverage and live performances increased auspiciously. Musicians have consciously reoriented much of their music toward local values and identity; nevertheless, they remain partially dependent on the tourist market and continue to resent the pressure of the music industry to record trivial songs in keeping with the mainlanders' artificial and romantic image of Hawaii.[8]

Modern Hawaiian music, in the synchronic perspective, encompasses a range of styles, most of which share a set of distinguishing characteristics. Some of these features can be traced to ancient music (primarily *hula ku'i* chant), while others are syncretic traits which, although distinctively Hawaiian, are products of dialectical acculturation.

The use of harmony and Western instruments in modern Hawaiian music may obscure, on a superficial hearing, the important retentions of ancient features in Hawaiian music, which have been illuminated by R. Anderson Sutton.[9] First, many Hawaiian popular songs employ textual features of ancient chant; these include the absence of end-rhyme, the practice of "linked assonance" (whereby the commencement of one line phonetically echoes the end of the previous line), and, most commonly, the commencement of the final verse with the phrase "Ha'ina ('ia) mai (ana) ka puana"—a traditional cadential line meaning, roughly, "thus ends my song" or "the tale is told." Fast recitation (as in the *hapa haole* hit "Hawaiian Cowboy") and whimsical modulations of vocal timbre are also features present in, and presumably derived from certain types of chant.

Secondly, melodic contours of some modern songs bear close affinities with those of chant. Most chant melodies are quite simple, often consisting of a reciting tone which alternates with a lower pitch (especially, a third or fourth lower); some chants use other lower pitches which may outline an inverted major triad (with the top pitch being the reciting tone). Such melodic structure is common in popular songs, although it is often masked by the presence of harmony and diatonic passing tones.[10]

Another atavism of modern Hawaiian music is the use, in stylized form, of the most familiar rhythm played on the *'ipu*, a gourd drum; this rhythm, which itself is referred to as *'ipu*, could be played:

or, more simply,

These rhythms are often incorporated into modern popular music, albeit generally at slower tempi, in the form of guitar or ukulele patterns; hence, Hawaiian musicians speak of the "'*ipu* strum."[11]

Other distinctive features of Hawaiian popular music cannot be traced to pre-contact music. Most notable among these traits is the use of falsetto, which is, indeed, one of the trademarks of Hawaiian music. The origins of this tradition in Hawaii are conjectural, and its extensive use in ancient music seems dubious (especially in view of its absence in chant as surviving today). Nevertheless, by the late 1800s, falsetto singing had become an important trait of acculturated music on the islands. Hawaiians have used falsetto in a variety of ways. Some singers cultivate yodeling techniques; vocalists like the Hoopii Brothers sing some pieces entirely in falsetto; in other cases, falsetto passages may be introduced in individual melodic lines, especially in the case of upward leaps at the ends of lines.[12] In recent decades the use of falsetto has declined somewhat; many contemporary Hawaiian singers avoid it entirely.

Along with falsetto singing, the steel or Hawaiian guitar is the most celebrated and distinctive feature of Hawaiian music. The Hawaiian guitar technique (in which the strings are stopped by a movable tuve, rather than by depressing the string on the frets with the fingers) appears to have originated in Hawaii itself. A few accounts refer to isolated experiments by local musicians to play the guitar in this manner before 1885. But it is generally agreed that the technique was developed and popularized primarily by Joseph Kekuku in the last decade of the nineteenth century. A series of subsequent improvements dramatically changed the instrument and accompanied refinement and development of playing style. First, the strings were raised higher above the fretboard to avoid buzzing; in the early 1920s, the National and Dobro guitars were devised on the mainland with steel, rather than wooden bodies; the National used metal resonating discs which enhanced the volume. Guitarists, laying the instrument horizontally on their laps, experimented with a variety of different tunings. In the thirties, the electric steel guitar came into vogue, enabling it to be heard easily in ensembles; with the eventual addition of pedals controlling tuning and volume, the steel guitar gradually assumed its modern form. By this time the instrument had become popular in country-western music as well as Hawaiian music. The mass media played an essential part in popularizing the steel guitar, especially in the peak years of the twenties and thirties.[13] Unfortunately, use of the instrument in Hawaiian music has declined since then, such that at present it is scarcely heard in Hawaii.

Still vital, however, are the "slack key" guitar styles, in which the strings of the (Spanish) guitar are loosened (slackened) to achieve different tunings. In these tunings (such as D G D G B D) the lower three strings are generally used to reiterate tonic and dominant pedal tones, while a variety of melodic, arpeggiated, and chordal figures are plucked on the remaining strings. Although primarily an accompaniment style, slack key guitar patterns are celebrated for their complexity and difficulty. The associated styles are also regarded as distinctively Hawaiian, especially for their frequent use of chant-derived rhythms like the aforementioned 'ipu beat.[14]

There are several other typical characteristics of Hawaiian music which together contribute to its distinctive quality. These include the general avoidance of minor keys, the gentle, non-percussive sound (few bands use drums), certain characteristic melodic patterns, a fondness for major chords incorporating the sixth degree, and the following cadential phrase:

The presence of these characteristics situates Hawaiian music within the continuum of pan-Pacific popular musics, and indeed, Hawaiian music has been extremely influential in the development of these styles throughout the Pacific.

As of 1987, Hawaiian music continues to flourish, although the gifted generation of Gabby Pahinui and his colleagues has largely passed away. In the absence of a continued mainland vogue of Hawaiian music, record production—mostly by small, local independent firms—and performances are oriented primarily toward consumption in Hawaii itself, whether for tourists or for all manner of local affairs from political rallies to canoe club parties; as a result, there is less commercial pressure to adulterate Hawaiian music in accordance with mainland trends. While young locals may prefer rock music for dancing and partying, they as well as the older generations continue to regard Hawaiian music as an important part of island heritage. Thus, in spite of increasing tourism and economic development, locals—especially non-whites—continue to pride themselves on their culture and to regard *haoles* as outsiders. Modern Hawaiian music, along with ancient chant and such activities as canoe racing, is an important symbol of ethnic identity. Hence, even as knowledge of the Hawaiian language continues to dwindle, it seems clear that Hawaiian music will continue to play a significant role in state culture.

Papua New Guinea

Musical culture in New Guinea encompasses a multitude of regional rural traditional musics, as well as set of acculturated genres reflecting various degrees and kinds of European influence. While large portions of New Guinea remain isolated from external cultural influences, the audiences for Western and native acculturated musics are steadily increasing due to rural development, the spread of radio and cassettes, and urbanization.

The various kinds of acculturated musics in New Guinea include military and constabulary brass bands, musics associated with missions

and choirs, and secular entertainment genres.[15] Hymns introduced by
Protestant missionaries have been especially important in the development of secular as well as church-related musics. Since the 1950s, most
schools have had choirs, which employ simple tonic sol-fa and staff
notations; the choirs and church hymns have been the most important
vehicles for Western musical acculturation and education.

Aside from choral music, the strongest influence on secular entertainment music in Papua New Guinea is that of the standard Pacific
style. The acculturated music in this style is generally referred to in PNG
as "string band" music. Although a few commercial recordings of string
band music were made as early as the fifties, the style is perhaps better
regarded as an urban folk music than as a popular music.[16] Sheridan has
documented the popularity of the guitar at informal urban "cup-tea
sing-sings," in hospitals (where music-making is encouraged as
therapeutic), among cargo cultists, in villages, and, above all, in taverns.[17] Niles further observes that string band music is generally sung in
local languages (rather than pidgin), and is performed at a variety of
non-traditional village events; string bands are popular, in regionally
distinct substyles, throughout the country.[18]

Since 1962, when drinking was legalized, the taverns have served as
the most important locales for modern secular entertainment music.
Gradually, elements of contemporary Western pop have been incorporated into string band music, such as electric guitars, drums, and rock
rhythms. Hence one can speak of a continuum of styles from "traditional" acoustic string band music to mainstream rock. Similar to the
former are songs using conventional string band style, with the addition
of one or more percussion instruments. Towards the modern end of the
continuum lie rock-oriented songs whose vocal harmonies suggest choral and/or string band roots.

The rock bands—referred to as "power bands"—developed in the
sixties, and were originally dominated by more affluent mixed-race musicians. At present, however, there are many Papua New Guinean
bands, performing songs in regional languages as well as pidgin English, the lingua franca. Cover versions of foreign hits have always been
an important part of the power band repertoire, but local compositions
have gradually increased in number and quality. The power bands perform primarily in urban taverns and hotels, for predominantly male
audiences who drink heavily during shows.[19]

The rise of power bands and more modernized string band styles
appears, not surprisingly, to have been closely related to the advent of
the mass media in PNG. Until the mid-1970s, only a handful of commercial recordings of string band music had been produced. By the early
1980s, however, the cassette industry was flourishing in PNG as in
much of the third world, disseminating tapes of string bands, power
bands, and choirs (primarily from Central and East New Britain
provinces). Niles's comprehensive discography documents the pro-

digious output of the cassette companies, almost all of which are locally owned.[20] While most of the power bands perform derivative rock music, a few—especially the group "Sanguma"—have experimented with the self-conscious syncretic use of traditional PNG music elements. Such innovative groups, according to Niles, appear to be more popular overseas—for example, in New Zealand—than at home. Nevertheless, the perserverance of regional traditional styles, as well as the growth of nationalism suggest that such syntheses may become increasingly important and appreciated in PNG as modern popular music extends its domain.

Notes

Chapter 1. Perspectives

1. *Popular Music* (1981), 1.
2. See John Baily, "Cross-cultural perspectives in popular music: The case of Afghanistan," *Popular Music* 1 (1981), 105–23.
3. Bruno Nettl, "Persian popular music in 1969," *Ethnomusicology* 16/2 (1972), 218.
4. Wallis and Malm, *Big Sounds*, 9.
5. Pekka Gronow, "The record industry: Growth of a mass medium," *Popular Music* 3 (1983), 53–76.
6. "State maintains tight grip on broadcasting," *Far Eastern Economic Review* 7/18/85, p. 42.
7. See, for example, Gaur, *The Other Side of the Coin.*
8. Antoine Hennion, "The production of success: An anti-musicology of the pop song," *Popular Music* 3 (1983), 159–94.
9. Jamal Rasheed, "Video-cassette boom stalks creative culture," *Far Eastern Economic Review* 6/3/86, p. 55.
10. Wallis and Malm, *Big Sounds,* 4–5.
11. *Ibid.,* 85ff.
12. *Ibid.,* 298.
13. *Ibid.,* 288.
14. See, for example, Swingewood, *Mass Culture,* 94.
15. See, for example, *ibid.*
16. See Hall and Whannel, *Popular Arts,* 364–84, for a summary of these and other arguments presented here regarding popular art and mass art.
17. See Chapter 2 in Adorno's *Sociology of Music.*
18. See, for example: Max Paddison, "The critique criticised: Adorno and popular music," *Popular Music* 2 (1982), 201–18; Edward Shils, "Daydreams and nightmares: Reflections on the criticism of mass culture," *Sewanee Review* 45/4 (Autumn 1957), 596–606; and Swingewood, *Mass Culture.*
19. Adorno, in Paddison, "The critique criticised," 202.
20. Adorno, in *ibid.,* 213; also see Jay, *Adorno,* 120.
21. Marothy, *Music and the Bourgeois,* 485ff. Marothy here comments specifically on the proletarianization of African urban culture and its influence on popular music. Marcuse's late (1969) work *An Essay on Liberation,* which may strike modern readers as a rather over-optimistic celebration of 1960s counterculture, also praises blues and jazz for what Marcuse regards as their liberating and affirmative content (p. 38).
22. Wallis and Malm, *Big Sounds,* 247.
23. See Blacking, *How Musical Is Man?*
24. *Ibid.,* 279.
25. Swingewood, *Mass Culture,* 108–9.

26. Jon Weiner, "Beatles buy-out," *The New Republic* 5/11/87, p. 14.

27. Music's ability to promote passive sublimation rather than active affirmation is articulated in Jean-Paul Sartre's oft-quoted statement in reference to Algerian reactions to French colonial domination: "It is in this way that an obsessed person flees from his deepest needs. . . . They dance; that keeps them busy; it relaxes their painfully contracted muscles; and the dance mimes secretly, often without their knowing, the refusal they cannot utter and the murders they dare not commit." (Preface to Fanon, *The Wretched of the Earth*, 19).

28. José Limón, "Texas-Mexican popular music and dancing: Some notes on history and symbolic process," *Latin American Music Review* 4/2 (1983), 229–46.

29. Marothy, *Music and the Bourgeois*, 530.

30. See Richard Middleton, "Popular music, class conflict, and the music-historical field," in *Popular Music Perspectives*, 24–46, and Stuart Hall, "Notes on deconstructing 'the popular,'" in *People's History and Socialist Theory*, ed. R. Samuel.

31. See Douglas Kellner, "Critical theory and the culture industries: A reassessment," *Telos* 17/4, (Winter 1984–85), 196–206.

32. David Coplan, "The urbanisation of African music: Some theoretical observations." *Popular Music* 2 (1982), 116.

33. David Coplan, "Marabi culture: Continuity and transformation in African music in Johannesburg, 1920–1940," *African Urban Studies* 6 (Winter 1979–80), 51, and "Go to my town, Cape Coast! The social history of Ghanaian highlife," in *Eight Urban Musical Cultures*, ed. Bruno Nettl, 110.

34. Turner, *Dramas, Fields, and Metaphors*, 233, 252–59.

35. See, for example, Bruno Nettl, "Some aspects of the history of world music in the twentieth century: Questions, problems, and concepts," *Ethnomusicology* 22/1 (1978), 123–36.

36. Coplan, "Go to my town, Cape Coast!," 99.

37. See Nettl, *Music in Primitive Culture*, 80, and Meyer, *Music, the Arts and Ideas*, 32.

38. Shepherd et al., *Whose Music?*, 111.

39. Marothy, *Music and the Bourgeois*.

40. Hauser, *The Social History of Art*, Vol. II, p. 15. For further discussion of these matters in relation to popular music, see Peter Manuel, "Formal structure in popular music as a reflection of socio-economic change," *International Review of the Aesthetics and Sociology of Music* 16/2 (1985), 163–80.

Chapter 2. Latin America and the Caribbean

1. Ulpiano Vega Cobiellas, *Nuestra America y la evolución de Cuba* (Havana: 1944), 74–75.

2. Carpentier, *La Música en Cuba*, 92–98.

3. Most *charanga* groups include the word *orquesta* in their titles, for example, *Orquesta Aragon*.

4. This ostinato is characteristic of the *Banda* and *Petro voudoun* dances.

5. In Carpentier, *La Música en Cuba*, 67.

6. See Sowell, *Ethnic America*, 193.

7. In Carpentier, *La Música en Cuba*, 136–41.

8. A number of alternate patterns for the *palitos* and, to a lesser extent, the *clave* are occasionally used. *Rumba* instrumentation also varies; for example, wooden boxes (*cajones* or *cajoncitos*) could replace the drums. The *clave* pattern itself is of West African origin, according to art historian and ethnomusicologist Robert Thompson. For further discussion of the *rumba*, see Larry Crook, "A musical analysis of the Cuban rumba," *Latin American Music Review* 3/1 (Spring–Summer 1982), 93–123.

9. Díaz Ayala, *Música Cubana*, 115. Díaz's book is a particularly valuable source for data on twentieth-century Cuban popular music. But see the review by Peter Manuel, "Cuban popular music literature: Progress and Polemics," *Studies in Latin American Popular Culture* vol. 5, 1986, pp. 253–56.

10. Díaz Ayala, *Música Cubana*, 145.
11. *Ibid.*, 15–21.
12. The introduction of structured, closed song form into the *canto* is a particularly clear illustration of the influence of bourgeois aesthetics on a formerly pre-capitalist musical genre. For a more expansive discussion of this phenomenon in the *son* and elsewhere, see Manuel, "Formal structure in popular music."
13. For discussion of this and other aspects of Cuban musical evolution, see the fine summary by Roberta Singer and Robert Friedman, "Puerto Rican and Cuban musical expression in New York," liner notes to New World Records 244.
14. Díaz Ayala, *Música Cubana*, 174.
15. For further discussion of the evolution of the *guaracha*, see León, *Del canto y el tiempo*, 166–78; Robert Stevenson, "The Afro-American musical legacy to 1800," *The Musical Quarterly* 54 (October 1968), 498; and Roberts, *Black Music of Two Worlds*, 98.
16. The archetypical *guaracha* rhythm combines a prominent conga stroke on the fourth beat of the bar with the *güiro* and/or *maracas* pattern:

♩ ♫ ♩ ♫

17. The bolero bass pattern may be seen as a simplification of the isorhythm of its antecedent, the *habanera*. See Peter Manuel, "The anticipated bass in Cuban popular music," *Latin American Music Review* 6/2 (1985), 249–61.
18. Compare, for example, Arcaño's recordings of the tune "Mambo" on Cariño DBM1-5806 and Areito C-3724.
19. The scholarly works of folklorist and anthropologist Fernando Ortíz (1881–1969) contributed greatly to this acceptance of Afro-Cuban culture.
20. Note, for example, Eddie Palmieri's adaptation of the traditional *rumba* "Consuélete" in his salsa hit "Ritmo Alegre" (on "Cheo y Quintana"—Coco CLP-109XX). This *rumba* is recorded in traditional style by Carlos Embale on Areito LD-3428.
21. Díaz Ayala, *Música Cubana*, 213–15.
22. See, for example, Roberta Singer, "Tradition and innovation in contemporary popular music in New York City," *Latin American Music Review* 4/2 (1983), 189–91. Audiences at concerts often spontaneously clap the *clave* pattern.
23. For a discussion of the evolution of the anticipated bass, and an analysis of its role in the ensemble, see Manuel, "The anticipated bass."
24. Crook, "A musical analysis of the Cuban rumba."
25. From the solo by Charlie Palmieri on Ray Barreto's "La Cuna" (CTI 9002). The author cannot guarantee the complete accuracy of the transcription. Note how, as in jazz piano, double-octave lines are generally spaced in alternate, rather than adjacent octaves.
26. Zoila Gómez, "Panorama de la canción cubana," *Revolución y Cultura* 84 (1979), 22–24.
27. Ché Guevara, for example, envisioned the Cuban revolution as "revolution with *pachanga*." For further discussion of Cuban music since 1959, see Peter Manuel, "Marxism, nationalism and popular music in revolutionary Cuba," *Popular Music* 7 (1987), 161–78. For the disparaging point of view, see Díaz Ayala, *Música Cubana*, 267–321.
28. Mesa-Lago, *Cuba in the 1970s*, 106.
29. Díaz Ayala, *Música Cubana*, 286–87.
30. Fidel Castro, address to the First Congress of the Communist Party of Cuba, 1975.
31. See Manuel, "Marxism, nationalism and popular music in revolutionary Cuba."
32. For further readings on *nueva trova*, see the following: Manuel, *ibid.*; Rina Benmayor, "'La nueva trova': New Cuban song," *Latin American Music Review* 2/1 (1981), 11–44; Pirard Carrasco, "The nueva canción in Latin America," *International Social Science Journal* 34/4 (1982), 599–623; and Jan Fairley, "Annotated bibliography of Latin-Amer-

ican popular music with particular reference to Chile and *nueva canción,"* in *Popular Music* 5 (1985), 305–56.

33. Acosta, *Canciones de la nueva trova,* 22.
34. Argeliers León, interviewed by the author in 1984.
35. Compare, for example, González's "salsa"-style rendition of Pablo Milanés' "Canción" (on Areito C-3972) with the vocal and guitar version recorded by Milanés and Lilia Vera (on Areito LD-3988).
36. Carrasco, "The nueva canción in Latin America," 616.
37. Hector Vega, "Some musical forms of African descendants in Puerto Rico: Bomba, Plena and Rosario Frances"; Francisco López Cruz, *La música folklórica de Puerto Rico,* 47–50.
38. López Cruz, *La música folklórica de Puerto Rico,* 69.
39. In the traditional *plena* "Santa María," for example, the choral refrain commences in minor key while the stanzas modulate to the relative major.
40. The first Puerto Rican radio station was established in 1922. See Pedro Malavet Vega, *La vellonera está directa: Felipe Rodríguez (La Voz) y los años '50,* 61.
41. See, for example, Canario's "Llegó de Roma" (reissued on Ansonia ALP 1232).
42. Rodríguez Julia, *El entierro de Cortijo,* 31–32.
43. *Ibid.,* 32, 71.
44. See for example, Sega, *Requiem para una cultura.*
45. See Weil et al., *Area Handbook for the Dominican Republic,* 31–48.
46. Little has been published about the *merengue;* to date, the most thorough study of the subject has been the M.A. thesis of Paul Austerlitz, "A history of the Dominican merengue highlighting the role of the saxophone" (Wesleyan, 1986).
47. *Ibid.,* 13–27.
48. *Ibid.,* 27, 31, 36, 47ff. According to Austerlitz, the most important groups in the first half of the twentieth century were those of Juan Bautista Espíñola Reyes, Juan Pablo "Pavin" Tolentino, Luis Alberti, and Avelino Vásquez.
49. *Ibid.,* 57–60.
50. *Ibid.,* 66.
51. *Ibid.,* 122.
52. Personal communication with John Murphy, ethnomusicologist and saxophonist for a contemporary New York *merengue* group.
53. From "El Gringo y El Cibaeño," Wilfrido Vargas (Karen KLP 87); saxophone parts are notated in concert pitch. The *tambora* pattern is abstracted from the recording, and from the most typical pattern, as illustrated to the author by John Murphy.
54. The song cited in footnote 53, depicting an encounter between a *gringo* and a rustic peasant from Cibao, is a particularly explicit example of this sort of mediation.
55. "Wilfrido Vargas se queja de los promotores," in *Notícias del Mundo* 4/10/87, p. 17.
56. Singer and Friedman, "Puerto Rican and Cuban musical expression in New York."
57. The term "salsa," however, is generally used in a more specific sense as denoting the Cuban-derived dance styles; thus, for example, Dominicans distinguish between *merengue* and salsa.
58. For Cuban perspectives on salsa, see Manuel, "Marxism, nationalism and popular music in revolutionary Cuba," 168–71.
59. In Mayra Martínez, "La salsa: ¿Un paliativo contra la nostalgia?"
60. Roberts, *Black Music of Two Worlds,* 111.
61. *Ibid.,* 186–87.
62. In Marre and Charlton, *Beats of the Heart,* 80.
63. Don Randel, "Crossing over with Ruben Blades." Paper presented at the annual conference of the International Association for the Study of Popular Music (American Chapter), in Pittsburgh, 4/87.
64. In Marre and Charlton, *Beats of the Heart,* 82.
65. Lydia Chavez, "Badillo's run highlights lack of Hispanic gains," the *New York Times,* 10/12/86, p. E9.

66. Enrique Fernández, "Is salsa sinking?," in the *Village Voice*, 9/2/86, p. 19. In the same article, Cuqui Ceijo, vice-president of the Federation of Musicians Local 468 in San Juan, states, "Eighty percent of our musicians are out of work. . . . In New York anyone can get a visa [to work in Puerto Rico]. Dominicans come here to play and stay all year if they want to." As of 1987, however, proposed changes in immigration laws are expected to exert considerable impact on the Latino music scene.

67. Abadía Morales, *La Música Folklórica Colombiana*, 94.

68. See, for example, Ocampo López, *El Folclor y los Bailes Típicos Colombianos*, p. 184.

69. Quiroz Otero, *Vallenato: Hombre y Canto*, 16–17.

70. *Ibid.*, 27–32.

71. *Vallenato* accompanies a couple dance which, unlike the traditional *cumbia* and *currulao*, is invariably performed with the partners touching, rather than in a ring or line format. See Consuelo Araujo de Molina, *Vallenatología*, 38.

72. Quiroz Otero, *Vallenato: Hombre y Canto*, 213–21.

73. *Ibid.*, 107–13.

74. Marre and Charlton, *Beats of the Heart*, 124.

75. For example, the *vallenato-protesta* of Armando Zabaleta. See Araujo de Molina, *Vallenatología*, 125–37.

76. Marre and Charlton, *Beats of the Heart*, 132.

77. Quiroz Otero, *Vallenato: Hombre y Canto*, 111.

78. Marre and Charlton, *Beats of the Heart*, 129.

79. Geijerstam, *Popular Music in Mexico*, 110.

80. *Ibid.*, 13–14.

81. Mendoza, *Panorama de la música tradicional de Mexico*, 93–94, and *La música tradicional española en Mexico*, 93; and Mayer-Serra, *Panorama de la música mexicana*, 62–70. Musicologists Carmen Sordo Sordi and Juan Garrido deny, however, that Italian influence extended beyond urban audiences. See Geijerstam, *Popular Music in Mexico*, 62.

82. Some purists have deplored the commercialization of the *haupango*; Reuter, for example, (*La música popular de Mexico*, 167), speaks disparagingly of singers seeking fame in the capitalist media "by singing 'La Malagueña' in Italian operatic style."

83. This aspect of commercialization of the *son huasteco* is discussed in greater detail in Peter Manuel, "Formal structure in popular music as a reflection of socio-economic change."

84. Geijerstam, *Popular Music in Mexico*, 103, notes that Trio Los Panchos recorded over forty LPs.

85. See David Stigberg, "Foreign currents during the 60s and 70s in Mexican popular music: Rock and roll, the romantic ballad and the cumbia," *Studies in Latin American Popular Culture* 4 (1985), 170–84.

86. See Reuter, *La música popular de Mexico*, 139; and Geijerstam, *Popular music in Mexico*, 67, 125–30.

87. See Geijerstam, *ibid.*, 67–69.

88. Reuter, *La música popular de Mexico*, 140, writes, "The cinema continued to present the popular 'idol' in the forties: the valiant *charro* [skilled horseman], the gambler and sybarite, always ready with his pistol, ever in love, but with a profound contempt for women, especially after having obtained his favors; jealous and boastful, drunken and racy, idolizing his mother and the Virgin of Guadalupe and, above all, radiating a tremendous personal sympathy—this figure of the Mexican macho was personified in stars like Jorge Negrete and Pedro Infante" (translation mine).

89. José Alfredo Jiménez's "El Rey" may be taken as a sort of manifesto of this individualistic male credo.

90. Especially, Peña's *The Texas-Mexican Conjunto*.

91. See Guy Bensusan, "A consideration of *norteña* and Chicano music," *Studies in Latin American Popular Culture* 4 (1985), 158–64. Mexicans of the central urban highlands may continue to regard *norteño* music as insignificant; for example, the nine-record set *Historia moderna de la música popular mexicana*, produced in 1976 by Juan Garrido, does not contain a single example of *norteño* music.

92. See Peña, *The Texas-Mexican Conjunto*, 10–11.

93. These developments are discussed in detail in *ibid.*, 19–69.

94. *Ibid.*, 70–99.

95. Bensusan, "A consideration of *norteña* and Chicano music," 161–64.

96. See Peña, *The Texas-Mexican Conjunto*, 100–110.

97. *Ibid.*, 150–51.

98. These small record producers are featured in Jeremy Marre's film, *Beats of the Heart: Tex-Mex*, his accompanying book, *Beats of the Heart*, 108, and in Les Blanc's documentary film *Chulas Fronteras*.

99. Marre and Charlton, *Beats of the Heart*, 104–5.

100. *Ibid.*, 154–55, and Manuel Peña, "Ritual structure in a Chicano dance," *Latin American Music Review* 1 (Spring 1980), 47–73.

101. Peña, *The Texas-Mexican Conjunto*, 149–50, 158–60.

102. Limón, "Texas-Mexican popular music and dancing," p. 238.

103. Peña's own informant seems to suggest this when he speaks of workers going to dances "to forget the sorrows." *The Texas-Mexican Conjunto*, 154.

104. Limón, "Texas-Mexican popular music and dancing," 241.

105. For exposition of these arguments, see Matamoro, *La Ciudad del tango*, 10–14; Donald Castro, "Popular culture as a source for the historian: The tango in its era of la guardia vieja," *Studies in Latin American Popular Culture* 3 (1984), 70–73; Gerard Behague, "Tango," in *New Grove's Dictionary of Music and Musicians*; and Vega, *Danzas y canciones argentinas*, 231–47.

106. Matamoro, *La ciudad del tango*, 13–14.

107. Rossi, *Cosas de negros*.

108. Matamoro, *La ciudad del tango*, 15–36.

109. *Ibid.*, 33–40; also see Julie Taylor, "Tango: Theme of class and nation," *Ethnomusicology* 20/2 (1976), 274–75.

110. See, for example, Taylor, *ibid.*, 276–81.

111. Matamoro, *La ciudad del tango*, 49–53, 115–29.

112. See Donald Castro, "Popular culture as a source for the historian: The tango."

113. Matamoro, *La ciudad del tango*, 56.

114. Ramon Pelinski, "From tango to 'rock nacional': A case study of changing popular music taste in Buenos Aires," in *Popular Music Perspectives* 2 (1985), 288.

115. See Taylor, "Tango: Theme of class and nation," and Donald Castro, "Popular culture as a source for the historian: Why Carlos Gardel?," *Studies in Latin American Popular Culture* 5 (1986), 144–59.

116. See Castro, *ibid.*, 152–53. Pelinski, "From tango to 'rock nacional,'" 291n, reports that Osvaldo Fresedo recorded an average of 180 tunes a year between 1925 and 1928.

117. Adolfo Sierra, *Historia de la orquesta típica*, 77–79.

118. Canton, *Gardel, ¿a quién le cantas?*, 15–19.

119. Pelinski, "From tango to 'rock nacional,'" 291.

120. *Ibid.*, 293.

121. A. Ford, "El tango," in *Literatura contemporanea*, Vol. 38, (Buenos Aires, 1971), and *Homero Manzi* (Buenos Aires: Centro Editor de America Latina, 1971), in Pelinski, "From tango to 'rock nacional,'" 292; also see Matamoro, *La ciudad del tango*, 213ff.

122. The development of modern popular musics out of these genres has been thoroughly documented in Gerard Behague, "Popular music currents in the art music of the early nationalistic period in Brazil, circa 1870–1920." Ph.D. diss. Tulane Univ., 1966.

123. Alvarenga, *Música popular brasileira*, 148–49.

124. Appleby, *Music of Brazil*, 60–61.

125. Summarized in *ibid.*, 61, 68.

126. Alvarenga, *Música popular brasileira*, 150–51.

127. *Ibid.*, 284–86.

128. *Ibid.*, 292.

129. These include the *tarol* (military drum), *tamborim* (small, round frame drum), *pandeiro* (tambourine), *surdo* (large double-headed drum), *cuíca* (friction drum), *agogô* (iron

double bell), and *chocalho* (rattle). For discussion of these instruments and other aspects of the *samba,* see Gardel, *Escolas de Samba,* 121–61.

130. *Ibid.,* 158–59.

131. Alvarenga, *Música popular brasileira,* 297–98; and Gerard Behague, "Popular music in Latin America," *Studies in Latin American Popular Culture* 5 (1986), 56.

132. Alvarenga, *Música popular brasileira,* 298.

133. Compare, for instance, J. B. de Carvalho's "Juro" with Carlos Galhardo's "Não pode ser," on RCA 803.347 ("Reminiscencias" Vol. 5).

134. See Robert Levine, "Elite intervention in urban popular culture in modern Brazil," *Luso-Brazilian Review* 21/2 (Winter 1984), 13–15.

135. See Marre and Charlton, *Beats of the Heart,* 216–18.

136. Levine, "Elite intervention," 16.

137. See the presentations in Marre's film *Beats of the Heart: Spirit of Samba.*

138. *Bossa nova* harmonies are often complex even by the standards of contemporary jazz; note, for instance, the avoidance of standard progressions in the bridge of "Girl from Ipanema" (F#maj B7+11 F#min9 D7+11 Gmin9 Eb7+11 Amin9 . . .).

139. For more detailed discussion of *bossa nova,* see Gerard Behague, "Bossa and bossas: Recent changes in Brazilian urban popular music," *Ethnomusicology* 17/2 (1973); or the similar article by the same author, "Brazilian musical values of the 1960s and 1970s: Popular urban music from bossa nova to tropicalia," *Journal of Popular Culture* 14/3 (1980), 437–52.

140. See, e.g., translations of "Construção" and "Deus lhe pague" in Behague, "Brazilian musical values."

141. See Walnice Galvão's criticism in *ibid.,* 447–48.

142. Veloso states, "Back in the late 1960s, the Brazilian singers all wore dark suits and ties when they performed. And then we came out of Bahia with long hair, wearing whatever we liked, and everyone seemed to hate us. The leftist students thought we were selling out to imperialism by playing rock, and the Government thought our songs were subversive and put us in jail. We caused a big scandal, but we had a lot of fun." In Robert Palmer, "Veloso brings newest beat from Brazil," *New York Times* 7/20/83, p. C17.

143. Behague, "Brazilian musical values," 451–52.

144. *Nueva canción,* in accordance with its importance as a socio-cultural phenomenon, has been the subject of several studies, which should be consulted by the interested reader. See Jan Fairley, "Annotated bibliography of Latin-American popular music with particular reference to Chile and to *nueva canción,*" *Popular Music* 5 (1985), 305–56.

145. Wallis and Malm, *Big Sounds,* 100–101.

146. Fairley, "Annotated bibliography," 308; see p. 307 for a somewhat different interpretation of the use of *altiplano* elements.

147. The vicissitudes of *nueva canción* after the coup are illuminated by Nancy Morris in "Canto porque es necesario cantar: The new song movement in Chile, 1973–83," *Latin American Review* 12/2 (1986), 117–36.

148. Fairley, "Annotated bibliography," 308.

149. Wallis and Malm, *Big Sounds,* 131–34.

150. Martha de Ulhoa Carvalho, "Canto Nuevo" (manuscript).

151. Fairley, "Annotated bibliography," 308.

152. Reuter, *La música popular de Mexico,* 143.

153. Note, for example, *New Grove's* entry on Haiti, which, aside from work songs, does not even mention secular music.

154. The early evolution of the *méringue* and *carabinier* is outlined in Fouchard, *La méringue: danse nationale d'Haiti.* According to Fouchard, the term *méringue* derives from a Bantu dance, the *mourringue,* introduced by slaves from Mozambique. Fouchard denies with nationalistic fervor the alleged Dominican origin of the *méringue.*

155. Fouchard, *La méringue,* 152–55.

156. According to arranger and producer Harry Leroy, *cadence* differs from *compas* only in the addition of a second conga part.

157. Congolese influence is particularly clear in the music of Coupé Cloué, whose band does not use horns. Note that the term *compas* continues to be applied to the music of "mini-jazz" bands.

158. According to Leroy, Haitians refer to the *cinquillo* pattern as *kata*—a term traditionally denoting the log segment struck with wooden sticks in *voudoun* music. In the cymbal pattern shown above, the last stroke is frequently stressed by being open, rather than damped.

159. For further discussion of reggae see Davis and Simon, *Reggae International*; Davis and Simon, *Reggae Bloodlines*; Bergman, *Hot Sauces: Latin and Caribbean Pop*; Pamela O'Gorman, "An approach to the study of Jamaican popular music," *Jamaica Journal* 6/3 (1972), 50–54; and Clarke, *Jah Music: The Evolution of the Popular Jamaican Song*.

160. Davis and Simon, *Reggae International*, 41.

161. O'Gorman, "An approach to the study of Jamaican popular music," 51.

162. Most common is the mento-like strum. See Davis and Simon, *Reggae International*, 55, for further analysis of reggae guitar and keyboard patterns.

163. Clarke, *Jah Music*, 61.

164. Davis and Simon, *Reggae International*, 126.

165. *Ibid.*, 109.

166. See Krister and Malm, *Big Sounds*, 97–100, for a discussion of CBS's inability to penetrate Jamaica due to nationalistic hostility to the multinationals.

167. See, e.g., *ibid.*, 138. The exploitation of reggae musicians is well dramatized in *The Harder They Come*.

168. Hebdige, *Subculture: The Meaning of Style*, 31–35.

169. See Clarke, *Jah Music*, 52–53, 57.

170. Garth White, "Reggae—A musical weapon," *Caribe* (Dec. 1980), 10. Also see the Jamaican music bibliography in the same issue.

171. See the interview with Seaga in Davis and Simon, *Reggae International*, 176–79.

172. The flip sides of most reggae singles in Jamaica contain instrumental versions of the "A" side, for use by rappers.

173. George De Stefano, "Remember Reggae?" *The Nation*, 1/26/85, p. 91.

174. Hill, *The Trinidad Carnival: Mandate for a National Theatre*, 71–2.

175. See *ibid.*, 45, 58, 60–61.

176. See Warner, *Kaiso! The Trinidad Calypso: A Study of the Calypso as Oral Literature*, 23–24.

177. See *ibid.*, Ch. 3, and the bibliography in the same book.

178. See *ibid.*, Ch. 4.

179. Merle Hodge, in *ibid.*, 99.

180. Wallis and Malm, *Big Sounds*, 14, 84–85, 236, 271, and 381.

181. *Ibid.*, 271.

182. *Ibid.*, 279.

183. From "Women and Money," by the Mighty Conqueror's *Socamania* (Makossa M 24242). For further discussion of soca, see Bergman, *Hot Sauces: Latin and Caribbean Pop*, ch. 3.

184. From "Calypso Clowns," on the same record, *Socamania*.

Chapter 3. Africa

1. Bergman, *Goodtime Kings: Emerging African Pop*, 9, 82.

2. David Coplan, "Go to my town, Cape Coast! The social history of Ghanaian highlife," in *Eight Urban Musical Cultures*, ed. Bruno Netl, 99.

3. David Coplan, "The urbanisation of African music: Some theoretical observations," *Popular Music* 2 (1982), 125.

4. Kazadi wa Mukuna, "The origin of Zairean modern music: A socio-economic aspect," *African Urban Studies* 6 (Winter 1979–80), 31–40.

5. See, e.g., James Koetting, "The organization and functioning of migrant Kasena flute and drum ensembles in Nima/Accra," *African Urban Studies* (Winter 1979–80), 17–30; and David Coplan, "Marabi culture: Continuity and transformation in African music in Johannesburg, 1920–1940," *African Urban Studies* (Winter 1979–80), 49–76.

6. Coplan, "Go to my town," 110. However, since pan-Africanism waned in the seventies, highlife, *juju,* and other genres have tended to favor song texts in regional ethnic languages rather than pidgin English or another lingua franca.

7. Hugh Tracey relates how the Ibo translation of one hymn phrase, "There is no sorrow in heaven," when set to three different church tunes, came to mean, respectively, "There are no tears on the bicycle," "There is no clothing among the crowd," and "There are no eggs in the sky." Cited in Bergman, *Goodtime Kings,* 34.

8. Coplan, "Go to my town," p. 98.

9. *Ibid.*, 98, and Bergman, *Goodtime Kings,* 34.

10. See Gerhard Kubik, "Neo-traditional popular music in East Africa since 1945," *Popular Music* 1 (1981), 92–93; Bergman, *Goodtime Kings* 35; and Coplan, "Marabi culture," 58–59.

11. Collins, *African Pop Roots,* 73–74.

12. See Naomi Ware, "Popular music and African identity in Freetown, Sierra Leone," in *Eight Urban Music Cultures,* ed. Bruno Nettl, 303; Kubik, "Neo-traditional popular music in East Africa," 92–3; and Collins, *African Pop Roots,* 74.

13. Roberts, *Black Music of Two Worlds,* 242.

14. See *ibid.,* 250, and Ware, *Eight Urban Music Cultures,* 311.

15. Bergman, *Goodtime Kings,* 82.

16. Coplan, "Go to my town," 108–11.

17. G. T. Nurse, "Popular songs and national identity in Malawi," *African Music* 3 (1964), 3.

18. Veit Erlmann, "Black political song in South Africa: Some research perspectives," *Popular Music Perspectives* 2 (1985), 187–209.

19. Collins, *African Pop Roots,* 115–18.

20. The role of the recording industry in Kenya and Tanzania is complex; see Wallis and Malm, *Big Sounds,* 30–33, 64, 257–61, 350–56, and 376–80.

21. Andrew Kaye, "A field methods report-in-progress: Ko Nimo and the problem of Ghana's contemporary musical culture" (Manuscript). Kaye also reports, however, that in 1985 Ghana passed a law which, if enforced, would protect local musicians from copyright infringements. A number of African countries do appear to be attempting to address copyright problems in some manner.

22. Personal communication with Ghanaian ethnomusicologist Francis Saighoe.

23. The development of West African popular musics is documented in considerable detail in Collins, *African Pop Roots,* Bergman, *Goodtime Kings,* and Coplan, "Go to my town."

24. Coplan, *ibid.,* 101.

25. See James Koetting, "Africa/Ghana," in *Worlds of Music,* ed. Jeff Titon, 100. For examples of early highlife and other African popular musics, see John Roberts' "Original Music" recordings, e.g., *Africa Dances* (Authentic 601).

26. Kaye, "A field methods report-in-progress."

27. Coplan, "Go to my town," 100–101.

28. See *The Hit Sound of the Ramblers Dance Band* (Afrodisia WAP 25) and *Hi-Life International* (Rounder 5014).

29. For example, the Ramblers Dance Band record mentioned above contains songs in Efik, Twi, Fanti, Ga, Ewe, and English. See Coplan, "Go to my town," 109–11.

30. See *Traditional Brass Band Music—Ghana* (Agora AG-LM-001), which contains examples of highlife, *adaha, agbadza,* and *adowa.*

31. Coplan, "Go to my town," 110–11.

32. Kaye, "A field methods report-in-progress."

33. See Collins, *African Pop Roots,* 46–51.

34. Roberts, *Black Music of Two Worlds,* 250–51. Also see Collins, *African Pop Roots,* 19–22, and Bergman, *Goodtime Kings,* 74–93.

35. Chris Waterman, "Juju," in *The Western Impact on World Music*, ed. Bruno Nettl, 87–90.

36. Note, for example, the *guaguancó* pattern played on the talking drum in Obey's *Celebration* (WAPS 538), side 2. Obey's first name is often spelled "Ebeneezer."

37. See Bergman, *Goodtime Kings*, 92–93.

38. See Collins, *African Pop Roots*, 22.

39. Bergman, *Goodtime Kings*, 65.

40. See, e.g., recordings of Moussa Doumbia (from Mali).

41. Cape Verdean emigration commenced during the whaling period, and has escalated markedly in the period of severe drought which has afflicted the archipelago since 1967. Gei Zantzinger's film "Songs of the Badius" documents the neo-African musics of Santiago.

42. According to United Nations statistics, Zaire (population ca. 35 million) enjoys the fifth lowest standard of living in the world. Profits from the export of the country's tremendous mineral wealth go primarily to Western multinationals and the tiny native elite.

43. The Congo cultural region comprises Zaire, the Central African Republic, and the Peoples Republic of the Congo; also heavily influenced are neighboring Uganda, Cameroon, Kenya, and Tanzania.

44. David Rycroft, "The guitar improvisations of Mwenda Jean Bosco." Parts I and II, *African Music* 2/4 (1962), 81–98, and 3/1 (1962), 86–102.

45. Roberts, *Black Music of Two Worlds*, 244–45.

46. See John Roberts' tape, "Afro-Cuban comes home: The birth and growth of Congo music," for a clear presentation of the evolution of Congolese style out of traditional and imported musics.

47. Roberts, *Black Music of Two Worlds*, 253. Congolese music is now often referred to as Zairian or Zairois, but such terms obscure the contributions of neighboring countries.

48. From Rocherau, "Residence Marina," and Franco, "Farceur" (Disco Stock Makossa DM 5005).

49. Tabu Ley Rocherau (with Mbilia Bel), "Residence Marina."

50. Lingala is also the language used by the military, and is the native tongue of Zairian dictator Mobutu Sese Seko. An informant related that the use of Lingala in *soukous* constitutes, for many, the major incentive to learn that language. Franco is one of the few *soukous* singers to have dared to criticize the Western-backed government of Mobutu (whose personal fortune is estimated to be roughly equivalent to Zaire's national debt). When Franco was shot (not fatally) in Paris in the mid-eighties, Mobutu henchmen were widely assumed to be responsible for the attack.

51. Kubik, "Neo-traditional popular music in East Africa," 1945," 83–104.

52. *Ibid.*, 93–99. Also see Gerhard Kubik, "Donald Kachamba's montage recordings: Aspects of urban music history in Malawi," *African Urban Studies* 6 (Winter 1979–80), 89–122.

53. Roberts, *Black Music of Two Worlds*, 255.

54. *Ibid.*, 255–56.

55. *Ibid.*, 257.

56. Wallis and Malm, *Big Sounds*. See the index of that book for the numerous scattered references to Tanzania and Kenya.

57. See John Roberts' recording "Songs the Swahili sing" (Original Music OMA 103).

58. Sudanese popular music bears affinities with that in Ethiopia, although Arab influence is much more pronounced there, as illustrated, for example, in the extensive use of the ʿud as an accompanying instrument.

59. Data on Ethiopian music presented here are derived primarily from analysis of recordings and personal communication with Yohannes Haileyesus, producer of Voice of America's Amharic service.

60. Kubik, "Neo-traditional popular music", 96.

61. See, e.g., recordings of Angolan expatriate Bonga. Many Brazilian slaves came originally from Angola.

62. The other major ethnic group in Zimbabwe is the Ndebele; their traditional music is

primarily vocal and has not lent itself to syncretic modernization as has Shona music. See Bergman, *Goodtime Kings*, 119–20, for discussion of Mapfumo and *chimurenga* music.

63. See Robert Kauffman, "Tradition and innovation in the urban music of Zimbabwe," *African Urban Studies* 6 (Winter 1979–80), 41–48.
64. John Waenda, "African Melody," on *Take Cover: Zimbabwe Hits* (AFRI LP 01).
65. Berliner, *The Soul of Mbira*, 26–27.
66. Veit Erlmann, "Black political song in South Africa—Some research perspectives," *Popular Music Perspectives* 2 (1985), 187–209.
67. Coplan, "Marabi culture," 51.
68. Coplan, *In Township Tonight!*, 92ff.
69. Coplan, "Marabi culture," 54–56.
70. Erlmann, "Black political song in South Africa," 196 ff.; also see Coplan, *In Township Tonight!*, 107.
71. See Coplan, "Marabi culture," 66.
72. Gerhard Kubik, "Kwela," in *New Grove's Dictionary of Music and Musicians* 329–30. The term "kwela" has often been applied indiscriminately to any black township music. Also see Coplan, *In Township Tonight!*, 157ff.
73. For example, the Manhattan Brothers' "Bawo wetu," which is based on "Take the A Train." "Jive" is not to be confused with "penny whistle jive" (a term applied to some *kwela* music), or with the more contemporary "Zulu jive." Since the forties, mainstream, post-bop jazz has also had a place in the South African musical scene, although the best musicians have tended to emigrate.
74. Coplan, *In Township Tonight!*, Ch. 6.
75. Bergman, *Goodtime Kings*, 116.
76. See Andersson, *Music in the Mix*, 37–59. Andersson also exposes how the ultra-right-wing Broederbond organization dominates SABC (South African Broadcasting Company) policies (pp. 85–97).
77. See Erlmann, "Black political song in South Africa," 202.
78. Robin Cohen, review of Muff Andersson, *Music in the Mix*, in *Popular Music* 4 (1984), 317–19; also see Coplan, *In Township Tonight!*, 150.
79. See Ben Mandelson's *Madagasikara Two: Current Popular Music of Madagascar* (Globe Style ORBD 013).
80. Liner notes to *ibid*.
81. See Jacques Maunick, liner notes to *Ile Maurice: Sega ravanne mauricien et Sega tambour de l'Ile Rodrigues* (Ocora 558 601).

Chapter 4. Europe

1. Liner notes to Monitor MF 374. Many fine recordings of *fado*, complete with text translations, are issued on the Monitor label.
2. Alicia Svigals, in an unpublished manuscript based on interviews conducted in 1985 by her and myself with *fadistas* in Providence, Rhode Island; singer Dinis Paiva and instrumentalist Tony Carlos were particularly informative.
3. Barreto, *Fado*, 17–21, 37–45.
4. *Ibid.*, 29, 125, and Pinto de Carvalho, *Historia do fado*, 42.
5. Barreto, *Fado*, 183, enumerates the following classical *castiço fados*:
   for six-line poems: Cravo, Despedida, Marceneiro, Manuel Maria, Triplicado, Franklin I, and Bacalhau;
   for five-line poems: Seixal and Tango;
   for four-line poems: Corrido, Menor, Mouraria, Dois Tons, Meia Noite, Noronha, Franklin II, Vianinha, and Torres Mondego.
   For further discussion of the evolution of *fado* in the nineteenth century, see Pinto de Carvalho, *Historia do fado*, 93ff.

6. Gallop, *Portugal*, 248–54.

7. Alberto Pimentel, cited in *ibid.*, 265.

8. Interview with Paiva et al. Traditional *fados* are to be distinguished from popular folk songs like "Uma Casa Portuguesa" which are often performed in *fado* style.

9. Svigals, unpublished manuscript.

10. See, for example "Partir e Morrer um Pouco" on Coimbra PR-8030.

11. Paiva. Coimbra-style *fado corrido* may be sung in slow tempo, as on Philips 831.206.

12. Aubrey Bell, in Gallop, *Portugal*, 262.

13. Gallop, *ibid.*, 264.

14. From the Monitor LP *Musical Treasures of Portugal*.

15. Barreto, *Fado*, 7.

16. A nineteenth-century *fado* of the court of Amoso, in *ibid.*, 503.

17. Gallop, *Portugal*, 264, cites the following excerpt from an ode to a deceased soccer player:

Foi um astro, foi um sol,	He was a star, he was a sun,
Nos campos de futebol.	On the football field.

18. Dinis Paiva.

19. Svigals, unpublished manuscript.

20. Pinto de Carvalho, *Historia do fado*, 287–88.

21. Jesús Ordovás, "Historia de 'Rock'," in *El Pais* (Madrid), 6/21/87, p. 384.

22. For a cursory sketch of the major groups, see Ordovás, *Historia de la música pop española*, 165–75.

23. From "Dragones y mezquitas" (RCA PK 35579).

24. For further discussion of *nueva canción andaluza*, see Claudín, *Canción de autor en España*, 272–79.

25. Sotirios Chianis, "Greece: IV—Folk music," in *New Grove's Dictionary of Music and Musicians*, 677. Also personal communication with Angeliki Keil.

26. Angeliki Keil, introduction to *Markos Vamvakaris*, ed. A. Keil.

27. Much of the information on *rebetika* in this section derives from Butterworth and Schneider, *Rebetika*, and from Holst, *Road to Rembetika*. Readers interested in the subject are urged to consult these fine books. An indispensable and very enjoyable source of recordings is the six-volume set *History of the Rebetika* (EMI-Regal *Historia Rebetike*). I am also indebted to Angeliki and Charles Keil for their constructive comments on the original draft of this section.

28. *Rebetes* is singular and plural; adjective forms are *rebete* and *rebetiko; mangas* is singular, *manges* plural.

29. Holst, *Road to Rembetika*, 48.

30. Butterworth, *Rebetika*, 12–13.

31. Keil, introduction to *Markos Vamvakaris*.

32. "I'm a Junkie," a *khasapiko* by Tsaousis, popular in the 1920s; from Butterworth and Schneider, *Rebetika* 101.

33. "My Mind as if Bewitched," a *khasapiko* by Bayianteras, first recorded in 1938; from *ibid.*, 47.

34. Angeliki Keil, personal communication.

35. Holst, *Road to Rembetika*, 20, 64–5.

36. *Ibid.*, 26–27, 35, 41–42.

37. See, e.g., the song "Among the Beauties of Athens," on *Historia Rebetike*, Vol. 1, A, 1, with improvised violin *taxim* and *layali*-like vocal passages sung in the style of the *amané* songs.

38. Holst, *Road to Rembetika*, 65.

39. *Ibid.*, 68.

40. *Ibid.*, 68–69, and Markos Dragomis, in Butterworth and Schneider, *Rebetika*, 19.

41. Holst, *Road to Rembetika*, 66–67.

42. *Ibid.*, 64.

43. In Butterworth and Schneider, *Rebetika*, 29.

44. *Ibid.*, 31–32.
45. *Ibid.*, 32–33.
46. See Holst, *Road to Rembetika*, 66. Turkish *Ussak* resembles Arab *Bayati*.
47. *Ibid.*, 44. The *Piraiotiko* is said to come from Piraeus.
48. *Ibid.*, 45.
49. From EMI Regal 2J048-70366, B, 4 (*Play Bouzoukis*).
50. From *Historia Rebetike*, Vol. 3, A,4. *Bouzouki* riffs following the solo verse segments are not notated. Holst, *Road to Rembetika*, 141, translates the verse: "True sunset—the hour when it gets dark; stooped I go my way, sorrow is wearing me out."
51. Holst, *Road to Rembetika*, 53–54.
52. Angeliki Keil, personal communication.
53. Holst, *Road to Rembetika*, 54–59.
54. *Ibid.*, 63.
55. *Ibid.*, 61.
56. Such functions and festivals are also the predominant context for Greek pop in the numerous and active Greek immigrant communities in the USA; one professional Chicago bandleader told me that very few of the numerous Greek restaurants and clubs in that city feel the need to offer live music, since Greek music is performed so frequently in other contexts.
57. Holst, *Road to Rembetika*, 60.
58. Keil, introduction to *Markos Vamvakaris. Syrtaki* is the diminutive form of *syrtos*.
59. See condemnations in Butterworth and Schneider, *Rebetika*, 14–15, 25, and Holst, *Road to Rembetika*, 14, 60ff.
60. It is significant that all the ethnic groups in Yugoslavia enjoy full protection of their rights in regard to linguistic and cultural autonomy; in this sense Yugoslavia differs markedly from other East European countries, whether socialist (e.g., Bulgaria), or capitalist (e.g., Greece). Most of the data in this section derive from an unpublished manuscript by Jane Sugarman regarding popular music in Macedonia. I am further indebted to Sugarman for her constructive comments on this section.
61. Ljerka Vidić, "The Musical practice of the nomadic Rom of Bosnia and Hercegovina," 83–84.
62. Sugarman, unpublished manuscript.
63. Koraljka Kos, "New dimensions in folk music: A contribution to the study of musical tastes in contemporary Yugoslav society," *International Review of the Aesthetics and Sociology of Music* 3/1 (1972), 61–73 (cited in Vidić, "Musical practice," 61).
64. Vidić, "Musical Practice," 67.
65. *Ibid.*, 67–79.
66. Sugarman, unpublished manuscript.
67. Personal communication with Mark Forry.

Chapter 5. The Arab Middle East

1. Although Arab theorists developed a system of musical notation as early as the thirteenth century, only in the twentieth century has notated music been commonly used.
2. Habib Hasan Touma, "History of Arabian music—A study," *The World of Music* 22 (1980), 72. Transliteration of Arabic words generally follows the Library of Congress guidelines, except that *ayn's* have been dropped from the name Abd and diacritics omitted in proper names.
3. For two excellent discussions of historical writings on Islam and music see Nelson, *The Art of Reciting the Qur'ān*, and M. L. Roy Choudhury, "Music in Islam," *Journal of the Asiatic Society, Letters* 23/2 (1957), 43–103. It should be noted that, judging by the descriptions by Nettl and others, attitudes toward music and musicians in Iran have been decidedly more conservative than in the Arab world. See, for instance, Nettl, *The Western Impact on World Music.*

Notes 257

4. Ali Jihad Racy, "Music in contemporary Cairo," *Asian Music* 13/1 (1981), 4–26.
5. Cf. Jean-Claude Chabrier's observation that "Artistic renown derives from Cairo," in "Music in the fertile crescent: Lebanon, Syria and Iraq," *Cultures* 1/3 (1974), 40.
6. Not incidentally, many of the professional musicians, music teachers in schools and universities, and administrators of radio and television facilities throughout the Arab world have been Egyptian expatriates.
7. See, for instance, the attitudes toward popular culture and music expressed by an Egyptian lady, Huda Shacarawi, in her memoirs, *Harem Years: Memoirs of an Egyptian Feminist.*
8. Although it has occasionally been used in secular contexts, the title *shaykh* usually carries religious overtones.
9. Raja' al-Naqqash, "al-Mashāyikh wa al-Fann" ("The Mashayikh and Art") in *al-Kawākib* (The Stars) 1965, repr. in *Lughz Umm Kulthūm* (The Secret of Umm Kulthum), 98.
10. Pierre Cachia (comp.), "The Egyptian mawwal: Its ancestry, its development, and its present forms" *Journal of Arabic Literature* 8 (1977), 77–103, especially p. 85.
11. Ibrahim Shafiq in *Turāthunā al-Mūsīqiyyah* (Our Musical Heritage), Vol. 3, p. A.
12. Umm Kulthum, Lebanese popular singers Lur Dakash and Sucad Muhammad, and Syrians Nadirah and Sabah Fakhri, are among those whose musical skills were attributed in part to study of the old *muwashshahāt.*
13. Sulayman Jamil, *al-Inshād fī al-Ḥaḍrah al-Ṣūfiyyah* (Religious Song in the Sufi Ḥaḍrah) (Cairo: Maṭbācat al-Kilāfī, ca. 1970, 17; also Kamal al-Najmi, "al-Fananūn wa al-Azhar" (Artists and the Azhar), in *Qiṣṣat al-Azhar* (The Story of the Azhar), 155–56, and al-Naqqash, "al-Mashāyikh wa al-Fann," 104.
14. al-Shaykh Yunis al-Qadi, "al-Aghānī" ("Songs"), *al-Masraḥ* (The Theater) No. 35 (Aug. 16, 1926), 26; also Mahmud Kamil, "Alḥān Zamān" (Music of Yesterday [radio broadcast] Jan. 18, 1986); Hafiz, *Tarīkh al-Mūsīqā wa al-Ghinā' al-cArabī* (History of Arabic Music and Song), 243; Abd al-Muncim Arafah *Tarīkh Aclām al-Mūsīqā al-Sharqiyyah* (History of the Stars of Eastern Music), 54–56, 81–82; and Rizq, *al-Mūsīqā al-Sharqiyyah wa al-Ghinā' al-cArabī* (Eastern Music and Arabic Song), Vol. 4, p. 103.
15. The careers of these foreigners were facilitated by a liberal immigration policy for entertainers, long maintained by the Egyptian government. See al-Tabaci, *Asmahān Tarwi Qiṣṣatahā* (Asmahan Tells Her Story), 102–3; Fu'ad, *Umm Kulthūm wa cAṣr min al-Fann* (Umm Kulthum and an Era of Art), 261.
16. For instance, playwright and composer Kamil al-Khulaci who traveled in the Levant in order to learn Turkish and Syrian musical styles, touring singers Fathiyyah Ahmad, Nadirah, actress-singer Munirah al-Mahdiyyah who, during the apex of her career, was said to have enthralled audiences in Istanbul with her command of Turkish music, and others.
17. The licentious aspects of these songs and the associated objectionable public behavior were blamed on the foreign troops on leave in Cairo during and after World War I, whose freewheeling habits were believed to have adversely affected the young people in Egypt.
18. "al-Sayyidah Nacīmah al-Maṣriyyah," *Rūz al-Yūsuf* No. 107 (Nov. 24, 1927), 20; notices and advertisements published in *Rūz al-Yūsuf, al-Ṣabāḥ, al-Masraḥ* during the 1920s and 1930s.
19. The forthcoming section is heavily indebted to Ali Jihad Racy's Ph.D. dissertation on the recording industry in Egypt, "Musical Change and Commercial Recording in Egypt, 1904–1932," especially chapter 3.
20. Racy, "Musical Change," 79, 93.
21. Pekka Gronow, "The record industry comes to the Orient," *Ethnomusicology* 25 (1981), 251–84.
22. Racy, "Musical change," 114.
23. "Ascār al-Muṭribīn wa al-Muṭribāt" (The Prices of Singers) *Rūz al-Yūsuf* No. 48 (Sept. 29, 1926), 14.
24. cAwad, *Umm Kulthūm alātī Lā Yacrafuhā Aḥad* (The Umm Kulthum Nobody Knows), 28.

25. Racy, "Words and music in beirut: A study of attitudes," *Ethnomusicology* 30 (1986), 420; also Chabrier, "Music in the fertile crescent," 39–40.

26. Racy, "Musical Change," 129, 125–27.

27. This information has been culled from a survey of theatrical periodicals dating from 1924–1935 which I made using the resources of the Egyptian National Library.

28. el-Shawan, "al-Mūsīká al-ᶜArabiyyah: A category of urban music in Cairo, Egypt, 1927–77," 114.

29. Douglas A. Boyd, *Egyptian Radio: Tool of Political and National Development*, Journalism Monographs No. 48 (Feb. 1977); see his chart of transmission power, p. 10; for dates of the establishment of new stations, their wave lengths and transmission power, see *Yearbooks* published by the Egyptian government.

30. See, for instance Mosharrafa, *Cultural Survey of Modern Egypt* Vol II, 61; complaints of singer Suᶜad Muhammad in *al-Usbūᶜ* (Sept. 1, 1975), 66; and the characterization of radio broadcasting by Mahfuz, *Bidāyah wa Nihāyah*, 149.

31. Fakhouri, *Kafr el-Elow*, 102–3; also Ibrahim Abu-Lughod's survey of six Delta villages in the 1960s, which prompted him to conclude that "the radio is the most effective medium for reaching villagers, even literate ones." Abu Lughod, "The mass media and Egyptian village life," *Social Forces* 42, (1963), 101; Boyd, *Egyptian Radio*, 4.

32. Wahba, *Cultural Policy in Egypt*, 53.

33. Translations of texts are as follows: Ex. A: "Sitting up alone, drowning in my passion, tears flowing down my cheeks, I whisper to the phantom of you that comes to me in the night"; Ex. B/2: "Hope of my life, O precious love never ending"; Ex. B/3: "And let me dream . . . If only I never had to awaken." The excerpt from "Sahrān li-waḥdī" (Ex. A, here transcribed up a fourth) is taken from the beginning of the song, which is in the mode Huzam. "Amal hayāti" (Ex. B) is in the mode Kurd. "al-Awwilah fil gharām" (Ex. C) is in Nahawand; however, the excerpt transcribed here, taken from near the end of the song, is suggestive of Hijaz transposed to begin on G. These transcriptions serve to illustrate the points made in the text and should not be viewed as comprehensive. Sources for the examples are Sawt al-Qahirah tapes nos. 84, 76041, and 75074, respectively. A downward arrow in the notations denotes the interruption of a sustained melodic line by an emphasized consonant. Other supplementary signs are as follows: * for falsetto; ' for breath; and bah for *bahhah*, a deliberate vocal hoarseness.

34. Raja' al-Naqqash, "Liqā' maᶜa Umm Kulthūm" (A Meeting with Umm Kulthum) in *Lughz . . .* , 48–49; repr. from *al-Kawākib* (1965) (paraphrased here).

35. For an early account, see J. Desparmet, "Les chansons de geste de 1830 à 1914 dans la Mitidja," *Revue Africaine* 83 (1939), 192–226.

36. See for instance, Susan Slyomovics, "Arabic folk literature and political expression," *Arab Studies Quarterly* 8 (1986), 178–85.

37. For Abduh's remarks, see "Muṭrib al-ᶜArab Muḥammad ᶜAbduh yataḥaddath ᶜan Umm Kulthūm wa ᶜAbd al-Ḥalīm Ḥāfiẓ wa Farīd al-Aṭrash" (The Singer of the Arabs Muhammad Abduh talks about Umm Kulthum, Abd al-Halim Hafiz and Farid al-Atrash) *al-Idhāᶜah wa al-Tilīfizyūn* (Radio and Television) 2681 (Aug. 2, 1986), 19.

38. A recent example might be the Algerian "rai" style of Cheb Khaled and Ensemble, "Hada Raykoum" Triple Earth TERRA 102, p1985.

39. Ali Jihad Racy, "Legacy of a star," in *Fayrouz: Legend and Legacy*, 37.

40. Chabrier, "Music in the fertile crescent," 39.

41. Racy, "Legacy of a star," 41; for similar observations on the "back country and exogenous strains" of Lebanese music, see Chabrier, *ibid.*, 36, 46.

42. Chabrier, *ibid.*, 48–49.

43. Poul Røvsing Olsen, "La musique africaine dans la Golfe persique" *Journal of the International Folk Music Council* 19 (1967), 28–36; also his "Enregistrements faits à Kuwait et à Bahrain" *Les Colloques de Wégimont* 4 (1964), 137–170; and Jargy, *La Musique Arabe*, 93.

44. Al-Haddad, *Cultural Policy in the Yemen Arab Republic*, 41, 43, and al-Mani and as-Sbit, *Cultural Policy in the Kingdom of Saudi Arabia*, 61–62.

45. Gronow, "The record industry comes to the Orient," 255, 263–64, 266.
46. Jürgen Elsner, "Ferment nationalen Bewusstseins: Die Musikkultur Algeriens" *Musik und Gesellschaft* 33/8 (1983), 459; Baghli, *Aspects of Algerian Cultural Policy*, 39. Little is known about popular music in Libya.
47. Philip Schuyler, "A folk revival in Morocco." The Moroccan information presented here derives from this manuscript.
48. *Ibid.*
49. For further discussion see, especially Majdi Wahba, "Cultural planning in the Arab world" *Journal of World History* 14/4 (1972), 800–813.

Chapter 6. The Non-Arab Middle East

1. Modern Turkish urban music has been entirely neglected by Western scholars (the entry in *New Grove's Dictionary of Music and Musicians* is representative in this respect). For information on the development of urban music in Turkey since 1750, I am indebted to Walter (Zev) Feldman (Univ. of Pennsylvania), an authority on Turkish music and oral literature. *Saz* artist Mehmet Yorukoglu and keyboard player Nedim Katgi also provided useful data on modern popular styles.
2. The goblet-shaped drum *dombak* has also been in common use in urban music since World War II. Feldman observes, however, that the *dombak* had fallen out of use since the early eighteenth century, and was virtually unknown in rural music, where percussion would not traditionally be used for an indoor music genre like *türkü*.
3. Recep Kaymak, "365 gün yandı ha yandı." The transcription is transposed; the 4/8 meter (used here to accommodate the eleven-bar verses) should not be taken as implying a Turkish conception of the rhythm.
4. The *djumbus*, a twentieth-century invention, resembles a short, fretless banjo, but is tuned and played like an *ud*. A fine recording of Turkish gypsy music is *Turquie: Musique Tzigane* (Ocora 558 649).
5. Cengiz Coşkuner, "Parasizlik" (Raks TS 2240).
6. Bruno Nettl, "Persian popular music in 1969," *Ethnomusicology* 16/2 (1972), 218–39.
7. See Zonis, *Classical Persian Music*, 35–40.
8. *Tahrir* is a vocal technique whereby individual or repeated notes are articulated by falsetto or head-voice breaks.
9. Iranian policy in this regard may be contrasted with that of neighboring Pakistan, which, since 1977 has also been ruled (directly or indirectly) by a regime espousing Islamic fundamentalism. The Pakistani government's discouragement of music has taken the form of curtailing state support for art and folkloric musics, such that while these genres suffer, commercial film music, with its hedonistic and thoroughly un-Islamic ethos, flourishes as never before.
10. See Erik Cohen and Amnon Shiloah, "Major trends of change in Jewish oriental ethnic music in Israel," *Popular Music* 5 (1985), 199–224. While the fondness of many Oriental Jews for the musics of their Arab homeland is quite natural, it remains ironic in view of the hostility with which many of them regard Arab Muslims themselves. For a discussion of this ambivalence, with reference to musical tastes, see A. Hoder, "Oriental Jews in Israel—Collective schizophrenia," in *Khamsin* 5 (1978), 11, 36–37.
11. See Cohen and Shiloah, "Major trends of change," 215–19.
12. Thomas L. Friedman, "Using songs, Israelis touch Arab feelings," *New York Times*, 5/3/87, pp. 1, 44.
13. See e.g., recordings of Zohar Argov, Moshe Giat, and Chaim Moshe.
14. Friedman, "Using songs," states that according to Shafik Salman, disc jockey for the Arabic service, by 1987 Arab listeners from Morocco to Damascus were sending the service several hundred letters monthly, most of which were requests for favorite hits in the new style. Oriental pop's mass popularity in the Arab world, however, should not be overestimated; my own informants based in Cairo at the time, for example, were unaware of the music.

Chapter 7. South Asia

1. For the sake of convenience and because of India's dominance in the subcontinent, "South Asian" cinema, popular music, etc., will henceforth be referred to as "Indian." Popular music styles and industries in Pakistan, Bangladesh, and to a lesser degree, Sri Lanka, bear similarities with those of India, but the reader should bear in mind that regional styles and specific productive conditions do to some extent distinguish these countries.

2. Ranade, *On Music and Musicians of Hindoostan*, 64. Low literacy rates (about 35 percent in India and 23 percent in Bangladesh) naturally enhance the importance of cinema. In Pakistan, the functional literacy rate has been estimated as low as 8 percent.

3. Pradip Krishen, "Introduction," *India International Centre Quarterly* (March 1981), 3.

4. The influence of folk *jātra* and *nautanki* on Indian cinema is discussed in Sarkar, *Indian Cinema Today*, 16; and in William Beeman's "The use of music in popular film: East and West," *India International Centre Quarterly* (March 1981), 83.

5. Sarkar, *Indian Cinema Today*, 131.

6. *Ibid.*, 19, and Burra, *Looking Back: 1896–1966*, 79–80.

7. The film *Awara* is typical in this respect. For discussion of this phenomenon, see Barnow and Krishnaswamy, *Indian Film*, 158–59. A similar reluctance to depict anything but glitter is evident in the recent production of Premchand's *Mazdur*; here the surface message is an almost socialistic celebration of proletarian victory over corporate exploitation; but the film's protagonists—a family of labor leaders—become rich early on in the film, such that scenes of their original lower-middle class domicile can be kept to a minimum.

8. See Sarkar, *Indian Cinema Today*, 118.

9. A musical interlude in "Tīn Deviyan" is not atypical: at a formal, black-tie party in a luxurious mansion, the protagonist croons a sentimental ballad while seated at a grand piano; for comic relief, another tuxedo-clad guest kicks a pie into the face of a servant, who smiles disarmingly while wiping himself off.

10. Marre and Charlton, *Beats of the Heart*, 150.

11. Rangoonwalla, *75 Years of Indian Cinema*, 140.

12. Sarkar, *Indian Cinema Today*, 103.

13. *Ibid.*, 104–5.

14. Beeman, "The use of music in popular film," 83.

15. Sarkar, *Indian Cinema Today*, 108.

16. *Ibid.*, 110.

17. In Pakistan, since the 1977 military coup and subsequent Islamization program, film censorship has become considerably more strict than in India. Aside from banning any negative portrayals of policemen or government officials, the military regime has forbidden such acts as singing and dancing on a rocking boat or in a rainstorm, and abduction by the hero of "two female artistes at one and the same time." A mother is not allowed to hug her son on screen, and lovers are forbidden to touch, much less kiss. (Jamal Rasheed, "Formula for mediocrity," in *Far Eastern Economic Review*, 6/12/86, p. 51).

18. See Rangoonwalla, *75 Years of Indian Cinema*, for a summary of the early history of Indian cinema.

19. *Ibid.*, 82.

20. Krishen, "Introduction," 6.

21. Girish Karnad, in "Comments from the gallery," *India International Centre Quarterly* (March 1981), 103.

22. Interview with Malayalam film poet Kavalam Pannikar.

23. See Ranade, *On Music and Musicians of Hundoostan*, 64.

24. Burra, *Looking Back*, 50; Sarkar, *Indian Cinema Today*, 113.

25. Sarkar, *Indian Cinema Today*; Burra, *Looking Back*, 51.

26. Amunugama, *Notes on Sinhala Culture*, 71.

27. See, e.g., the foxtrot "Ham āp ki āṅkhoṅ," from *Pyasa* (1957).
28. See Peter Manuel, "The Light-Classical Urdu Ghazal-Song," and "The relationship between musical and prosodic rhythms in the light-classical Urdu Ghazal-Song," in *Studies in the Urdu Ǧazal and Prose Fiction* (Madison: Univ. of Wisconsin Press, 1979), 101–19.
29. Urdu scholar Bruce Pray has discussed these matters in "The Qawwāli in Hindi films," a paper presented at the Conference on South Asia, University of Wisconsin-Madison, November 1984.
30. Use of harmony in the Light-Classical *ghazal* is discussed in Manuel, "The light-classical Urdu Ghazal-song."
31. See Siddhartha Basu, Sanjay Kak, and Pradip Krishen, "Cinema and society: A search for meaning in a new genre," *India International Centre Quarterly* (March 1981), 57–76. In Pakistan, films dealing with social issues have been almost completely replaced by action films relying on foreign sets, car chases, special effects and the like. Government censorship effectively prohibits social commentary (Rasheed, "Formula for mediocrity," 51–53).
32. See, e.g., the Tamil films *Urangatha Ninaiyugal* and *Thani Kattu Raju.*
33. Marre and Charlton, *Beats of the Heart,* 141–42.
34. Ranade, *On Music and Musicians of Hindoostan,* 77.
35. Beeman, "The use of music in popular film," 83.
36. Scott Marcus, personal communication.
37. For discussion of *ṭhumri* and the decline of contemporary courtesan culture, see Peter Manuel, "The evolution of modern thumri," *Ethnomusicology* 30/3 (Fall 1986), 470–90.
38. Scott Marcus, personal communication.
39. Anil Biswas, "The ghazal in Indian film," *Sangeet Natak* 37 (1975), 12–15.
40. Sreekant Khandekar, "Classical music: The new awakening," *India Today* 3/15/86, p. 156.
41. Jagannath Dubashi, "Cassette piracy: High stakes," *India Today* 3/31/86, p. 112.
42. For information on Banaras, I am indebted to Scott Marcus, who conducted extensive field work there in 1983–1984. I am also grateful for his constructive comments on this chapter.
43. Amunugama, *Notes on Sinhala Culture,* 69–70.
44. For further discussion of Afghan urban music, see John Baily, "Cross-cultural perspectives in popular music: Afghanistan," *Popular Music* 1 (1981), 105–21, and Sakata, *Music in the Mind.* Information in this section is derived primarily from these sources and from my visit to Kabul and Herat in 1976.
45. Mark Slobin, "Afghanistan," in *New Grove's Dictionary of Music and Musicians,* 136–44.
46. Baily, "Cross-cultural perspectives in popular music."
47. For further discussion of Afghan modal use, see John Baily, "A system of modes used in the urban music of Afghanistan," *Ethnomusicology* 25/1 (1981), 1–40.
48. *Mughlai* (*mughlî*) is also the name of a seven-beat *tāl* used in Rajasthani folk music and occasionally in Hindustani light classical music.
49. Baily, "Cross-cultural perspectives in popular music," 109.

Chapter 8. Southeast Asia

1. The early development of *cai luong* is summarized in Duy, *Musics of Vietnam,* Ch. 4, and in Addiss, liner notes to *Music from North and South Vietnam* (Folkways FE 4219); the latter article is also included in Addiss' "Theater music of Vietnam," *Southeast Asia: An International Quarterly* 1/1–2 (1971), 129–52.
2. Duy, *Musics of Vietnam,* 146.
3. Addiss, "Theater music of Vietnam" 144.
4. See Addiss, liner notes to Folkways FE 4219.
5. From *Hành Khât Ðại Hiêp* (Songhac—bāng nhac "Vietnam").

6. Interview with Pham Duy, Nov. 1985.

7. *Ibid.*

8. The Vietnamese modal system is discussed briefly in Tran Van Khe, "Vietnam," in *New Grove's Dictionary of Music and Musicians,* 744–52.

9. John Trainor, "Significance and development in the vọng cổ' of South Vietnam," *Asian Music* 7/1 (1975), 50–59.

10. Addiss, "Theater Music of Vietnam," 148.

11. The expansion process is explained, albeit ambiguously, in Trainor, "Significance and development in the vong co," and Addiss, "Theater music of Vietnam." I am grateful to Pham Duy for further elucidating it to me, and for his constructive comments on an earlier draft of this section.

12. From *Dũng Thanh Lâm I* (produced in southern California).

13. Addiss, "Theater music of Vietnam," 148.

14. Speech before the Fourth Party Congress, in Duiker, *Vietnam Since the Fall of Saigon,* 24.

15. Barbara Grossette, "A slice of Hanoi night life: Hear a tale of Saigon," in the *New York Times,* 1/17/86, p. 2.

16. Duiker, *Vietnam,* 10.

17. Grossette, "A slice of Hanoi night life."

18. See, e.g., recordings of Yodruk Saragjai. The more Westernized *luk tung* may be virtually indistinguishable in style from *sakon* and rock.

19. Marre and Charlton, *Beats of the Heart,* 204.

20. *Ibid.,* 203–4.

21. *Ibid.,* 206–7.

22. Martin Hatch, "Popular music in Indonesia," *Popular Music Perspectives* 2, (1985), 210–12.

23. *Ibid.,* 214–15. Hatch reports that by 1981, at least eight million newly recorded cassettes were being issued every month.

24. "Commercial cassette recordings of traditional music in Java: Implications for performers and scholars," *The World of Music* 27/3 (1985).

25. See Hatch, "Popular music in Indonesia," for a discussion of some of these genres and sub-genres, which, aside from those discussed in this chapter, include *pop umum, pop contemporer, nostalgia, pop anak-anak, pop daerah, pop jawa, pop sunda,* and *pop minang.*

26. Ernst Heins, "Kroncong and tanjidor: Two cases of urban folk music in Jakarta," *Asian Music* 7/1 (1975), 20–32.

27. Personal communication from R. Anderson Sutton.

28. *Op. cit.,* and Judith Becker, "Kroncong, Indonesian popular music," in *Asian Music* 7/1 (1975), 14–19.

29. Becker, *ibid.,* 14–15.

30. William Frederick, "Rhoma Irama and the dangdut style: Aspects of contemporary Indonesian popular culture," *Indonesia* 34 (1982), 106.

31. Becker, "Kroncong, Indonesian popular music," 16–17. Hatch ("Popular music in Indonesia," p. 217) estimates that 5 percent of current cassette releases are *kroncong.*

32. Vibrato is also commonly used in a similar manner in Indonesian traditional musics.

33. Hatch, "Popular music in Indonesia," 217.

34. The title of an old-style *kroncong* piece, "Kafrinyo," cited by Heins, "Kroncong and tanjidor," (p. 23), brings to mind the Portuguese-Sri Lankan genre *kaffrinna.*

35. Becker, "Kroncong, Indonesian popular music,"

36. These similarities are illustrated in greater detail by Heins, "Kroncong and tanjidor." *Celumpung* is a plucked zither; *ketuk* is a small pot gong.

37. See Frederick, "Rhoma Irama and the dangdut style," for a thorough and insightful discussion of the social history and status of *dangdut.*

38. Hatch, "Popular music in Indonesia," 218.

39. See Frederick, "Rhoma Irama and the dangdut style."

40. *Ibid.,* 122.

41. *Ibid.,* 125. See Frederick for further discussion of these issues.

42. *Ibid.*, 113, 119, and elsewhere.
43. For a more detailed discussion of *jaipongan,* see Peter Manuel and Randall Baier, "Jaipongan: Indigenous popular music of West Java," in *Asian Music* 18/1 (Fall/Winter 1986), 91–110.
44. For a different perspective on the development of the *pesindhen's* role, see R. Anderson Sutton, "Who is the pesindhen? Notes on the female singing tradition in Java," in *Indonesia* 37 (1984), 118–31.
45. Sutton (personal communication) reports seeing *jaipongan* dance schools as far away as Malang, in East Java.
46. Harrel, in "Some aspects of Sundanese music," *Selected Reports in Ethnomusicology* 2/2 (1975), 81–101, discusses in some detail the intervallic relationships in Sundanese mode, but some aspects of his treatment—including the concepts of 10-, 15-, and 17-pitch *salendro*—may be more reflective of the theoretical ideas of his particular informants than of most Sundanese practicing musicians.
47. "Mat Peci," by Ucit (Entin Suhartini), on Sunda Kliningan Biola. The third line of the transcription represents a composite played on two interlocking *sarons;* the pitches were occasionally unclear.
48. Sutton, "Commercial cassette recordings."
49. Hatch, "Popular music in Indonesia," 222.
50. *Ibid.*

Chapter 9. China

1. See Alan Thrasher, "The sociology of Chinese music: An introduction," *Asian Music* 12/2 (1981), 17–53. The neglect of opera music in this chapter should not lead the reader to question the importance of this genre. Opera music, a true "people's art," is perhaps the single most popular and vital form of music in China today; moreover, it is widely disseminated on the media, and its appeal is not limited to any one socio-economic or ethnic group. Opera style, however, has not dramatically changed in its association with the mass media, and hence it is not a "popular music" in the same sense as the other genres treated in this volume.
2. Nettl, *The Western Impact on World Music,* 23ff.
3. Scott, *Literature and the Arts,* 127.
4. Thrasher, "The sociology of Chinese music," 47, asserts that Confucian ethics placed a low priority on performance, discouraged innovation and emotive performance. To the extent that this is true, the customary low status of traditional music may have rendered it particularly vulnerable to Westernization.
5. Nettl, *The Western Impact on World Music,* 75.
6. In Scott, *Literature and the Arts,* 134. One of the most popular cabaret songs, paradoxically, was a tune introduced by the Japanese troops, "China Night" (which has since been adopted, in altered fashion, by American Indians of the Southwest—some of whom presumably encountered it when they served as GI's in post-war Japan).
7. See *ibid.*, 65–83, for a summary of the development of Chinese cinema.
8. Yan-zhi Chen, "Observations on Chinese popular songs: A historical comparative study" (manuscript).
9. Isabel Wong, "*Geming Gequ:* Songs for the education of the masses." *Popular Chinese Literature and Performing Arts in the People's Republic of China 1949–1979,* ed. Bonnie McDougall, 112–16.
10. *Ibid.*, 121.
11. *Ibid.*, 126.
12. Malm, *Music Cultures of the Pacific,* 168.
13. Wong, "*Geming Gequ,*" 120.
14. See Scott, *Literature and the Arts,* 135–37, for a discussion of Nie Er and Xing-hai Xian.
15. In developing countries (including czarist Russia), the small size of the elite classes

may make their influence and control of patronage and the media seem especially incommensurate.

16. See McDougall, *Mao Zedong's Talks*.
17. See Arnold Perris, "Music as propaganda: Art at the command of doctrine in the People's Republic of China," *Ethnomusicology* 27/1 (1983), 1–28.
18. See, e.g., Chieh Fu, "Let us write songs in praise of the heroic workers, peasants and soldiers," *Chinese Literature* 11 (1967), 108–20.
19. Yin Cheng-Chung, "How the piano concerto "Yellow River" was composed," in *Chinese Literature* 11 (1974), 97–102.
20. Personal communication with Isabel Wong. I am grateful to Dr. Wong for her comments on an earlier draft of this chapter.
21. Perris, "Music as propaganda."
22. Cheng-Chung, *Chinese Literature*, 100. Similarly, a Chinese intellectual writing in the latter part of the Cultural Revolution, described as "outrageous" the notion that musical works without titles have no inherent socio-political content (Chao Hua, "Do musical works without titles have no class character?" *Chinese Literature* 4 (1974) 89–94).
23. Scott, *Literature and the Arts*, 139–52.
24. For example, the song "Breakers Leaping on the Honghu Lake," from the modern opera "Honghu Red Guards."
25. Wong, "Geming Gequ," 133.
26. Two typical songs in this respect are "Everybody Says Our Hometown Is Fine" (from the film *The Red Sun*), and "Farmers Are Flowers Toward the Sun."
27. See Scott, *Literature and the Arts*, 146.
28. Wong, "Geming Gequ," 131.
29. Scott, *Literature and the Arts*, 140.
30. Chieh Fu, "Let Us Write Songs," 108.
31. Garside, *Coming Alive: China After Mao*, 80.
32. *Ibid.*, 28.
33. *Ibid.*, 62.
34. In John Fitzgerald, "Deng's development drive and the dawn of decadence," *Far Eastern Economic Review* (FEER), 4/5/85, p. 44.
35. *Ibid.*
36. Typical songs are "Our Lives Are Full of Sunlight." "The Grapes of Tulufan Are Ripe," and "The Sea, My Homeland."
37. Clare Hollingworth, "Letter from Baotou," *FEER*, 7/4/85, p. 84.
38. Randy Chiu, "Disike takes the floor as youth culture takes the stage," in *FEER*, (May 9, 1985), 61.
39. "Millions strum in China," in the *Los Angeles Times*, 12/13/85, p. 24.
40. See John Minford, "Picking up the pieces," in *FEER*, 8/8/85, pp. 30–32.
41. John Fitzgerald, "Deng's development drive."
42. Robert Delfs, "The controversial fame of China's first rock star," *FEER*, 12/25/85, p. 40. Under the Spiritual Pollution campaign, dancing was banned as unhealthy and immoral. Subsequent policy, as articulated by Jiao Yongfu, a prominent cultural bureaucrat in Beijing, tolerates dancing as long as it is "civilized and wholesome," and not excessively sensual. See Edward Gargan, "Is Deng still supreme? Envoys study the omens," the *New York Times*, 3/16/87, p. A4.
43. Robert Delfs, "Cool gusts menace the warm mood of liberalism," and "What's love but a second hand emotion?" *FEER*, 12/26/85, pp. 45–47. In December 1986, revolutionary China's first commercial radio station—featuring Chinese rock, advertisements, and variety programming—was established in Canton. Edward Gargan, "Commercial radio arrives in southern China," the *New York Times*, (March 8, 1987).
44. Geremie Barme, "Revolutionary opera arias sung to a new, disco beat," *FEER*, 2/5/87, p. 38.
45. *Ibid.*, 37.

Chapter 10. The Pacific

1. We employ henceforth the standard designation of "ancient" for pre-Western-contact music, "old" or "traditional" for nineteenth-century acculturated music, and "modern" for twentieth-century styles.

2. The degree of acculturation is also reflected in miscegenation and language. Only a tiny minority of locals are of pure Hawaiian ancestry today, as Filipino, Japanese, Korean, Chinese, Polynesian, Latino, Caucasian, Hawaiian, and other racial and ethnic groups have been intermarrying for generations. The Hawaiian language is presently known only by some two thousand people. Most composers, not to mention performers, of modern Hawaiian songs are not fluent speakers of the Hawaiian language. Music thus serves to perpetuate the language. It should be remembered that darker-complected islanders have an acute sense of ethnic identity, whether as Hawaiian or simply "local," as opposed to *haoles* (whites), tourists, and other outsiders.

3. Elizabeth Tatar, in George Kanahele, *Hawaiian Music*, xxv–xxvii.

4. Jerry Hopkins, in *ibid.*, 325–26.

5. Robert Armstrong, in *ibid.*, 19.

6. This resentment is voiced repeatedly in the interviews in Kasher and Burlingame, *Da Kine Sound*. Also see George Lewis, "Beyond the reef: Role conflict and the professional musician in Hawaii," *Popular Music* 5 (1985), 189–98.

7. In Kasher and Burlingame, *Da Kine Sound*, 131. Also see Tatar, in Kanahele, *Hawaiian Music*, xxvi. A note on pronunciation of Hawaiian orthography may be appropriate here. Doubled vowels indicate intermediate glottal stops (often indicated by apostrophes); thus, the name Hoopii, frequently mangled by *haoles* as "Whoopie", is pronounced Ho'opi'i.

8. Lewis, "Beyond the reef," 196.

9. Sutton, "The persistence of tradition in Hawaiian music: Ancient features in contemporary popular music" (Manuscript).

10. Sutton mentions Leina'ala Haili's "Ka'uiki" as an example. A few ancient-style chants have themselves been adapted to modern instrumentation and style; the most familiar of these is "He'eia," as recorded by Gabby Pahinui (on Hula HCS H-506, and Panini PS 1002).

11. Sutton cites the *'ipu* strum in Genoa Keawe's "Makaha" (GK-102) as typical. The *'ipu* itself consists of two gourds of unequal size attached at the neck, forming a distended hourglass shape; the instrument is struck with the hand and beaten against the earth. Swing rhythm (with triplet subdivision of the beat) is also popular in Hawaii, and is referred to as "chang-a-lang."

12. For use of yodeling, see the Hoopii Brothers recording of "Hawaiian Cowboy" (on Poki SP 9006), or Karen Keavehawaii's recordings. Hui Ohana employs a more *himeni*-derived approach to falsetto, with languid three-part harmonies in slow tempos. Further discussion of the use of falsetto is found in Tatar, in Kanahele, *Hawaiian Music*, 86–92.

13. See Donald Kilolani Mitchell, in Kanahele, *ibid.*, 365–79. Hawaiian guitar technique bears obvious affinities to blues bottleneck guitar playing, although claims of a Hawaiian origin of that style are questionable.

14. See Tatar, in *ibid.*, 350–60.

15. These are outlined by R. J. Sheridan, "Music," in *Encyclopaedia of Papua and New Guinea*, vol. II, ed. Peter Ryan, pp. 818–21.

16. Niles, *Commercial Recordings of Papua New Guinea Music 1949–1983*, 5.

17. *Ibid.*, 817–20.

18. Personal communication. I am obliged to Niles for the informative publications, recordings, and correspondence he has sent me.

19. *Ibid.*

20. *Ibid.*

Glossary

apala—traditional and popular music genre of northern Nigeria.

baila—(Port. and Sp., "dance") Portuguese-derived traditional and popular music genre of Sri Lanka.

balada—Sp., "ballad"; in Mexico, a sentimental *canción* in mainstream international pop style.

batuque—(1) archaic Brazilian urban secular song and dance; (2) in Cape Verde, a traditional African-derived music and dance form.

biguine—music and dance genre of Martinique, in fast duple meter.

bolero—in Latin America, a song form in slow 4/4 with a characteristic bass pattern of a half note followed by two quarter-notes.

bomba—Puerto Rican folk dance and music genre.

bouzouki—Greek long-necked lute, related to the Turkish *saz*.

cadence—syncretic popular music genre of Haiti and the French Caribbean, closely resembling *compas*.

cải lương—modern Vietnamese light opera form, and the most important context for contemporary Vietnamese popular music.

cambouley—archaic processional dance and music of Trinidad, associated with Carnival, imitating plantation fire drill.

canción—Sp., "song," especially a through-composed, sentimental slow song not associated with dance.

canto nuevo—Chilean "new song," especially that which has flourished since the military coup of 1973.

chachachá—Cuban popular dance and music genre in medium-tempo, quadratic meter, popularized in the early 1950s; most typically played by *charanga* ensembles.

charanga—Cuban dance music ensemble consisting, usually, of flute, two violins, piano, bass, percussion, and vocals.

çifte telli—gypsy improvised music genre of Turkey, in up-tempo quadratic rhythm; also used in Greek *bouzouki* music.

cinquillo—ostinato in the Cuban *danzon:*

clave—(Sp., lit., "key") (1) pair of hard wooden sticks used as idiophones in Cuban and Dominican music; (2) a characteristic ostinato played on the above.

coladera—in Cape Verde: (1) a procession with song; (2) a modern popular music genre in fast duple meter.

compas—(1) Haitian syncretic popular music genre; (2) Sp.: "bar, measure", hence, in flamenco, the distinguishing structural harmonic and rhythmic ostinato of a *cante*.

conga—(1) Afro-Cuban drum, played with the hands; (2) Afro-Cuban music and dance genre, predominantly secular, traditionally rendered with voices and percussion, associated with Carnaval processions (*comparsas*).

conjunto—Sp., "ensemble"; in Cuba, it implies a standard dance band of two to four horns, piano, bass, and percussion; in *norteño* and Tex-Mex music, it denotes an ensemble featuring accordion, *bajo sexto*, guitar, bass, and occasionally, one or two horns.

cueca—Chilean folk song and dance, in 6/8 meter; often used in *nueva canción*.

cumbia—Columbian folk and popular genre.

dangdut—Indian- and rock-derived popular music genre of Indonesia.

danzón—light-classical Cuban genre originating in the late 1800s.

fado—Portuguese urban folk (and now popular) genre.

fuji—Nigerian dance and music genre, resembling *juju* without melodic instruments.

funana—Cape Verdean folk genre, sung with accompaniment of accordion and percussion.

garba—folk song and dance of Gujerat, often modernized as a pop genre, as in "disco *garba*."

ghazal—(1) poetic form used in Persian, Urdu, Turkish, and other Central Asian literatures; (2) in India, Turkey, and elsewhere: a musical genre based on the *ghazal* poetic form.

guaguancó—the most popular kind of *rumba*.

guaracha—Cuban syncretic song form, often with bawdy or picaresque lyrics, bearing some affinities with the *son*; also cultivated in Puerto Rico.

güiro—Cuban gourd scraper (Dominican Republic: *güira*).

hapa haole—Hawaiian, "half-white," referring, for example, to Hawaiian-style songs with English texts.

highlife—popular syncretic music genre of West Africa, especially Ghana.

huayno—traditional folk genre of Andean Indians.

jaipongan—indigenous popular music and dance form of West Java.

jaleo—the final section of a Dominican *merengue*, resembling the *montuno* of the Cuban *son* in the use of call-and-response vocals over a simple harmonic ostinato.

jive—term for various syncretic South African popular musics.

juju—syncretic popular music genre of Nigeria.

kaffrinna—in Sri Lanka, a Portuguese-derived folk genre closely related to *baila*.

karsilama—a Turkish urban gypsy dance and song form, in nine-beat meter; also occasionally used in Greek *bouzouki* music.

ketuk tilu—a folk music and dance form of West Java, from which *jaipongan* evolved.

kiliwāli—Afghan urban popular music genre.

kroncong—(1) folk and semi-popular music genre of Jakarta, Sumatra, and southern Malaysia; (2) Portuguese-derived ukulele-like instrument used in (1).

kwela—syncretic music genre of South Africa, originally played on penny whistle and guitar.

lāvni—folk song of Maharashtra, now modernized into an urban popular genre.

longa—Rumanian gypsy genre, incorporated into Turkish urban entertainment music in the late nineteenth century.

luk tung—acculturated popular music genre of Thailand, based on rural folk songs.

lundu—(1) African-derived dance and song of Brazil; (2) nineteenth century Brazilian salon piece derived from (1).

makossa—rock-oriented popular music of Cameroon.

makwaya—archaic syncretic choral genre of South Africa.

mambo—(1) up-tempo, predominantly instrumental Cuban genre, featuring antiphonal sectional writing for horn and reed sections; (2) alternate term for instrumental sections of the *jaleo* of the Dominican *merengue*.

maqām (Turkish: *makam*)—melodic mode, used as a basis for improvisation or composition in Arab, Turkish, and Persian musics.

marabi—South African syncretic urban music genre.

mawwāl—Arab traditional folk strophic song genre, with topical text in colloquial Arabic, set in five-line stanzas.

maxixe—archaic Brazilian urban popular dance and music form.

mbaqanga—the predominant black South African commercial popular music genre since the 1950s.

mbube—South African syncretic urban style, archetypically sung by male chorus without accompaniment.

merengue—(1) predominant secular folk and popular dance and music genre of the Dominican Republic, in fast duple meter; (2) in the modern Dominican *merengue*, the "song"-like section which precedes the *jaleo*; (3) a dance and song genre in triple meter used in the Colombian *vallenato*.

méringue—Haitian Europeanized folk dance and song form; an important source for pop *compas*.

modinha—Italian- and Portuguese-influenced urban Brazilian salon ballad of the eighteenth and nineteenth centuries, generally consisting of sentimental vocal text, sung in Italian- and Portuguese-influenced style, accompanied by guitar and/or piano.

montuno—(1) the final part of a Cuban *rumba* or *son,* employing call-and-response vocals; (2) the recurring pattern played, for example, on the piano, in the *montuno* of a *son.*

nueva canción—Sp. "new song," that is, Latin American progressive song.

nueva trova—Cuban efflorescence of *nueva canción.*

orkes melayu—archaic Malaysian and Sumatran syncretic genre, constituting an early influence on *dangdut.*

paseo—the predominant song genre, in duple meter, used in Columbia *vallenato.*

perico ripiao—the traditional folk *merengue* form and ensemble of Cibao, Dominican Republic; lit., "ripped parrot."

plena—syncretic song and dance form of Puerto Rico, featuring vocals accompanied by *panderetas* (frame drums) and one or more melodic instruments, or, in modernized form, by standard dance band instrumentation.

qāsidah—Arab poetic and musical genre, based on sophisticated, extended, generally serious text in classical Arabic.

rās—Gujerati stick dance, often modernized into a pop music and dance genre.

rebetika—urban Greek lumpen proletarian music of the early twentieth century.

rumba—Cuban traditional secular dance and music genre, rendered by vocals with percussion; incorporated dance-band instrumentation as the genre blended with the *son.*

sakon—Thai Westernized pop music.

samba—Brazilian secular music and dance form, spanning continuum from traditional percussion- and vocal-dominated street styles, to more modernized popular renditions.

şarkı—Turkish urban art song, flourishing from the late nineteenth century.

sega—traditional and popular song and dance genre of Mauritius and the Reunion Islands.

sirto—a folk music and dance form of the Greek islands, with a lively 3+3+2 rhythm, incorporated into Greek *bouzouki* music and Turkish urban gypsy music.

soca—modernized calypso, with greater orientation toward dance.

son—(1) the predominant secular popular music genre of twentieth-century Cuba; (2) folk genre, in regional variants, of Mexico.

soukous—Zairian folk dance and music genre, modernized into the predominant Congolese popular music form since the late 1960s.

taqsīm (taksim, taxim)—in Arab, Turkish, and Greek music, an improvisation in one or more melodic modes, in free-rhythmic style.

taqtuqah—Arab light, strophic, popular song genre, especially of the first half of the twentieth century, with text in colloquial Arabic.

tarabu—syncretic song form of coastal Tanzania, Kenya, and Zanzibar, reflecting Arab, Indian, African, and some Western influence.

trova—Cuban urban folk and popular music category, comprising in particular the *bolero* and *canción*.

türkü—Turkish rural folk music genre, with text lines of specific syllabic counts, for indoor listening; since the 1950s, *türkü* has become widely used in urban popular music.

ughniya—generic designation for modern, through-composed Arab popular song.

vallenato—accordion- and vocal-dominated folk and popular genre of northeastern Columbia.

vọng cô'—(1) a specific Vietnamese urban art song dating from around 1919; (2) a specific Vietnamese mode; (3) any Vietnamese urban or popular piece, set in the mode of the same name, and using the pitches of the *vọng cô'* song as structural cadential points.

zebekiko (zembekiko)—Greek and Turkish secular dance and music genre, in nine-beat meter, widely used in *rebetika* and *bouzouki* music.

zemenawi—Ethiopian modern urban music.

Bibliography

Abadía Morales, Guillermo. *La Música Folklórica Colombiana*. Columbia: Universidad Nacional de Colombia, 1973.

ᶜAbd al Munᶜim ᶜArafah. *Tarīkh Aᶜlām al Mūsiqá al Sharqiyyah* (History of the Stars of Eastern Music). Cairo: Maṭbāᶜat ᶜAnānī, 1947.

Abu Lughod Ibrahim, "The mass media and Egyptian village life." *Social Forces* 42: 97–104 (1963).

Acosta, Leonardo. *Canciones de la nueva trova*. Havana: Editorial Letras Cubanas, 1981.

Addiss, Stephen. Liner notes to *Music from North and South Vietnam*. Folkways Records FE 4219.

———. "Theater music of Vietnam." *Southeast Asia, an International Quarterly* 1/2 (1971).

Adolfo Sierra, Luis. *Historia de la orquesta típica: evolución instrumental del tango*. Buenos Aires: Orestes S.E.C., 1966.

Adorno, Theodor. *Introduction to the Sociology of Music*. New York: Seabury, 1976.

Alvarenga, Oneyda. *Música popular brasileira*. Rio de Janeiro: Editora Globo, 1950.

Amunugama, Sarath. *Notes on Sinhala Culture*. Colombo: Gunasena, 1980.

Andersson, Muff. *Music in the Mix: The Story of South African Popular Music*. Johannesburg: Ravan, 1981.

Appleby, David. *The Music of Brazil*. Austin: Univ. of Texas Press, 1983.

Araujo de Molina, Consuelo. *Vallenatología*. Bogotá: Ediciones Tercer Mundo, 1973.

Austerlitz, Paul. "A history of the Dominican merengue highlighting the role of the saxophone." M.A. thesis, Wesleyan Univ., 1986.

'Awad, Mahmud. *Umm Kulthum alātī lā Yaᶜrafuhā Aḥad* (The Umm Kulthum Nobody Knows). Cairo: Mu'assasat Akhbār al-Yawm, n.d.

Baghli, Sid-Ahmad. *Aspects of Algerian Cultural Policy*. Paris: Unesco, 1978.

Baily, John. "A system of modes used in the urban music of Afghanistan." *Ethnomusicology* 25/1 (1981).

———. "Cross-cultural perspectives in popular music: The case of Afghanistan." *Popular Music* 1: 105–22 (1981).

Barnow, Erik, and S. Krishnaswamy. *Indian Film*. New York: Oxford Univ. Press, 1980.

Barreto, Mascarenhas. *Fado: Origens Liricas e Motivação Poética—Lyrical Origins and Poetic Motivation.* Lisbon: Aster, n.d. (English translation by George Dykes).

Basu, Siddhartha, Sanjay Kak, and Pradip Krishen. "Cinema and society: A search for meaning in a new genre." *India International Centre Quarterly* 8/1: 57–76 (March 1981).

Becker, Judith. "Kroncong, Indonesian popular music." *Asian Music* 7/1: 14–19 (1975).

Beeman, William. "The use of music in popular film: East and west." *India International Centre Quarterly* 8/1: 77–87 (March 1981).

Behague, Gerard. "Popular music currents in the art music of the early nationalistic period in Brazil, circa 1870–1920." Ph.D. diss., Tulane Univ., 1966.

———. "Bossa and bossas: Recent changes in Brazilian urban popular music." *Ethnomusicology* 17/2 (1973).

———. "Tango," in *New Grove's Dictionary of Music and Musicians.* Ed. Stanley Sadie. New York: Macmillan, 1980.

———. "Interpretation of traditional and popular musics in the city of Salvador, Bahia." See Heartz and Wade, *Report of the Twelfth Congress of the American Musicological Society,* Berkeley 1977, Kassell: Barenreiter, 1977.

———. "Brazilian musical values of the 1960s and 1970s: Popular urban music from bossa nova to Tropicalia." *Journal of Popular Culture* 14/3: 437–52 (1980).

———. "Popular music in Latin America." *Studies in Latin American Popular Culture* 5: 41–67 (1986).

Benmayor, Rina. "'La nueva trova': New Cuban Song." *Latin American Music Review.* 1/1: 11–44 (1981).

Bensusan, Guy. "A consideration of norteña and Chicano music." *Studies in Latin American Popular Culture* 4: 158–69 (1985).

Bergman, Billy. *Hot Sauces: Latin and Caribbean Pop.* New York: Quill, 1985.

———. *Goodtime Kings: Emerging African Pop.* New York: Quarto, 1985.

Berliner, Paul. *The Soul of Mbira.* Berkeley: Univ. of California Press, 1978.

Biswas, Anil. "The ghazal in Indian film." *Sangeet Natak* 37: 12–15 (1975).

Blacking, John. *How Musical Is Man?* Seattle: Univ. of Washington Press, 1973.

Borraza, Fernando. *La nueva canción chilena.* Casilla, Chile: Editora Nacional Quimantu, 1972.

Burra, Rani. *Looking Back: 1896–1966.* New Delhi: Directorate of Film Festivals, 1981.

Butterworth, Katherine, and Sara Schneider. *Rebetika: Songs from the Old Greek Underworld.* Athens: Komboloi, 1975.

Cachia, Pierre. "The Egyptian mawwal: Its ancestry, its development, and its present forms." *Journal of Arabic Literature* 8: 77–103 (1977).

Canton, Dario. *Gardel, ¿a quién le cantas?* Buenos Aires: Ediciones de la Flor, 1972.

Carpentier, Alejo. *La Música en Cuba.* Mexico City: Fondo de Cultura Económica, 1979 (reprint of 1945 edition).

Carrasco, Pirard. "The nueva canción in Latin America." *International Social Science Journal* 34/4: 599–623 (1982).

Carvalho, Martha de Ulhoa. "Canto Nuevo" (Manuscript), 1987.

Castro, Donald. "Popular culture as a source for the historian: The tango in its era of la guardia vieja." *Studies in Latin American Popular Culture* 3: 70–85 (1984).

————. "Popular culture as a source for the historian: Why Carlos Gardel?" *Studies in Latin American Popular Culture* 5: 144–62 (1986).

Chabrier, Jean-Claude. "Music in the fertile crescent: Lebanon, Syria and Iraq." *Cultures* 1/3: 35–58 (1974).

Chen, Yan-zhi. "Observations of Chinese popular songs: A historical comparative study." (Manuscript), 1985.

Cheng-Chung, Yin. "How the piano concerto 'Yellow River' was composed." *Chinese Literature* 11: 97–102 (1974).

Chianis, Sotirios. "Greece: IV—Folk music," in *New Grove's Dictionary of Music and Musicians*. Ed. Stanley Sadie, New York: Macmillan, 1980.

Chieh Fu. "Let us write songs in praise of the heroic workers, peasants and soldiers." *Chinese Literature* 11: 108–120 (1967).

Clarke, Sebastian. *Jah Music: The Evolution of the Popular Jamaican Song*. London: Heinneman Educational Books, 1980.

Claudin, Victor. *Canción de autor en España*. Jucar 1981.

Cohen, Erik, and Amnon Shiloah, "Major trends of change in Jewish Oriental ethnic music in Israel." *Popular Music* 5: 199–224 (1985).

Collins, John. *African Pop Roots*. London: Foulsham, 1985.

Coplan, David. "Go to my town, Cape Coast! The social history of Ghanaian highlife," in *Eight Urban Musical Cultures*. Ed. Bruno Nettl. Urbana: Univ. of Illinois Press, 1978.

————. "Marabi culture: Continuity and transformation in African music in Johannesburg, 1920–1940." *African Urban Studies* 6: 49–76 (Winter 1979–80).

————. "The urbanisation of African music: Some theoretical observations." *Popular Music* 2: 113–30 (1982).

————. *In Township Tonight! South Africa's Black City Music and Theatre*. New York: Longman, 1985.

Crook, Larry. "A musical analysis of the Cuban rumba." *Latin American Music Review* 3/1: 93–123 (Spring-Summer 1982).

Davis, Stephen. *Reggae Bloodlines*. Anchor Press, 1977.

————, and Peter Simon. *Reggae International*. New York: R&B, 1982.

Díaz Ayala, Cristobal. *Música Cubana del Areyto a la Nueva Trova*. San Juan: Cubanacan, 1981.

Dubashi, Jagganath. "Cassette piracy: High stakes." *India Today*, March 31, 1986, 112.

Duiker, William. *Vietnam since the Fall of Saigon*. Athens, Ohio: Ohio Univ. Press, 1985.

Duy, Pham. *Musics of Vietnam*. Carbondale: Southern Illinois Univ. Press, 1975.

Efege, Jota. *Figuras y coisas de música popular brasileira*. Rio de Janeiro: Edição Funarte, 1980.

Elsner, Jürgen. "Ferment nationalen Bewusstseins: Die Musikkultur Algeriens." *Musik und Gesellchaft* 33/8: 456–63 (1983).

Erlmann, Veit. "Black political song in South Africa: Some research perspectives," in *Popular Music Perspectives 2*. Ed. David Horn. Salisbury: May & May, 1985.

Fairley, Jan. "Annotated bibliography of Latin-American popular music with particular reference to Chile and *nueva canción*." *Popular Music* 5: 305–56 (1985).

Fakhouri, Hani. *Kafr el-Elow: An Egyptian Village in Transition*. New York: Holt, Rinehart & Winston, 1972.

Fanon, Frantz. *The Wretched of the Earth*. New York: Grove Press, 1963.

Fouchard, Jean. *La méringue*. Ottawa: Editions Lemeac, 1973.

Frederick, William. "Rhoma Irama and the dangdut style: Aspects of contemporary Indonesian popular culture." *Indonesia* 34: 102–130 (1982).

Fu'ad, Niᶜmat Ahmad. *Umm Kulthum wa ᶜAṣr min al-Fann* (Umm Kulthum and an Era of Art). Cairo: al-Hay'ah al Miṣriyyah al-ᶜAmah lil-Kitāb, 1976.

Gallop, Rodney. *Portugal: A Book of Folk-ways*. Cambridge, U.K.: Cambridge Univ. Press, 1936.

Gardel, Luis. *Escolas de Samba*. Rio de Janeiro: Livraria Kosmos Editora, 1967.

Garrido, Juan S. *Historia de la Música Popular en Mexico: 1896–1973*. Mexico City: Editorial Extemporaneos, S.A., 1974.

———. "Historia moderna de la música popular mexicana." Liner notes to RCA Victor MKLA-115 (1976).

Garside, Roger. *Coming Alive: China after Mao*. New York: Mentor, 1981.

Gaur, Madan. *The Other Side of the Coin: An Intimate Study of the Indian Film Industry*. Bombay: Trimurti, 1973.

Geijerstam, Claes. *Popular Music in Mexico*. Albuquerque: Univ. of New Mexico Press, 1976.

Gómez, Zoila. "Panorama de la canción cubana." *Revolución y cultura* 84: 22–24 (1979).

Greco, Juan. *La Guitarra Flamenca*. Madrid: Union Musical Española, 1973.

Gronow, Pekka. "The record industry comes to the Orient." *Ethnomusicology* 25/2:251–84 1981).

———. "The record industry: Growth of a mass medium." *Popular Music* 3: 53–76 (1983).

al-Haddad, Abdul-Rahman. *Cultural Policy in the Yemen Arab Republic*. Paris: Unesco, 1982.

Hafiz, Muhammad Mahmud Sami. *Tarīkh al-Mūsīqá wa al-Ghinā' al-ᶜArabī* (History of Arabic Music and Song). Cairo: Maktabat al-Anjlū al Miṣriyyah, 1971.

Hall, Stuart. "Notes on deconstructing 'the popular,'" in *People's History and Socialist Theory*. Ed. R. Samuel. London: Routledge, 1981.

Hall, Stuart, and Paddy Whannel. *The Popular Arts*. New York: Random House, 1965.

Harrel, Max. "Some aspects of Sundanese music." *Selected Reports in Ethnomusicology* 2/2: 81–101 (1975).

Hatch, Martin. "Popular music in Indonesia," in *Popular Music Perspectives 2*. Ed. David Horn. Salisbury: May & May, 1985.

Hauser, Arnold. *The Social History of Art*. New York: Vintage, 1952.

Heartz, Daniel, and B. Wade. *Report of the Twelfth Congress of the American Musicological Society, Berkeley 1977*. Kassel: Barenreiter, 1977.

Hebdige, Dick. *Subculture: The Meaning of Style*. New York: Methuen, 1979.

Heins, Ernst. "Two cases of urban folk music in Jakarta." *Asian Music* 7/1 (1975).

Hennion, Antoine. "The production of success: An anti-musicology of the pop song." *Popular Music* 3: 159–95 (1983).

Hill, Errol. *The Trinidad Carnival: Mandate for a Popular Theatre*. Austin: Univ. of Texas Press, 1972.

Holst, Gail. *Road to Rembetika*. Athens: Denise Harvey, 1975.

Horn, David, ed. *Popular Music Perspectives 2*. Salisbury: May & May, 1985.

Jargy, Simon. *La Musique Arabe*. Paris: Presses Universitaires de France, 1971.

Jay, Martin. *Adorno*. Boston: Harvard Univ. Press, 1984.

Kanahele, George, ed. *Hawaiian Music and Musicians: An Illustrated History*. Honolulu: Univ. of Hawaii Press, 1979.

Karnad, Giresh. "Comments from the gallery." *India International Centre: Quarterly*, (March 1981).

Kasher, Robert Kamohalu, and Burl Burlingame. *Da Kine Sound: Conversations with the People Who Create Hawaiian Music*. Hawaii: Press Pacifica, 1978.

Kauffman, Robert. "Shona urban music and the problem of acculturation." *Yearbook of the International Folk Music Council* 4: 47–56 (1972).

———. "Tradition and innovation in the urban music of Zimbabwe." *African Urban Studies* 6: 41–48 (Winter 1979–80).

Kaye, Andrew. "A field methods report-in-progress: Ko Nimo and the problem of Ghana's contemporary musical culture" (Manuscript), 1987.

Kazadi wa Mukuna. "The origin of Zairean modern music: A socioeconomic aspect." *African Urban Studies* 6: 31–9 (Winter 1979–80).

Keil, Angeliki, ed. *Markos Vamvakaris, Autobiography*. Athen: Papazissis Editions, 1972.

Khandekar, Sreekant. "Classical music: The new awakening." *India Today*, March 15, 1986, 152–53, 155–56.

Khe, Tran Van. "Vietnam," in *New Grove's Dictionary of Music and Musicians*. Ed. Stanley Sadie. New York: Macmillan, 1980.

Koetting, James. "The organization and functioning of migrant Kasena flute and drum ensembles in Nima/Accra." *African Urban Studies* 6: 31–40 (Winter 1979–80).

Kos, Koraljika. "New dimensions in folk music: A contribution to the study of musical tastes in contemporary Yugoslav society." *International Review of the Aesthetics and Sociology of Music* 3/1: 61–73 (1972).

Krishen, Pradip. "Introduction." *India International Centre: Quarterly* (March 1981).

Kubik, Gerhard. "Kwela," in *New Grove's Dictionary of Music and Musicians*. Ed. Stanley Sadie. New York: Macmillan, 1980.

———. "Donald Kachamba's montage recordings: Aspects of urban music history in Malawi." *African Urban Studies* 6: 89–122 (Winter 1979–80).

———. "Neo-traditional popular music in East Africa since 1945." *Popular Music* 1: 83–104 (1981).

León, Argeliers. *Del canto y el tiempo*. Havana: Editorial Letras Cubanas, 1984.

Levine, Robert. "Elite intervention in urban popular culture in modern Brazil." *Luso-Brazilian Review* 21/2: 9–23 (Winter 1984).

Lewis, George. "Beyond the reef: Role conflict and the professional musician in Hawaii." *Popular Music* 5: 189–98 (1985).

Limón, José. "Texas-Mexican popular music and dancing: Some notes on history and symbolic process." *Latin American Music Review* 4/2: 229–246 (1983).

Lomax, Alan. *Folk Song Style and Culture*. New Brunswick: Transaction Books, 1968.

López Cruz, Francisco. *La música folklórica de Puerto Rico*. Sharon, Conn.: Troutman, 1967.

Loza, Steven. "Music and the Afro-Cuban experience: A survey of the Yoruba tradition in Cuba in relation to the origins, form, and development of contemporary Afro-Cuban rhythms." M.A. thesis, UCLA, 1979.

Mahfuz, Najib. *Bidāyah wa Niwāyah.* Cairo: Dār Miṣr lil-Tabācah, 1949.

Malavet Vega, Pedro. *La vellonera está directa: Felipe Rodríguez (La Voz) y los años '50.* Rio Piedras: Taller Huracan, 1984.

Malm, William. *Music Cultures of the Pacific, the Near East, and Asia.* 2d ed. Englewood Cliffs: Prentice-Hall, 1977.

al-Mani, Muhammad, and Abd ur-Rahman Sbit as-Sbit. *Cultural Policy in the Kingdom of Saudi Arabia.* Paris: Unesco, 1981.

Manuel, Peter. "The Light-Classical Urdu Ghazal-song." M.A. thesis, UCLA, 1976.

———. "Formal structure in popular music as a reflection of socio-economic change." *International Review of the Aesthetics and Sociology of Music* 16/2: 163–80 (1985).

———. "The anticipated bass in Cuban popular music." *Latin American Music Review* 6/2: 249–61 (1985).

———. "The evolution of modern thumri." *Ethnomusicology* 30/3: 470–90 (Fall 1986).

———. "Marxism, nationalism and popular music in revolutionary Cuba." *Popular Music* 7: 161–78 (1987).

Manuel, Peter, and Randall Baier. "Jaipongan: Indigenous popular music of West Java." *Asian Music* 18/1: 91–110 (Fall/Winter 1986).

Marcuse, Herbert. *One-Dimensional Man.* Boston: Beacon Press, 1964.

———. *An Essay on Liberation.* Boston: Beacon Press, 1969.

Marothy, Janos. *Music and the Bourgeois, Music and the Proletarian.* Budapest: Akademiai Kiado, 1974.

Marre, Jeremy, and Hannah Charlton. *Beats of the Heart: Popular Music of the World.* New York: Pantheon, 1985.

Martínez, Mayra. "La salsa: ¿Un paliativo contra la nostalgia?" Havana: CID-MUC. Mimeo.

Matamoro, Blas. *La ciudad del tango.* Buenos Aires: Editorial Galerna, 1969.

Mayer-Serra, Otto. *Panorama de la música mexicana.* Mexico City: Fondo de Cultura Economica, 1941.

McDougall, Bonnie. *Mao Zedong's Talks at the Yan'an Conference on Literature and Art.* Ann Arbor: Univ. of Michigan Press, 1980.

Mendoza, Vicente. *La música tradicional española en Mexico.* Mexico City: Fondo de Cultura Económica, 1953.

———. *Panorama de la música tradicional de Mexico.* Mexico City: Letras Mexicana, Fondo de Cultura Económica, 1954.

Mesa-Lago, Carmelo. *Cuba in the 1970s.* Albuquerque: Univ. of New Mexico Press, 1978.

Meyer, Leonard. *Music, the Arts and Ideas.* Chicago: Univ. of Chicago Press, 1967.

Middleton, Richard. "Popular music, class conflict, and the music-historical field," in *Popular Music Perspectives.* Ed. David Horn. Salisbury: May & May, 1985.

Montes, Jorge. *The History of Tango.* Buenos Aires: Sicamericana, 1977.

Morris, Nancy. "Canto porque es necesario cantar: The new song movement in Chile, 1973–83." *Latin American Review* 12/2: 117–36 (1986).

———. "The Latin American new song movement: An overview." (Manuscript), 1984.

Mosharrafa, Moustafa. *Cultural Survey of Modern Egypt.* London: Longmans, Green, 1947.

al-Najmi, Kamal. "al-Fananūn wa al-Azhar" (Artists and the Azhar), in *Qiṣṣat al-Azhar* (The Story of the Azhar). Cairo: Dār al-Hilāl, n.d., 155–56.

al-Naqqash, Raja. "Liqā' maᶜa Umm Kulthūm" (A Meeting with Umm Kulthum), and "al-Mashāyikh wa al-Fann" (The Mashāyikh and Art), in *Lughz Umm Kulthūm* (The Secret of Umm Kulthum). Cairo: Dār al-Hilāl, 1965.

Nelson, Kristina. *The Act of Reciting the Qur'an*. Austin: Univ. of Texas, 1985.

Nettl, Bruno. *Music in Primitive Culture*. Cambridge: Harvard Univ. Press, 1956.

———. "Persian popular music in 1969." *Ethnomusicology* 16/2: 218–39 (1972).

———. "Some aspects of the history of world music in the twentieth century: Questions, problems, concepts." *Ethnomusicology* 22: 123–36 (1978).

———, ed. *Eight Urban Musical Cultures: Tradition and Change*. Urbana: Univ. of Illinois Press, 1978.

———. *The Western Impact on World Music*. New York: Schirmer Books, 1985.

Niles, Don, comp. *Commercial Recordings of Papua New Guinea Music 1949–1983*. Boroko: Institute of Papua New Guinea Studies, 1984.

Nurse, G. T. "Popular songs and national identity in Malawi." *African Music* 3: 3 (1964).

Ocampo López, Javier. *El folclor y los bailes típicos colombianos*. Manizales: Biblioteca de Escritores Caldenses, n.d.

O'Gorman, Pamela. "An approach to the study of Jamaican popular music." *Jamaica Journal* 6/3: 50–54 (1972).

Ordovás, Jesús. *Historia de la música pop española*. Madrid: Alianza Editorial, 1986.

Paddison, Max. "The critique criticized: Adorno and popular music." *Popular Music* 2: 201–18 (1982).

Pelinski, Ramon. "From tango to 'rock nacional': A case study of changing popular music taste in Buenos Aires," in *Popular Music Perspectives* 2. Ed. David Horn. Salisbury: May & May, 1985, pp. 287–95.

Peña, Manuel. "Ritual structure in a Chicano dance." *Latin American Music Review* 1: 47–73 (Spring 1980).

———. *The Texas-Mexican Conjunto: History of a Working-Class Music*. Austin: Univ. of Texas Press, 1985.

Perris, Arnold. "Music as propaganda: Art at the command of doctrine in the People's Republic of China." *Ethnomusicology* 17/1: :1–28 (1983).

Pinto de Carvalho, Jose. *Historia do Fado*. Lisbon: Publicaçoes Dom Quixote, 1982.

Pray, Bruce. "The Qawwali in Indian films." Paper presented at the Conference on South Asia, Nov. 1984, Univ. of Wisconsin, Madison, WI.

Quiroz Otero, Ciro. *Vallenato: Hombre y Canto*. Bogota: Icaro Editores, 1983.

Racy, Ali Jihad. "Musical change and commercial recording in Egypt, 1904–1932." Ph.D. diss., Univ. of Illinois, 1977.

———. "Legacy of a star," in *Fayrouz: Legend and Legacy*. Eds. Kamal Boullata and Sargon Boulous. Washington, D.C.: Forum for International Art and Culture, 1981.

———. "Music in contemporary Cairo." *Asian Music* 13/1: 4–26 (1981).

———. "Music," in *The Genius of Arab Civilization: Source of the Renaissance*. Cairo: American Univ. Press, 1983, pp. 121–41.

———. "Words and music in Beirut: A study of attitudes." *Ethnomusicology* 30: 413–27 (1986).

Ranade, Ashok. *On Music and Musicians of Hindoostan*. New Delhi: Promilla, 1984.

Randel, Don. "Crossing over with Ruben Blades." Paper delivered at 1987 conference of International Association for the Study of Popular Music, North American Chapter, April 1987, Pittsburgh, PA.

Rangoonwalla, Firoze. *75 Years of Indian Cinema*. New Delhi: Indian Book Co., 1975.

Reuter, Jas. *La música popular de Mexico*. Mexico City: Panorama Editorial, 1981.

Rizq, Qistandi. *al-Mūsīqa al-Sharqiyyah wa al-Ghinā' al-ᶜArabī* (Eastern Music and Arabic Song). Cairo: al-Maṭbāᶜah al-ᶜAṣriyyah, ca. 1936.

Roberts, John Storm. *Black Music of Two Worlds*. New York: Praeger, 1972.

————. *The Latin Tinge: The Impact of Latin American Music on the United States.* New York: Oxford University Press, 1979.

Rodríguez Juliá, Edgardo. *El entierro de Cortijo*. Rio Piedras: Ediciones Huracan, 1983.

Rossi, V. *Cosas de negros*. Buenos Aires, 1926.

Rycroft, David. "The guitar improvisations of Mwenda Jean Bosco." Parts I and II. *African Music* 2/4: 81–98, and 3/1: 86–102 (1962).

Sakata, Hiromi Lorraine. *Music in the Mind: Concepts of Music and Musicians in Afghanistan*. Kent: Kent State Univ. Press, 1983.

Sarkar, Kobita. *Indian Cinema Today: An Analysis*. New Delhi: Sterling, 1975.

Schuyler, Philip. "A folk revival in Morocco." (Manuscript.)

Scott, A. C. *Literature and the Arts in Twentieth Century China*. Garden City: Doubleday, 1963.

Sega, Eduardo. *Requiem para una cultura*. (Rio Piedras: Ediciones Bayoan, 1980).

Sevilla, Paco. "Flamenco: The early years—Part II." *Guitar and Lute*: 28–36 (March 1983).

Shaarawi, Huda. *Harem Years: Memoirs of an Egyptian Feminist*, trans. and introduction by Margot Badran. London: Virago, 1986.

Shafiq, Ibrahim. *Turāthunā al-Mūsīqiyyah* (Our Musical Heritage). Cairo: al-Lajnah al-Mūsīqiyyah al-ᶜUlyá, 1969.

el-Shawan, Salwa. "al-Mūsīka al-ᶜArabiyyah: A Category of Urban Music in Cairo, Egypt, 1927–77." Ph.D. diss., Columbia Univ., 1980.

Shepherd, John, Phil Verder, Graham Vulliamy, and Trevor Wishart. *Whose Music? A Sociology of Musical Languages*. London: Latimer New Dimensions, 1977.

Sheridan, R. J. "Music" in *Encyclopaedia of Papua and New Guinea*, Vol. II. Ed. Peter Ryan. Melbourne: Melbourne Univ., 1972.

Shils, Edward. "Daydreams and nightmares: Reflections on the criticism of mass culture." *Sewanee Review* 45/4: 596-606 (Autumn 1957).

Singer, Roberta. "Tradition and innovation in contemporary popular music in New York City." *Latin American Music Review* 4/2: 183–202 (1983).

Singer, Roberta, and Robert Friedman. "Puerto Rican and Cuban musical expression in New York." Liner Notes to New World Records 244, 1977.

Slobin, Mark. "Afghanistan," in *New Grove's Dictionary of Music and Musicians*. Ed. Stanley Sadie. New York: Macmillan, 1980, 136–44.

Slymovics, Susan. "Arabic folk literature and political expression." *Arab Studies Quarterly* 8: 178–85 (1986).

Sowell, Thomas. *Ethnic America: A History*. New York: Basic Books, 1981.

Stevenson, Robert. "The Afro-American musical legacy to 1800." *Musical Quarterly* 54 (Oct. 1968).

Stigberg, David. "Foreign currents during the '60s and '70s in Mexican popular music: Rock and roll, the romantic ballad and the cumbia." *Studies in Latin American Popular Culture* 4: 170–84 (1985).

Sugarman, Jane. Untitled manuscript regarding popular music in Macedonia, 1984.

Sutton, R. Anderson. "Commercial cassette recordings of traditional music in Java: Implications for performers and scholars." *The World of Music* 27/3: 23–46 (1985).

———. "The persistence of tradition in Hawaiian music: Ancient features in contemporary popular music." (Manuscript).

Svigals, Alicia. Unpublished manuscript regarding *fado*.

Swingewood, Alan. *The Myth of Mass Culture*. Atlantic Highlands, N.J.: Humanities, 1977.

al-Tabaʿi, Muhammad. *Asmahān Tarwi Qiṣṣatahā* (Asmahan Tells Her Story). Cairo: Maṭbāʿat Rūz al-Yūsuf, 1965.

Taylor, Julie. "Tango: Theme of class and nation." *Ethnomusicology* 20/2: 273–91 (1976).

Thrasher, Alan. "The sociology of Chinese music: An introduction." *Asian Music* 12/2: 17–53 (1981).

Titon, Jeff, ed. *Worlds of Music*. New York: Schirmer, 1984.

Touma, Habib Hasan. "History of Arabian music—A study." *The World of Music* 22: 66–75 (1980).

Trainor, John. "Significance and development in the vọng cô' of South Vietnam." *Asian Music* 7/1 (1975).

Turner, Victor. *Dramas, Fields, and Metaphors*. Ithaca, New York: Cornell, 1974.

Vega, Carlos. *Danzas y canciones argentinas*. Buenos Aires, 1936.

Vega, Hector. "Bomba, plena and Rosario Frances. Some musical forms of African descendants in Puerto Rico." M.A. thesis, Hunter College, 1969.

Vega Cobiellas, Ulpiano. *Nuestra America y la evolución de Cuba*. Havana, 1944.

Vidić, Ljerka. "The musical practice of the nomadic Rom of Bosnia and Hercegovina." M.A. thesis, Wesleyan Univ., 1987.

Wahba, Magdi. *Cultural Policy in Egypt*. Paris: Unesco, 1972.

———. "Cultural planning in the Arab world." *Journal of World History* 14/4: 800–813 (1972).

Wallis, Roger, and Krister Malm. *Big Sounds from Small Peoples: The Music Industry in Small Countries*. New York: Pendragon, 1984.

Ware, Naomi. "Popular music and African identity in Freetown, Sierra Leone," in *Eight Urban Musical Cultures*. Ed. Bruno Nettl, Urbana: Univ. of Illinois Press, 1978.

Warner, Keith. *Kaiso! The Trinidad Calypso: A Study of the Calypso as Oral Literature*. Washington, D.C.: Three Continents, 1985.

Waterman, Chris. "Juju," in Bruno Nettl, *The Western Impact on World Music: Change, Adaptation, and Survival*. New York: Schirmer, 1985.

Weil, Thomas, et al. *Area Handbook for the Dominican Republic*. Washington D.C.: American Univ. 1973.

White, Garth. "Reggae—A musical weapon." *Caribe*, Dec. 1980: 6–10.

Wong, Isabel. "Geming Gequ: Songs for the education of the Masses," in *Popular Chinese Literature and Performings Arts in the People's Republic of China 1949–1979*. Ed. Bonnie McDougall. Berkeley: Univ. of California Press, 1984.

Zonis, Ella. *Classical Persian Music: An Introduction*. Cambridge: Harvard Univ. Press, 1973.

Index

Caluza, Reuben, 108
Calypso, 12, 79–83
Cambouley, 79, 266
Camerón de la Isla, 122, 124
Cameroon, 93
"Canario," Manuel Jiménez, 41–42
Canaro, Francisco, 6
Canción, 266; in Cuban music, 36; in
    Mexico, 55–56
Canción ranchera, 55–57
Candombé, 59
Candomblé, 64
Cano, Carlos, 126
Canto nuevo, 71, 266
Cape Verde, 95–97
Carabinier, 72–73
Carmo, Carlos do, 117
Carnival: in Brazil, 65; in Cuba, 28; in
    Spain, 126; in Trinidad, 79–80
Caro, Julio de, 62
Cassette technology, 6–7, 104; in India,
    191–92; in Indonesia, 206–7; and piracy,
    7, 81, 89, 104, 191
Castriota, Samuel, 62
Cazimero, Roland, 238
Censorship, 7, 67, 70–71, 88, 100, 110,
    157, 228, 231, 253, 260–61
chachachá, 31–32, 47, 87, 266
Chapottín, Felix, 32
Charanga, 27, 30, 31, 37, 245, 266
Charango, 69–70
Chen, Ruby, 170
Chica, 73
Chicano. *See* Tex-Mex music
Chichos, Los, 124
Chile. *See Nueva canción*
Chimurenga, 88, 105
China, 15, 221–35
Chiquitete, 126
Choro, 65
Choudhrey, Salil, 179
Christian missionary music. *See* Hymns,
    Christian
Chunguitos, Los, 124
Çifte telli, 127, 129, 131, 162, 266
Cinema and popular music, 5; in the Arab
    world, 149–50; in China, 224; in India,
    173–90; in Indonesia, 208, 210–12; in
    Turkey, 167
Cinquillo, 27–28, 74, 251, 266
Clave, 29, 33, 3, 267; in Africa, 90–91; in
    sega, 113
Cliff, Jimmy, 76
Cobián, Juan Carlos, 62
Coladera, 96, 267
Colombia, 50–53. *See also* Cumbia;
    Vallenato
Colon, Willie, 48
"Como el Agua," 124
Compas, 73, 251, 267
Concepción, Cesar, 41–42

Conga (genre), 28, 67
Conga (drum), 41, 267
Congolese music: influence elsewhere in
    Africa, 86, 101–3, 104–5, 110, 111;
    influence in Haiti, 73
Conjunto, 267. *See also* Tex-Mex music
Contradanza, 27
Contredanse, 27, 73
Copyright, 7, 252
Corrido, 58
Cortijo, Rafael, 42
Coskuner, Cengiz, 165
Coupé Cloué, 251
Courtesans in India, 176, 187
Criolla, 36
Cruz, Celia, 4
Cuatro, 39, 41, 43, 79
Cuba, 15, 20, 24, 26–39; influence in
    Africa, 86–87, 91, 97–98, 103, 106;
    influence in Mexico, 53–54; influence in
    Spain, 122; influence in Vietnam, 199.
    See also particular musical style
Cueca, 70, 267
Cugat, Xavier, 47
Cultural Revolution (China), 15, 230–32
Cumbia, 11, 50–53, 267
Cuni, Miguelito, 32

Dabkah, 158
Dādra, 177, 189
Dairo, I.K., 93
Dangdut, 206, 210–12, 267
Danza, 39
Danzón, 26–28, 39, 267
Darko, George, 92
Darwish, Sayyid, 156, 158
Dawr, 147
Décima, 28, 38
Deng Li-Chun, 221, 233
Deng Xiaoping, 231–34
Detribalization, 17, 85
Disco. *See* Rock
Dominican Republic, 42–46. *See also*
    Merengue
Douglas, Chieftain Walter, 79
"Dunya meň," 183

Egypt, 142–59; impact of television, 5
Electric guitar: in Africa, 87, 93–94, 98–99,
    102–5, 110, 111, 113; in calypso, 82; in
    China, 233; in India, 186; in Spain, 125;
    in Vietnam, 200
"Entre dos Aguas," 124
Eliot, T.S., 9
Ethiopia, 103

Fado, 3, 24, 60, 115–21, 209, 267
Failde, Miguel, 27
Fakhri, Sabah, 159, 257
Fandango, 122
Fania Records, 48